MOSES THE EGYPTIAN

Moses the Egyptian

THE MEMORY OF EGYPT
IN WESTERN MONOTHEISM

Jan Assmann

HARVARD UNIVERSITY PRESS

CAMBRIDGE, MASSACHUSETTS

LONDON, ENGLAND

First Harvard University Press paperback edition, 1998

Library of Congress Cataloging-in-Publication Data

Assmann, Jan.
Moses the Egyptian : the memory of Egypt in western monotheism /
Jan Assmann.
p. cm.
Includes bibliographical references and index.
ISBN 0-674-58738-3 (cloth)
ISBN 0-674-58739-1 (pbk.)
1. Moses (Biblical leader) 2. Egypt—Religion.
3. Monotheism—History of doctrines. I. Title.
BS580. M6A79 1997
222'.1'092—dc21
96-51600

To Moshe Barasch

Contents

Illustrations

Preface

In the introduction to his book *Freud's Moses* (1991), Yosef Hayim Yerushalmi drew a line starting with Freud and leading backward via Friedrich Schiller and John Spencer to Strabo, Manetho, Apion, and Celsus which he suggests would be interesting to explore "had we but world enough and time." In *Monotheismus und Kosmotheismus* (1993), I started from the opposite end with Akhenaten and his religious revolution and sketched out the story of Moses' reception via Manetho, Strabo, Apion, and Tacitus up to Schiller and Sigmund Freud—only to break off with a similar feeling of resignation. But then, quite unexpectedly, I was given world enough and time in the form of an invitation to spend a year (1994–95) in California, and I used it for a preliminary exploration of this vast terrain between Akhenaten and Freud.

I am grateful to the J. Paul Getty Center for the History of Arts and the Humanities and especially to its director, Salvatore Settis, for the invitation, for the particularly fruitful atmosphere of cooperation and dialogue which he created, and for several stimulating discussions. I thank those who participated in the continuing discussions on "memory" (the topic for that year), especially Julia Annas, Mary Carruthers, Francois Hartog, Christian Jacob, Anne and Patrick Poirier, Krzysztof Pomian, Jacques Revel, Michael Roth, Carlo Severi, and also Aleida Assmann and Carl E. Schorske, with whom I had the chance to share some of the problems and concepts this book is about and who contributed many stimulating suggestions. I feel particularly indebted to my immediate office-neighbors at the center: to Carlo Ginzburg, whose seminars on "enstrangement" proved an inexhaustible source of information and stimulation and whose critical interest in my work forced me to clarify my position and saved me from many imprecisions; and to Stuart Harten, who was working on the motif of the veiled image at Sais and who shared with me many of his bibliographical discoveries.

Cristiano Grottanelli and Mauro Pesce drew my attention to some recent Italian contributions and provided me with books and articles which I otherwise would have missed. My research assistant, Louise A. Hitchcock, not only provided books and photocopies but also read the manuscript, corrected my English, and contributed many valuable suggestions. A special word of gratitude is also due my friend and *collega in aegyptiacis* Antonio Loprieno, who was most helpful in making me feel at home in Los Angeles, even Egyptologically. On the occasion of a symposium on Ancient Egyptian Literature which we organized together, I met Dana M. Reemes. We discovered by chance that we shared an interest and a delight in a book which I was then reading in the Special Collections Room at the UCLA Research Library: Ralph Cudworth's *True Intellectual System of the Universe*. He not only gave me a copy of this book so that I could use it at home, but also provided a wealth of related material from his inexhaustible private library (which I acknowledge in the notes). Moreover, he read the manuscript of this book, made helpful suggestions, and did much to improve its style. I am grateful to Lindsay Waters for his encouragement during the preparation of this book and to Nancy Clemente for her skillful editing of the manuscript.

My stay in Santa Monica considerably increased the burdens of my colleagues at Heidelberg University who had to assume my duties; and among the many to whom I feel obliged, I am especially grateful to my assistants Martin Bommas, Heike Guksch, Andrea Kucharek, and Friederike Seyfried, as well as to Stephan Seidlmayer, who took on my teaching and administrative duties at the Institute of Egyptology, which prospered under his careful and stimulating directorship.

This book grew out of a project of the study group Archaeology of Literary Communication, concerned with secrecy and mystery, which Aleida Assmann and I have been pursuing in the form of a series of conferences and publications (*Schleier und Schwelle*, volumes 1–3). The discussions during these conferences contributed much to the formation of the basic ideas for this book. I feel particularly indebted to Aleida Assmann, Moshe Barasch, and Wolf-Daniel Hartwich. I dedicate this book to Moshe Barasch, whose encouragement kept me writing it.

MOSES THE EGYPTIAN

CHAPTER ONE

Mnemohistory and the Construction of Egypt

The Mosaic Distinction

Draw a distinction.
Call it the first distinction.
Call the space in which it is drawn the space severed or cloven
    by the distinction.

It seems as if George Spencer Brown's "first Law of Construction"[1] does not apply solely to the space of logical and mathematical construction. It also applies surprisingly well to the space of cultural constructions and distinctions and to the spaces that are severed or cloven by such distinctions.

The distinction I am concerned with in this book is the distinction between true and false in religion that underlies more specific distinctions such as Jews and Gentiles, Christians and pagans, Muslims and unbelievers. Once the distinction is drawn, there is no end of reentries or subdistinctions. We start with Christians and pagans and end up with Catholics and Protestants, Calvinists and Lutherans, Socinians and Latitudinarians, and a thousand more similar denominations and subdenominations. Cultural or intellectual distinctions such as these construct a universe that is not only full of meaning, identity, and orientation, but also full of conflict, intolerance, and violence. Therefore, there have always been attempts to overcome the conflict by reexamining the distinction, albeit at the risk of losing cultural meaning.

Let us call the distinction between true and false in religion the "Mosaic distinction" because tradition ascribes it to Moses. We cannot be sure that Moses ever lived because there are no traces of his earthly existence outside the tradition. But we can be sure that he was not the first to draw the distinction. There was a precursor in the person of an Egyptian king who called himself Akhenaten and instituted a monotheistic religion in the fourteenth century B.C.E. His religion, however, spawned no tradition but was forgotten immediately after his death. Moses is a figure of memory but not of history, while Akhenaten is a figure of history but not of memory. Since memory is all that counts in the sphere of cultural distinctions and constructions, we are justified in speaking not of Akhenaten's distinction, but of the Mosaic distinction. The space severed or cloven by this distinction is the space of Western monotheism. It is this constructed mental or cultural space that has been inhabited by Europeans for nearly two millennia.

It is an error to believe that this distinction is as old as religion itself, though at first sight nothing might seem more plausible. Does not every religion quite automatically put everything outside itself in the position of error and falsehood and look down on other religions as "paganism"? Is this not quite simply the religious expression of ethnocentricity? Does not the distinction between true and false in reality amount to nothing other than the distinction between "us" and "them"? Does not every construction of identity by the very same process generate alterity? Does not every religion produce "pagans" in the same way that every civilization generates "barbarians"?

However plausible this may seem, it is not the case. Cultures not only generate otherness by constructing identity, but also develop techniques of translation. We have to distinguish here between the "real other," who is always there beyond the individual and independent of the individual's constructions of selfhood and otherhood, and the "constructed other," who is the shadow of the individual's identity. Moreover, we have to realize that in most cases we are dealing not with the "real other," but with our constructions and projections of the other. "Paganism" and "idolatry" belong to such constructions of the other. It is this inevitable construction of cultural otherness that is to a certain degree compensated by techniques of translation. Translation in this sense is not to be confused with the colonializing appropriation of the "real" other. It is simply an attempt to make more transparent the borders that were erected by cultural distinctions.

Ancient polytheisms functioned as such a technique of translation.

They belong within the emergence of the "Ancient World" as a coherent ecumene of interconnected nations.[2] The polytheistic religions overcame the primitive ethnocentrism of tribal religions by distinguishing several deities by name, shape, and function. The names are, of course, different in different cultures, because the languages are different. The shapes of the gods and the forms of worship may also differ significantly. But the functions are strikingly similar, especially in the case of cosmic deities; and most deities had a cosmic function. The sun god of one religion is easily equated to the sun god of another religion, and so forth. Because of their functional equivalence, deities of different religions can be equated. In Mesopotamia, the practice of translating divine names goes back to the third millennium B.C.E. (as will be shown in Chapter 2). In the second millennium, this practice was extended to many different languages and civilizations of the Near East. The cultures, languages, and customs may have been as different as ever: the religions always had a common ground. Thus they functioned as a means of intercultural translatability. The gods were international because they were cosmic. The different peoples worshipped different gods, but nobody contested the reality of foreign gods and the legitimacy of foreign forms of worship. The distinction I am speaking of simply did not exist in the world of polytheistic religions.

The Mosaic distinction was therefore a radically new distinction which considerably changed the world in which it was drawn. The space which was "severed or cloven" by this distinction was not simply the space of religion in general, but that of a very specific kind of religion. We may call this new type of religion "counter-religion" because it rejects and repudiates everything that went before and what is outside itself as "paganism." It no longer functioned as a means of intercultural translation; on the contrary, it functioned as a means of intercultural estrangement. Whereas polytheism, or rather "cosmotheism," rendered different cultures mutually transparent and compatible, the new counter-religion blocked intercultural translatability. False gods cannot be translated.

All cultural distinctions need to be remembered in order to render permanent the space which they construct. Usually, this function of remembering the fundamental distinctions assumes the form of a "Grand Narrative," a master story that underlies and informs innumerable concrete tellings and retellings of the past. The Mosaic distinction between true and false in religion finds its expression in the story of Exodus. This means that it is symbolized by the constellation or opposition of Israel and Egypt. Books 2 through 5 of the Pentateuch unfold the distinction in a narrative and in a normative form. Narratively, the distinction is represented by the story of Israel's Exodus out of Egypt. Egypt thereby came to symbolize the rejected, the religiously wrong, the "pagan." As a consequence, Egypt's most conspicuous practice, the worship of images, came to be regarded as the greatest sin. Normatively, the distinction is expressed in a law code which conforms with the narrative in giving the prohibition of "idolatry" first priority. In the space that is constructed by the Mosaic distinction, the worship of images came to be regarded as the absolute horror, falsehood, and apostasy. Polytheism and idolatry were seen as the same form of religious error. The second commandment is a commentary on the first:

1. Thou shalt have no other gods before me.
2. Thou shalt not make unto thee any graven image.

Images are automatically "other gods," because the true god is invisible and cannot be iconically represented.

Both the story and the law code are symbolically expressive of the Mosaic distinction. The story is more than simply an account of historical events, and the Law is more than merely a basis for social order and religious purity. In addition to what they overtly tell and establish, they symbolize the distinction. Exodus is a symbolical story, the Law is a symbolical legislation, and Moses is a symbolical figure. The whole constellation of Israel and Egypt is symbolical and comes to symbolize all kinds of oppositions. But the leading one is the distinction between true religion and idolatry.

Both the concept of idolatry and the repudiation of it grew stronger and stronger in the course of Jewish history.[3] The later the texts, the more elaborate the scorn and abomination which they heap on the idolators. Some poignant verses in Deutero-Isaiah and Psalm 115 develop into whole chapters in the apocryphal *Sapientia Salomonis* and long sections in Philo's *De Decalogo* and *De Legibus Specialibus*.[4]

This hatred was mutual and the "idolators" did not fail to retaliate. Understandably enough, most of them were Egyptians. For example, the Egyptian priest Manetho, who wrote an Egyptian history under Ptolemy II, represented Moses as a rebellious Egyptian priest who made himself the leader of a colony of lepers. Whereas the Jews depicted idolatry as a kind of mental aberration, of madness, the Egyptians associated iconoclasm with the idea of a highly contagious and bodily disfiguring epidemic. The language of illness continues to typify the debate on the Mosaic distinction down to the days of Sigmund Freud. In the following chapter, I try to show that this story about the lepers originally referred not to Moses, but to Akhenaten, who was the first to establish a monotheistic counter-religion and to draw the distinction between true and false. But after his death, his religion was abolished, and his name fell into complete oblivion. The traumatic memories of his revolution were encrypted and dislocated; eventually, they came to be fixed on the Jews.

It is important to realize that we are dealing here with a strong mutual loathing that is rooted not in idiosyncratic aversions of Jews and Egyptians but in the Mosaic distinction as such, which was originally Akhenaten's distinction. And while it is true that many arguments of the "idolators" lived on in the discourse of Anti-Semitism, and that the fight against the Mosaic distinction seemed to have anti-Semitic implications, it is also true that many of those who, in the eighteenth century, attacked Moses' distinction, such as John Toland or Gotthold Ephraim Lessing, fought for tolerance and committed themselves to the equality of the Jews. The struggle against the Mosaic distinction could also assume the character of a fight against anti-Semitism. The most outspoken destroyer of the Mosaic distinction was a Jew: Sigmund Freud.

When Sigmund Freud felt the rising tide of German anti-Semitism outgrowing the traditional dimensions of persecution and oppression and turning into a murderous attack, he—remarkably enough—did not ask the obvious question of "how the Germans came to murder the Jews"; instead he asked "how the Jew came to attract this undying hatred." He embarked on a project very different from his normal work. This "historical novel," as he first planned to call it,[5] was a rather private undertaking, a kind of "day-dreaming,"[6] which underwent many transformations before it was finally published as a book. It became a text on Moses in which Freud intended to come to terms with his own Jewishness in particular, and with Judaism and religion in general, by reflecting on the origins, the development, and the meaning of Moses' fundamental distinction between Jews and Gentiles. His quest for origins took him as far back as Akhenaten and his monotheistic revolution.

In making Moses an Egyptian and in tracing monotheism back to ancient Egypt, Freud attempted to deconstruct the murderous distinction. It is the same method of deconstruction by historical reduction that Nietzsche had used in his *Genealogy of Morals.*

I had always felt the challenge that Freud's book posed for both Egyptology and Comparative Religion and wondered why there had been so little response on the part of these disciplines.[7] It was a question not of correcting Freud's historical errors but of learning to remember the fundamental questions which the present addresses to the past and which Egyptology is at least expected to be concerned with, if not to answer. It is in a rather personal attempt to "come to terms with," similar to Freud's, that I embark on the writing of this study about Moses the Egyptian. The present text reflects my situation as a German Egyptologist writing fifty years after the catastrophe which Freud saw approaching, knowing the full extent of the genocide which was still unthinkable in Freud's time, and having turned to ancient Egypt thirty-five years ago with questions that are all too easily forgotten as soon as one enters an academic discipline. Disciplines develop questions of their own and by doing so function as a mnemotechnique of forgetting with regard to concerns of a more general and fundamental character. In this book I try to remember and recover the questions, not to answer them. I attempt a mnemohistory of religious antagonism insofar as this antagonism is founded on the symbolic confrontation of Israel and Egypt. In this respect, I hope to contribute to a historical analysis of anti-Semitism.

A Tale of Two Countries

The Mosaic distinction is expressed as the distinction between Israel and Egypt. On the map of physical and political geography, Ancient Israel and Ancient Egypt were two neighboring countries in the eastern Mediterranean. Each of them had other neighbors as well. Sharing the common historical and political world that was the Mediterranean and the Near East, the two countries were related to each other as well as to their other neighbors by a network of political, commercial, and ideological ties which were sometimes friendly, often conflictual, but always complex. Yet on the map of memory Israel and Egypt appear as antagonistic worlds. The complexity and the plurality of a geopolitical continuum disappear. Historical reality is reduced to a figure of memory which retains just the two of them as the basic symbol of the Mosaic distinction. Israel embodies truth, Egypt symbolizes darkness and error. Egypt loses its historical reality and is turned into an inverted image of Israel. Israel is the negation of Egypt, and Egypt stands for all that Israel has overcome. This antagonistic constellation assumed the form of a Grand Narrative: the myth of the Exodus. It is a "constellative myth," a "Tale of Two Countries," and the semantic focus of the tale is the tension which the constellation of these extreme poles creates. The construction of cultural otherness and confrontation which the myth of the Exodus effects in the course of its formation, transmission, and transformation cannot be reduced to some historical experiences in the late Bronze Age.

Monotheistic religions structure the relationship between the old and the new in terms not of evolution but of revolution, and reject all older and other religions as "paganism" or "idolatry." Monotheism always appears as a counter-religion. There is no natural or evolutionary way leading from the error of idolatry to the truth of monotheism. This truth can come only from outside, by way of revelation. The narrative of the Exodus emphasizes the temporal meaning of the religious antagonism between monotheism and idolatry. "Egypt" stands not only for "idolatry" but also for a past that is rejected. The Exodus is a story of emigration and conversion, of transformation and renovation, of stagnation and progress, and of past and future. Egypt represents the old, while Israel represents the new. The geographical border between the two countries assumes a temporal meaning and comes to symbolize two epochs in the history of humankind. The same figure reproduces itself on another level with the opposition between the "Old" and the "New" Testaments. Conversion presupposes and constructs an opposition between "old" and "new" in religion.[8]

Remembering Egypt could fulfill two radically different functions. First, it could support the distinction between true religion and idolatry. We may call this function of memory the "memory of conversion." In the context of Jewish and Christian ritual memory, the memory of the Exodus forms and supports an identity of conversion. Conversion defines itself as the result of an overcoming and a liberation from one's own past which is no longer one's own. Remembering their disowned past is obligatory for converts in order not to relapse.[9] "Those who cannot remember the past are condemned to repeat it" (George Santayana). Remembering is an act of constant disowning. Egypt must be remembered in order to know what lies in the past, and what must not be allowed come back. The theme of remembering is therefore central to the Exodus myth and to the constellation of Egypt and Israel. This is not only a myth to be remembered but a myth about remembering, a myth about past and future. It remembers the past in order to win the future. Idolatry means forgetting and regression; monotheism means remembering and progression.

Second, and inversely, remembering Egypt is important for any attempt to reexamine the Mosaic distinction. We may call this function of memory the "deconstructive memory." If the space of religious truth is constructed by the distinction between "Israel in truth" and "Egypt in error," any discoveries of Egyptian truths will necessarily invalidate the Mosaic distinction and deconstruct the space separated by this distinction. This method or strategy of historical deconstruction became especially important in the context of the Enlightenment, when all distinctions were viewed as opposed to Nature, and Nature came to be elevated to the rank of the highest ideal. Spinoza's (in)famous formula *deus sive natura* amounted to an abolition not only of the Mosaic distinction but of the most fundamental of all distinctions, the distinction between God and the world. This deconstruction was as revolutionary as Moses' construction. It immediately led to a new appraisal of Egypt. The Egyptians were Spinozists and "cosmotheists." Ancient cosmotheism as a basis for intercultural translation was rediscovered. In the discourse of the Enlightenment, it was reconstructed as an international and intercultural mystery religion in the fashion of Freemasonry.

The first form of memory functions as a means of cultural identity formation and reproduction, whereas the second form functions as a technique of intercultural translation.

The Aims of Mnemohistory

The present study attempts to investigate the history of Europe's remembering Egypt, especially in the second form in which the remembering of Egypt is brought to bear on a modification or even deconstruction of the Mosaic distinction. We may call this particular form of historical investigation "mnemohistory." Unlike history proper, mnemohistory is concerned not with the past as such, but only with the past as it is remembered. It surveys the story-lines of tradition, the webs of intertextuality, the diachronic continuities and discontinuities of reading the past. Mnemohistory is not the opposite of history, but rather is one of its branches or subdisciplines, such as intellectual history, social history, the history of mentalities, or the history of ideas. But it has an approach of its own in that it deliberately leaves aside the synchronic aspects of what it is investigating. It concentrates exclusively on those aspects of significance and relevance which are the product of memory—that is, of a recourse to a past—and which appear only in the light of later readings. Mnemohistory is reception theory applied to history.[10] But "reception" is not to be understood here merely in the narrow sense of transmitting and receiving. The past is not simply "received" by the present. The present is "haunted" by the past and the past is modeled, invented, reinvented, and reconstructed by the present. To be sure, all this implies the tasks and techniques of transmitting and receiving, but there is much more involved in the dynamic of cultural memory than is covered by the notion of reception. It makes much more sense to speak of Europe's having been "haunted" by Egypt than of Egypt's having been "received" by Europe. There were, of course, several discoveries and receptions of Egypt in the same way as there were multiple discoveries and receptions of China, India, or Mexico. But independent of these discoveries there was always the image of Egypt as the past both of Israel and of Greece and thus of Europe. This fact makes the case of Egypt radically different from that of China, India, or "Orientalism" in general.

The aim of a mnemohistorical study is not to ascertain the possible truth of traditions such as the traditions about Moses but to study these traditions as phenomena of collective memory. Memories may be false, distorted, invented, or implanted. This has been sufficiently shown in recent discussions in the fields of forensic psychiatry, psychoanalysis, biography, and history.[11] Memory cannot be validated as a historical source without being checked against "objective" evidence. This is as true of collective memory as of individual memory, a fact which will be illustrated by a rather striking example in the next chapter. But for a historian of memory, the "truth" of a given memory lies not so much in its "factuality" as in its "actuality." Events tend to be forgotten unless they live on in collective memory. The same principle applies to fundamental semantic distinctions. There is no meaning in history unless these distinctions are remembered. The reason for this "living on" lies in the continuous relevance of these events. This relevance comes not from their historical past, but from an ever-changing present in which these events are remembered as facts of importance. Mnemohistory analyzes the importance which a present ascribes to the past. The task of historical positivism consists in separating the historical from the mythical elements in memory and distinguishing the elements which retain the past from those which shape the present. In contrast, the task of mnemohistory consists in analyzing the mythical elements in tradition and discovering their hidden agenda. Mnemohistory does not ask, "Was Moses really trained in all the wisdom of the Egyptians?" Instead, it asks, why such a statement did not appear in the book of Exodus, but only appeared in Acts (7:22), and why the Moses discourse in the seventeenth and eighteenth centuries almost exclusively based its image of Moses not on Moses' elaborate biography in the Pentateuch, but on this single verse in the New Testament. In the Exodus story as it is remembered by the Pessah Haggadah, there is no mention of Moses at all. The Moses discourse of the Enlightenment, on the other hand, leaves God out of the narrative.

The approach of mnemohistory is highly selective. A historical—either Egyptological or Biblical—investigation of the traditions about Moses and Egypt would be far more comprehensive. It would certainly take into account the considerable amount of available epigraphical, archaeological, and philological evidence. As an Egyptologist, I am aware of what I am leaving aside in this study. I am dealing with the Amarna experience only insofar as it lives on in the tradition about the "lepers," and I am dealing with this tradition, and Egyptian anti-Semitism in general, only insofar as it informs the later discourse on Moses and Egypt. I am reading Maimonides only in the light of Spencer, John Spencer in the light of William Warburton, Warburton in the light of Reinhold and Schiller, and of Freud insofar as he partakes in this discourse and reflects on its issues. For each of these men's writings, a strictly *historical* approach would proceed in a very different way. There is certainly much more to be said about John Spencer than the reader will learn in the course of this study. Specialists of the intellectual history of the seventeenth century such as Frances A. Yates or Frank E. Manuel would have drawn a radically different picture. In the case of

Friedrich Schiller, and even more so in that of Sigmund Freud, the mnemohistorical approach becomes extremely selective and spotlights aspects of their oeuvre which would appear marginal in a purely historical perspective. I am following a vertical line of memory and shall, to a large extent, exclude the horizontal continuum of history.

I have given the name of "Moses the Egyptian" to this vertical line of memory which I am investigating from the times of Akhenaten up to the twentieth century. I shall not even ask the question—let alone, answer it—whether Moses was an Egyptian, or a Hebrew, or a Midianite. This question concerns the historical Moses and thus pertains to history. I am concerned with Moses as a figure of memory. As a figure of memory, Moses the Egyptian is radically different from Moses the Hebrew or the Biblical Moses. Whereas Moses the Hebrew is the personification of confrontation and antagonism—between Israel = truth and Egypt = falsehood—Moses the Egyptian bridges this opposition. In some respect he embodies the inversion or at least the revision of the Exodus myth. Moses the Hebrew is the Deliverer from Egypt and therefore the symbol of Egyptophobia. The Hebrew Moses of the Bible has kept an image of Egypt alive in Western tradition that was thoroughly antithetic to Western ideals, the image of Egypt as the land of despotism, hubris, sorcery, brute-worship, and idolatry. While the Biblical Moses personifies the Mosaic distinction, Moses the Egyptian embodies its mediation. He personifies the positive importance of Egypt in the history of humankind.

The importance of the discourse on Moses and Egypt for the cultural memory of Europe lies in the foregrounding of the Egyptian subtext in the Bible, in the restoration of its polemical disfigurements, and in the mobilization of all available extra-biblical sources in order to make this subtext readable again. The Egyptian subtext appears in the Bible only as the discarded image against and upon which the Biblical text is written. We may compare the importance of Moses the Egyptian for the struggle of the Enlightenment against clerical institutions and theological distinctions to the importance of Paul the Jew in the context of the modern Jewish-Christian dialogue. Paul the Jew bridges the opposition between Jews and Christians in the same way as Moses the Egyptian did in the religious controversies of the Age of Enlightenment.

The Jewish Paul personifies an ambivalent Christian image of Judaism: Christianity's own past, the chosen people, the maternal womb out of which Christianity sprang. He also embodies an ambivalent Jewish image of Christianity: an offspring of Jewish messianism, a typical Jewish heresy that belongs to Judaism in the same sense as, for instance, the movement of Sabbatai Tzvi in the seventeenth century.[12] Paul the Jew embodies what is common to Judaism and Christianity. In the same way, Moses the Egyptian embodies what is imagined to be common to Ancient Egypt and Israel. Both Moses and Paul are figures of memory, symbolizing a first distinction, the cutting of an umbilical cord.

Still, we must not forget that Moses the Hebrew and Moses the Egyptian are by no means equal. There is a strict hierarchy of center and periphery. The Biblical story as told in Exodus, with additional material in the third to fifth books of Moses, is canonical and normative, while the other stories are apocryphal if not outright heretical. Certainly, Moses the Egyptian does not belong to the canonical tradition. Seen as a figure of memory, he belongs to a kind of counter-memory. By counter-memory I mean a memory that puts elements to the fore that are, or tend to be, forgotten in the official memory. It is well known—Akira Kurosawa's film *Rashomon* (1950) and Alain Resnais's film *L'année dernière à Marienbad* (1961) have impressively demonstrated this principle—that individual memories remember the same event in many different ways. But counter-memory goes a step further in that it explicitly contradicts another memory. "You remember it this way, but I remember it differently because I remember what you have forgotten."[13] If it becomes codified in the form of a traditional story or even in a work of written historiography, counter-memory corresponds to what Amos Funkenstein and David Biale have proposed to call "counterhistory."[14] Moses the Egyptian is a typical example of counterhistory. Thus, as a figure of memory, he is indicative of certain countercurrents in the Western tradition. This makes Moses an extremely interesting figure, quite independent of the possibility that there may be excellent evidence (and I think indeed, there is, but that is another story) that Moses, if there ever existed a historical figure of that name, was indeed an Egyptian.[15]

Mnemohistory is nothing new. For instance, studying the vertical lines of transmission and reception: the *Wanderstrassen* of cultural memory, was the project of Aby Warburg. Only the distinction between history proper and mnemohistory is new. Without an awareness of this difference, the history of memory, or mnemohistory, turns all too easily into a historical critique of memory. For example, Martin Bernal turned, without further warning, from being a historian of memory (at which he is brilliant) in volume 1 of his monumental quest for "Black Athena" into being a historian of "facts" (at which he is doing less well) in volume 2.[16] Bernal's distinction between the "ancient model" and the "new model" in the imaging of Greece and his analysis of the hidden agenda that was active in the eclipse of the old model and the rise of the new one forms an important contribution to the mnemo-historical analysis of Eurocentrism and its cultural memory.

In the first volume, Bernal demonstrates that the Philhellenic move-ment in German Romanticism was inextricably combined with Judeo-phobia and Egyptophobia. This new image of Greece was instrumental in shaping a new image of Germany. The "Aryan myth" had a big share in this retrojective self-modeling, along with Herder's concepts of national genius and originality. But Bernal should have realized that the "ancient model" is as much an imaginary construction as the "new model." Therefore, he should have refrained from crossing the borders of mnemohistory and embarking on the project of proving its historical truth. In dealing with late eighteenth and early nineteenth century Germany, Bernal shows a keen awareness of the biases of cultural memory. But in dealing with ancient Greece he ignores these biases and accepts the most fabulistic accounts in Hecataeus and Diodorus as decisive evidence.[17] Hecataeus of Abdera was a Hellenist of the very first generation. He wrote his history in conformity with Alexander the Great's program of building a multicultural empire.[18] His interest in constructing interconnections between different cultures and inventing stories about migrations, disseminations, and contacts is as easily un-derstandable as Karl Otfried Müller's quest for cultural purity and exclusivity. Bossuet's discourse on universal history was undertaken to enlighten the dauphin and to improve the political situation.[19] This project was shared by large parts of the Enlightenment, for example by the circle of British intellectuals who wrote the *Athenian Letters*[20] and by the Austrian Freemasons who pinned their hopes on Joseph II and wrote on the Egyptian Mysteries.[21] They found what they sought in Diodorus' description of ancient Egyptian monarchy, which was based on Hecataeus' account. Hecataeus had pursued the same project, want-ing to enlighten Ptolemy I. The "ancient model" was so important in early Hellenism and in the Enlightenment not because it was historically correct but because its concept of an enlightened monarchy was politically useful. All of these efforts relate to the dynamics of cultural memory and to the ongoing process of shaping an identity by reconstructing its past. The proper way of dealing with the workings of cultural memory is mnemohistory.

Looming large in this debate is the infelicitous opposition between history and myth, leading to an all-too antiseptic conception of "pure facts" as opposed to the egocentrism of myth-making memory. History turns into myth as soon as it is remembered, narrated, and used, that is, woven into the fabric of the present. The mythical qualities of history have nothing to do with its truth values. For example, Masada is both a complex of uncontested historical facts and a powerful component of modern Israel's national mythology. Its mythological function does not in the least invalidate its historicity, nor would its demythization enlarge our historical knowledge. As soon as the term "Holocaust" was adopted, the genocide of the Jews that was perpetrated by Nazi Germany assumed mythical status in America and in Israel. Then meanings were created which made even this complex of events narratable, transmittable, and representable in the system of cultural memory. The same mythopoetic process has not yet begun in Germany and will perhaps take much longer to develop, because in the country of the perpetrators this part of the past is much more difficult to incorporate into the present than in the countries of the victims. Even the word "Holocaust" does not seem adequate in the German context. All of this does not, however, affect the historicity of the events themselves in the least. The historical study of the events should be carefully distinguished from the study of their commemoration, tradition, and transformation in the collective memory of the people concerned.[22]

Seen as an individual and as a social capacity, memory is not simply the storage of past "facts" but the ongoing work of reconstructive imagination. In other words, the past cannot be stored but always has to be "processed" and mediated. This mediation depends on the semantic frames and needs of a given individual or society within a given present.[23]

If "We Are What We Remember,"[24] the truth of memory lies in the identity that it shapes. This truth is subject to time so that it changes with every new identity and every new present. It lies in the story, not as it happened but as it lives on and unfolds in collective memory. If

"We Are What We Remember," we are the stories that we are able to tell about ourselves. "We have, each of us, a life-story, an inner narrative—whose continuity, whose sense, is one's life. It might be said that each of us constructs and lives, a 'narrative,' and that this narrative is us, our identities."[25] The same concept of a narrative organization of memory and self-construction applies to the collective level. Here, the stories are called "myths." They are the stories which a group, a society, or a culture lives by. Myths in the sense of traditional narratives play a very important role in the formation of ethnic identities ("ethnogenesis"). Ethnogenetic movements typically derive their dynamics from some master narratives which act as a "mythomoteur."[26] As far as contemporary events are experienced and interpreted by contemporaries in the light of such metanarratives, history (in the sense of *res gestae*) is already imbued with narrative, quite independently of its being told or written in the form of narrative. Narrative structures are operative in the organization of action, experience, memory, and representation.

Mnemohistory and Discourse History

Mnemohistory investigates the history of cultural memory. The term "cultural memory" is merely a translation of the Greek name Mnemosyne. Since Mnemosyne was the mother of the nine Muses, her name came to stand for the totality of cultural activities as they were personified by the different Muses. By subsuming these cultural activities under the personification of memory, the Greeks were viewing culture not only as based on memory but as a form of memory in itself. The memory-line I am concerned with is, however, much more specific. It is just one of the many *Wanderstrassen* of cultural memory, as Aby Warburg called it. Further, its investigation involves a methodology of its own which must not be confounded with the much more general concerns of mnemohistory. This is the history of discourse. By "discourse" I understand something much more specific than what this term has come to refer to in the wake of Michel Foucault and others.[27] I am referring to a concatenation of texts which are based on each other and treat or negotiate a common subject matter. In this view, discourse is a kind of textual conversation or debate which might extend over generations and centuries, even millennia, depending on institutionalizations of permanence such as writing, canonization, educational and clerical institutions, and so forth.

Discourse (in this restricted sense of debate) is organized by a thematic frame and a set of (unwritten) rules as to how to deal both with antecedent texts and with the subject matter. These include rules of conversation, argumentation, quotation, verification, and many others. A mnemohistorical discourse analysis investigates this concatenation of texts as a vertical line of memory and seeks out the threads of connectivity which are working behind the texts: the intertextuality, evolution of ideas, recourse to forgotten evidence, shifts of focus, and so forth. In dealing with a specific topic within the general frame of imaging Egypt in European cultural memory (Mozart's *Magic Flute* and its Egyptian associations), Siegfried Morenz spoke of the "Lebenszusammenhang [vital coherence] of Egypt-Antiquity-Occident." This term is not very illuminating; indeed, it is somewhat mystifying.[28] Cultural memory is the principle that organizes a "vital coherence," and one of its forms is "discourse."

Discourse is more than intertextuality. Besides the textual dimension there is always the material or thematic dimension *(Sachdimension)*. A discourse is defined by the double relationship of a text to the chain of its predecessors (textual dimension) and to the common theme (material dimension). Normally discourse creates a stronger affinity between texts than does authorship. For example, the first two essays in Freud's *Moses and Monotheism* are much closer to Schiller's *Die Sendung Moses* than to Freud's other writings. Warburton's *Divine Legation of Moses* is closer to Spencer than to his own writings on Pope and Shakespeare. The same even applies to my own text, which seems to me to have much more in common with the texts I am commenting on than with my Egyptological work (except for the sixth chapter, where I introduce some Egyptian material which I consider to be related to the general problem of monotheism).

The similarity among texts participating in a discourse (as opposed to those forming the oeuvre of a specific writer) is reminiscent of Claude Lévi-Strauss's concept of myth as the totality of its versions. This raises the question as to whether the notion of "myth" would not be equally adequate with regard to the Moses-Egypt tradition. It is a story that unfolds in innumerable versions much in the same way as the stories of Hercules or Prometheus. The only difference is that the

Moses-Egypt story is told not by poets but by scholars. Nevertheless, the dynamics that are operative in the unfolding of the story seem much the same as those operating in what Hans Blumenberg has called *Arbeit am Mythos* ("work on myth").

Here I insert a personal note about the concept of "discourse" because it seems to me to be generally instructive. In embarking on this study of Moses the Egyptian I experienced becoming involved in, even being possessed by, a thematic complex which has held sway over me ever since I first looked at Spencer's *De Legibus Hebraeorum Ritualibus* in the Special Collections Room of the UCLA Research Library—by intertextual contagion, as it were. That was in October 1994 and I immediately started writing this study as if under a spell and in what for me (and in a foreign language) was an incredibly short time. I also found it extremely difficult to put this project aside after having finished the first draft of the manuscript and to turn to other tasks. This personal experience with the "Moses/Egypt discourse" opened my eyes to the kind of fascination which the lines of Spencer, Warburton, Reinhold, Schiller, and Freud so obviously bespeak. It also sharpened my awareness of the kind of continuity and connectivity which reading and writing can create and which I refer to as "discourse." Metaphorically speaking, a discourse has a life of its own which reproduces itself in those who are joining in it. It is this "life of its own" that might be related to the mythical aspect of discourse in Lévi-Strauss's sense. Behind, beside, and beneath the discourse that takes place in the realm of the written word, there is the myth of Egypt, which transcends this realm and which works its "mythomotoric" spell from behind the stage. In the eighteenth century one would have personified this mythomotoric fascination as the "genius of the discourse." For us, this kind of helpful mystification is, of course, illicit and so is the use of unanalyzed concepts like "discourse" and "cultural memory." I can only hope that the foregoing remarks have sufficiently clarified my use of the terms.

Moses and the Egyptian Revival

An analysis of the discourse on Moses and Egypt brings to light a phase in the reception of Ancient Egypt which has up to now remained neglected. Normally, this reception is conceived of as comprising two periods of Egyptian "revival" or "Egyptomania" that are associated with two events in the history of Europe: the Renaissance and Napoleon's expedition to Egypt.

The first revival consists mainly in the discovery of alleged "Egyptian texts," such as the treatise on the Egyptian hieroglyphs by Horapollo and the *Corpus Hermeticum*.[29] Marsilio Ficino and other writers of the Italian Renaissance from Francesco Colonna to Athanasius Kircher reconstructed Hermetic philosophy as ancient Egyptian theology and wisdom. These authors deemed themselves able to fill out the Classical image of Egypt as it was designed by Greek and Latin authors with the cosmological, theological, and philosophical content which they were able to extract from the Hermetic writings. By combining the Hermetic tradition and the Classical image of Egypt, Ficino was able to give a name to a founder and master of what to him appeared to be the content of Egyptian wisdom. Hermes Trismegistus was able to confront the Biblical Moses on at least an equal footing as far as chronology was concerned and could even be called "Moses Aegyptiacus." In contrast to the extremely Egyptophobic image that the Bible drew and transmitted of ancient Egypt, the Classical image of Egypt was almost unanimously and unequivocally Egyptophilic. The Renaissance revival of ancient Egypt branches out into several different discourses:

1. The "Hermetic" discourse[30]—Egypt as the source of wisdom, "prisca theologia" and "philosophia perennis."[31]
2. The "Hieroglyphic" discourse—the Egyptian script (mis)understood as pure conceptual writing *(Begriffsschrift)*—the emblematic tradition.[32]
3. The historical discourse or the discovery of time[33]—Egypt as the civilization whose documented history stretches well beyond Biblical chronology. The discourse on history directly opposes Classical and Biblical chronology and, for this reason, is particularly controversial.

The Renaissance is generally held to be the Golden Age of Egyptophilia. Its image of Egypt was a real reinvention of tradition and a stupendous achievement of the retrojective imagination which had very little to do with history. Nevertheless, that image exerted an enormous influence on cultural memory. What is more, it continued to do so long after the successful destruction of Ficino's imaginings by historical critique.[34]

The second event that sparked an Egyptian revival is the Napoleonic expedition to Egypt, which led to the first systematic survey of its monuments. This project eventually led to the decipherment of the hieroglyphic script by François Champollion and the rise of Egyptology as an academic discipline. But this enterprise is to be seen not as the trigger of a new Egyptian revival but rather as one of the more spectacular results of a new wave of Egyptomania which swept Europe in the later part of the eighteenth century. This has been established by a series of recent studies, especially on architecture.[35] We shall see that the Moses/Egypt discourse plays an important part in this development.

What has been generally overlooked is a stage in the mnemohistory of Egypt that starts in the latter half of the seventeenth century and culminates in the time of Napoleon. This discourse on Egypt is different from that of the Egyptophilic Renaissance in that it has worked through the critique of Isaac Casaubon and the hostile reactions of orthodoxy and has built its reconstructions on the solid foundations of rationalism and historical criticism. Whereas the Renaissance Egyptophiles were operating within an extremely large definition of Christianity and were able to deem themselves good Christians while toying with ideas that later came to be denounced as heretical, the scholars of the later phase were working in a climate of sharp boundaries and decisions where an interest in Egypt had to be legitimized. Therefore, this later phase is primarily concerned with Egypt as the historical background of Moses, monotheism, and revelation. Its protagonists were no longer philosophers and physicians with magical, alchemistic, and cabalistic inclinations. Its context was Biblical historical criticism as practiced by scholars such as Gerard Joannes Vossius (1577–1649), Samuel Bochart (1599–1667), John Selden (1584–1654), Richard Simon (1638–1712), Jean Le Clerc (1657–1737), John Marsham (1602–1685), Herman Wits (1636–1708), Pierre-Daniel Huet (1630–1721), and many others. Of these, I will concentrate on John Spencer (1630–1693) because his contribution became the starting point of the discourse on Moses and Egypt.   .

This new interest in Egypt was kindled by the religious and political conflicts of the time, the terrible experience of the religious wars in the first half of the century and the controversies about atheism, pantheism, Deism, free-thinking, and other heresies in the wake of Thomas Hobbes and Baruch Spinoza. Egypt was appealed to in the theological, political, historical, and philosophical debates of the time. Claimed to be the common "origin of all cults," it was used as an example to argue for the ultimate convergence of reason and revelation, or nature and Scripture. Some of those who sympathized with Spinozism spoke of "Egypt" when they meant Spinoza, not daring to explicitly mention the name of the anathematized philosopher.

Despite its obvious polytheistic and idolatrous appearance, Egyptian religion was described as containing an esoteric and original monotheism or pantheism. This was not simply a return to Athanasius Kircher, who modeled his uncritical image of Egypt on the *Corpus Hermeticum.* On the contrary, it did full justice to Casaubon's textual criticism and late dating of the Hermetic texts. Kircher has to be seen as the last of the Renaissance Egyptologists, while the new phase of Egyptology belongs within the frame of the Enlightenment and its method of historical critique. The wisdom of Hermes Trismegistus seemed to have fallen from favor after 1614, when Isaac Casaubon (1559–1614) exposed the *Corpus Hermeticum* as a late compilation and a Christian forgery. Since then, the Hermetic tradition seemed to have survived only in the form of occult undercurrents such as Rosicrucianism, alchemy, theosophy, and so forth. This, at least, is the picture Frances Yates has drawn of the Hermetic tradition. But Frances Yates's declaration of demise of Hermeticism was premature. Hermes Trismegistus had a triumphant comeback in the eighteenth century, and this was due to Ralph Cudworth's rehabilitation. In rescuing Hermes Trismegistus from Casaubon's devastating critique, Cudworth inaugurated a new phase of Egyptophilia, which in Germany, coincided with a wave of Spinozism. The names associated with this phase besides those of Spinoza and Cudworth are those of the French and English Deists, the Cambridge Platonists, the free-thinkers, and the Freemasons.[36] Of these, I will concentrate on William Warburton, whose extremely detailed demonstration of the divine character of Moses' legislation might pass for the most comprehensive and representative codification of those ideas he wanted to refute. The object of the esoteric monotheism or the "mysteries" of the ancient Egyptians came to be identified as "Nature."[37] In the idea of Nature as the deity of an original, nonrevealed monotheism, which survived in Egyptian religion under the almost impenetrable cover of symbols and mysteries, the Hermetic, hieroglyphic, and Biblical discourses on Egypt merge. This development led to the height of Egyptomania in the late eighteenth century, Mozart's *Zauberflöte* and Napoleon's expedition being two particularly notable examples.

🕮 IN DEALING with discourses on "Moses the Egyptian," I shall be taking "Egyptian" in a large sense, as comprising not only ethnic but also cultural identity. For different reasons, Manetho, Strabo, Toland, and Freud took Moses to be a real Egyptian in the ethnic and cultural sense. In contrast, Spencer, Warburton, Reinhold, and Schiller remained faithful to the canonical tradition in which Moses was a Hebrew. But they viewed Moses as totally assimilated and, what is more, initiated into the "hieroglyphic wisdom and mysteries" of the Egyptians. It might be asked what an Egyptologist could possibly contribute to such a project, which obviously requires very different qualifications. It is not necessary to know Egyptian to study the works of these men, who themselves did not know Egyptian. What is required is the combined competencies of a classicist, a scholar of patristic literature, a Hebraist, a Renaissance scholar, a historian of ideas, and a Freudian scholar, whose field is now a discipline in itself. I cannot claim any of these competencies for myself. I am perfectly (and painfully) aware of the all too preliminary character of my observations, which, of course, need to be extended, reviewed, and corrected by the respective specialists. But there is something here which only an Egyptologist can discover, and that is the original impetus which got this discourse started and which survives in an almost miraculous way through all of its transformations and ramifications. As a branch of history, mnemohistory cannot do without history. It is only through continual historical reflection that the workings of memory become visible. But it is only through mnemohistorical reflection that history (that is, Egyptology) becomes aware of its own function as a form of remembering.

Therefore, the question is not only what Egyptology can contribute to the study of the imaging of Egypt in the intellectual history of Europe, but what the study of this history can teach Egyptology. Memory and history are different but inextricably related. There are historians but no "memorians." Memory and history are poles of the same range of activities, some of which are closer to one pole than to the other. It is important to keep the two poles apart in order not to lose sight of their constant interaction. Memory tends to inhabit the past and to furnish it with images of its own making, whereas history in its radical form of positivism tends to neutralize the past and to make it speak in its own voices, strange as they may sound. Nothing was more detrimental to the image of Egypt in the cultural memory of Europe than confronting it with historical discovery and reconstruction. It was not Johann Winckelmann who eclipsed or marginalized Egypt, but Egyptologists such as Adolph Erman, Kurt Sethe, and Sir Alan Gardiner, who pursued a project of demystification. Nobody will belittle the immense achievements of positivism. Egyptology had to become a positivistic and philological science in order to lay out its foundations. But in the course of Egyptology's establishment as a discipline of its own in the context of Classics and Orientalism, its original questions fell into oblivion and the growing gap between Egyptomania and Egyptology created a no man's land of mutual incomprehension.

It is certainly no coincidence that a reaction against this kind of positivism was started in postwar Germany by Egyptologists such as Joachim Spiegel,[38] Eberhard Otto,[39] Hellmut Brunner,[40] Siegfried Morenz,[41] and Walther Wolf,[42] all of whom had witnessed the catastrophic events of World War II and the horrors of German fascism. They looked to Egypt not only as territory for archaeological, historical, and philological discoveries and problem-solving but also with the—more or less unconscious—hope of gaining insight into the fundamentals of moral and religious orientation. This project of entering into a dialogue with ancient Egypt instead of making it the mere object of decipherment and discovery, and of integrating it again into the cultural memory of Europe instead of closing the "canon" with the Biblical and Classical traditions, aims at colonizing the no man's land between Egyptomania and Egyptology and reconnecting Egyptology with its mnemohistory.

CHAPTER TWO

Suppressed History, Repressed Memory: Moses and Akhenaten

Akhenaten: The First Counter-Religion

Unlike Moses, Akhenaten, Pharaoh Amenophis IV, was a figure exclusively of history and not of memory. Shortly after his death, his name was erased from the king-lists, his monuments were dismantled, his inscriptions and representations were destroyed, and almost every trace of his existence was obliterated. For centuries no one knew of his extraordinary revolution. Until his rediscovery in the nineteenth century, there was virtually no memory of Akhenaten.[1] Moses represents the reverse case. No traces have ever been found of his historical existence. He grew and developed only as a figure of memory, absorbing and embodying all traditions that pertained to legislation, liberation, and monotheism.

Immediately after the first publication of the rediscovered inscriptions of Akhenaten it was realized that he had done something very similar to what memory had ascribed to Moses: he had abolished the cults and idols of Egyptian polytheism and established a purely monotheistic worship of a new god of light, whom he called "Aton." In his Berlin dissertation, *De Hymnis in Solem sub Rege Amenophide IV. Redactis* (1894), the young American scholar James Henry Breasted demonstrated the importance of Akhenaten's monotheistic revolution for the interpretation of Biblical monotheism. Arthur Weigall, another Egyptologist with a less solid philological background, established the parallel between Egyptian and Biblical monotheism or between Akhenaten and Moses even more closely. Was Psalm 104 not a Hebrew translation of Akhenaten's hymn? Were not the Egyptian "Aton" and the Hebrew

"Adonai" the same name?[2] When Sigmund Freud embarked on his "historical novel" about Moses and monotheism, he followed these lines and made Moses an Atonist, close to the throne but not identical with the king himself. This identification did not fail to be made by several other authors working in a field which could be characterized as "science fiction" applied to the past instead of the future.[3]

Was Akhenaten the Egyptian Moses? Was the Biblical image of Moses a mnemonic transformation of the forgotten pharaoh? Only "science fiction" can answer these questions by a simple "yes." But mnemohistory is able to show that the connection between Egyptian and Biblical monotheism, or between an Egyptian counter-religion and the Biblical aversion to Egypt, has a certain foundation in history; the identification of Moses with a dislocated memory of Akhenaten had already been made in antiquity. Therefore, let me begin this history of religious antagonism at the very beginning, with King Amenophis IV, who ruled Egypt for about seventeen years in the middle of the fourteenth century B.C.E.

One could perhaps go even further back in history to the seventeenth century B.C.E., when the Hyksos, a population of Palestinian invaders, settled in the eastern delta and went out to rule Egypt for more than a hundred years. The Jewish historian Flavius Josephus saw the ancestors of Israel in these foreign rulers of Egypt. But there was certainly no religious conflict between the Hyksos and the Egyptians. The Hyksos were neither monotheists nor iconoclasts. On the contrary, their remaining monuments show them in conformity with the religious obligations of traditional Egyptian pharaohs, whose role they assumed in the same way as did later foreign rulers of Egypt such as the Persians, the Macedonians, and the Romans. They adhered to the cult of Baal, who was a familiar figure for the Egyptians, and they did not try to convert the Egyptians to the cult of their god. The whole concept of conversion seems absurd in the context of polytheistic religions. No—if we look for the first outbreak of a purely religious conflict in the historical records, we find something very different.

The first conflict between two fundamentally different and mutually exclusive religions in the recorded history of humankind occurred in Egypt in the fourteenth century B.C.E. This event is especially extraordinary because it took place within one society and did not involve any aggression from the outside. In its radical rejection of tradition and its

violent intolerance, the monotheistic revolution of Akhenaten exhib-
ited all the characteristic features of a counter-religion. Within the first
six years of his reign, Pharaoh Amenophis IV changed the whole cultural system of Egypt with a revolution from above in a more radical
way than it ever was changed by mere historical evolution. The discussion of the theology of this new religion would take me too far afield
right now and I will deal with that topic in a separate chapter. Here, it
is the aspect of religious antagonism which is of primary interest and
the traumatic impression which this experience must have made on the
Egyptians of that generation. It is this trauma which in some way
constituted the original impetus for the history that I seek to reconstruct. What I want to show is that the recollections of Akhenaten's
revolution, which were banned from official and historical memory,
survived in the form of traumatic memory. As Aleida Assmann has
shown, trauma can act as a stabilizer of memory.[4]

THE MONOTHEISTIC revolution of Akhenaten was not only the
first but also the most radical and violent eruption of a counter-religion
in the history of humankind. The temples were closed, the images of
the gods were destroyed, their names were erased, and their cults were
discontinued. What a terrible shock such an experience must have dealt
to a mentality that sees a very close interdependence between cult and
nature, and social and individual prosperity! The nonobservance of
ritual interrupts the maintenance of cosmic and social order. The
consciousness of a catastrophic and irreparable crime must have been
quite widespread. But there is even more. At the end of the Amarna age,
a political crisis broke out between the Hittite Empire and Egypt. The
Hittites raided an Egyptian garrison in Syria and took prisoners. These
prisoners brought a plague to Anatolia which swept over the entire
Near East—probably including Egypt—and raged for twenty years. It
was the worst epidemic which this region knew in antiquity. It is more
than probable that this experience, together with that of the religious
revolution, formed the trauma that gave rise to the phantasm of the
religious enemy.

One could perhaps argue that the people at large were little affected
by the discontinuation of the cults, which would have concerned only
the priests. The belief in cosmic coherence was probably characteristic

of the priestly classes, but this was scarcely the case for the rest of the population. However, the discontinuation of the cults and the desolation of the temples also implied the cessation of festivals, which must have affected the whole population. The religious feast in ancient Egypt was the one occasion when the gods left their temple and appeared to the people at large. Normally, they dwelt in complete darkness and seclusion inside the sanctuaries of their temples, inaccessible to all except the priest in service. But on the occasion of a feast, these boundaries between secrecy and publicity, sacred and profane, inner and outer, were breached. The gods appeared to the people outside the temple walls. Every major Egyptian religious feast was celebrated in the form of a procession.[5]

The Egyptian idea of the city was thus centered on and shaped by the religious feasts. The city was the place on earth where the divine presence could be sensed by everyone on the occasion of the main processional feasts. The more important the feast, the more important the city. The feasts promoted not only religious participation but also social identification and cohesion. The Egyptians conceived of themselves as members of a town or city rather than as members of a nation. The city was where they belonged and where they wanted to be buried. Belonging to a city primarily meant belonging to a deity as the master of that city. This sense of belonging to a god or goddess was created and confirmed by participating in the feasts. The abolition of the feasts must have deprived the individual Egyptians of their sense of identity and, what is more, their hopes of immortality. For following the deities in their earthly feasts was held to be the first and most necessary step toward otherworldly beatitude. In the Theban tomb of Pairi there is a graffito which the scribe Pawah wrote in the time of Smenkhkare, the last of the Amarna kings. It is a lamentation for the absent god and it begins with the words: "My heart longs to see you!" Its theme is nostalgia for the sight of Amun in his feast.[6]

I stress these facts because I am trying to reconstruct the frames of experience within which the average Egyptian of the Amarna period must have lived. These are also the frames of recollection. It is only through such frames that an event becomes experienceable, communicable, and memorable. It seems to me quite clear that the Amarna period must have meant the utmost degree of sacrilege, destruction, and horror for the Egyptians: a time of divine absence, darkness, and

disease. Some intimations of their suffering reverberate in short allu-
sions in Tutankhamun's "Restoration Stela":

> The temples of the gods and goddesses were desolated
> from Elephantine as far as the marshes of the Delta,
> their holy places were about to disintegrate,
> having become rubbish heaps, overgrown with thistles.
> Their sanctuaries were as if they had never been,
> their houses were trodden roads.
> The land was in grave disease [*znj-mnt*].
> The gods have forsaken this land.
> If an army was sent to Syria to extend the borders of Egypt,
> it had no success at all.
> If men prayed to a god for help,
> he did not come.
> If men besought a goddess likewise,
> she came not at all.
> Their hearts had grown weak in their bodies,
> because "they" had destroyed what had been created.[7]

The metaphor of "grave disease" will appear time and again in the
course of my story. But if you consider the plague which afflicted the
successors of Akhenaten, this description is not so metaphorical after
all. According to my theory, the trauma resulting from the events of the
Amarna period reflected both the experience of religious otherness and
intolerance and the suffering caused by a terrible epidemic. Indeed, the
Egyptian name for this epidemic was "the Asiatic illness."[8] This fact
may have contributed to the conflation of Amarna recollections with
the image of the Asiatic, which, as we shall see, occurred again in later
tradition.

We have every reason to imagine the Amarna experience as traumatic and the memories of Amarna among the contemporary generation as painful and problematic. The recollection of the Amarna
experience was made even more problematic by the process of systematic suppression whereby all the visible traces of the period were deleted
and the names of the kings were removed from all official records. The
monuments were dismantled and concealed in new buildings. Akhenaten did not even survive as a heretic in the memory of the Egyptians.

His name and his teaching fell into oblivion. Only the imprint of the shock remained: the vague remembrance of something religiously unclean, hateful, and disastrous in the extreme.

For the Egyptians, the Amarna religion was their first and—until their encounter with the Jews and perhaps an earlier encounter with the Persians—their only experience of an alien religion.[9] They were familiar with alien deities, such as Baal, Anat, Astarte, Qedeshet, Reshep, Teschup, Marduk, and Aschur but they did not know about structurally alien religions. Religion was felt to be much the same everywhere and so were most of the gods since their names could be easily translated from one language and one religion into another. Some of these alien gods were even integrated into Egyptian mythology. It is quite impossible that the kind of religious confrontation and conflict which is so prominent in the story of the Exodus could have occurred in Egypt except in the Amarna age, at least until the Persian conquest (525 B.C.E.). To the Egyptians this must have meant a confrontation with extreme alterity, even more extreme than their confrontation with the Hyksos.

Since every trace of the Amarna period had been eradicated, there was never any tradition or recollection of this event and its cultural expression until the nineteenth century, when the archaeological traces of this period were discovered and interpreted by modern Egyptology. The memories of this period survived only in the form of trauma. The first symptoms of this may have become visible as early as some forty years after the return to tradition, when concepts of religious otherness came to be fixed on the Asiatics, who were Egypt's traditional enemies. In this context, the dislocated Amarna reminiscences began to be projected onto the Hyksos and their god Baal, who was equated with the Egyptian god Seth. In a Ramesside novel, we read that Apophis, the Hyksos king, practiced a monolatric religion:

> King Apophis chose for his lord the god Seth.
> He did not worship any other deity in the whole land except
>   Seth.[10]

Presumably by this time, other memories and experiences had invaded the void in the collective memory which had been created both by trauma and by the annihilation of historical traces. The Hyksos conflict was thus turned into a religious conflict. This process of distortion continued through the centuries as events occurred that fit into the story of religious otherness and its dangerous semantics of abomination and persecution. It was in the course of this process that the Egyptian god Seth gradually began to incorporate these traits of religious otherness and to assume the characteristics of both a devil and an Asiatic. The Assyrian and Persian invasion of Egypt enriched the story with new details. The void which had been created by the cultural repression of the Amarna period tended always to be filled by new experiences, which in their turn had roots in the semantic frame of this nascent image of the Asiatic foe.

Lepers and Jews: Moses as Akhenaten in Greek and Latin Texts

In one of his most brilliant pieces of historical reconstruction, Eduard Meyer was able to show as early as 1904 that some reminiscences of Akhenaten had indeed survived in Egyptian oral tradition and had surfaced again after almost a thousand years of latency.[11] He demonstrated that a rather fantastic story about lepers and Jews preserved in Manetho's *Aigyptiaka* could refer only to Akhenaten and his monotheistic revolution. Rolf Krauss and Donald B. Redford were able to substantiate Meyer's hypothesis by adducing more arguments and much new material.[12] Moving along a different track, I arrived at the same conclusion. My aim was not to identify the actual historical event to which this legend refers, but to find any traces the Amarna experience might have left within the Egyptian tradition.[13] This difference in perspective is important. In claiming Manetho's story only as a trace of the Amarna experience, this interpretation fully meets the criticism which Raymond Weill has justly brought forward against any attempt to identify "the" one historical event that is reported in this story. Raymond Weill rejected Meyer's explanation of the origin of Manetho's story as being too monocausal. He advocated a multidimensional explanation according to which the tradition about the "Asiatiques impies" originated with the expulsion of the Hyksos and developed over the centuries into the form in which it appears in Hellenistic historiography.[14] According to Weill, the Amarna experience might have contributed to this development, but it would be a mistake to explain the story by reducing it to one particular event in history.

Both Weill and Meyer were right. The story as told by Manetho and others integrated many different historical experiences, among them the expulsion of the Hyksos from Egypt in the sixteenth century B.C.E. But the core of the story is a purely religious confrontation, and there is only one episode in Egyptian history that corresponds to these characteristics: the Amarna period. This axial motif of religious confrontation became conflated with the motif of foreign invasion. The Amarna experience retrospectively shaped the memories of the Hyksos occupation, and it also determined the way in which later encounters with foreign invaders were experienced and remembered. This explanation takes full account of Weill's criticism without giving up Meyer's important insight. The significance of this discovery for the project of mnemohistory is immense. Not only does it prove how trauma can serve as a "stabilizer of memory" across a millennium, but it also shows the dangers of cultural suppression and traumatic distortion. The Egyptian phantasm of the religious enemy first became associated with the Asiatics in general and then with the Jews in particular. It anticipated many traits of Western anti-Semitism[15] that can now be traced back to an original impulse. This impulse had nothing to do with the Jews but very much to do with the experience of a counter-religion and of a plague.

❧ MANETHO was an Egyptian priest who wrote his history of Egypt under Ptolemy II in the first half of the third century B.C.E.[16] We know his account from two excerpts by Flavius Josephus in his *Contra Apionem*. In this book, Josephus tries to refute the various calumnies which the Egyptian historian Apion and other Hellenistic historiographers—mostly of Egyptian provenance—had attributed to the Jews. His text is an extremely valuable codification of extra-Biblical accounts of Jewish history that tell the "tale of two countries," Egypt and Israel, from the Egyptian side. Especially important are two long excerpts which Josephus takes from Manetho. He adduces the first excerpt as proof of the great antiquity of the Jewish people and the second as an example of anti-Jewish calumny. The first excerpt is offered as truth, the second as falsehood. The first excerpt deals with the Hyksos, who are said to have conquered Egypt without resistance and to have treated the population with utmost cruelty. They reigned for more than five hundred years until the king of Thebes finally rebelled against them and besieged their capital at Avaris.[17] The Hyksos emigrated into Syria and finally settled in what is now called Judaea.

The second excerpt[18] opens the series of anti-Jewish calumnies which Josephus wants to refute. Here, Manetho is treated not as a witness but as an enemy. According to Josephus, Manetho's first version follows the "sacred Scripture" *(ta hiera grammata)*, but his second version is based on popular tales and legends *(mutheuomena kai legomena)*. In Manetho's account, King Amenophis wanted to see the gods. The sage Amenophis, son of Hapu, tells him that he may see the gods if he cleanses the land of lepers. The king sends all lepers with priests among them into the quarries in the eastern desert. Amenophis the sage predicts divine punishment for this inhuman treatment of the sick: they will receive help from outside, conquer Egypt, and reign for thirteen years. Not daring to tell the king this in person, he writes everything down and commits suicide. The lepers are allowed to settle in Avaris, the ancient capital of the Hyksos. They choose Osarsiph, a Heliopolitan priest, as their leader.[19] He makes laws for them on the principle of normative inversion, prescribing all that is forbidden in Egypt and forbidding all that is prescribed there. The first and foremost commandment is not to worship the gods, not to spare any of their sacred animals, not to abstain from other forbidden food. The principle of normative inversion consists in inverting the abominations of the other culture into obligations and vice versa. When this principle is applied on the alimentary level, the eating of pork, for example, would be commanded, not because it is cheap or tasty or nutritious, but only because it visibly demonstrates the fact that one does not belong to a community that abominates this food. Inversely, the consumption of meat together with dairy products would be prohibited, not because the combination of meat and milk is unbecoming or unsavory, but because keeping them apart demonstrates separation from a society where consuming this combination is customary, perhaps even obligatory. I will have ample opportunity to treat such questions in greater detail because normative inversion plays a dominant role in Maimonides' and Spencer's hermeneutics.

The second commandment proscribes association with people from outside. The first of these two commandments seems most characteristic of the negative force of a counter-religion: the negation of the traditional gods with their images, sacrifices, and dietary taboos. The second commandment, on the other hand, seems typical of an "enclave culture" (Mary Douglas' term), the culture of a threatened minority that develops a multitude of purity laws in order not be swallowed up by the majority culture. As Mary Douglas has brilliantly shown, Judaism is the classic case of such an "enclave culture."[20] Therefore, it is very probable that the second commandment, the prohibition of intercourse with outsiders, refers to the Jews rather than to the Amarna religion, especially since the notion of exclusivism, or "amixia," came to be a stereotype of the Classical discourse on Jews and Judaism. The second of the two commandments of Osarsiph would then have to be explained as a secondary motif that entered the tradition only after the Egyptians encountered the Jews. This encounter could have occurred as early as the sixth century, when refugees from Judah came to Egypt and when Jewish mercenaries were settled in colonies such as the colony at Elephantine. But the possibility can by no means be ruled out that even the second commandment stems from the older experience. The Amarna religion shows some traits of an enclave culture as well. The most conspicuous manifestation of this aspect of Amarna is the many boundary stelae that mark the borders of the city and that record the solemn oath of the king never to cross those boundaries. Was this done for fear of contagion with the plague that was possibly ravaging Egypt at that time, as Hans Goedicke suggested? Or was it the search for purity and the fear of contagion of a more spiritual kind that engendered this policy so untypical of and even paradoxical for the pharaoh? In any event, it is revealing to look at Amarna as an enclave culture and to associate the commandment of segregation with the (however distorted) memory of the Amarna experience. Moreover, the prohibition of contact with outsiders can be more generally interpreted as the negation of mutual religious translatability. It has then to be seen against the background of ancient polytheism, which encouraged and enforced intercultural communication.

After the establishment of his counter-religious institutions, Osarsiph fortified the city and invited the Hyksos, who were driven out of Egypt some two or three hundred years earlier, to join the revolt. The Hyksos returned. King Amenophis then remembered the prediction, declined to fight the rebels, hide the divine images, and emigrated with the sacred animals to Ethiopia. The lepers and the Hyksos ruled Egypt for thirteen years in a way that makes the former Hyksos rule appear like a Golden Age in the memory of the Egyptians. At this time, not only were the towns and temples laid waste and the holy images destroyed, but the sanctuaries were turned into kitchens and the sacred animals roasted on fires. Osarsiph took the name "Moses." Finally, Amenophis and his grandson Ramses returned from Nubia and drove out the lepers and their allies.

This is Manetho's version of the story, which I shall call version A. It might be broken down into five main episodes:

1. The original state of lack or distress: the invisibility of the gods, which prompted the king to want to see them.
2. The steps taken by the king to overcome this situation: concentration and enslavement of the lepers in the quarries, then their ghettoization in Avaris.
3. The organization of the lepers under the leadership of Osarsiph and his legislation, which inverted the laws and customs of Egypt, especially laws forbidding the worship of the (Egyptian) gods and consorting with other people.
4. The thirteen years of reign of terror by the Hyksos and the lepers, and their war against the temples, cults, images, and animals.
5. The liberation of Egypt, and the expulsion of the lepers and the Hyksos.

This is the extraordinary story in which Akhenaten in the guise of "Osarsiph" alias Moses reenters the literary tradition of Egypt. Amos Funkenstein has recently drawn attention to Manetho's version of the legend of the lepers as the earliest example of what he proposes to call "counterhistory." In his words, counterhistories "form a specific genre of history written since antiquity . . . Their function is polemical. Their method consists of the systematic exploitation of the adversary's most trusted sources against their grain . . . Their aim is the distortion of the adversary's self-image, of his identity, through the deconstruction of his memory."[21] This is a precise description of Josephus' reading of Manetho's text. But it hardly does justice to Manetho's intentions. Manetho does not refer to the Jews at all, let alone to the Bible. He speaks of Egyptian outcasts under the leadership of an Egyptian priest, whose equation with Moses is a gloss, because it comes only at the end and as an afterthought.[22] Manetho does not display intertextuality by "turning the Bible on its head" (Funkenstein), but instead records an orally transmitted legend. As will be shown, the story of Moses circulated in many different versions among the ancient historiographers. Manetho is sharing a widespread tradition. Therefore, it is obvious that they are not only copying from each other but using different (oral) sources. The story must consequently predate the first possible acquaintance of an Egyptian writer with the Hebrew Bible.[23] But Manetho is the only one to call the hero of the story "Osarsiph." All the other versions call him Moses, most of them making him an Egyptian. Manetho must have been aware of this discrepancy because the story occurs in an older history of Egypt that he must have known. There, the name of the leader is given as Moses. I think that Manetho himself (and not a later redactor) added the gloss about Osarsiph's assuming the name Moses in order to reconcile the different versions.

The author of the earliest non-Biblical account of the Exodus is Hecataeus of Abdera, who came to Egypt in about 320 B.C.E.[24] In his version, the story begins at a moment of distress: a plague is ravaging Egypt. The Egyptians interpret this as divine punishment for the presence of aliens and the introduction of alien rites and customs. Consequently, the aliens are expelled. Some, under the leadership of Kadmos and Danaos, colonize Greece,[25] while others, under the leadership of Moses, colonize Palestine. Hecataeus belonged to the very first generation of Hellenistic intellectuals who came to live in Alexandria and to take an active part in the cultural life of the new empire. His ecumenic vision of Egyptian history was perfectly fitting for the new world order that was emerging at Alexandria.[26]

According to Hecataeus, Moses forbade the making of divine images "because God does not own a human shape. Rather, heaven alone who encompasses the earth is God and lord of all, and he cannot be depicted in images."[27] Again, the revolutionary, counter-traditional character of the new religion is emphasized; it is depicted as aniconic, cosmic monotheism. The other versions of the story (more than a dozen) adduce more material. Sometimes, the name of a king is given; in some sources, he is called Bocchoris,[28] in others Amenophis.[29] Most of these versions exhibit a very pronounced anti-Jewish tendency and strike many themes that would linger in European collective memory until the advent of modern anti-Semitism.[30]

Lysimachos, whose particularly polemical account might have been written in the second century B.C.E., begins the story with a famine in the reign of King Bocchoris. The oracle ordered the king to cleanse the temples of the unpure and impious people *(anagnōn kai dyssebōn)* that had settled there—a reference to the Jews who sought refuge from leprosy and other diseases. Bocchoris gave orders to drown the lepers and to expel the others into the desert. The outcasts gathered around one Moses, who led them out of the country and ordered them not to think well of anybody *(mēte anthrōpōn tini eunoēsein)* and to destroy every temple and altar of the gods *(theōn te naous kai bōmous anatrepein)*. These two motifs occur again and again, the first one is termed "amixia" (exclusivity) or "misanthropeia," the second one "asebeia" (impiety, or even atheism).[31]

Chaeremon, an Egyptian who lived in the first half of the first century B.C.E. as a priest and pedagogue in Alexandria and after 49 in Rome as the tutor of Nero, gives yet another version of the story.[32] The goddess Isis appeared to King Amenophis in a dream and reproached him because of the destruction of her temple in times of war. The priest and scribe Phritibantes ("the chief of the temple") advised him to propitiate the goddess by "purging" Egypt of the lepers. The king gathered 250,000 lepers and expelled them from Egypt. Their leaders were Moses and Joseph, whose Egyptian names were Tisithen and Peteseph. In the city of Pelusium they were joined by 380,000 would-be emigrants who had been refused permission to leave the country. Here, for the first time, we meet with a distinct intrusion of Biblical motifs into the story. The united forces of the lepers and the emigrants conquered Egypt and compelled the king to seek refuge in Nubia. Only his son and successor, Ramses, succeeded in reconquering Egypt and driving the "Jews" into Syria.

A very interesting variant of the Moses tradition can be found in Pompeius Trogus' *Historicae Philippicae*. Here, Moses appears not as an Egyptian but as the son of Joseph. But the cult he institutes in Jerusalem is characterized as "sacra Aegyptia." When leaving Egypt, Moses "secretly took the sacred objects of the Egyptians. In trying to recover these objects by force, the Egyptians were forced by storms to go home." Therefore, the cult Moses founded in Jerusalem must have been the cult of these "sacra"—a veritable "translatio religionis." The reason for the Exodus is the same as in most of the other sources: an epidemic. "But when the Egyptians had been exposed to the scab and to a skin infection, and had been warned by an oracle, they expelled [Moses] together with the sick people beyond the confines of Egypt lest the disease should spread to a greater number of people." This "hygienic" reason for the expulsion of the infected persons from Egypt also accounts for the exclusive character of Moses' legislation: "And because he remembered that they had been expelled from Egypt due to fear of contagion, they took care not to live with outsiders lest they become hateful to the natives for the same reason (i.e., fear of contagious infection). This regulation which arose from a specific cause, he [Moses] transformed gradually into a fixed custom and religion."[33] The "hygienic" explanation of the Law would become enormously important: Friedrich Schiller would point to a similar link between the circumstances of the expulsion and the extreme importance which the Law ascribes to leprosy, its early diagnosis and its treatment.

The most extreme portrait of Moses the Egyptian was drawn by Artapanos, the Jewish author of a (lost) book called *On the Jews.* In his representation, Moses appears ethnically as a Jew but culturally as the founder of Egyptian religion and civilization. He is not compared to Hermes Trismegistus, as he is in later works by Marsilio Ficino and other writers of Renaissance Hermetism, but literally identified as Hermes the inventor of hieroglyphics, the author of sacred writings, and the founder of the very religion which the Moses of both Strabo and the Bible so strongly opposed. He divided Egypt into thirty-six nomes and assigned a deity, sacred objects, idols, and even animals to be worshipped in each. Artapanos' Moses embodies the dream of assimilation. Not only does he assimilate, but he contributes to the foreign culture.[34] Artapanos inverts the idea that Moses was an Egyptian priest taking his institutions from Egypt, and makes him a Jew who first established the civil and religious institutions of Egypt. Yet by so doing, he only intensifies the connection between Moses and Egyptian religion. Moses is not its translator, but its founder. His picture of Moses is pure counterhistory in Funkenstein's sense of the term: it is the exact inversion of Hecataeus' and Manetho's Moses, written in contradiction to their texts[35] and with very little reference to the Bible or other Jewish traditions.

✿ TACITUS gives a summary that combines several versions of the Exodus tradition.[36] Egypt is stricken by an epidemic that leads to bodily deformities; King Bocchoris consults the oracle and learns that he must "purge" the country of this race *(genus)* because the gods detest it *(ut invisum deis)*. The Jews are driven into the desert, but find a leader in Moses who brings them to Palestine and founds Jerusalem. In order to consolidate his authority, Moses institutes a new religion which is the exact opposite of all other religions *(novos ritus contrariosque ceteris mortalibus indidit)*. Tacitus, as well as Hecataeus and Strabo, characterizes the Jewish concept of god as monotheistic and aniconic: "The Egyptians worship many animals and monstrous images; the Jews conceive of one god, and that with the mind only: they regard those who make representations of god in man's image from perishable materials as impious; that supreme and eternal being is incapable to them of representation and is without end."[37] With typical conciseness, Tacitus defines the basic principle of this new religion as what might be termed "normative inversion": the Jews consider everything that we keep sacred as profane and permit everything that for us is taboo *(profana illic omnia quae apud nos sacra, rursum concessa apud illos quae nobis incesta)*. In their temples they consecrate a statue of a donkey and sacrifice a ram "in order to ridicule the god Amun" *(in contumeliam Ammonis)*. For the same reason, they sacrifice a bull because the Egyptians worship Apis. In Tacitus, the characterization of Jewish monotheism as a counter-religion which is the inversion of Egyptian tradition and therefore totally derivative of, and dependent on, Egypt reaches its climax.

The strange and particularly absurd motif of the god of the Jews being represented in the statue of an ass finds its explanation in Plutarch, who tells the story in a completely mythologized form. The god Seth, the murderer of Osiris, is driven out of Egypt and spends seven days fleeing into Palestine. There he fathers two sons, whom he calls Hierosolyma and Juda.[38] Seth is usually associated with the donkey in Egyptian mythology. In Greco-Egyptian texts, the god Iao—the Greek rendering of the Hebrew Tetragrammaton[39]—is equated with Seth and the ass because the name—obviously onomatopoietic—sounded like the Egyptian word for ass.[40]

Apion, himself the target of Flavius Josephus' polemics, seems to have treated the topic of the Exodus in the context of his lost Egyptian history. For Apion, the Exodus is an event of Egyptian rather than

Jewish history. He declares Moses to be an Egyptian priest from Heliopolis. According to Apion, Moses led the Jews out of Egypt and
nevertheless taught them a religion that remains true to the tradition
of his native country. He built open temples without any roofs in
various quarters of the city. All of them were oriented toward the east
because this is the way the temples are oriented in Heliopolis. Instead
of obelisks, he erected pillars with a model of a boat underneath. The
shadow which the pillar cast on the basin containing the boat was
supposed to inscribe a circle analogous to the circuit of the sun.[41] Apion
does not describe the religious institutions of Moses as revolutionary;
on the contrary he portrays them as being quite in conformity with
Egyptian tradition. But the Egyptian tradition which Apion attributes
to Moses is a very special one. The sun cult of Heliopolis is the closest
traditional analogy with what Akhenaten taught in the form of a monolatric worship of light. It is not a counter-religion, but a kind of alter-
native religion, which is very different from other Egyptian cults.

🕮 THE HISTORIAN who came closest to a construction of Moses'
religion as monotheistic and as a pronounced counter-religion was
Strabo. It is in this source that Moses the Egyptian makes his most
triumphant and, from a mnemohistorical point of view, his most con-
sequential appearance. This portrait of Moses was to be recognized in
the eighteenth century as that of "a pantheist or, to speak according to
more recent usage, Spinozist."[42] It is this text which comes closest to
Freud's reconstruction of Moses' identity and of the origin of monotheism.

According to Strabo, an Egyptian priest named Moses, who felt
dissatisfied with Egyptian religion, decided to found a new religion and
emigrated with his followers into Palestine. He rejected the Egyptian
tradition of representing the gods in zoomorphic images. His religion
consisted of the recognition of only one divine being whom no image
can represent: "which encompasses us all, including earth and sea, that
which we call the heavens, the world and the essence of things—this
one thing only is God."[43] The only way to approach this god is to live
in virtue and in justice. Later on, the Hebrews deviated from the purity
of this doctrine and developed superstitious rules such as dietary prohibitions and the requirement that males be circumcised.[44]

This passage is important in two ways:

1. It defines monotheism as a counter-religion. Its defining quality lies not in the belief in one god as opposed to the belief in many gods, but in its radical and complete break with traditional religion. It typically views and abhors tradition in terms of superstition and idolatry, and as a complex of ritualistic magic and fetishism. In many aspects this seems to be a more adequate notion of monotheism than the modern one, which centers on the purely theological questions of the one and the many. The ancients were concerned not so much with theological issues, such as the conceptualization of the divine, as with religious pragmatics, such as questions of ritual and sacrifice, images and temples, prescriptions and taboos.[45] The decisive feature of the monotheistic movements is their revolutionary, "idolophobic," or iconoclastic character. They are counter-religions which are born out of "dissatisfaction" with tradition.

2. The passage also quite bluntly and explicitly declares Moses to be an Egyptian priest and his new religion to be an Egyptian counter-religion.

THE STORY of the lepers can thus be explained as a conspicuous case of distorted and dislodged memory. In this tradition Egyptian recollections of Akhenaten's monotheistic revolution survived. But because of the banishment of Akhenaten's name and monuments from cultural memory, these recollections became dislocated and subject to many kinds of transformations and proliferations. To use a term of psychoanalysis, they became "encrypted," that is, inaccessible to conscious reflection and processing.[46] The formation of a "crypt" in collective memory may be caused by strong traumatic experiences. Some even maintain that "encryption" is a much more faithful form of preserving traumatic memories than conscious remembering.[47] But the Amarna case shows that suppression or encryption renders an original experience vulnerable to many kinds of distortion and transformation rather than preserving it in a pure state. Instead of pursuing this process through all its stages of transformation and proliferation, I would like to bring a third version of the Exodus story into focus: the Biblical account. The Biblical text has a very complex and multilayered structure which contains much more material than is relevant to the present discussion. But some of its themes and elements are directly associated with the tradition I am considering and constitute just another version of the same events. These are:

1. Concentration and enslavement with forced labor and oppression, which provokes divine wrath, as in Manetho's version;
2. A plague enforcing Egypt's separation from the "aliens," as in Hecataeus' version. This motif appears here tenfold, as ten plagues.
3. The separation, realized here in the form of a finally and reluctantly conceded emigration rather than an expulsion, and the Exodus under the leadership of Moses;
4. The legislation of Moses, along with the prohibition against worshipping (other) gods as the most prominent commandment.

The most striking common denominator of Manetho's version and the Biblical version is the dark affective shading of the narrative. Both versions are suffused with mutual hatred and abomination. Both accounts also translate the experience of counter-religion. In the Biblical version, the Egyptians are shown as torturers and oppressors, idolators and magicians. In the Egyptian version, the "Jews" are shown as lepers, as impure people, atheists, misanthropes, iconoclasts, vandals, and sacrilegious criminals. But equally striking are the differences between the two versions because they relate to each other in the form of an exact inversion. All the extra-Biblical versions agree that the aliens, or impure ones, are driven out of Egypt. In the Bible, the Hebrews are retained in Egypt against their will and they are allowed to emigrate only after divine interventions in the form of the plagues. But even in this version the account of the emigration contains elements of expulsion.

Of course, it would be most instructive to confront these different versions with what could constitute historical evidence, but there is almost no such evidence. The only historical event which is both archaeologically provable and semantically comparable with the content of these different versions of the expulsion/emigration story is the sojourn of the Hyksos in Egypt.

If we apply the same question asked previously about the Amarna experience to the Hyksos tradition and if we remain on the lookout for what might have become of the memories that must have been shared by the expelled tribes about their stay in, and domination of Egypt, we find ourselves again referred to the Exodus tradition. I completely agree with Flavius Josephus and Donald B. Redford, who has held in various publications that the Hyksos' sojourn in, and withdrawal from, Egypt was all that happened in terms of historical fact. Further, he argued that different memories of these events lived on in the traditions of Canaan and Egypt. The Hebrews merely fell heir to the Canaanite part of these memories. If we accept this theory, we are in a position to evaluate the stages of its transformation and to recognize its direction. The Hyksos stayed in Egypt not as slaves but as rulers. They withdrew from Egypt not as finally released slaves but as expelled enemies. The inversions which the Hebrew tradition imposed on the historical facts find their explanation in the semantic frame of the covenant-and-election theology. This is a semantics of small beginnings and great promises. Within this frame the withdrawal from Egypt could not be understood other than as a rise from nothingness to identity, from bondage to freedom, from impurity to purity, and from forlorness to alliance. In the context of oral tradition, narrative inversions such as these met with no resistance because "no fixed narrative or king-list held imagination in check."[48]

In Egypt, the experience of the Hyksos invasion and expulsion entered the official king list tradition. It was therefore safe from overly radical alterations. But the king-list tradition was devoid of any semantic specification or narrative fleshing-out. These documents listed the names of the rulers and the regnal years, but no evaluation of the kings. My thesis is that the Hyksos tradition received its semantic coloring and its character as a predominantly religious conflict only after the Amarna age, or, to be more precise, after the extinction of the contemporary generation, when the Amarna reminiscences tended to get conflated with the Hyksos tradition. Only then did the Hyksos begin to play the role of adherents of an alien and antagonistic religion. The Amarna experience shaped the Hyksos tradition and created the semantic frame of the "religious enemy," which was afterward filled by the Assyrians, the Persians, the Greeks, and finally the Jews.

My question, to resume, is not about "what really happened," but rather about what became of the recollections that must have existed in the form of individual remembrances and collective traditions, both in Canaan (of the Hyksos' sojourn in Egypt) and in Egypt (of the Amarna revolution). In my opinion, it is much easier to explain the survival of these memories until the Hellenistic period than their complete disappearance. Herodotus and demotic literature abound with tales, anecdotes, and fables that must have lived on in oral tradition for centuries or even a millennium.[49]

🏵️ THE STORY of the lepers is about purity and defilement. A situation of lack (invisibility of the gods) or distress (famine, plague) is explained by an oracle or an inspired sage as the result of pollution. The country suffers from defilement by the presence of "strangers" and can only be cured by their expulsion. In her fascinating and convincing analysis of the book of Numbers, Mary Douglas has discovered a cyclical structure which closely relates the laws to drive out the lepers (Numbers 5:1–4) and to expel the idolators (Numbers 33:50–56).[50] Leprosy and idolatry are among the most dangerous forms of pollution because they prevent God from "dwelling amidst his people." The Egyptian story tells us about the corresponding fears and abominations on the side of the "idolators." It sheds light on the opposite term of idolatry. Idolatry does not merely denote a certain religious attitude based on the worship of "idols" or images; in this sense, the opposite term would be "aniconism." But idolatry means more than iconism. It is a polemical term which expresses a strong cultural/religious abomination and anxiety. With the term "idolatry," the "aniconists" refer to the "iconists" as the group where the strongest menace resides. Idolatry is the umbrella term for what must be warded off by all means. There is a marked crescendo to be observed in the texts dealing with idolatry. As has already been stated, both the concept of idolatry and the repudiation of it grew stronger and stronger in the course of Jewish history. The prevailing metaphor, however, is not leprosy, but madness. Idolatry is conceived of as a mental aberration, not as a bodily disease. Leprosy is the metaphor used by the other side, the iconists, in order to characterize the "iconoclasts."

This is what the story of the lepers tells us. Under certain conditions of danger, the "iconists" develop similar fears and abominations. Like "aniconism," "iconism" is a form of ensuring divine presence under strong conditions of purity. Destroying the images and killing the sacred animals means the same kind of danger for the "iconists" as idolatry means for the "aniconists." These actions defile the country and render it uninhabitable for the gods. Iconoclasm has the destructive power of a deadly pollution, and can only be compared to a strongly contagious and defiling disease such as leprosy or the plague. In the same way that "idols" destroy the contact between Israel and its invisible god, the defilement or destruction of images destroys the contact between Egypt and its deities. Iconism and aniconism are mutually exclusive means of ensuring divine presence.[51]

The Egyptian form of religious symbolism made such fears and anxieties controllable by personification. In the Late Period, the god Seth became the personification of all the threats directed against divine presence as ensured by iconism. Seth, the mythical murderer of Osiris, became the prototypical iconoclast. He was first associated with the Persians and then with the Jews. I have already quoted the passage in Plutarch where Seth appears as the ancestor of the Jews. A demotic papyrus of the Roman period deals with the Jews as "lawbreakers" (*paranomoi*) "once expelled from Egypt by the wrath of Isis." The text is a prophecy describing future distress and prescribing the way of salvation: "Attack the Jews" for "impious people will despoil your temples" and "your largest temple will become sand for the horses." The Jews will even "inhabit the city of Helios."[52]

The image of the Jew as the religious enemy par excellence—as atheist, iconoclast, sacrilegious criminal—turns out to be a matter not of experience, but of memory, that is, the return of the suppressed memory of Akhenaten. The Egyptian encounter with the Jews had already taken place within the prefabricated semantic frame of the sacrilegious Asiatic as the religious enemy. With the possible exception of Manetho, who wrote not about Jews, but about Egyptian lepers, all the others, especially Flavius Josephus, conflated the story of the lepers with the account of the Jewish Exodus from Egypt. Tacitus[53] and Orosius transmitted this pseudo-historical tradition to the Occident. Tacitus' authority as a historian imparted the dignity of authentic historical research to this product of imagination, projection, and distorted memory.

The story of the lepers has always been interpreted as an Egyptian prelude to European anti-Semitism.[54] It has been explained as being expressive of an Egyptian reaction to the Jews who came to settle in Egypt after the Babylonian conquest of Jerusalem. My mnemohistorical reading of the story has uncovered its traumatic dimension, which links it to the Amarna experience. But despite these possible origins, it is only too true that the story became focused on the Jews and thus the tale became a component of European anti-Semitism. Apart from this general history of its reception, the story of the lepers had a very specific aftermath in the fourteenth century, as has been pointed out by Carlo Ginzburg.[55] In 1321, Jews and lepers were accused of a conspiracy against Christianity, leading to their persecution, extermination, and confinement. The lepers were accused of having strewn poisonous powders in the fountains, wells, and rivers, so as to transmit leprosy to the healthy. The Jews were believed to be accomplices in this crime. Some versions fixed the ultimate responsibility for the entire scheme on the Muslim king of Granada, who had offered the Jews a huge amount of money to destroy Christianity. In turn, the Jews had instigated the lepers to spread their disease. The chronicles tell the story in many different versions: the lepers alone; the Jews and the lepers; the Muslims, the Jews, and the lepers. We find a complete reenactment of the Egyptian scenario: the native lepers, the resident aliens, and the foreign kingdom operating from afar. Again we find the identical pattern of a strongly contagious and bodily disfiguring disease, a counter-religious attack, and a political conspiracy.[56]

When the plague started to ravage Europe less than thirty years later, attempts were widely made to attribute the responsibility for the epidemic to the Jews.[57] The phantasm of the religious Other and the phobic idea of contagion and conspiracy never ceased to haunt Europe. The anti-Semitic discourse in nineteenth-century Germany, especially that of Richard Wagner and Emperor Wilhelm II, who had a strong influence on Adolf Hitler, used precisely the same language of conspiracy and contagion. Our own century has seen the greatest excesses of this collective psychosis. Therefore, it is important to trace this history back to its origin, with the hope that this anamnesis and "working-through" may contribute to a better understanding and an overcoming of the dynamics behind the development of cultural or religious abomination.

Counter-Religion and Religious Translatability in the Ancient World

The dynamics of counter-traditional religions can only be understood properly if seen against the background of that level of intercultural translatability at which the different civilizations and polytheisms of the Ancient World had arrived during the second millennium B.C.E. The conviction that God or the gods are international was a characteristic of the polytheistic religions of the ancient Near East. We must not think of polytheism as something primitive and tribal. The polytheistic religions of the ancient Near East and Ancient Egypt represent highly developed cultural achievements that are inseparably linked to the political organization of the early state and are not to be found in tribal societies. Tribal religions are characterized by their scarcely humanized and only weakly articulated and differentiated concept of the divine, which is worshipped in the form of ancestral spirits, and which is adored without any ritual worship in the form of a very remote high god, or *deus otiosus*. By contrast, in the context of "high-cultural" polytheisms the deities are clearly differentiated and personalized by name, shape, and function. The great achievement of polytheism is the articulation of a common semantic universe. The gods are given a semantic dimension, by means of mythical narratives and theocosmological speculations. It is this semantic dimension that makes the names translatable. Tribal religions are ethnocentric. The powers that are worshipped by one tribe are different from the powers worshipped by another tribe. In contrast, the highly differentiated members of polytheistic pantheons lend themselves easily to cross-cultural translation or "interpretation." Well-known cases are the *interpretatio Latina* of Greek divinities and the *interpretatio Graeca* of Egyptian ones. Translation functions because the names have not only a reference, but also a meaning. The meaning of a deity is his or her specific character as it is unfolded in myths, hymns, rites, and so on. This character makes a deity comparable to other deities with similar traits. The similarity of gods makes their names mutually translatable. But in historical reality, this correlation has to be reversed. The practice of translating the names of the gods created a concept of similarity and produced the idea or conviction that gods are international.

The tradition of translating or interpreting foreign divine names goes back to the Mesopotamian *Listenwissenschaft* of the third millennium B.C.E. In the context of these innumerable glossaries equating Sumerian and Akkadian words, there also appear lists of gods giving the divine names in two or even three languages, such as Emesal (women's language, used as a literary dialect), Sumerian, and Akkadian.[58] The most interesting of these sources is the explanatory list *Anu ša Ameli* which contains three columns, the first giving the Sumerian names, the second the Akkadian names, and the third the functional definition of the deity.[59] This explanatory list gives what may be called the "meaning" of divine names, making explicit the principle which underlies the equation or translation of divine names. As long as this search for theological equations and equivalents was confined to the two languages, Sumerian and Akkadian, one could argue that it remained within the frame of a common religious culture. The translation here operates translingually, but not transculturally. But in the Kassite period of the late Bronze Age, the lists are extended to include languages spoken by foreign peoples. There is an "explanatory list of gods" that gives divine names in Amorite, Hurritic, Elamite, and Kassite in addition to Sumerian and Akkadian.[60]

In these cases, there can be no doubt that the practice of translating divine names was applied to very different cultures and religions. The conviction that these foreign peoples worshipped the same gods is far from trivial and self-evident. Quite the contrary, this insight must be reckoned among the major cultural achievements of the Ancient World. The powerful influence of this insight can be seen in the field of international law and in the practice of forming treaties with other states and peoples. This, too, seems a specialty of Mesopotamian culture. Treaties had to be sealed by solemn oaths and the gods that were invoked in these oaths had to be recognized by both parties. The list of these gods conventionally closes the treaty. They necessarily had to be equivalent as to their function and in particular as to their rank. Intercultural theology became a concern of international law.

It seems probable to me that the interest in translations and equations for gods of different religions arose out of the Akkadian assimilation of the Sumerian pantheon and developed in the context of foreign policy. I do not assume that something like a conviction of living in a common world and worshipping common gods went before and formed the fundamentals of this political practice. Rather, I see it the other way round: the growing political and commercial interconnectedness of the Ancient World and the practice of cross-cultural translation of everything including divine names gradually led to the concept of a common religion. The argument runs as follows: Peoples,

Cultures, and political systems may be different. But as long as they have a religion and worship some definite and identifiable gods, they are comparable and contactable because these gods must necessarily be the same as those worshipped by other nations but under different names. The names, iconographies, and rites—in short, the cultures— differ, but the gods are the same. This concept of religion as the common background of cultural diversity and the principle of cultural translatability eventually led to the late Hellenistic mentality for which the names of the gods mattered little in view of the overwhelming natural evidence of their existence, and it was this mentality of Late Antiquity that the Deism of the seventeenth and eighteenth centuries returned to.

🌸 THE DEITY whose theology was most strongly informed by this universalist concept was Isis—not in her traditional Egyptian form, but in the form she assumed in Greco-Egyptian syncretism. The eleventh and last book of the *Metamorphoses* by Apuleius of Madaurus, written in the time of Marcus Aurelius, not only gives expression to this cos- motheistic conviction in a very explicit and articulated form, but in a way also transcends it. The book opens with a beautiful and highly significant scene. Lucius, a young man who has been transformed into an ass after carelessly dabbling in magic, awakens at the shore of the Mediterranean as the full moon rises from the sea. Books 1 through 10 had told of his trials and misfortunes, and Apuleius' Latin text seems to closely follow his Greek original. But with the eleventh book the tone changes from the colorful and sometimes burlesque style of a pica- resque novel into what A. D. Nock characterized as "the high-water mark of the piety which grew out of the mystery religions."[61] A new chapter is opened and a new hope rises with the moon, which Lucius addresses as follows:

> O Queen of Heaven—whether thou art Ceres, the primal and
> bountiful mother of crops . . .; or whether thou art heavenly Ve-
> nus who . . . art worshiped in the shrine of Paphos; or the sister
> of Phoebus who . . . art now adored in the temples of Ephesus; or
> whether as Proserpine . . . thou art propitiated with differing
> rites—whoever thou art . . ., by whatever name *(nomine)* or cere-

mony *(ritu)* or face *(facie)* thou art rightly called, help me now in the depth of my trouble.[62]

Lucius addresses a nameless power which he feels is immanent in and revealed by the moon with four names: Ceres (Demeter), Venus (Aphrodite), Diana (Artemis), and Proserpina (Persephone). This is the tradition of invoking a deity with the "names of the nations" which I will consider soon. The specific names, rites, and shapes are far less important than the manifest cosmic power. The goddess answers him in a dream, presenting herself in a similar way. She, too, ends her self-presentation with a catalogue of names:

> Lo, I am with you, Lucius, moved by your prayers, I who am the mother of the universe, the mistress of all the elements, the first offspring of time, the highest of deities, the queen of the dead, foremost of heavenly beings, the single form that fuses all gods and goddesses; I who order by my will the starry heights of heaven, the health giving breezes of the sea, and the awful silences of those in the underworld: my single godhead is adored by the whole world in varied forms, in differing rites and with many diverse names.
>
> Thus the Phrygians . . . call me Pessinuntia . . .; the Athenians . . . call me Cecropeian Minerva; the Cyprians . . . call me Paphian Venus, the . . . Cretans Dictynna, the . . . Sicilians Ortygian Proserpine; to the Eleusinians I am Ceres . . ., to others Juno, to others Bellona and Hecate and Rhamnusia. But the Ethiopians . . . together with the Africans and the Egyptians who excel by having the original doctrine honor me with my distinctive rites and give me my true name of Queen Isis.

The goddess also correlates names and nations. The name *is* important, but only for a specific group who adores the goddess in a specific form and through specific rites. Besides all these ethnic names, however, she also has a "true name" *(verum nomen)*, which remained in use only among the nations with the most ancient and authentic tradition: the Egyptians and their southern neighbors.

Apuleius is a borderline case. On the one hand, he shares the view about the conventionality of divine names and the natural evidence of the divine essence. On the other hand, there is this concept of *verum nomen*, which clearly transcends the frame of natural evidence and belongs to the frame of revelation. The names which the deity is given by the various nations are not revealed, but constitute the culturally specific answer to general nature. But the *verum nomen* is exclusively revealed to the Egyptians and the Ethiopians. We are dealing with mystery as a transitional stage between nature and revelation.[63] Revelation is the opposite of nature. A revealed name cannot be translated. But there is no opposition, let alone counter-religious antagonism between the Egyptian worship of Isis based on the "true name" and the worship of the various nations based on their conventional names for the same goddess. The concept of the "true name" does not turn the other nations into "pagans," but only makes believers of a lower level of initiation. All worship the same deity and it is this natural identity transcending all cultural differences that counts.

THE TRADITION of invoking Isis by the names by which the various nations address her (a tradition which I will refer to, for brevity's sake, as "the names of the nations") was widespread in Greco-Roman Isis religion. There are several Isis-texts from Egypt that address the goddess in this way. The earliest is a hymn which Isidorus of Narmuthis had engraved on pillars in the temple of Thermuthis at Medinet Madi (first century B.C.E.).[64]

> All mortals who live on the boundless earth,
> Thracians, Greeks and Barbarians,
> Express your fair name, a name greatly honored among all,
> [But] each speaks in his own language, in his own land.
> The Syrians call you: Astarte, Artemis, Nanaia,
> The Lycian tribes call you: Leto, the lady.
> The Thracians also name you as Mother of the gods,
> And the Greeks [call you] Hera of the Great Throne,
>   Aphrodite,
> Hestia the goodly, Rhea and Demeter.
> But the Egyptians call you Thiouis[65] [because they know] that
>   you, being one, are all other goddesses invoked by the races
>   of men.[66]

Another text is provided by a papyrus from Oxyrhynchos. It contains a long hymn to Isis starting with a very long though badly fragmented list of names and places.[67] There we read:

> . . . at Aphroditopolis [. . .], one in the house of Hephaestus [. . .] chmuenis; who at [. . .]ophis art called Bubastis, [. . .]; at Letopolis Magna [. . .] one; at Aphroditopolis in the Prosopite nome fleet-commanding, many-shaped Aphrodite; at the Delta giver of favors . . . at Nithine in the Gynaecopolite nome, Aphrodite; at Paphremis, Isis, queen, Hestia, mistress of every country;. . . in the Saite nome, Victorious Athena . . .; in Sais, Hera, queen, full grown; in Iseum, Isis; in Sebennytos, intelligence, ruler, Hera, holy; in Hermupolis, Aphrodite, queen, holy; . . . in Apis, Sophia; in Leuke Akte, Aphrodite, Mouchis, Eseremphis; at Cynopolis in the Busirite nome, Praxidike; at Busiris, Good Fortune [*Tukhe agathe*]; . . . at Tanis, gracious in form, Hera [. . .] etc.

After a long list correlating Egyptian towns with names of Isis, the text continues by naming places outside Egypt such as Arabia, where she is the "great goddess"; in Lycia, "Leto"; at Myra, "sage, freedom"; at Cnidus, "dispeller of attack, discoverer"; at Cyrene, "Isis"; on Crete, "Dictynnis"; at Chalcedon, "Themis"; in Rome, "warlike"; in the Cyclades, "of threefold nature"; on Patmos, "young [. . .]"; at Paphos, "hallowed, divine, gentle"; on Chios, "marching"; at Salamis "observer"; on Cyprus, "all-bounteous"; and so forth, including foreign names: at Bamyce, "Atargatis"; among the Indians, "Maia"; at Sidon, "Astarte." The list closes with a striking formula: "the beautiful essence of all the gods" *(theôn hapánton tò kalòn zôon).*

🧠 BUT THE MOTIF of "the names of the nations" and the relativization of all cultural and national differences as mere surface phenomena to be set off against the background of a common universal religion is not exclusively related to Isis. It is typical of the idea of a "Supreme Being" (the Greek expression is *Hypsistos,* "the Highest One").

It consists in the belief in a supreme being comprising in its essence not only the myriads of known and unknown deities, but above all those three or four gods who, in the context of different religions, play the role of the highest god (usually Zeus, Sarapis, Helios, and Iao = YHWH). This super-deity is addressed by appellations like *Hypsistos* ("supreme"),[68] and by the widespread "One-God" predication *Heîs Theós*.[69] Oracles typically proclaim particular gods to be identical with other gods. The oracles concerning Sarapis are well known:

> One Zeus, one Hades, one Helios is Sarapis.[70]

> One Zeus, one Hades, one Helios, one Dionysos,
> One god in all gods.[71]

Where Iao, the God of the Jews, is elevated to the rank of the One-and-Supreme Being, he has to give up his transcendent other-worldliness in order to become an immanent cosmic entity. In one of these oracles he is proclaimed the god of time (Olam-Aion) appearing as Hades in winter, Zeus in springtime, Helios in summer, and Abros Iao in autumn.[72] In these oracles and predications, there becomes manifest a quest for the sole and supreme divine principle beyond the innumerable multitude of specific deities. This quest is typical of the "ecumenic age" and seems to correspond to efforts to achieve political unification.[73] The belief in the "Supreme Being" *(Hypsistos)* has a distinctly cosmopolitan character. Typical of this conception is the combination of names from different languages and religions.

The hallmark of this cosmopolitan religiosity is the tradition of invoking the Supreme Being by the "names of the nations." A consecration text in Papyrus Leiden I, 384, addresses the Supreme God Iao (= YHWH)-Sabaoth-Abrasax in the following words:

> I invoke you as do the Egyptians: "Phno eai Iabok,"
> As do the Jews: Adonaie Sabaoth,
> As do the Greeks: king, ruling as monarch over all,
> As do the high priests: hidden one, invisible one, who looks
>   upon all,
> As do the Parthians: OYERTO almighty.[74]

A magical invocation starts as follows:

> I invoke thee who encompasses the universe,
> in every voice and in every dialect *(pasē phonē kai pasē
>   dialektō)*[75]

Hippolytus, in his report on the sermon of the Naassenians (a Gnostic sect), includes the liturgical chant from the cult of Attis invoking Attis by the names of the gods of the various peoples which forms the "text" of the sermon:

> Whether the offspring of Kronos or the blessed son of Jove or
>   of the great Rhea,
> hail to thee, Attis, sad message of Rhea.
> The Assyrians call thee thrice desired Adonis,
>   all Egypt calls thee Osiris,
> Greek wisdom the heavenly horn of the moon,
> the Samothracians "dignified Adamna,"
> the Haemonians Korybas,
> the Phrygians now Papas, then Tot or God,
> or "Without-Fear," goat-herd, mown ear,
> or man, born by the almond with many fruits, flute-player.[76]

Of particular interest in the context of this study is an epigram by Ausonius, because it was to play a major role in the discourse about Moses the Egyptian.[77] It is epigram 48, entitled "Mixobarbaron Liberi Patris Signo Marmoreo in Villa Nostra Omnium Deorum Argumenta Habenti."[78] I give the text according to the edition and translation by Hugh G. Evelyn White[79]:

> Ogygiadae[80] me Bacchum vocant,
> Osiris Aegypti putant,
> Mysi Phanacen nominant,
> Dionyson Indi existimant,
> Romana sacra Liberum,
> Arabica gens Adoneum,
> Lucaniacus Pantheum.
>
> The sons of Ogyges call me Bacchus,
> Egyptians think me Osiris,
> Mysians name me Phanaces,
> Indians regard me as Dionysus,
> Roman rites make me Liber,
> The Arab race thinks me Adoneus,
> Lucaniacus[81] the Universal God.

This tradition of invoking the highest god by the names of the various nations expresses a general conviction in Late Antiquity about the universality of religious truth and the relativity of religious institutions and denominations. Mozart's masonic Cantata K. 619 and Goethe's monologue "Wer darf ihn nennen" bespeak the same conviction in very similar terms.

The conception of the conventionality and therefore the translatability of the divine names was based on natural evidence, that is, on reference to experiences that were accessible to all humankind. Seneca refers to visible evidence in precisely this sense: "This All, which you see, which encompasses divine and human, is One, and we are but members of a great body."[82] According to Servius, the Stoics taught that there is only one god whose names merely differ according to actions and offices.[83] Varro, who knew about the Jews from Poseidonios, was unwilling to see any difference between Jove and Yahweh *nihil interesse censens quo nomine nuncupetur, dum eadem res intelligatur* ("because he was of the opinion that it mattered little by which name he was called as long as the same thing was meant").[84] Porphyry, a Neoplatonic philosopher of the third century C.E. held the opinion that the names of the gods were purely conventional.[85] In a pamphlet against the Christians called *Alethes Logos,* Celsus argued that "it makes no difference whether one calls god 'Supreme' *[Hypsistos]* or Zeus or Adonai or Sabaoth or Ammon such as the Egyptians do or Papaios as the Scythians."[86] The name does not matter when it is evident what or who is meant.

In his treatise on Isis and Osiris, Plutarch succinctly conveys this general conviction by stating that behind the differing divine names are always common cosmic phenomena: the sun, the moon, the heavens, the earth, the sea. Just as all people live in the same world, they adore the same gods who are the lords of this world: "nor do we regard the gods as different among different nations nor as barbarian and Greek and as southern and northern. But just as the sun, moon, heaven, earth and sea are common to all, though they are given various names by the varying nations, so it is with the one reason *[logos]* which orders these things and the one providence which has charge of them, and the assistant powers which are assigned to everything: they are given different honors and modes of address among different nations according to custom, and they use hallowed symbols."[87] The divine names are translatable because there is always a referent serving as a *tertium comparationis.* This referent is the concept of a functionally divided and divinely animated or inspirited universe in which humankind finds and maintains its place by recognizing and adoring the operative powers, by giving them names and iconographies, temples and ceremonies.

In the realm of this general religious conviction which I call cosmotheism (a term use by F. H. Jacobi, to whom I will return later), there was no room for religious antagonism. That is why the antagonistic power of counter-religions such as Judaism and Christianity was so much resented by pagan intellectuals. The opposition between cosmotheism and monotheism, or between nature and revelation, was never resolved, but merely suppressed in the victorious development of the church. Its return during the Renaissance and its controversial history in the formation of European modernity forms the subtext of the discourse on Moses the Egyptian with which the following chapters will be concerned.

CHAPTER THREE

Before the Law: John Spencer as Egyptologist

The boundaries of intranslatability which the Jewish, the Christian, and somewhat later the Islamic monotheisms erected in the name of revelation must be viewed against the background of the firm cosmotheistic belief in translatability in the name of nature. With the decline and fall of the Roman Empire, the cosmotheistic conviction disappeared. The Middle Ages were safely contained within the bounds of Biblical monotheism. There was no place for a figure such as Moses the Egyptian who would blur the boundaries of counter-religion. Egypt was viewed as the "other" and not as the origin.

The situation changed only with the Renaissance, when Egypt became recoverable through sources other than the Bible and the Church Fathers. The landmarks in the rediscovery or reinvention of Egypt were two books: the *Hieroglyphica* by Horapollo and the *Corpus Hermeticum*. Through them it became clear what was meant by "all the wisdom of Egypt," which Moses was said to have been "well versed in"—in this single verse in the Bible (Acts 7:22) that deals with Moses' Egyptian education.[1] Thus a process of fundamental cultural, religious, and historical reorientation started. In the light of what was seen as strong parallels between Biblical and Hermetic texts, the wall of intranslatability collapsed and Egypt began to appear as the origin, rather than the "other," of Biblical monotheism.

John Spencer was a latecomer in the history of this first stage of Egyptology. The reason for choosing him as a starting point, rather than Marsilio Ficino, Giordano Bruno, Robert Fludd, Athanasius

Kircher, and others who wrote on Egypt, its hieroglyphs, and its Hermetic doctrines, was explained in the first chapter and need not be repeated here. With Spencer and some of his contemporaries such as Marsham and Cudworth, the discourse on Egypt leaves the confines of Hermeticism and other mystical and occult traditions and begins to speak the language of the Enlightenment. Seen from the vantage point of the Enlightenment, Spencer appears to be not a latecomer, but a pioneer. With him, and not with Giordano Bruno or Athanasius Kircher, begins a debate that will be continued by Schiller and via Schiller by Freud.

John Spencer (1630–1693) was an English Hebraist[2] who in 1667 was appointed Master of Corpus Christi College at Cambridge. He published his doctoral dissertation, *Urim and Thummim*, in 1670 and his monumental monograph *De Legibus Hebraeorum Ritualibus et Earum Rationibus Libri Tres* in 1685.[3] For Spencer, Moses is not an Egyptian but an "Egyptianized" Hebrew. However, Moses did not need to be born an Egyptian in order to be able to "translate" Egyptian mysteries into Hebrew laws. It is sufficient that he was intimately acquainted with Egyptian wisdom. And this is precisely what St. Stephanus asserts in the short recapitulation of sacred history included in his speech of apology and farewell before his execution: that "Moses was well versed in all the wisdom of the Egyptians." For Spencer's project, this short sentence was absolutely crucial. It was the one foundation on which he could build his entire edifice, and it was the one testimony that could save him from being accused of heresy. Serving as leitmotifs throughout the whole line of the Moses debate, which started with Spencer and which ends with Freud, are this sentence and a short passage from Philo of Alexandria in *De Vita Mosis* in which he says that Moses was initiated into the "symbolic" philosophy of the ancient Egyptians.[4]

Spencer's project was to demonstrate the Egyptian origin of the ritual laws of the Hebrews. In order to understand the novelty and the boldness of this undertaking, we must briefly consider how Spencer dislodged two crucial tenets of Christian theology. The first is the traditional Christian distinction between moral Law, political Law, and ritual Law within the body of the 613 prescriptions and prohibitions contained in the Torah. Moral Law is the Decalogue, political and ritual Law is all the rest. Moral Law is eternal, political and ritual Law is temporal.[5] The validity of the ritual Law is limited to the timespan between Moses and Jesus. The second presupposition is the orthodox view that every coincidence between a Biblical law and a pagan rite is a work of the devil, who is an ape of God. The Hebrew Law is the original model, and the pagan religions are diabolic institutions imitating this model.[6] Spencer contradicted the second presupposition by showing that Egypt was the origin and the model for the ritual Law. Concerning the first presupposition, Spencer did quite a revolutionary thing: he shifted the focus from the timeless moral Law to the long abolished ritual Law, and, even more significant, he tried to use this body of prescriptions and institutions to reconstruct the long forgotten "atrocities" of Egyptian idolatry. Notwithstanding his strategic professions of Egyptophobia, his extremely diligent and well-documented representation of Egyptian rites became one of the most important reference books for Egyptophiles of the eighteenth century.

Normative Inversion as a Mnemotechnique of Forgetting: Maimonides

Spencer's project is the rational explanation of the Mosaic law. It is the same project that Rabbi Moses ben Maimon (Maimonides, 1135–1204) pursued in his famous *Guide for the Perplexed* (*Dalalat al-ha'irin*, Hebrew *Moreh Nebukhim*).[7] Spencer fully acknowledges this debt to Maimonides. But Spencer's method of rational explanation differs widely from Maimonides' in that it proceeds mainly by historicization. Spencer explains Moses' legislation by reconstructing its historical context. Yet even in the method of historical explanation, he is following Maimonides, whose "apologetic purpose consequently involves him in a historical task, obliging him to give an account of ancient oriental paganism."[8] However, Maimonides' reconstruction of oriental paganism not only lacks any authentic historical interest and understanding, but is also mistaken. Instead of taking Ancient Egypt as the proper background against which to set off the contradistinctive force of Moses' legislation, he talks about the "Zabii" or "Sabians." The Sabians are twice mentioned in the Koran along with Jews and Christians as a people believing in God and thus protected by the Law.[9] It is still an open question which religion or sect the Koran could have meant. In Spencer's time, the Sabians were mostly associated or even identified with the Persians, Zoroastrians, or "Eastern Chaldaeans," and their religion was described as astrology and idolatrous worship of the celestial bodies.[10] More recently, some have thought of the Mandaeans or a similar movement;[11] Funkenstein sees in them the "small remnants of a gnostic sect of the 2nd or 3rd century A.D."[12] From 830 on the term was used to refer to the people at Harran who had managed to remain pagans and who still adhered to the cult of Sin, the Mesopotamian moon god. Threatened by persecution, they claimed to be Sabians, and claimed Hermetic writings as their sacred book.[13] By 1050, however, they had been forced to convert to Islam or one of the tolerated religions, and they thus disappeared from the scene. Maimonides, who wrote a century later, could refer to the astrologers and Hermetists at Harran who remained well known through their books;[14] but he could also refer to the Gnostic sect, about which he might have learned from Ibn Wahshiyya's *Nabataean Agriculture* (tenth century).[15] In fact, however, there never existed in history a polytheistic universal religious community *(umma)* by that name like the one Maimonides wrote about.

Maimonides' Sabians are an imagined community which he created by applying Manetho's principle of normative inversion in the opposite direction. Manetho was familiar with Egyptian tradition and imagined a counter-community based upon the inverted mirror image of Egyptian mores. Maimonides was familiar with normative Judaism and imagined a pagan counter-community—the *'ummat Ṣa'aba*—as the counter-image of Jewish law. If the Law prohibits an activity x there must have existed an idolatrous community practicing x. The truth of both counter-constructions lies in the negative potential and antagonistic force of revelation or counter-religion.

Maimonides had excellent reasons for choosing the Sabians instead of the historically more appropriate ancient Egyptians for his reconstruction of a historical context for Mosaic law. It is precisely their complete insignificance which serves his purpose. He describes his Sabians as a once powerful community. The fact that the remnants of its memory survive only in some works of extremely specialized scholarship is the best proof of the truth of his explanation of the Law. He explains the function of the Law as a kind of "ars oblivionis," a withdrawal therapy of Sabian idolatry. Umberto Eco may be right in postulating that there is no possible art of oblivion on the level of individual memory.[16] But Eco's arguments do not apply on the level of collective memory. The most efficient way of erasing a memory is by superimposing on it a counter-memory. This is less an "art" than a strategy which works on both the individual and the collective level. Hence the best way to make people forget an idolatrous rite is to put another rite in its place. The Christians followed the same principle by building their churches on the ruins of pagan temples and by observing their feasts on the dates of pagan festivals. For the same reason, Moses (or divine "cunning and wisdom," manifesting itself through his agency)[17] had to institute many dietary and sacrificial prescriptions in order to occupy the terrain held by the Sabians and their idolatrous ways, "so that all these rites and cults that they practiced for the sake of the idols, they now came to practice in the honor of god."[18] The divine strategy was so successful that the Sabians and their once mighty community fell into oblivion.

Spencer's respect for Maimonides was so great that he took considerable pains to find out about the identity of the Ṣa'aba only to arrive at the truly ingenious solution of interpreting the term "Sabians" in its largest possible sense of "paganism."[19] He then felt free to introduce into the concept of "Sabiism" all the historical knowledge about Ancient Egypt which he was able to extract from Classical sources and which is so conspicuously absent from Maimonides' attempts at historical contextualization. It is this knowledge that makes Spencer's work a precursor of what will later be called the history of religions and even Egyptology.[20] Maimonides and Spencer agree on the contradistinctive meaning of the Law and the negative potential of counter-religion. The reason of the Law shines forth only when it is seen against the background of a discarded tradition called *idololatria*, idolatry.[21] But whereas Maimonides contents himself with what he is able to find out about the community of the Ṣa'aba, Spencer engages in a full-fledged historical investigation.

❧ THERE IS yet another categorical difference between Spencer's and Maimonides' method of historical reasoning. It did not occur to Maimonides that his method of historical explanation might have disastrous effects on the timeless validity of the Law. Normally, historical explanation is strictly opposed to thinking in legal terms. So long as a law is valid, it has no time index. In court, all that counts is whether a law is valid or invalid, not whether it dates from fifty years ago or has been issued only recently. Commentaries might deal with the historical circumstances of its origin in order to elucidate its meaning. But this is a different discourse; in court, this kind of historical and contextual explanation of a law would rarely go so far as to contest a judgment that is based upon such a law. The Romans, it is true, paid great attention to the historical circumstances and the original intention of a law (rather than to its literal formulation);[22] but the purpose of this kind of historical thinking was basically conservative. History was studied in order to save the law, not to abolish it. A law was saved by generalizing the original intention, or the set of facts to which it was originally applied, and by establishing its timeless relevance. This is also the method of Maimonides. He contends that the original intention of the Law was to destroy idolatry and demonstrates this by reconstructing the historical *circumstantiae* with reference to the Sabians. His intention, however, is conservative; he wants to save the Law. Therefore, he generalizes the crime of idolatry so as to fit metahistorical problems and arrives at his well-known purely philosophical and ahistorical concept of idolatry. For Maimonides, the Law remains in force in spite of historical circumstances because of the timeless danger of idolatry. In the legal context, historical reasoning serves the essentially ahistorical purpose of "undating" the Law, making its time index invisible and retaining its timeless validity.

By definition, a historical law is a law of the past that is no longer in force. It interests the historian, not the lawyer. Juridical or—to use a term more appropriate in the present context—*halakhic* use of the past is essentially ahistorical in that it seeks to prevent the Law from becoming historical.[23] Maimonides argued within the frame of juridical/*halakhic* thinking. He would not admit that the Law had lost some of its function or "reason" after the disappearance of the Sabians. His historicization of the Law never went so far as to present it as "historical." Spencer, by contrast, went beyond *halakhic* interpretation and argued within the frame of historical thinking. This marks the decisive difference between these two attempts at historical explanation. Spencer's method of historicization is based on a Christian evolutionism which knows not only of an origin, but also of an end of the Law. Spencer admires Maimonides' rationalization and historicization of the Law, but wonders why his Jewish readers refuse to draw the obvious conclusion: "Utinam Judaei hodierni, qui tot laureis Mosis huiusce tempora redimire solent, ad haec verba mentes adverterent! Tunc enim fervor illi animi quo in ritus Mosaicos feruntur, statim refrigesceret; nec Messiam nostrum (cuius nomen unguentum effusum est) tot maledictis & convitiis proscindere vellent, quod Mosis Leges, earum ratione iam cessante, penitus abrogaverit." ("If only the Jews of today who used to hold the times of this same Moses in such a high esteem, would pay attention to these words! For then, the mental fervor which they show towards these rites would immediately cool; and they would not wish to abuse our Messiah with so many curses and insults for his having completely abolished the Mosaic law *because of the cessation of its reason.*"[24]

The Sacrifice of the Paschal Lamb

Strangely enough, in his search for historical explanations, Maimonides had recourse to the same principle of "normative inversion" that was used by pagan writers such as Manetho and Tacitus in order to accuse the Jews of plagiarism: They did not create their own laws; they merely inverted the Egyptian laws. Maimonides does not seem to have seen any anti-Jewish tendencies in this argument. If Tacitus declares that the Jews sacrifice rams *in contumeliam Ammonis* he comes very close to Maimonides' explanation of the sacrifice of the paschal lamb.[25] This is one of the rare places where Maimonides refers to the Egyptians instead of the Sabians. His explanation is based on Exodus 8:22 and its interpretation by Onqelos. Moses asks Pharaoh for three days leave in order to celebrate their annual feast in the desert. At Pharaoh's injunction that they should celebrate their feast in Egypt instead of in the desert, he objects: "Lo, if we shall sacrifice the abomination ["taboo"] of the Egyptians, will they not stone us?" Onqelos explains the words "the abomination of the Egyptians" as referring to their worship of "the sign of Aries" as their supreme god. He obviously refers to the constellation and is understood in this way by other commentators who would be adduced by the indefatigable Spencer. But the ram was sacred for other than astronomical reasons: it was the animal of Amun, the highest god of the Egyptians, and also of Khnum, the local god of Elephantine. The latter god is of particular interest here because in the vicinity of his temple occurred the very incident which Moses tried to avoid. The case is so spectacular that it justifies a short excursus into actual history.

The incident took place in the fifth century B.C.E. on the island of Elephantine, near the southern border of Egypt.[26] The island hosted not only a small and crowded town, but also a military colony of Jewish mercenaries. They seem to have come there before the Josian reform because their form of Judaism is somewhat unorthodox. They built a temple to their god YHW (this, instead of YHWH, is the form in which the divine name occurs in the papyri)[27] instead of a mere synagogue, which was a severe violation of Jerusalem's claim to a monopoly on temples. In addition, they worshipped besides "Yahu" a female companion of his. But apart from these deviations from the post-exilic orthodoxy of normative Judaism, they were fervent adherents of Yahu; most of their names contained the divine name[28] and they undoubtedly considered themselves Jews.[29] Among the remnants of family archives and other documents of this group written in Aramaic there are fragments of a correspondence that sheds light on a most unexpected and surprising chain of events. One of these is a letter by Jedaniah, the leader of the community, asking Bagohi/Bagoas, the Persian representative in Judah, for formal permission to rebuild the temple of Yahu. This temple had been destroyed three years earlier by Egyptian soldiers under the command of a Colonel Nefayan and by order of his father, the Persian governor *(frataraka)* Ogdanes (Vidranga). The writer accuses the priests of Khnum of taking advantage of the temporary absence of the satrap Arsham/Asarmes in order to bribe Vidranga to undertake this destruction. The letter says that Vidranga, Nefayan, and all the others involved in the affair have since been executed, to the great satisfaction of the Jews. But their temple had still not been rebuilt and the community continued fasting and mourning for three years. Jedaniah supports his plea with a very interesting historical argument: when Cambyses conquered Egypt in 525 B.C.E., he destroyed all the Egyptian temples, but did nothing against their temple.[30] The hostile attitude shown by Cambyses toward Egyptian temples and cults is a common theme in Greek and Egyptian literature. He is even purported to have murdered the Apis bull.[31] All of this has usually been dismissed as legend and Greek propaganda because no contemporary Egyptian document contains any hint of such an incident.[32] Cambyses' successor, Darius I, even built a temple for Amun in the el-Khargeh oasis. Diodorus (or Hecataeus) counts Darius among the great legislators of Egypt and tells the reader that the Egyptians deified this Persian king immediately after his death.[33] But the extraordinary piety of Darius may have been an act of atonement and reconciliation. Admittedly, Jedaniah writes more than a hundred years after these events, but he cannot possibly refer to anti-Persian propaganda if he wants to win Bagohi/Bagoas' help for his cause. There must have existed a kind of anti-Egyptian (counter-)religious solidarity between Achaemenid Zoroastrianism and Jewish Yahwism to which Jedaniah is appealing.

Another document contains Bagohi/Bogoas' answer. He recommends the rebuilding of the temple and the performance of two types of offerings: cereal-offering *(mincha)* and incense. Not mentioned and therefore not permitted is a third kind of offering that Jedaniah asked for: holocaust *(ola)*, in which the victim is completely burnt on the altar. A third document explicitly stipulates that "sheep, oxen, and goats are not to be offered there as holocaust, but only incense and meal-offering."[34] The conclusion is obvious: such burnt offerings, especially of sheep, had been the cause of the conflict. The priest of the god Khnum, whose sacred animal was the ram, and whose temple and animal necropolis were immediately adjacent to the temple of Yahu, must have taken offense at the Jewish sacrifice of the paschal lamb. Thus there happened at Elephantine precisely what Moses was afraid of according to Exodus 8:22.[35]

This affair is a wholesome reminder that there is a reality outside the texts and that we are dealing not exclusively with a world of imagination and construction, but also with a world of factual experience. In the context of normative inversion, experience and imagination form a vicious cycle. Imagination is fueled by experience, and experience is framed and preinformed by imagination. The truth lies in the antagonistic character of counter-religion, which the Egyptians experienced for the first time with the Amarna movement and which, from that time on, they would expect from the "Asiatics." When the Jews settled in Egypt, they filled and confirmed a preconceived frame. But we must not forget that Egyptian history of the Late Period and the Greco-Roman era is replete with stories about conflicts of this sort between neighboring nomes that accused each other of breaking their respective taboos. In this time of foreign occupation and domination, each temple developed its own system of dietary and sacrificial laws. Since Egypt lacked such general concepts as "nation" and "people," the search for normative self-definition and (contra)distinctive identity centered on smaller units, so that the nome, its capital, and the temple of the tutelary deity of that capital came to be the points of focus for nativistic movements.

Yet these conflicts, as far as we know, never went so far as the destruction of a temple. This is the historical background for the oral traditions about the "expulsion of the lepers" which gives such a negative and polemical turn to the principle of normative inversion.

🙾 SPENCER's interpretation of the paschal lamb follows Maimonides in the application of normative inversion. The lamb is sacrificed because it corresponds to the most sacred animal of the Egyptians, the ram, which is the sacred animal of their highest god, Amun. Spencer links the Hebrew names of the Egyptian ancestors, Ham and Misraim, with "(H)ammon" and "Misori vel Osiris." In this way, he explains why Ammon with the ram and Osiris with the bull were the highest gods and the most sacred symbols for the Egyptians.[36] In prescribing the sacrifice of the lamb and the bull, God was directly opposing his strongest adversaries, the gods Amun and Osiris. Therefore, he had excellent reasons to be precise about the species and the gender of the animals.[37] To Spencer, it seems evident "that God wanted to vilify, in his law, those animals which meant the most to the Egyptians," and he even quotes Tacitus *(in contumeliam Ammonis)* with approval.[38] Among all the historiographers of Classical Antiquity who wrote on the Jews, Tacitus is the one who gave to the principle of normative inversion its most concise and most polemical expression. It is interesting to see the same principle of normative inversion applied by writers such as Maimonides and Spencer, who use it not polemically from without but approvingly from within. God was right in giving the Jews a law that was simply the Egyptian custom turned upside down, because the Jews had to be de-Egyptianized. It would be more than unjust to accuse Spencer of merely continuing the anti-Semitic insinuations of Manetho, Lysimachus, and Tacitus.[39] He is arguing "from within," where normative inversion appears not as a human strategy of destruction, rebellion, and revolution, but as "divine cunning" and a cure for idolatry. What is more, he is fully aware of the ambivalent character of this argument and explicitly distances himself from its dangerous aspects. Spencer devotes a whole chapter to this problem: *Cur Deus tot Leges & ritus eorum moribus oppositas instituerit* ("why God installed so many laws and rites which were opposed to their [the Sabians'] customs").[40] The question is answered first *negative*, then *positive*. He contradicts Maimonides by saying that God certainly did not decree those laws merely for the sake of contradiction or for the sole reason of making his people as different as possible from all other nations. Spencer distances himself from the Classical tradition, explicitly refuting Diodorus, Lysimachus, and Tacitus, holding that Moses cannot possibly have instituted the laws out of mere hatred of other people's customs. Another argument he seeks to refute is the *quia absurdum* rationale: that God imposed these seemingly "absurd and useless" laws only to make clear his absolute will and imperium. *Haec opinio,* he says, *digna est, quae Satyris potius quam argumentis explodatur*— "this opinion is worthy of being rejected more by satire than by arguments."

Spencer's explanation is purely historical: The sacrifice of the lamb is to be seen as a symbolic renunciation and self-distanciation. In their entirety, the paschal rites reenact and reenforce the separation from Egypt and from idolatry. The main concern of his argumentation— and the main interest of his beautifully structured and richly documented text— is historical rather than theological. He wrote at a time when the very fundamentals of chronology and history were still much debated. Therefore, he adduces an enormous wealth of Biblical, Classical, ecclesiastical, and Rabbinic sources in order to prove that ancient Egyptian "zoolotria"[41] antedates Moses' time by many years. Even this much had still to be proven. It is this truly historical concern that distinguishes his treatment of the topic from Maimonides' and that makes his work appear, not without reason, "as a first antecedent to a modern, historical-comparative science of religion."[42]

There are many other quite extraordinary examples that show this historical approach even more clearly. I confine myself— reluctantly— to only two of them: the prohibition not to "seethe the kid in his mother's milk" *(lex hoedi coctionem in lacte matris prohibens)*[43] and the prohibition of mourning at the occasion of the offering of the first fruits *(non comedi ex eo in dolore meo [be-'oni];* "I have not eaten thereof in my mourning").[44]

The Prohibition "Not to Seethe the Kid in His Mother's Milk"

Before giving his own explanations for this prohibition, Spencer classifies the traditional explanations into four categories: (1) pity, (2) "normative inversion" of some idolatrous rite, (3) a prohibition against fertility magic, and (4) hygiene: the avoidance of unwholesome overeating *(quod cibus crassissimus sit, nimiamque repletionem generet)*.

Spencer rules out (1) quoting Philo, *De Misericordia*, Ibn Ezra, Isaac Arama, and Simeon de Muis, who view this and similar laws as having the educational purpose of preventing cruelty and encouraging gentleness, compassion, and civilization. This interpretation is currently held by scholars such as Othmar Keel, who devoted an entire monograph to this particular law.[45] Spencer contends that a dead animal would not recognize being cooked in the milk of its mother. He also discards (4), quoting Maimonides. This would become the favorite explanation of late-nineteenth-century Jewish apologetics. Spencer's objection is no less rational. For the purpose of gourmandise, any milk would do. The hygienic theory fails to explain why it is just the maternal milk that is forbidden.[46]

Therefore, Spencer favors both (2) and (3), which do not exclude each other. Like a true historian of religion, he searches for a pagan fertility rite involving the cooking of a kid in the milk of its mother. What does he find? From Isaac Abravanel's commentary on Exodus, he extracts information about a Spanish feast called *mesta* which was celebrated by shepherds twice a year with kids and milk. God surely wanted to prevent the Israelites from partaking in such pagan rites. But for that reason he would have forbidden the "eating" *(comestio)* not the "cooking" *(coctio)* of the kid. And, indeed, Spencer finds "an ancient anonyme Karaite"[47] who reports "a custom among the ancient gentiles, after having collected all fruits, of cooking a kid in the milk of its mother and then, *drk ksph*, 'by way of magic,' of sprinkling this milk over trees, fields, gardens, and orchards in the belief that by doing so they would ensure their fertility for the following year." He is even able to confirm this rather isolated testimony with a quotation from another rather apocryphal source, Rabbi Menachem, who states: "I have heard that it was customary among the Gentiles to boil meat with milk, especially of goat and lamb, and when they grew trees, to make a fumigation with the seed of those trees and to pour the milk into it so that they had more and more fast maturing fruits . . . etc."[48] It did not occur to Spencer that his *vetus Karaita anonymus* and Rabbi Menachem might have made up this pagan fertility rite in the same way Maimonides invented his Sabians: by applying the principle of normative inversion in the opposite direction. If there was a law forbidding the cooking of the kid in the milk of its mother, there must have existed a pagan rite which consisted of precisely this same activity—and imagination goes off to invent a rustic scene with a group of shepherds cooking kids in milk and sprinkling it on trees, fields, and orchards.

The principle of normative inversion or the construction of cultural otherness is obviously working retroactively too. Starting from a given order, it imagines a culture based upon the inverted mirror image of that order and, by this very procedure of retrospective inversion, turns the past into "a foreign country."[49] Spencer's own explanation is built upon these Rabbinic testimonies and he supplements them with a contextual observation. As he shows, God gave four sets of instructions pertaining to the three great feasts: Passover, Pentecost *(Schavuot)*, and Tabernacles *(Sukkot)*. These instructions are: (1) do not offer fermented bread; (2) do not leave relics of the sacrifice until morning; (3) bring the first fruits to the house of God; and (4) do not "seethe the kid in his mother's milk." Since (1) and (2) refer to Passover and (3) refers to Pentecost, (4) must refer to *Sukkot*. Thus, (4) should correspond precisely to the occasion of performing fertility rites. He closes his exposition with a quotation from Horace which beautifully illustrates a fertility rite involving meat and milk on the occasion of a feast concluding the collection of fruits,[50] and a passage from the *Commentary in Exodum* (question 37) of Abulensis, who had already brought together the poet and the Bible: "The gentiles offered milk to Sylvanus and pork to Ceres in order to have plenitude of fruits. Whether they cooked a kid in the milk they offered to Sylvanus is not clear from the poets, but sufficiently probable." Frazer could not have done better. Spencer, however, is interested not only in the origin of the Biblical prescription but also in its actual application by the Jews. He devotes several pages to the description of the Jewish custom of keeping the dishes for meat and dairy products strictly separated ("quod vasa duplicia, altera ad carnes, altera ad cibos lactarios, coquendos comparent: cultros duos, unum ad carnem, alterum ad caseum, scindendum deferant. Duo etiam in mensa salina habere solent, ne carnes & lacticinia uno eodemque sale condiantur: duo etiam pro utrisque mantilia, notis aut literis distinctis inscripta, ne ab incautis permisceantur") and emphasizes the extreme importance that modern Jewry ascribes to this particular prescription.[51]

The Forbidding of Mourning at the Occasion of Offering First Fruits

Spencer's explanation of the prescription not to consume the first fruits *(be-'oni) in luctu meo* ("in my mourning") shows him to be not only a historian of religion but also an Egyptologist. What could be the meaning of this *locus perobscurus?* In this case, the Sabians, against whom this prohibition is directed, can be identified as the Ancient Egyptians. Diodorus reports that on the occasion of the first fruit offerings, the Egyptians broke into loud lamentations invoking Isis.[52] Spencer illustrates this passage by a more detailed description of these rites by Julius Firmicus Maternus:

> In the innermost part of their temples *[in adytum]* they buried an idol of Osiris: this they annually mourned, they shaved their heads, they beat their breast, tore their members, etc., in order to bewail the pitiful fate of their king. . . the defenders of this mourning and those funerals give a physical explanation: the seed, they say, is Osiris, the earth Isis, the heat Typhon. And because the fruit is ripe as a result of heat, it is collected for the living of men and thus separated from earth's company, and when winter comes it will be sowed into the earth in what they interpret as the death and burial of Osiris. But the earth will become pregnant and bring forth new fruits.[53]

This is a fair description of the Egyptian Khoiak rites, especially of the rite *ḫbs t3*, "hoeing the earth," and I cannot resist the temptation of completing Spencer's documentation by adducing some Egyptian testimonies which were inaccessible to him. A papyrus in the British Museum contains a description of the catastrophes following the death of Osiris, which is lamented during the rites of Khoiak:

> The earth is devastated,
> The sun does not rise.
> The moon hesitates, it no longer exists.
> The ocean sways, the land turns upside down,
> The river dries up.
> Everybody is wailing and lamenting,
> Gods and goddesses,
> Humans, spirits, and the dead,
> Cattle and livestock are crying.[54]

The burial of the seed is celebrated in the form of a funeral. The feast of "hoeing the earth" is a nocturnal rite. We read in another papyrus: "O Sokaris Osiris, when this disaster occurred for the first time, there was a sanctuary erected at Busiris in order to mummify you and to make your smell pleasant . . . I and my sister Nephthys kindled the torch at the entrance of the sanctuary. Since that time the great ceremony of 'Hoeing the Earth' is celebrated for you."[55] The following day is called "The Great Mourning" *(mega penthos)* and the whole country mourns for the dead Osiris. The festival cycle closes eight days later with "the erection of the Djed pillar."

But let us return to Spencer's argument. He proceeds from the Egyptians to the Phoenicians, who, following Eusebius, "dedicated compassion, commiseration, wailing, weeping, and lamenting to the aging germs of the earth."[56] This refers to the mourning of Adonis, which Spencer illustrates with quotations from Ammianus Marcellinus[57] and Lucian.[58] He is thus able to show that in the whole cultural context of the ancient Hebrews in Egypt and in Syria, the collecting and offering of the fruits was accompanied by ceremonies of a funerary character. This, to his mind, is the most plausible explanation of the Hebrew *be-'oni,* "in mourning of me." The expression is rendered by the Septuagint not by *lupe* or *pothos,* but by *en odunē mou,* which is the strongest expression of mourning, applied, for example, to Jacob's mourning for Rachel. It is the only other instance where Hebrew *'on* is rendered *"odunē"* by the Septuagint. Yahweh would not want to be offered the fruits with funerary demonstrations of mourning as if he had died in the way Osiris and Adonis died. In strong contrast to Osiris and Adonis, the Biblical god is a living god; death is his principal taboo and everything connected with death and dying, such as mourning a corpse, is redolent of defilement and would render the offering unacceptable.[59]

Accommodation: The Enculturation of the Law

Spencer regards the concept of normative inversion, which he takes from Maimonides and the ancient sources, as only one possible category of historical explanation. He devotes the second of his three books to explanations of this type. The other two concepts are enculturation and reception. *Enculturation* is to be understood here as the historical embodiment of a system of ideas in a concrete society, such as the semantic frames and pragmatic customs of a given historical culture. *Reception* refers to the reception of ideas, images, customs, and so forth, of one culture by another culture and their subsequent integration into the latter. These notions are not Spencer's, but the distinction is his and my terms are offered only to highlight distinctions which underlie the structure of his book. He makes the distinctions by devoting his first book to what I propose to call "enculturation" and the third book to "reception," but he subsumes both categories of historical explanation under concepts such as *accommodatio, translatio, mutatio,* and *derivatio.*

Accommodation and translation are terms that apply to the categories of both acculturation and reception. The term "accommodation" is used to stress the historical circumstances of the Law, its time index; and "translation" is used to stress its cultural determination and framing, its cultural index. But the direction of translation is different: enculturation here means the translation of something divine into the language of a specific culture, a cultural "incarnation" of sorts. Reception means the translation of a set of forms and ideas from one culture into another culture.

The hypothesis that Spencer wants to substantiate in the first book is the assumption that the culture into which God had to translate his truth was an Egyptian or "Egyptianizing" one. The Israelites, to whom the Law was given, were culturally Egyptians. During their long sojourn in Egypt they had become totally assimilated to Egyptian culture. For them, Yahweh was an unknown god in the same sense that he was unknown to Pharaoh.[60] What we today would call their "ethnicity" or "cultural identity," which would set the Israelites apart from their Egyptian host culture, did not yet exist because the construction of this identity was precisely the function of the Law. In his infinite benevolence and "condescendence," God did not choose to superinscribe his laws above the cultural texts already in existence, culturally treating the Israelites as a *tabula rasa.* Instead, he chose to translate his legislative system into their cultural background text and to "accommodate" his truth to their historically and culturally limited and predetermined Egyptian forms of understanding.

Spencer developed his concept of accommodation by starting with a beautiful sentence by Isidor of Pelusium, which he used as a motto:[61]

Hōsper tês mèn selénēs kalês oúsēs, toû dè Hēlíou kreíttonos, heîs estin ho demiourgòs; hoútō kaì palaiâs kaì kainês diathékēs heîs nomothétēs, ho sophôs, kai katallélōs toîs kairoîs nomothetésas.

Quemadmodum et pulchrae Lunae, et pulchrioris Solis, unus idemque effector est; eodem modo et Veteris et Novi Testamenti unus atque idem est Legislator, qui sapienter, et ad tempora accommodate, leges tulit.

Just as there is only one single creator of both the beautiful moon and the even more beautiful sun, there is also only one single legislator of both the Old and the New Testaments, who gave the laws wisely and with respect to temporal circumstances.

This sentence best expresses Spencer's historical interest in reconstructing the "temporal circumstances" of Moses' laws. It is his conviction that the meaning of the Law can only be reconstructed within what Herder, a century later, would call Zeitgeist. Spencer almost literally anticipates this term by speaking of *genius seculi*, "the spirit of the century."[62] It is this interest in reconstructing the historical background or frame of the Mosaic Law that guides his proto-Egyptological investigations because it is his conviction that it was Ancient Egypt which formed that historical context.

In Spencer's time, Egypt's place in history had not been established.[63] Even the basic chronological facts were open to discussion. He took great pains to show that Egyptian civilization was older than Moses' legislation; the words *diu ante Mosis tempora* are a leitmotif in his exposition. Spencer was not interested in questions of chronology. All that mattered for him was the direction of translation and reception: who received from whom. The prevailing theory of the time, advocated by a number of scholars including the famed Athanasius Kircher and just enunciated again *ex cathedra* by Cardinal Pierre-Daniel Huet[64]—two authors Spencer knew very well—viewed the Egyptians as plagiarizing Moses' laws.

Spencer opposed this theory with his concept of assimilation.[65] Given the greater age and more advanced stage of Egyptian civilization, the Israelites became so fully assimilated to the Egyptian customs and rites that "it was not possible to find a single difference in the way of life of both nations"[66] Spencer quotes from a Rabbinic source: "Wherever the Israelites settled down in the desert, they started making themselves idols."[67] The idols they made were Egyptian ones. The clearest proof is the Golden Calf, which ancient sources such as Philo, Lactantius, Hieronymus, and the *Targum Hierosolymitanis* had identified as the Apis bull.[68] The Israelites prayed to the God they knew and not to the "unknown God" of Moses.

Eusebius called the Law *curatrix quaedam et gubernatrix*. Spencer likewise drew his metaphors from the fields of medicine and education. Both metaphors depict images of progress emphasizing the historical character or the historicity of the Law. The Law served a purpose within a progress that can be compared to the progress of healing and the progress of learning. In the first volume of his *De Legibus*, Egypt is constructed as a historical context and a period, a stage in an evolutionary process. As such, it appears in a rather negative light, as a stage to be transcended. The Law is given to an Egyptianized people with the purpose of initiating a process of gentle de-Egyptianization. The key term of the first book is "historical accommodation." The divine legislation had to make allowances for historical circumstances. This explains why it receives and "translates" so many Gentile, especially Egyptian, elements.

The key concept of the second volume is normative inversion, although Spencer does not use the term. Normative inversion is another form of historical contextualization, another relation of system and environment. Instead of reception and translation, we have direct contradistinction. The historical context appears here in a still more negative view, as a counterculture, to be opposed, superseded, and finally forgotten. Spencer adopts this concept from Maimonides, and also adopts his term for this counterculture, which is not Egypt, but *'ummat Ṣa'aba*, the Sabian community.

It is only in the third (and by far the most voluminous) book that Egypt appears in a more favorable light. The key term for the third volume is "translation." This term appears in the title of the first "dissertation," "which deals in a more general way with the rites that are translated into the Law from the customs of the Gentiles" (*qua generaliùs agitur de Ritibus è Gentium moribus in Legem translatis*). Translation is the positive form of accommodation. It refers to rites and customs that are received from Egypt not in order to be supplanted and eventually overcome, but in order to be preserved as valuable. It is in this context that the Egyptian education of Moses comes to the fore.

Moses certainly knew hieroglyphic writing, which Spencer takes to be a secret code by which the Egyptian priests transmitted their wisdom to the initiated. His sources include Philo of Alexandria, *De Vita Mosis*, book 1, where we read that Moses learned from his Egyptian masters, among other subjects, *tēn dia symbolōn philosophian.*

For the nature of the hieroglyphic script, Spencer draws on Porphyry and Clement of Alexandria. From Clement, he also takes the fascinating idea that some of the laws are in fact hieroglyphs because they relate to the symbolic value of things.[69] In the eight dissertations that form the third volume of *De Legibus*, Spencer tries to prove the origin, in most cases Egyptian, of certain institutions such as the sacrifices, the lustrations, the lunar feasts, the ark and the Cherubim, the temple, the scapegoat, and Urim and Thummim (the breastplate to be worn by the high priest).[70] The last-mentioned treatise is based on his doctoral dissertation of 1670.

Spencer's formula for this type of accommodation is that God did not want his cult to lacking anything which his people had learned to adore as holy during their stay in Egypt *(nec quicquam cultui suo deesse quod in ceremoniis Aegypti deperire solebant et venerari).*[71] A more general formulation of this principle would be that God did not want his religion to lack visibility. Visible religion is Spencer's main concern. He is not interested in theology or mythology, but in the visible and bodily forms in which religion is expressed and practiced.[72]

Spencer's thesis is that the visible dimension of religion is more or less universal, and that in this respect ancient Hebrew religion was much closer to its cultural environment—especially to Ancient Egypt —than in its beliefs. By this principle, to achieve visibility God even conceded to his people images which were strictly forbidden on the theoretical or theological level. The ark of the covenant and the Cherubim are to be understood as visualizations of the divine presence *(presentiae divinae symbolum, cultus divini medium, rerum sacrarum repositorium);*[73] Spencer interprets the ark as the combination of a *cista mystica* and an Egyptian coffin.

The problem with the Cherubim is that they so bluntly violate the strict aniconism of the Israelite cult. They are tolerable only as "hieroglyphs" or symbols. Their Egyptian origin is most evident in their appearance. Ezekiel describes them as "creatures" or "beasts" *(khayyot)*, each with the face of a man, a lion, a bull, and an eagle. As such they reappear in the Book of Revelations (4:6, 7). They are, therefore, *multiformis* or composite in the same way as Egyptian gods and hieroglyphics. Even if there are no exact parallels in Egyptian iconography (as Spencer does not fail to point out), they look so very Egyptian that they must have functioned in the same way as Egyptian hieroglyphs, that is, as a secret code for conveying or hiding a sacred truth.

In reading Spencer, one easily gets the impression that he tries to find Egyptian origins everywhere and for everything. That is not so. That he handles his sources with true critical scholarship is shown by his dissertation on Urim and Thummim, which he interprets as two different pectorals or breastplates worn by the high priest on different occasions and used for oracular purposes. Urim is associated with questions of warfare, Thummim with jurisdiction. Concerning Urim, Spencer explicitly rejects the thesis of an Egyptian origin brought forward by Athanasius Kircher.

Like Spencer, Kircher identified Urim with Teraphim. But he went further and identified Teraphim with Seraphim and derived Seraphim from Serapis. Spencer reacted to this kind of etymology with scorn. Notwithstanding his insistence on the superior antiquity of Egyptian rites and institutions, Spencer was perfectly aware that Serapis was a newcomer to the Egyptian pantheon and that his cult had only been introduced by Ptolemy III. It is reassuring to see Spencer arguing this way. By so doing he prepares his readers for his own interpretation.

Urim has nothing to do with Egypt, but Thummim is taken from Egypt. Thummim has a Hebrew etymology; it comes from *tam*, "to be perfect," and means something like perfection, integrity, wholeness. But in the Septuagint it is mostly rendered not by *teleia*, "perfection," but by *aletheia*, "truth." The explanation Spencer gives for this strange rendering is indeed most convincing: the translators were aware of the fact that in Egypt the supreme judge wore a figure of Aletheia as a pectoral and that Thummim was just the Hebrew adaptation of this Egyptian custom. For this information, Spencer quotes Aelian and Diodorus, who in this case turn out to be reliable sources.[74] The Vizier, who acted as supreme judge, indeed wore an emblem of Maat, the goddess of truth, on his breast. Spencer is thus referring to an authentic Egyptian custom.[75]

🌸 SPENCER's work proved ground-breaking in two different respects. First, it is remarkable that he investigated historical origins at all, since orthodoxy would have clung to the notion of revelation. He followed Maimonides in asking the reasons for each particular law and institution, but he differed from Maimonides in his strictly historical understanding of the concept of reason or explanation. To explain something, for Spencer, meant to discover its origin. In this respect, Spencer is a precursor of practitioners of historicism and comparative religion. Second, his work proved ground-breaking in that it revealed Egypt as the origin of most of the legal institutions of Moses. He certainly went much too far in tracing almost everything back to Egypt, but by doing so he collected virtually all the information that in his time was available on Ancient Egyptian religion and civilization. The point of Spencer's theories of origin is not whether they hit the historical truth or not, but how much of Ancient Egyptian culture they make visible and accessible. Spencer's propensity for tracing almost everything back to an Egyptian origin looks like Egyptomania. As far as the Cherubim are concerned, the Assyrian associations seem far closer than the Egyptian ones. But Assyria and Babylonia—hiding perhaps behind the enigmatic "Sabians"—were lost and forgotten civilizations in Spencer's time, whereas Egypt was somehow preserved in the cultural memory of Europe owing to the great attention paid it by Classical authors. Egypt, therefore, was almost the only civilization Spencer could refer to when looking for such origins.

Spencer's historical explanation of the Mosaic legislation led to a second rediscovery of Egypt, the first occurring in the Hermetic tradition that began at the end of the fifteenth century with Marsilio Ficino. Spencer's work opened a new and different window on ancient Egypt. Whereas the Hermetic view of Egypt was marked by extreme Egyptophilia, Spencer's image of Egypt was characterized by an equally extreme Egyptophobia. This might seem like a paradox in one who showed such a fervent interest in everything Egyptian and had done so much to recover any information about Egypt that could be got from Biblical, Classical, Christian, and Rabbinic sources. But Spencer was quite explicit in his opinion, and used very strong language when dealing with Egyptian religion. It is the same language of illness and pollution that we have met with in the extra-Biblical traditions about the Exodus. Spencer's text bristles with examples and I will quote just a few that occur on a single page: the Egyptian religion is called "faeces superstitionis Aegyptiacae," "idolomaniae pestis," "impietatis Aegyptiacae lues," "pestis Aegyptiaca." Further, he asks whether Abraham, who stayed only a short while in Egypt, could possibly have wished to "drink" that *faeces*, to bring this pestilence into *salutifera patris fidelium domus* instead of remaining pure and immune to this *lues* of Egyptian impiety. It is only during their later stay, which lasted for four hundred years, that the Hebrews became "infected" and "polluted" with the Egyptian pestilence of what one is tempted to call "idolitis."[76]

It is highly interesting to see the language of illness return in the very same context, that is, in the context of confrontation between Egypt and Israel. The motif of a contagious and disfiguring illness such as leprosy, pestilence, or scabies seems so central to the whole tradition about Moses and the Exodus that it occupied a prominent place not only in the normative texts of the Jews and the popular legends of the Egyptians, but also in the scholarly discourse of John Spencer. Illness seems to be the privileged metaphor of religious otherness. From the Egyptian point of view, the monotheistic iconoclasm appears as illness, while from the Jewish and Christian point of view, *idololatria*, is also a disease.[77] Eusebius had called the Law a *curatrix quaedam et gubernatrix; aut etiam, instar medici cuiusdam, universae Iudaeorum nationi, gravi Aegyptioque morbo laboranti, tradita est.* Note that the German Jewish poet Heinrich Heine speaks of *die alte, aus dem Niltal mitgeschleppte Plage, der ungesunde altägyptische Glaube* ("the plague dragged along from the Nile valley, the unhealthy beliefs of Ancient Egypt") and that Sigmund Freud quotes these lines in his book on Moses.[78]

Spencer continues this polemical pathology of religion where the leading distinction is not true versus false, but healthy versus ill, in a most elaborate form. Idolatry is constantly called *pestis*. But both his and Maimonides' favorite metaphor is that of addiction. The Law is administered to the people as a withdrawal program[79]—*ut Israelitis suis idololatriae pestae correptis medelam adhiberet*—and to deflect their minds from paganism.[80] The difference between illness and addiction lies in the emphasis on "inner man" and psychical or mental faculties. Seen as addiction, idolatry threatens the inner freedom of will, deliberation, selection, and decision-making. In this respect, the metaphor of addiction points in the same direction as the metaphor of adultery, which is used by the Biblical prophets, especially Hosea.[81] Adultery is misplaced desire and, like addiction, a question of emotional compulsion rather than cognitive aberration. Illness, addiction and adultery are metaphors for forbidden contact and its fatal consequences. "Adultery" means breaking the limits of matrimonial fidelity by contact with another partner, illness means a state of defection through contact with polluted persons and addiction refers to a polluting contact that has become a habit and a necessity.

Hieroglyphs into Laws: Sub Cortice Legis

But despite the strongly Egyptophobic imagery of illness and infection, there is also a more positive understanding of Egypt hidden in Spencer's pages. This is his concept of secrecy, of transmitting a veiled truth which he believed Moses had learned in Egypt and then translated into his law code. Spencer subscribed to the conventional theory about hieroglyphic writing that was based on Horapollo's two books on hieroglyphics[82] and especially on Athanasius Kircher's "decipher-ments."[83] According to this theory, hieroglyphs were iconic symbols that referred to concepts. They were used exclusively for religious purposes such as transmitting the "mystical" ideas that were to be kept secret from the common people. Spencer contends that a good many of the laws, rites, and institutions that God gave his people through the mediation of Moses show this hieroglyphic character.

The Law appears here as a "veil" *(velum)*, a "cover" *(involucrum)*, or a shell *(cortex)* which transmits a truth by hiding it. This "hieroglyphic" function of a law, a rite, or an institution constitutes the "secondary" reason for it in Spencer's system. Spencer makes the distinction between primary and secondary causes or reasons *(rationes)* right at the beginning of his work. The primary reason is the therapeutic or educa-tional function of the Law in overcoming idolatry, while the secondary reason is the "adumbration" of "certain mysteries."[84] In this distinction he is following Maimonides, whose concept of *verba duplicata* drew the distinction between *sensus literalis* and *sensus mysticus*.[85]

What is this "mystical" or "interior meaning" of the Law? Concern-ing this question, Jewish and Christian opinions differ widely. In the Jewish tradition, the mystical meaning of the Law concerns "celestial truths," that is, adumbrations of the mystical architecture of celestial palaces through which the adept ascends onto the divine throne. In the

Christian tradition, the mystical meaning of the Law consists in the foreshadowings of Christ. But Spencer is very cautious and circumspect; he explicitly distances himself from the *allegorizantium natio*, who do not recognize any limits on allegorical interpretation.[86] He limits the scope of allegorical or mystical interpretation to certain rites and institutions, and he allows for more than exclusively "evangelical" mysteries. The hidden meaning of a law could consist of (1) an image of celestial things *(imagines rerum coelestium)*, (2) certain philosophical secrets *(arcana quaedam philosophica)*, (3) images of evangelical mysteries *(mysteriorum evangelicorum simulacra)*, (4) moral secrets *(arcana quaedam ethica)*, or (5) historical secrets that might be hidden under the guise of Mosaic rites *(mysteria quaedam historica in rituum Mosaicorum involucris occultata)*. Ceremonies such as the paschal rites are commemorative institutions pointing to the Exodus from Egypt. Spencer closes this section with a quotation from Plutarch, claiming for the Hebrews what Plutarch says of the Egyptians: "Their sacred rites do not institute anything dissonant to reason, anything fabulous, anything smelling of superstition, but they contain in their recesses certain ethical and useful doctrines or philosophical or historical insights."[87]

The Law has to have a double meaning because it has to fulfill a double function. Its primary or "carnal" *(sarkikos:* in Greek, p. 161) function is to cure the people of their idolatric addiction and to educate them. Its secondary or "spiritual" *(pneumatikos)* function is to transmit higher truths to those who are capable of higher understanding. Eusebius made the same distinction: "Moses ordered the Jewish plebs to be committed to all of the rites which were included in the words of their laws. But he wished that the others, whose mind and virtue were stronger as they were liberated from this exterior shell, should accustom themselves to a philosophy more divine and superior to common man, and should penetrate with the eye of the mind into the higher meaning of the laws."[88]

Moses learned this principle of double encoding from his Egyptian masters. It is for this reason that God chose Moses as his first prophet: a man "nourished with the hieroglyphic literature of Egypt" *(hieroglyphicis Aegypti literis innutritum)*. "God wished that Moses should write the mystic images of the more sublime things. The hieroglyphic literature, in which Moses was educated, was fairly convenient for this purpose."[89] Spencer continues: It is probable that God transmitted certain sacred truths *(sacratiora quaedam)* in the Law under the veil of symbols and types *(symbolorum & typorum velis obducta)* in conformity with the practice of the pagan, especially Egyptian, sages. He refers to the "ancients" *(Veteres)* and to "the entire book on hieroglyphics" by Horapollo to substantiate his thesis that the practice of indicating all things of a more sublime character "in a mystical and, as it were, nebulous way" was very much in fashion among the Egyptians. Origen is quoted as attributing the same "mystical mode of philosophizing" to the Persians[90] and Clement of Alexandria is referred to as saying that "all theologians *[pantes theologēsantes]*, barbarians and Greeks, concealed the principles of reality *[tas men archas tōn pragmatōn apekrupsanto]* and transmitted the truth only by means of riddles, symbols, allegories, metaphors, and similar tropes and figures *[tēn de alētheian ainigmasi, kai symbolois, allēgoriais te, au kai metaphorais, kai toioutoisi tisi tropois parade-dōkasin]*."[91] I shall return to both these passages in the context of Cudworth's work, where they play a more central role.

Spencer concludes that it is therefore appropriate "to hold that God gave the Jews a religion that was carnal only in its frontispiece, but divine and wonderful in its interior in order to accommodate his institutions to the taste and usage of the time lest his Law and cult should seem deficient in anything transmitted in the name of wisdom."[92] In this same context he adduces one of those passages from Clement of Alexandria that were to become the cornerstones of Reinhold's and Schiller's construction of Egypt: *In adyto veritatis repositum sermonem revera sacrum, Aegyptii quidem per ea, quae apud ipsos vocantur adyta, Hebraei autem per velum significarunt.* "The Egyptians indicated the really sacred logos, which they kept in the innermost sanctuary of Truth, by what they called Adyta, and the Hebrews [indicated it] by means of the curtain [in the temple]. Therefore, as far as concealment is concerned, the secrets *[ainigmata]* of the Hebrews and the Egyptians are very similar to each other."[93] These sentences pave the way for a totally different understanding of the relationship between Egypt and Israel. Spencer does not go far down that road, but in the course of the eighteenth century these ideas would become more and more important, eventually leading to a new and positive imaging of Egypt. Egyptian religion is seen as the source of the same truth as Moses' monotheism. What Egypt kept secret under the veil of its hieroglyphs, Moses promulgated in the form—but also under the veil—of legislation.

Hen kai Pan: Egypt's Arcane Theology according to Ralph Cudworth

Spencer's investigations into Moses' Egyptian background concentrated on ritual. His concept of "translation" aimed at an interpretation of the laws as transformations of Egyptian rites. It seems strange that he did not consider the question of Moses' *theological* education. He does not seem to have been concerned with the question as to which concepts of the divine Moses might have been taught by his Egyptian masters. Spencer could omit this topic because it had just been dealt with in a comprehensive and impressive way in Ralph Cudworth's *True Intellectual System of the Universe*, which appeared in 1678.[94] There is every reason to suppose that Spencer and Cudworth, the leading Hebraists at Cambridge and representatives of that stupendously productive erudition typical of the seventeenth century, knew each other well. Spencer's reconstruction of Egypt's "visible religion" and Cudworth's reconstruction of Egypt's "arcane theology" supplement each other in a way that suggests a division of labor. The only difference is that Cudworth, unlike Spencer, did not cast his reconstruction in the form of an inquiry into Moses' Egyptian education.[95] He is concentrating on the Mosaic distinction, that is, the distinction between true and false in religion, not in its Biblical form, where it appears as the antagonism between Egyptian idolatry and Israelite monotheism, but in its abstract and philosophical form, where it is reduced to the distinction between God and the world. Cudworth belonged to the circle of the Cambridge Platonists, who constituted one of the forerunners of Deism. His god was the god of the philosophers, and his enemy was not idolatry but atheism or materialism. Therefore, his book does not overtly declare its relevance for the history of monotheism. This relevance only became clear in the course of its reception, when Cudworth's picture of Egyptian theology and Spencer's picture of Egyptian ritual were integrated into a comprehensive view of Egyptian religion.

The problem that Cudworth was addressing in his *True Intellectual System* was the problem of atheism. Without even mentioning the name of Spinoza it is clear who was the addressee of this "confutation." Cudworth was trying to launch a debate which did not really break out until a century later. I shall consider the "pantheism debate" in due course. But I should note here that it was the very formula by which

Cudworth chose to characterize Egypt's arcane theology that triggered the famous conflict between Jacobi and Mendelssohn and heavily influenced German and English pre-Romanticism. This formula was *Hen kai pan*, One and All.[96]

The concept that Cudworth was trying to substantiate with a vast collection of quotations from Greek and Latin authors is the idea of primitive monotheism, common to all religions and philosophies including atheism itself. What is common to all must be true and vice versa; this was the basic assumption of seventeenth-century epistemology and was also implicit in the idea of "nature" and in the concept of "natural religion." The recognition of one Supreme Being constitutes "the true intellectual system of the universe" because—as Lord Herbert of Cherbury had already shown in 1624—the assertion "that there is a Supreme God" is the most common notion of all.[97] Even atheism conforms to this common notion because the God whose existence it negates is precisely this one Supreme God and not one or all of the gods of polytheism.[98] This notion common to both theists and atheists can be defined as *"a Perfect Conscious Understanding Being [or Mind] Existing of it self from Eternity, and the Cause of all other things."*[99]

Cudworth then proceeds to prove that not only atheism but even polytheism shares this idea of One Supreme God. The "Grand Prejudice and Objection" which he is attacking next is the idea that all of the primitive and ancient religions were polytheistic and that only "a small and inconsiderable handful of the Jews" formed the idea of one God. Following the principle that "what is true must be natural" and "what is natural must be common to all," some had concluded that the idea of One God could not have any "Foundation in *Nature*," but must be considered "a mere *Artificial* thing, owing its Original [*sic*] wholly to *Private Phancies* and *Conceits*, or to *Positive Laws* and *Institutions*, amongst *Jews*, *Christians* and *Mahometans*."[100] It is to disprove this assumption that he embarks on his project to prove the "*Naturality* of that *Idea of God*" by demonstrating that even polytheism implied the idea of One Supreme God. This project leads him to a new appraisal of ancient Egyptian religion and its "arcane theology."

He begins by introducing a most useful distinction within the notion of "God": the distinction between "unmade and self-existent gods" and "native and mortal gods."[101] He then states that no pagans ever asserted a multitude of unmade self-existent deities. They always believed in only one such deity from whom all the other gods originated. He demonstrates this at great length, first for Greek polytheism (from Hesiod to Julian the Apostate), then for the Sibylline oracles, Zoroastrianism, Chaldaean religion, and Orphism. He allows for some forms of what he calls "ditheism" (= dualism) which acknowledges two self-existent deities, one the principle of good, the other of evil; among the "ditheists" he counts Plutarch, the Marcionites, and the Manichaeans, but neither Plato nor, surprisingly enough, Zoroaster (because "these Persian *Magi* did, in their *Arimanius,* either *prosopopoein,* personate Evil only, as we suppose the Egyptians to have done in *Typhon;* or else understand a *Satanical Power* by it.")[102] Cudworth ends this section with "the Orphick Kabala" and its *"Grand* Arcanum, *That* God is All".[103] From here, Cudworth concludes, "it is unquestionably Evident, that *Orpheus* with . . . the generality of Greekish Pagans acknowledged *One Universal* and *All-comprehending Deity, One* that was *All."*[104] With this first introduction of the One-and-All, the ground is prepared for the fifty pages of Egyptology which form section 18 of chapter 4.[105]

Cudworth presents Egypt as the homeland of learning. Egyptian knowledge and science were divided into history, philosophy, and theology. Egypt's written records stretched back to cosmogony and "attributed more antiquity to the world than they ought."[106] The Egyptians conceived of cosmogony as *creation* and not as *evolution* "made by chance without a God, as Anaximander, Democritus and Epicurus afterwards did," because Simplicius affirmed that the Mosaic creation account was "nothing but Egyptian fables." Egyptian philosophy included "Pure and Mix'd Mathematicks (Arithmetick, Geometry and Astronomy)" and the doctrines about the immortality of the soul. Egyptian theology was divided into a "Vulgar and Fabulous Theology" and another *"aporrhetos theologia, Arcane and Recondite Theology,* that was concealed from the Vulgar and communicated only to the Kings, and such Priests and others as were thought capable thereof."[107] Three passages are the basis for this extremely significant reconstruction of Egyptian "twofold" or "double-doctrine" theology, which would form the core of the discussion of Egyptian religion in the eighteenth century and even resonate in some Egyptological theories of our day, including Thomas Mann's concept of "esoteric monotheism."[108] Since I have only briefly mentioned these passages in the context of Spencer, I shall here quote them in Cudworth's translation:

The first one is by "Origen, whose very name is Egyptian, it being interpreted *Horo-genitus* . . . upon occasion of *Celsus* his boasting, that he thoroughly understood all that belonged to Christianity; *Celsus* (saith he) *seemeth here to me, to do just as if a man travelling into* Egypt, *where the Wise men of the Egyptians, according to their Country-Learning Philoso-phize much, about those things that are accounted by them Divine, whilst the Idiots, in the mean time, hearing only certain fables which they know not the meaning of, are very much pleased therewith:* Celsus, *I say, doth as if such a Sojourner in Egypt,* who had conversed only with those Idiots, and not been at all instructed by any of the Priests, in their Arcane and Recon-dite Mysteries, should boast that he knew all that belonged to the Egyptian Theology . . . *What we have now affirmed* (saith he) *concerning the difference betwixt the Wise men and the Idiots amongst the Egyptians, the same may be said also of the Persians, amongst whom the Religious Rites are performed Rationally by those that are ingenious, whilst the superficial Vulgar look no further in the observation of them, than the external Symbol or Ceremony. And the same is true likewise concerning the Syrians and Indians, and all those other Nations, who have besides their Religious Fables, a Learn-ing and Doctrine.*"[109]

The second passage is from Clement of Alexandria: "*The Egyptians do not reveal their Religious Mysteries promiscuously to all, nor communicate the knowledge of divine things to the Profane, but only to those who are to succeed in the kingdom, and to such of the Priests as are judged most fitly qualified for the same, upon account both of their birth and Education.*"[110]

The third piece of testimony for the arcane theology of the Egyptians comes from two famous passages in Plutarch's treatise on Isis and Osiris. One is on the Sphinx: "*When amongst the Egyptians there is any King chosen out of the Military Order, he is forthwith brought to the Priests, and by them instructed in that Arcane Theology, which conceals Mysterious Truths under obscure Fables and Allegories. Wherefore they place Sphinges before their Temples, to signifie that their Theology contained a certain Arcane and Enigmatical Wisdom in it.*"[111] The other is on Harpocrates as the symbol of mystic silence: "*The* Harpocrates *of the Egyptians is not to be taken for an Imperfect and Infant God, but for the President of mens Speech concerning the Gods, that is but imperfect, balbutient and inarticulate, and the Regulator or Corrector of the same; his finger upon his mouth being a symbol of Silence and Taciturnity.*"[112]

The Egyptians used two means of transmitting their secrets to the knowledgeable while concealing them from the common folk: allegories and hieroglyphics. Cudworth accepted the common explanation of hieroglyphs as "Figures not answering to sounds or Words, but immediately representing the Objects and Conceptions of the Mind,"[113] chiefly used "to express the Mysteries of their Religion and Theology, so that they might be concealed from the prophane Vulgar." This was the "Hieroglyphick Learning and Metaphysical Theory" Moses had been instructed in. According to Cudworth, there can be no doubt that it consisted in the "Doctrine of *One Supreme and Universal Deity the Maker of the whole World.*"[114] Cudworth defends this interpretation of Ancient Egyptian theology against two different interpretations.

The first says that the Egyptians were atheistic and materialistic; this view had been advocated by Porphyry in his *Letter to Anebo*. Porphyry holds that the Egyptians know of no other gods "but the Planets and those Stars that fill up the Zodiack . . ., and Robust Princes, as they call them," a passage Eusebius underscored by saying "that the very Arcane Theology of the Egyptians, Deified nothing but Stars and Planets, and acknowledged no Incorporeal Principle or Demiurgick Reason as the Cause of this Universe, but only the Visible Sun . . . See now what is become of this Arcane Theology of the Egyptians, that deifies nothing but sensless Matter or Dead Inanimate Bodies."[115] These depictions of Egyptian theology, which Cudworth finds quite mistaken, correspond precisely to his notion of "absolute atheism." Since they had already been refuted by Iamblichus, Cudworth can confine himself to a long quotation from *De Mysteriis*.

The second challenge to Cudworth's interpretation is encapsulated in a question which Cudworth asks of himself: "whether [the Egyptians] were not Polyarchists [= polytheists], such as asserted a Multitude of Understanding Deities Self-Existent or Unmade." With this question he turns to the *"Trismegistick Writings."* Unlike Athanasius Kircher and others who continued to look upon Hermes Trismegistus as the embodiment of *prisca theologia* as if nothing had happened since the days of Marsilio Ficino and Giordano Bruno, Cudworth is too conscientious a scholar not to take Casaubon's dating of the *Corpus Hermeticum* into account before exploiting these texts as an invaluable source of information on Egyptian arcane theology. Isaac Casaubon (1559–1614) had proved beyond reasonable doubt that the *Corpus Hermeticum* dated from Late Antiquity and that it was probably a Christian forgery.[116]

According to Frances Yates, the year 1614 in which his book was published has to be recognized as "a watershed separating the Renaissance world from the modern world."[117] Casaubon's dating of the Hermetic texts "shattered the basis of all attempts to build a natural theology in Hermeticism." It was no easy task to vindicate the *Corpus Hermeticum* in the face of such a devastating verdict. Cudworth did so with not altogether valid arguments, but nonetheless with brilliant success. This is the reason that the "watershed" effect did not work and that natural theologies continued to be "built in Hermeticism." Yates closed the book on the Hermetic tradition much too early. It was because of Cudworth's intervention and in Cudworth's interpretation that the Hermetic texts continued to be influential in the eighteenth century.

Cudworth criticized Casaubon for treating all sixteen treatises that form the *Corpus Hermeticum* as a single text. By doing so, Casaubon made the mistake of applying observations applicable to only one text to the whole corpus.[118] According to Cudworth, Casaubon's conclusion that the books were all Christian forgeries is true of only three of the sixteen: 1 *(Poemander)*, 4 *(Crater)* and 8 *(Sermon of the Mount)*. These are, Cudworth says, indeed Christian forgeries (modern philologists, it should be noted, agree they are not). The others, including Cudworth's favorite, *Asclepius*, contain genuine Egyptian theology. They might be of late date, but they were written "before the Egyptian Paganism and their Succession of Priests were yet extinct".[119] Even if some were Christian forgeries "yet must there needs have been some Truth at the bottom to give subsistence to them. This at least, that *Hermes Trismegist* or the Egyptian Priests, in their Arcane and True Theology, really acknowledged *One Supreme and Universal Numen.*"[120]

Still, Cudworth is very careful not to build his edifice on Hermetic texts alone. Before considering them, Cudworth marshals a host of what he thinks to be less suspect testimonies in order to prove "that the Egyptians acknowledged, besides their *Many Gods, One Supreme and All-comprehending Deity*".[121] Plutarch's treatise *De Iside and Osiride*, which must indeed be considered the best source on Egyptian religion available at the time, repeatedly states that the Egyptians called their Supreme God "the first god," the god "accounted by them an *Obscure and Hidden Deity*," symbolized (for various reasons) by a crocodile.[122] Horapollo "tells us, that the Egyptians acknowledging a *pantokrator* and *kosmokrator, an Omnipotent Being that was the Governor of the whole World,* did Symbolically represent him by a Serpent." This "first and most divine Being," according to Eusebius, *"is Symbolically represented by a Serpent having the head of an Hawk."*

Cudworth later reverts to a passage from Eusebius, who speaks of "Kneph" as the name of that *"One Intellectual Demiurgus"* and says that the "Reason and Wisdom, by which the world was made, is not easy to be found out but hidden and obscure . . . and from this Cneph was said to be Generated or Produced Another God, whom the Egyptians call Phtha and the Greeks Vulcan [= Hephaistos]."[123] "Kneph" is a quite exact rendering of the Egyptian *Km-3t=f,* "who completed his time," the name of "the first form" of Amun.

Cudworth then turns to "Divine Iamblichus," who does not fail to lend abundant support to his theory, concluding with a very interesting quote from Damascius: *"The Egyptian Philosophers that have been in our times, have declared the hidden truth of their Theology, having found in certain Egyptian Writings, that there was according to them, One Principle of all things, praised under the name of the Unknown Darkness, and that thrice repeated:* Which Unknown Darkness is a Description of that Supreme Deity, that is Incomprehensible."[124] In the "Vulgar Religion and Theology" this Supreme and Hidden God was named "Hammon" or "Ammon"; "Manetho Sebennites *conceives the Word* Amoun, *to signifie that which is Hidden"* (which is perfectly correct). Iamblichus explains the name as "the Demiurgical Intellect, and President of Truth, as with Wisdom it proceedeth to Generation, and produceth into light, the Secret and Invisible Powers of the hidden Reasons," which definition leads Cudworth to the conclusion "that *Hammon* amongst the Egyptians, was not only the name of the *Supreme Deity,* but also of such a one as was *Hidden, Invisible and Incorporeal."*[125]

The idea of the Hidden God sets the scene for the veiled image at Sais. Cudworth seems to be the first to give Plutarch's and Proclus' famous descriptions a prominent place in Egyptian religion. He renders Plutarch's version of the inscription "upon the Temple at Sais" as *"I am all that Hath been, Is, and Shall be, and my* Peplum *or Veil, no mortal hath ever yet uncovered"* and concludes that there can be no means of interpreting this idea of "all" as "sensless matter," because it is a personal "I" that speaks as *"One thing which was All."*[126] Cudworth interprets the veil as the symbol of a distinction between outer and inner, "something

Exterior and Visible" and "something Hidden and Recondite, Invisible and Incomprehensible to Mortals." He compares this characterization to "that description which God makes of himself to *Moses, Thou shalt see my Back parts, but my Face shall not be seen.*"[127] Philo "thus glosseth upon those words, '*it is sufficient for a wise man to know God a Posteriori, or from his Effects; but whosoever will needs behold the naked Essence of the Deity, will be blinded with the transcendent Radiancy and Splendor of his Beams.*'" It is precisely in this way that the veiled Isis is depicted as an allegory of nature, with puttos measuring her footsteps "a posteriori." What in the Biblical text is called the back parts of God and what Philo interprets as his works, the inscription "called the *Peplum,* the *Veil* and *Exterior Garment* of it, or else *God himself Veiled.* Wherefore it is plain," Cudworth continues, "that the Deity here described, cannot be the mere Visible and Corporeal World as Sensless and Inanimate, that being all Outside and Exposed to the View of Sense, and having nothing Hidden or Veiled in it."

Horapollo explains the Egyptian concept of "God" as "*a Spirit diffusing itself through the World, and intimately pervading all things.*" Cudworth links this up with Iamblichus' mention of a Saitic inscription which he takes to be the same as Plutarch's. A prophet named Bithys is purported to have "there [at Sais] declared the name of that God, who extends or diffuses himself through the whole World." Cudworth also stresses the fact that the "Athena of the Greeks, who was derived from the Egyptian Neith, was famous for her Peplum too." A peplum was annually consecrated to Minerva "in the Great Panathenaicks, with much Solemnity, when the Statue of this Goddess, was also by those Noble Virgins of the city, who embroidered this Veil, cloathed all over therewith." Cudworth thinks it is probable that "the statue of the Egyptian Neith also, in the temple at Sais, had likewise agreeably to its Inscription, such a *Peplum* or Veil cast over it." He then mentions Proclus' version, which adds the sentence "*And the Sun was the fruit or off-spring which I produced.*" This sentence proves that for the Egyptians "the Sun was not the Supreme Deity."

The "First God," Cudworth resumes, is the Supreme God of the Egyptians. They conceived him to be "Invisible and Hidden," before, outside, and independent of the world, but at the same time to be the world. "The First God," or *to Hen,* "and *to pan* or the *Universe,* were Synonymous expressions," "because the *First Supreme Deity,* is that which contains *All Things*, and diffuses it self through *All Things*." We are back to the One-and-All, and it is now clear that Orpheus derived this doctrine from the Egyptians: *hen ti ta panta, that all things were one*.[128] For the Egyptians, *to Hen*, the invisible source of everything, manifests and "veils" itself in everything. *Pan* is the exterior manifestation of *to Hen*. This sheds an entirely new light on the theology of the Arcadian god Pan. *(To) pan*, meaning "all things," is the same as nature, and the Arcadian Pan is the god of nature. Cudworth discusses some passages dealing with Pan in terms of pantheism, including Plutarch's famous story "Death of the Great Pan."[129] Later on, Berkeley would equate *to Pan* with Isis as the goddess of nature, that is, *natura naturata*, as opposed to Osiris, who is *natura naturans*.[130]

Only after having established the theology of *Hen kai pan* beyond any possible doubt as the "Arcane Theology" of the Egyptians, does Cudworth produce no less than twenty-three great passages from the sixteen treatises of the *Corpus Hermeticum* where this idea of the One-and-All is expounded with great clarity and explicitness. He quotes these passages both in their original Latin or Greek and in his beautiful translation. The effect of this presentation of accumulated pantheistic manifestoes on a reader who has followed him so far is simply overwhelming. "All the powers that are in me, praise the One and the All." It is small wonder that these radiant pages continued to illuminate the subject for more than a century. The Hermetic texts express from within what Plutarch describes from without. The Saitic inscription on the veiled image and the Hermetic texts all "undoubtedly assert *One God that was All things*."[131]

Another inscription confirms this equation of the Saitic inscription and the *Hen kai pan* of the Hermetic texts. It is an inscription on an altar at Capua that had been published by Athanasius Kircher and that reads (I reproduce Cudworth's layout):

TIBI.
UNA. QUÆ.
ES. OMNIA.
DEA. ISIS

"To you, one who is all, O goddess Isis."[132] Who does not think in this context of Apuleius' immortal theophany of Isis, which I discussed in

Chapter 2? Cudworth devotes some pages to Apuleius and his concept of Isis and then turns to Serapis. He knows, of course, as "Origen tells us, that this was a new upstart Deity, set up by Ptolemy in Alexandria"[133] Serapis declares himself in an oracle as follows: "The starry heaven is my head, the Sea my Belly, my Ears are in the Ether, and the bright Light of the Sun is my clear piercing Eye."[134] I have shown elsewhere and will discuss further in Chapter 6 that this description not only corresponds to the widespread Hellenistic concept of "le dieu cosmique" (André-Jean Festugière's phrase) but also has close parallels in Egyptian texts dating as far back as the thirteenth century B.C.E.[135]

It is not sufficient to say that Cudworth was wrong in taking the *Corpus Hermeticum* and other Greek and Latin texts as testimonies of genuine Egyptian theology because his arguments were erroneous. His aim was not to reshift the Hermetic tradition into highest antiquity, but to defend these texts against Casaubon's accusations of forgery. In this, he was right, and he would have been right also in the three cases which he yielded to Casaubon. For Cudworth, it was not a question of date but of authenticity. His aim was to get at the authentic "arcane theology" of the Egyptians by basing his argument not so much "upon the Sibylline oracles, and those reputed writings of Hermes Trismegist, the authority whereof hath of late been decried by learned men; nor yet upon such oracles of the Pagan deities as may be suspected to have been counterfeited by Christians; but upon such monuments of Pagan antiquity, as are altogether unsuspected and indubitate." Cudworth was thinking of Egyptian priests who knew Greek and availed themselves not only of the Greek language but even of Greek philosophic terminology in order to express their "arcane theology." By rehabilitating the Hermetic writings, he was successful in reestablishing the Hermetic tradition within the quest for Natural Religion, and this is what counts in the history of that tradition. Bishop Berkeley, the famous philosopher, was paraphrasing Cudworth's results when he wrote: "And though the books attributed to Mercurius Trismegistus were none of them wrote by him, and are allowed to contain some manifest forgeries; yet it is also allowed, that they contain tenets of the ancient Aegyptian philosophy, though dressed perhaps in a more modern garb. To account for which, Jamblichus observes, that the books under his name contain indeed mercurial opinions, though often expressed in the style of the Greek philosophers, as having been translated from the Egyptian into Greek[136] [. . .] Plato and Aristotle considered God as abstracted or distinct from the natural world. But the Aegyptians considered God and nature as making one whole, or all things together as making one universe. In doing this, they did not exclude the intelligent mind, but considered it as containing all things. Therefore, whatever was wrong in their way of thinking, it doth not, nevertheless, imply or lead to Atheism."[137]

Cudworth was probably wrong in equating the Greco-Egyptian philosophy of the One-and-All with an Egyptian theology ancient enough to make it possible for Moses to be initiated into it. But even here, there is much to be said in favor of Cudworth's view. Of course, such monuments as Cudworth was looking for could yield their secrets only after the decipherment of the hieroglyphs in 1822. What he took for "unsuspected and indubitate" evidence was just the same kaleidoscope of Classical quotations that we have already seen—with some exceptions for the sake of historical and textual critique. Only now are we in a position to examine those monuments and to read those inscriptions which Cudworth was vainly seeking. The hieroglyphic texts confirm Cudworth's intuitions in every way he could have desired. This will be shown in the second part of the sixth chapter.

CHAPTER FOUR

The Moses Discourse in the Eighteenth Century

A Deist's Point of View: John Toland

Almost simultaneously with the appearance of Spencer's dissertation *De Urim et Thummim* (1670) and well before his *De Legibus*, Sir John Marsham published his reconstruction of history and chronology (*Canon Chronicus*, 1672). Marsham's book had the same chronological implications as Spencer's argument and contradicted the orthodox view of history with its distinction between *historia sacra* and *historia profana*. Spencer's historicization of the Law abolished the traditional frames and fences of the Biblical truth, opening new vistas on the prehistory and historical context of the Bible. Spencer had shown that not only civilization but also religion and worship began "long before Moses' time" *(diu ante Mosis tempora)*. Marsham elaborated the same idea in the form of a new chronology.[1]

   Only a few years after Marsham's and Spencer's publications, John Toland[2] and Matthew Tindal[3] explained the theological consequences of the chronological revolution. These two writers worked from a different vantage point; they belonged to what Margaret Jacob aptly called "the radical Enlightenment." Whereas Spencer, Cudworth, and Warburton tried to change the orthodox distinctions from within, Toland and Tindal worked from without, trying to "ruin the sacred truths" in a revolutionary and sometimes aggressive way. Basing their work on the ideas of the French and English Deists as well as on those of the Hermeticists and the Spinozists, they sought a concept of natural religion common to all nations, above and beyond its historical forms in different cultures. In Spencer, they found the historical proof that

Egypt was the homeland and the origin of this religion. They combined Spencer's reconstruction of the Egyptian origins of the Mosaic Law with the Hermetic tradition and its reconstruction of Egyptian theology, the doctrine of the One being the All and the All being the One. Marsham had shown that Egyptian religion came first and predated Moses by eight or nine centuries. On the basis of the undoubted principle that "truth comes first, and what comes later is corruption," Egypt had to be regarded as the homeland of truth. Just as Marsham had abolished the distinction between *historia sacra* and *historia profana*, they abolished the distinction between natural religion and positive religion, or nature and Scripture.[4] In the eyes of the orthodox and much against his own intentions, Spencer's book thus became associated with the position of "Deists" like Pierre Bayle, Matthew Tindal, and John Toland.[5] As a result, he was accused by the defenders of orthodoxy not only of having paved the way for these ideas but of sharing them. Spencer's Egyptophobic vision of idolatry was completely obscured in the face of new enemies, such as Spinozism and Deism.

I shall briefly illustrate the position of the Deists by singling out from the innumerable books and treatises that appeared during the hundred and fifty years between the first and the last of the English Deists, Lord Herbert of Cherbury and Lord Bolingbroke, a small booklet by John Toland called *Origines Judaicae*. My sole reason for calling attention to this text is that it is a commentary on Strabo and the first attempt to give an account of Moses' life and work exclusively based on the extra-Biblical tradition discussed in Chapter 2.[6] Thus Toland's booklet forms a link between Strabo and Freud. While Spencer makes use of all of his Classical knowledge in order to make sense of the Biblical text, Toland plays the Classical authors off against the Bible. The difference between the two could not be more radical. Toland gives the discourse a decisively heretical turn, which Warburton will try in vain to counteract and which Karl L. Reinhold will bring to full fruition in his masonic text.

Toland's enemy is no longer called *idololatria*; now it is *superstitio*. And this notion referred not just to paganism, but to Biblical religion as well. By "religion" Toland understands "natural religion," "RELIGIO, quae est juncta cum cognitionae Naturae," as opposed to "positive religion," which is based on revelation. This amounts to a complete and radical abolition of the Mosaic distinction. With Toland, we are entering the ground of "radical enlightenment"[7] which is very different from the ground on which Spencer, Cudworth, and later Warburton were working. Toland's portrait of Moses is very much the same as that to be found in a blasphemous pamphlet that circulated in the late seventeenth and eighteenth centuries under the title *L'esprit de Monsieur Benoit de Spinosa: Traité des trois imposteurs,*[8] not to be confused with the somewhat older treatise *De Tribus Impostoribus.*[9]

Toland does not count Moses among the three impostors, but does count him among the six lawgivers. According to Diodorus, these are Mneves, Minos, Lycurgus, Zoroastres, Zalmoxis, and Moses. Each of them founded the laws of a specific people and referred to a specific deity as the source of the Law in order to give it more authority:

Mneves	Egypt	Hermes
Minos	Crete	Jupiter
Lycurgus	Lacedaemon	Apollon
Zoroastres	Arimaspoi	Bonus Genius (Ahura Mazda)
Zalmoxis	Getes	Communis Vesta
Moses	Judaei	Deus qui Iao dicitur

Here, Moses is presented as a lawgiver who followed the general principle of "inventing" *(finxisse)* God as the author of his legislation. This legal fiction of a superhuman source of legal authority is precisely the imposture of which Moses is accused in the *Traité des trois imposteurs.*[10]

In this proposition Toland is opposing Pierre-Daniel Huet, who had claimed Moses as the first lawgiver and as the source of all subsequent legislation, and who had produced the equation Mnevis = Osiris = Bacchus = Moses—"O praecarium & ridiculum argumentum!" Toland shows, not without glee, to what tortuous argumentation orthodoxy must have recourse in order to reconcile Biblical and Classical sources, or religion and reason. A religion that cannot stand up to reason will be termed superstition.

Toland's small booklet of some one hundred pages (with large characters printed on very small pages) is a commentary on Strabo's account of the origins of the Jewish people. He gives Strabo, Diodorus, and Tacitus more credit than "the 'scriptor' of the Pentateuch." Toland cannot understand why all those who have dealt with Jewish history such as Marsham and Spencer relied on the Pentateuch and passed over Strabo in silence.

For Toland—as for Freud two hundred and twenty-five years later—Moses was an Egyptian priest and nomarch. He takes the "priest" from Strabo and, referring to Diodorus, who says that the nomarchs were also priests, turns the priest into a nomarch.[11] Even the Bible retains a memory of his political power, for it knows not only that Moses was "well versed in all the wisdom of the Egyptians," but also that he was "powerful in words and deeds," which can only refer to the combination of *sacerdotium* and *praefectura*, and not to magic and miracles *ut plures volunt.* If he was a nomarch, his nome could have been Goshen, where the Hebrews settled.[12]

Strabo reports Moses' dissatisfaction with Egyptian religion. Each nome had its own deity because—according to Diodorus—a certain very sagely prince *(sapientissimus quidam princeps)* wanted to maintain the peace of the kingdom and introduced a pluralistic and polytheistic religion *(variam & miscellam induxit religionem),* to prevent a conspiracy among the Egyptians. Moses, however, was a deist and an iconoclast. Strabo and the Bible agree on these points. In the Bible, Moses insists on the invisibility of God: *nullam imaginem vidistis* (Deuteronomy 4:15). Tacitus says that the Egyptians worship many animals and monstrous images whereas the Jews conceive of one god only, and with the mind only *(mente sola unumque numen intelligunt);* they regard as impious those who make representations of gods in man's image from perishable materials; that supreme and eternal being is to them incapable of representation and without end *(profanos qui Deum imagines, mortalibus materiis in species hominum effingunt: summum illud & aeternum neque mutabile neque interiturum).* The Moses of Strabo held God to be "Nature, or matter, mechanically arranged and acting without conscience and intelligence" *(Naturam, vel mundi materiam mechanice dispositam et absque ulla conscia intelligentia agentem)* and was an enraged enemy of idolatry. Even Scripture shows that he did not make any mention of the immortality of the soul or of a future state of reward or punishment. The name by which he called his god merely means *necessariam solummodo existentiam,* necessary existence or "what exists by himself" *(quod per se existit),* in the same sense that the Greek *to on* denotes the incorruptible, eternal, and interminable world. Moses was not an atheist, but a "Pantheist, or, to speak in conformity with more recent usage, a Spinozist." His deity was the same as Cicero's *mundus:* "omnium autem rerum quae natura administrantur, seminator, & sator, & parens, ut ita dicam, atque Educator."[13]

The type of cult which "Moses Strabonicus" instituted did without massive expenditures for priests, temples, rituals, and ceremonial objects, without ecstatic inspirations and other "absurd actions."[14] This description is in contradiction to the innumerable and extremely lavish sacrifices and ceremonies which we find in the Bible and in which the Jews seem to have surpassed all other nations. Yet, according to Strabo, that was a later depravation. Moses instituted a cult of great purity and simplicity. The only feast was the Sabbath, the only law was Natural Law (Naturae lex) consisting of the ten commandments, and the only cult was the worship of the two tablets containing these commandments. Everything else—the discrimination between pure and impure food, circumcision, sacrifices, and so forth—is the result of later developments and decadence at a time when the Jews turned to idolatry and when God sent them the prophet Ezekiel speaking in the name of God: "But I shall give them statutes that are not good and laws by which they cannot live" ("Ego etiam dederam ipsis statuta non bona et Jura per quae non vivere possent").[15] In this way, religion turned into superstition. Toland sees the reason for this depravation of original religion in the exaggerated importance which the people attributed to dreams and ecstatic experiences. He refers to prophetic warnings against dreams such as those in *Jeremiah* 29:8 and *Joel* 2:28–29, but above all to Cicero's *De Divinatione*, which claims that dreams could never have any divine significance. If God would communicate with man, he would speak to the wakeful, not to the sleeping. *Somnia divina putanda non sunt.*

Toland closes his treatise by recapitulating his points:

1. The Jews were descendants of the Egyptians.
2. Moses, their leader and lawgiver, was an Egyptian priest and nomarch.
3. Nature was his supreme and sole deity (in other words, he was a deist).
4. He instituted a cult without expenses, ecstasies, or rites.
5. The laws of purity, circumcision, and other rites were introduced after his time.
6. Moses was one of a group of outstanding legislators such as Minos, Lycurgus, Zalmoxis and others. This means that he invented a personal deity and referred to that deity as the source

of the Law and of its authority. As Cicero had shown in the
first book of *De Natura Deorum*, gods are a political fiction.[16]
But Moses gave this god a name that scarcely concealed his
purely philosophical and physical concept of nature: Jehovah,
"necessary existence."

Mystery; or The Schizophrenia of Paganism: William Warburton

Sixty years after Spencer and thirty years after Toland, William Warburton, bishop of Gloucester (1698–1779), took up the same project of
the historical evaluation of Moses and his legislation, and in it he addressed the Deists and free-thinkers. In no less than nine books in three
volumes, Warburton pursued a rather strange plan. He fully subscribed
to the thesis advanced by Spinoza and the Deists that the Hebrew Bible
contained no hints of the immortality of the soul and "a future state of
reward and punishment."[17] However, he refuted the conclusions which
the Deists drew from this revolutionary discovery: that these ideas were
indispensable for every institution of religion coming from God and
that consequently the Mosaic institutions could necessarily be nothing
but a human fabrication, if not an imposture. Instead, Warburton saw in
the very absence of these ideas the proof of the divine origin of Moses'
legislation! This use of the same arguments for different ends renders
his argument twisted and convoluted. He first shows that every pagan
religion and society is based on two principles: (1) the assumption of the
immortality of the soul and a future state of rewards and punishments
and (2) secrecy or mystery. Every pagan or natural religion is organized
in the dual form of outside/inside, or surface/depth, or fore-
ground/background. He then goes on to show not only that these principles are absent from the Mosaic institutions, but that they are
consciously and carefully avoided. Moses is the only lawgiver who did
not have to depend on the principles of a hereafter and of secrecy
because he could depend on an "extraordinary providence." Moses
counted on God to reward virtue and punishing mischief in this world,
that is, in the realm of history. He dispensed with secrecy by teaching
the mysteries to everybody and creating a nation of initiates.

Warburton's book met with the same productive misreading as did
Spencer's sixty years before. Its importance was seen as residing not so

much in its thesis as in the material it made accessible. In trying to trace the Mosaic laws back to an Egyptian origin, Spencer created a very detailed picture of Egyptian religion and rituals, and became influential only by overturning orthodox chronology and reconstructing sacred history by putting Egypt above all else—including Israel. In attempting to demonstrate the divine character of a religion which did away with secrecy and immortality, Warburton attracted attention with his careful delineation of the role of secrecy in religion, the form and content of the ancient mystery cults, and the function of hieroglyphic writing. His section on the ancient mysteries extends over more than three hundred pages, including appendices and notes.

Warburton does a great deal more than just collect the pertinent quotations from Classical authors and the Christian Fathers. In interpreting these passages, he ventures into literary criticism, distinguishing hymns,[18] confessions,[19] and initiation speeches, attributing the fragments to speakers within the cultic liturgy, reconstructing the liturgical frame and the thematic points of focus. Warburton is able to show to what degree the language of philosophers, tragedians (especially Euripides), historians, and other Greek and Latin writers are imbued with mystical terminology. He detects the same terminology in a famous passage in Flavius Josephus (which I will discuss later), taking this as proof that Moses' lawgiving and religious teaching was modeled on initiation into the lesser and greater mysteries of Egypt. In following up these hints, Warburton got as involved in reconstructing pagan mystery cults as Spencer did in reconstructing Egyptian ritual; in the process both lost sight of their theological agendas. Or should one say that their theological concerns were just a pretext to do what in their time was not yet established as a discipline in its own right, namely, comparative religion? As a matter of fact, they were remembered not for their theology, but for their Egyptology.

Following in the footsteps of Spencer and especially Cudworth, Warburton helped construct the famous "dual religion" hypothesis in order to establish a sharp antagonism between the so-called overt and secret rituals of pagan religion. From Clement of Alexandria, he took the distinction between "lesser" and "greater mysteries." The lesser mysteries were essentially a hieroglyphic encasement, designed to captivate the populace at large through symbolic icons, sensual rituals, and sacred animals. But they disclosed their signification only to those who

proved able to understand their secret meaning, which generally consisted of teachings about the immortality of the soul and a future life
where virtue would be rewarded and vice would be punished. The
greater mysteries were administered only to the very few among the
initiates whose minds and virtues were strong enough to withstand the
truth. This truth was essentially negative: it consisted in abolishing the
illusionary imagery of polytheism. Initiation constitutes a process of
disillusionment. By passing the threshold between the lesser and the
greater mysteries, the initiate is supposed to abrogate his former beliefs,
to recognize their erroneous and fictitious nature, and "to see things as
they are."[20] The disillusionment of the initiate is brought about by
telling him that the gods are just deified mortals and that there is only
one invisible and anonymous God, the ultimate cause and foundation
of Being "who originated all by himself, and to him all things owe their
being." These phrases are taken from Eusebius and Clement of Alexandria, who both quote an Orphic hymn which Warburton interprets
as the words by which the hierophant in the Eleusinian mysteries
addressed the initiate (in Warburton's translation):

> I will declare a secret to the initiated; but let the doors be shut
> against the profane. But thou, O Musaeus, the offspring of bright
> Selene, attend carefully to my song; for I shall deliver the truth
> without disguise. Suffer not, therefore, thy former prejudices to
> debar thee of that happy life, which the knowledge of these
> sublime truths will procure unto thee: but carefully contemplate
> this divine Oracle, and preserve it in purity of mind and heart. Go
> on, in the right way, and contemplate THE SOLE GOVERNOR OF THE
> WORLD: HE IS ONE, AND OF HIMSELF ALONE; AND TO THAT ONE ALL
> THINGS OWE THEIR BEING. HE OPERATES THROUGH ALL, WAS NEVER
> SEEN BY MORTAL EYES, BUT DOES HIMSELF SEE EVERYONE.[21]

Since the Eleusinian mysteries are of Egyptian origin, according to
Diodorus and others,[22] this Orphic hymn must also be based on an
Egyptian model. According to Clement of Alexandria, this last and
highest initiation led to a point where all teaching ends. Discursive
instruction stops and immediate vision takes over. "The doctrines delivered in the Greater Mysteries are concerning the universe. Here all
instruction ends. Things are seen as they are; and Nature, and the

workings of Nature, are to be seen and comprehended."[23] In the final stage of initiation, the adept is speechlessly confronted with Nature.

Such were the pagan, especially Egyptian, initiations which Moses revealed to the Israelites:

> Josephus is still more express [than Eusebius].[24] He tells Appion [sic] that that high and sublime knowledge, which the Gentiles with difficulty attained unto, in the rare and temporary celebration of their *Mysteries*, was habitually taught to the Jews, at all times. And what was this sublime knowledge, but the doctrine of the UNITY? "Can any government (says he) be more holy than this? or any Religion better adapted to the nature of the Deity? Where, in any place but in this, are the whole People, by the special diligence of the Priests, to whom the care of public instruction is committed, accurately taught the principles of true piety? So that the body-politic seems, as it were, one great *Assembly*, constantly kept together, for the celebration of some sacred *Mysteries*. For those things which the Gentiles keep up for a few days only that is, during those solemnities they call MYSTERIES and INITIATIONS, we, with vast delight, and a plenitude of knowledge, which admits of no error, fully enjoy, and perpetually contemplate through the whole course of our lives. If you ask (continues he) the nature of those things, which in our sacred rites are enjoined and forbidden; I answer, they are simple, and easily understood. The first instruction relates to the DEITY, and teaches that GOD CONTAINS ALL THINGS, and is a Being every way perfect and happy: that he is self-existent, and the SOLE CAUSE of all existence; the beginning, the middle, and the end of all things, etc." Nothing can be more explicit than the testimony of this learned Jew. He not only alludes to the *greater Mysteries*, by the direct terms of teletes and mysteria, but uses several expressions relative to what the gentile Mystagogos taught therein . . . Thus, I think, it appears that the APORRHETA, in the *greater Mysteries*, were the detection of the origine of vulgar *Polytheism;* and the discovery of the doctrine of the *Unity*.[25]

Warburton takes this characterization of the Jewish Law by a Jew as proof of his thesis that the greater mysteries taught a conception of God similar to what Moses taught to the Hebrews. According to Josephus,

Moses' lawgiving was an attempt to make the highest and most exclusive mystical knowledge available to all by this means to transform his
people into a community of initiates.

It is difficult to see how Warburton could avoid the obvious conclusion which Reinhold would draw from this demonstration thirty-five
years later: that the God of the mysteries was the same as the God of
Moses and that the so-called revelation was nothing more than a huge
open-air performance of an initiation into the greater mysteries, meant
not for the select few, but for a whole people. Instead, Warburton made
great efforts to keep the God of the mysteries apart from the God of
the philosophers and especially from Spinoza's *deus sive natura*.[26] He did
not want to impute to these "atheistic" ideas the notions of high antiquity and original wisdom (which he attributed to the mysteries). But this
was exactly the effect of his book. His readers understood him to have
shown that the original esoteric wisdom of the Egyptians taught the
tenets of Spinozism and worshipped *deus sive natura*. A typical example
of this reception is P. A. d'Origny's book *L'Egypte ancienne*.[27] Here,
d'Origny expounds the idea that the ancient Egyptians were the first to
invest great efforts in cultural and spiritual achievements and to arrive
at an esoteric worship of nature because of the extraordinary produc-
tivity of their agriculture. While the people worshipped nature in the
shape of many local deities, the elite revered "the One infinite Being,
Creator and Preserver of All."[28] D'Origny explicitly defends the Egyptians against the accusation of atheism or materialism and refers to
Spinoza in this context: "S'il suffisait de s'être fait une chimère de
divinité pour n'être point Athée, les Égyptiens qui adoraient la nature
en general & même en detail dans leur sept dieux immortels, & dans
un grand nombre de dieux terrestres et animaux, n'etoient point
Athées: si au contraire l'ont doit regarder comme tels ceux qui, ainsi
Spinoza, ne reconnoissent pour dieux que la nature ou la vertu de la
nature répandue dans tous les êtres, les Égyptiens en general l'étoient
certainement."[29] The Deists and Spinozists of the eighteenth century
looked to Egypt as the origin and homeland of their concept of God
and they drew their evidence from Warburton.

❀ THE IDEA of a complete antagonism between official religion and
a mystery cult was especially influential. This was small wonder in a

time when the ideas of Spinozism and Deism were disseminated in forms of esotericism and concealment. Warburton constructed the relation of mysteries to official religion in terms of contradiction. One was the negation of the other. The mystery cults were counter-religions in that they would have destroyed the official religion if their greater mysteries were made public. But official polytheism was indispensable for the political order of the society. Warburton did not fully subscribe to the Deists' concept of pious fraud.[30] The official religion was not a deception; it was inevitable and therefore was a legitimate institution. It was coexistent and coextensive with the state. Only those who were chosen to rule the state were admitted to the greater mysteries. It was necessary for them to know the full, unveiled truth. For those who were to be ruled, knowledge of the veiled truth was much more appropriate. This was not fraud, but simply human necessity.

Warburton's great (re)discovery was the political function of secrecy, which he demonstrates with reference to a Greek text, the famous fragment of Critias.[31] According to Warburton, Egyptian religion is the prototype of all pagan religions, in that Egypt first founded a state and a mystery cult. State and religious secrecy are seen as interdependent. Secrecy, however, has a rather complex structure. The difference between outer and inner, or popular and mystery religion, recurs on the level of mystery as the difference between lesser and greater mysteries. The function of mystery or secrecy is political. Without secrecy, there is no civil society or political order. People must be kept in awe in order to be brought to obey the Law and to support the state. But secrecy has two faces and fulfills two functions. One is to excite curiosity: this is the function of the lesser mysteries. They teach the immortality of the soul and its destiny in the hereafter, the "future state of reward and punishment." The other function is to hide truths that must only be taught to the very few because otherwise the state would be overturned. These dangerous and exclusive truths can be reduced to two sentences:

1. The polytheistic pantheon is but an illusion, necessary for the people, but otherwise fictitious.
2. There is but one God, the sole creator and source of all Being.

Warburton further distinguishes three stages in the development of religion and philosophy:

1. The natural stage: Egyptian religion. Here, the premises and foundations of monotheism are laid out in the form of an esoteric pantheism.
2. The systematic stage: the stage of Greek materialistic philosophy which drew the conclusions from the Egyptian premises and built them into a coherent system, turning natural pantheism into a kind of atheism, monism, or "Spinozism."
3. The syncretistic stage: the stage of the Hermetic fallacy, when the Hermetic writings were forged in order to graft the Greek conclusions onto the Egyptian premises and to read "Spinozism" into the Egyptian origins.

What Moses—or rather God by the mediation of Moses—did, was to translate the Egyptian premises of monotheism into revealed truth.

Warburton's readers did not follow him in all his convoluted distinctions but jumped at the idea of revelation as translation, which to their mind, blurred and overcame the very distinction between revelation and reason or nature which Warburton meant to emphasize. Thus Warburton came to substantiate the views of the free-thinkers and Freemasons, which he wanted to refute. The idea that pagan religions developed and degenerated around a nucleus of original wisdom which they enshrined and sheltered in a complex and enigmatic architecture of hieroglyphics and ceremonies and which in the course of time became more and more antithetic to their public political institutions had special appeal in the Age of Enlightenment, when the most advanced ideas were communicated within the esoteric circles of secret communities.[32]

Things and Signs: The Grammatology of Idolatry and Mystery

The discovery of a manuscript of Horapollo's *Hieroglyphica* on the island of Andros in 1419 led to a linguistic and semiotic revolution. To make a long story very short, one could say (using terms first introduced by Aleida Assmann)[33] that the Aristotelian semiotics of "mediated signification" (*mittelbare Signifikation*, where signs signify what they denote by means of a conventional code) which prevailed during the Middle Ages gave way to the Platonic semiotics of "immediate signification" (*unmittelbare Signifikation*, where signs signify by natural participation). The ancient debate as to whether words referred to things and concepts "by nature" *(physei)* or "by convention" *(thesei),* which had been closed by Aristotle in favor of "convention," was re-opened with the discovery of a writing system that was (mis)interpreted to refer "by nature" to things and concepts. Owing to this discovery, the linguistic debate between "Platonists" and "Aristotelians" turned into a debate on writing. For this reason, "grammatology," a term coined by Ignace J. Gelb for "the study of writing"[34] and used by Jacques Derrida for "the philosophy of writing,"[35] appears to be a more appropriate term than the usual "linguistics"[36] to refer to the discourse on hieroglyphs and on the possibility of natural writing. The grammatological aspect of the Mosaic distinction consists in the opposition between nature and Scripture. The idea of a revealed or "positive" religion was closely linked to the technique of writing.

The dream of early modernity was a reconciliation of nature and Scripture or, to put it in the words of a book title of the eighteenth century: *Naturae et Scripturae Concordia.*[37] Traditionally, this project found its expression in the theory of the two books of God, the book of nature and the book of Scripture.[38] Now, a different, but related, solution presented itself in the possibility of a "Scripture of nature," a writing which would refer not to the sounds of language, but to the things of nature and to the concepts of the mind. Egyptian hieroglyphics were held to be such a script by many scholars from the fifteenth century to the early nineteenth century. This explains the enormous interest which early modern Europe invested in ancient Egypt and its hieroglyphs.

Hieroglyphs were interpreted as natural signs or "real characters" (Francis Bacon) which referred not to sounds, but to things.[39] God created the world as symbols and images and the Egyptians merely imitated the creator. Their system of writing was held to be as original and natural as Adam's language, which immediately translated God's creatures into words.[40] Immediacy is the key word in this context. To quote Ralph Cudworth's definition: "The Egyptian hieroglyphicks were figures not answering to sounds or words, but immediately representing the objects and conceptions of the mind."[41] This interpretation of the Egyptian hieroglyphs was based particularly on a passage in Plotinus:

The wise men of Egypt, I think, also understood this, either by scientific knowledge or innate knowledge, and when they wished to signify something wisely, did not use the form of letters which follow the order of words and propositions and imitate sounds and the enunciations of philosophical statements, but by drawing images *[agalmata]* and inscribing them in their temples, one beautiful image for each particular thing, they manifested the non-discursiveness of the intelligible world. Every image is a kind of knowledge and wisdom and is a subject of deliberation. And afterwards [others] deciphered [the image] as a representation of something else by starting from it in its concentrated unity, already unfolded and by expressing it discursively and giving the reasons why things are like this.[42]

This is how Marsilio Ficino commented on this passage: "The discursive knowledge of time is, with you, manifold and flexible, saying for instance, that time is passing and, through a certain revolution, connects the beginning again with the end . . . The Egyptian, however, comprehends an entire discourse of this kind by forming a winged serpent that bites its tail with his mouth."[43]

"For, using an alphabet of things and not of words," wrote Sir Thomas Browne in the first half of the seventeenth century, "through the image and pictures thereof they [the Egyptians] endeavoured to speak their hidden contents in the letters and language of nature," that is, of things. An alphabet of things and not of words, this was indeed "the best evasion of the confusion of Babel."[44]

The most elaborate, erudite, and influential exposition of this interpretation of Egyptian hieroglyphs was published by William Warburton in 1741. Warburton based his argument on two different but related historical investigations. One was the study of the ancient mystery cults, the other was the study of the origin of writing in general and of the Egyptian hieroglyphs in particular.[45] The common assumption, shared by ancient as well as modern authors, was that the Egyptians invented their hieroglyphs solely "to express the mysteries of their religion and theology, so that they might be concealed from the prophane vulgar."[46] Hieroglyphic writing was generally held to be an epiphenomenon of mystery, invented to protect the truth from abuse, misunderstanding, and vulgarization, and to protect the political institutions from truths that would shatter their foundations. According to the theory of the time, the origin of hieroglyphic writing was thus inextricably linked with the rise of that "twofold philosophy"[47] which distinguished between popular beliefs and esoteric wisdom. Natural religion in its primitive state of original monotheism had no need for writing. Writing became necessary only with the development of a state or "political society" (assumed to have first occurred in Egypt), when the people began to deify their first kings and lawgivers. Religion then began to split into the politically supportive but fundamentally fictitious beliefs of the people and the knowledge of the priests, which was potentially destructive. It was then that the priests had to invent a code for transmitting their dangerous wisdom. Hieroglyphics was the "veil" which they wrapped around their tradition in order to protect both the state and the truth.

Warburton's objection to this theory was simple and reasonable. He looked into the origins of other writing systems and found that no original writing was ever invented for the sole purpose of secrecy. Cryptography was always a secondary invention based on existing primary writing systems. The natural functions of writing were related to memorization and communication, but not to arcanization. Warburton based his demonstration on Chinese and Mexican scripts, using whatever information was available in his time from missionaries and travelers. He states that every original writing is a combination of pictures and arbitrary signs (his expression is: "marks of arbitrary institution"). The pictures or figures render the things instead of the words. The arbitrary signs refer to "mental conceptions." Both, however, refer to "things," not to "sounds." His example for arbitrary signs is the knotted cords of the Peruvians. The Chinese script also contains many arbitrary signs which, according to a theory of Martino Martini, were derived from knotted cords.[48] The Peruvians emphasized signs but used "paintings" as well, while the Mexicans emphasized figures but also used arbitrary signs. Thus every original writing system contained both types of characters and was devised for the purposes of perpetuating tradition and modes of communication.

But with these "hieroglyphic paintings" and "marks of arbitrary institution" we are still in the stage of "prewriting." Real writing systems developed only during a process of what Warburton calls "abridgment," that is, the introduction of rules and frames that limit the inventory of signs and transform it into a conventional system. This process has little to do with secrecy or arcanization and simply follows the laws of necessity and economy.

Warburton identifies three rules for reducing the figurative signs, which he takes from Horapollo's treatise on Egyptian hieroglyphics:

1. "The principal circumstance stands for the whole" (for example, "two hands, one holding a shield and the other a bow" for "battle"):[49] the "curiological hieroglyphics."[50]
2. "The instrument of the thing stands for the thing itself" (for example, an eye for "omniscience"):[51] the "tropical hieroglyphics."
3. Symbolic analogy (a serpent biting its tail for "universe"): the "symbolic hieroglyphics."

According to Warburton every writing system starts from this common point of departure and develops in different directions. He explains the differences by means of a concept which will later become associated with the name of Johann Gottfried Herder: the "genius of the people" *(Volksgeist)*.[52] According to Warburton, the Egyptians were extremely inventive and imaginative and therefore naturally inclined toward "symbolic and analogic marks." Consequently they cultivated the figurative signs and almost dropped the "marks by institution." With the Chinese the situation was the obverse. In conformity with their notorious uninventiveness and cultural stagnation (I am still paraphrasing Warburton),[53] they had little taste for pictorial symbolization and turned to abstraction. The Egyptian method of figurative writing, which pictured "things" and used the properties of things in order to denote undepictable meanings, requires a vast knowledge of natural history. This ingenious observation of Warburton explains the striking analogies between Horapollo's interpretations of hieroglyphics on the one hand and codifications of ancient natural sciences such as those by Aelianus and Pliny and the Physiologus on the other.[54] Unlike all other scripts, the Egyptian hieroglyphics remained a *Dingschrift* and thus a codification of cosmological and biological knowledge. Other writing systems lost this epistemological connection with the visible word and turned into purely conventional codes.

After this demonstration of origins, the ground was prepared for the next step: the question of "how hieroglyphs came to be used to conceal knowledge." Again, Warburton's explanation is most ingenious. Precisely because the Egyptian script did not follow the common progression from picture to letter,[55] it became complex and developed into polygraphy. While other peoples turned from pictures to letters, the Egyptians kept their pictorial script and invented additional nonpictorial scripts. Warburton starts with Porphyry and Clement of Alexandria and combines their somewhat divergent descriptions in order to arrive at a system of tetragraphy.

Porphyry distinguishes the epistolic, the hieroglyphic, and the symbolic scripts, Clement the epistolic, the sacerdotal, and the hieroglyphic. Both are referring to what in modern Egyptological usage is termed demotic, hieratic, and hieroglyphic. Hieroglyphic and Hieratic are related to the Classical Egyptian language; one is the monumental version, the other is the cursive version of what is basically the same writing system. Demotic, by contrast, is related to the vernacular. It is derived from hieratic, but has become extremely abstract and cursive. These facts, however, were not known by Warburton. Therefore, I am simply following Warburton's reasoning in recapitulating his system, which runs as follows: Warburton thinks that each is omitting a script that the other one mentions. Porphyry omits Clement's "sacerdotal" writing, Clement omits Porphyry's "symbolic" script. Thus, there were four scripts instead of just three: epistolic, sacerdotal, hieroglyphic, and symbolic.

But Warburton thinks that he must correct Clement's wonderfully precise description in yet another respect. Clement describes the curriculum of an Egyptian pupil. First, he learns the epistolic writing, then proceeds to the sacerdotal script, and only if he is exceptional does he master hieroglyphics, which is the last, most difficult, and most accomplished script. This is perfectly correct because the average scribe in fact learned only demotic and hieratic; only a very few who were to become artists also learned hieroglyphics. Warburton takes this curriculum for evolution and thinks that Clement is describing the development of Egyptian writing: starting with demotic, developing into hieratic, and ending with hieroglyphic. Warburton inverts this sequence. First came hieroglyphic, then sacerdotal, and finally epistolic. Symbolic is also a late development. According to Warburton, it is the "Symbolic" script that was developed for the purpose of secrecy, not hieroglyphics, as was commonly assumed. Warburton sees the difference between hieroglyphs and symbols in the use of what he calls tropes, the figurative functions of those signs which do not simply denote what they represent but which use metaphor or metonymy.

Tropical hieroglyphics use this method out of necessity. Symbolic hieroglyphics or tropical symbols, on the other hand, are riddles or enigmas. Warburton's example for a tropical hieroglyph is an image which never appears as a hieroglyph and which, moreover, was completely alien to the Egyptians: the Ephesian *Diana Multimammia*, which he takes to be a common hieroglyph denoting "Universal Nature." The interest of this misunderstanding lies in the fact that it was this same image that was generally identified with the veiled image of Sais and the Egyptian iconography of Isis.[56] Moreover, we learn from this example that Warburton does not distinguish between writing and iconography. For tropical symbols or symbolic hieroglyphs, which usually combine different things, Warburton gives two examples: the scarab pushing a dung ball as a symbol of the sun, and the disk with a serpent as a symbol of the universe. Both examples are taken from Clement.

The symbolic script, or cryptography, functions in three ways: by the creation of new "enigmatic" signs, by the multiplication of meanings of one sign, and by the multiplication of signs for one meaning. Strangely enough, this is a very exact description of how Egyptian cryptography works, although Warburton could not have had the slightest idea of this. If one adds cryptography to the normal scripts that were in use at the time of Clement and Porphyry, Warburton's system of tetragraphy is equally exact:

Epistolic = Demotic
Sacerdotal = Hieratic
Hieroglyphic = Hieroglyphic
Symbolic = Cryptography

Until the Late Period, cryptography is a very rare variant of hieroglyphic, used predominantly for aesthetic purposes, to arouse the curiosity of passers-by. But in the Greco-Roman period, an age of foreign domination, the methods of cryptography were integrated into the monumental script of hieroglyphics; this created enormous complexity and turned the whole writing system into a kind of cryptography. Clement and Porphyry reflect this latest stage of hieroglyphics.

From the vantage point of modern Egyptology, Warburton was perfectly right in refuting the grammatology of secrecy that attributes the invention and development of writing in Egypt to the wish of the priests to keep their philosophical religion secret from the superstitious masses and to the need of the rulers to protect the politically supportive polytheism from the subversive monotheism of reason and nature. But the grammatology of secrecy can find some confirmation if applied not to the origins of writing, but to its latest stages. This is precisely what Warburton had proposed. Even in this he was right. In the later periods of Ancient Egyptian history, when the country was under foreign domination, there was an obvious need for more secrecy. It is very possible that the Greek misunderstanding of the hieroglyphs as a secret code reflects the way the Egyptian priests themselves spoke (and probably also thought) about their hieroglyphs and religion. It is at least evident that during this time the hieroglyphic script developed an enormous complexity. Its repertoire of signs increased by 1000 percent (from about 700 to about 7000) and turned into a kind of "figurative writing,"[57] which was not so very far from what Horapollo represented it to be.[58] We must not forget that hieroglyphs had long since ceased to be a "normal" writing system. Their use was restricted to purely monumental and artistic functions. In the Late Period, when demotic and Greek were in use for everyday purposes, hieratic and hieroglyphic turned into sacred scripts. Their inaccessibility to even literate Egyptians created a cultural barrier between priests and laymen which could easily have given rise to the concepts of "double religion," mystery, and initiation. But this does not mean that there ever was antagonism between popular and priestly religion. Every elite reacts to a crisis such as foreign domination with a marked increase in finesse and complexity up to levels of virtuosity that are not easily matched by outsiders. In these final stages of Egyptian religion, secrecy indeed seemed to fulfill a social function in helping the sacerdotal class maintain elite status. However, the rise of secrecy and cryptography in Late Period Egypt does not seem to be connected with a differentiation within Egyptian religion between an esoteric monotheism and a popular polytheism.

Warburton now proceeds to explain the other scripts. The most interesting point is his theory about the epistolic writing. He takes this system to be alphabetic. As has already been shown, the difference between hieroglyphs and letters was defined with respect to their reference either to things or to sounds. Hieroglyphs signify immediately, whereas letters signify by the mediation of language.[59] The principle of nonlinguistic signification applied both to hieroglyphs and to what Warburton called signs of arbitrary institution, such as knotted cords. The Egyptians invented, or rather "found," the system of alphabetic letters that somehow lay hidden within their complex inventory of pictorial and arbitrary signs.

This invention occurred somewhere about midway in the long history of their civilization. A secretary of the pharaoh made this discovery, which originally was used only for the private correspondence of the king. Warburton refers in this context to Plato's famous passage in *Phaedrus*.[60] The king, in Warburton's reading of Plato's account, immediately sees both the advantages and the disadvantages of this invention. The advantage is that it makes communication much easier. The disadvantage is that it destroys memory. Plato, however, is opposing writing (in general) to oral communication, not phonographic writing to hieroglyphics. But Warburton's misreading of the tale opens a highly interesting window on the mnemotechnical properties of hieroglyphs.[61] In Warburton's interpretation, the king is afraid that Theut's invention of phonographic letters will destroy the *ars memoriae* of the hieroglyphic system. As Warburton had already shown, hieroglyphs presuppose a vast amount of knowledge about the nature of those things that are used for signs. Since virtually all existing things are used for signs, this knowledge amounts to a veritable cosmology and the hieroglyphic system amounts to a veritable *ars memoriae*. "Men's attention would be called away from things, to which hieroglyphics, and the manner of explaining them, necessarily attached it, and be placed in exterior and arbitrary signs, which would prove the greatest hindrance to the progress of knowledge."[62]

Giordano Bruno, the Hermetist and mnemonist, had expressed the same idea some hundred and fifty years earlier: "The sacred letters used among the Egyptians were called hieroglyphs . . . which were images . . . taken from the things of nature, or their parts. By using such writings and voices, the Egyptians used to capture with marvellous skill the language of the gods. Afterwards when letters of the kind which we use now with another kind of industry were invented by Theuth or some other, this brought about a great rift both in memory and in the divine and magical sciences."[63]

Neither Bruno nor Warburton knew that the Egyptian term for hieroglyphs was "divine words" (compare Bruno's expression "the language of the gods") and that they were coming very close to ideas which the Egyptians themselves held concerning hieroglyphs. Bruno's concept of divine language is obviously taken from Iamblichus.[64] Thanks to the wisdom of their kings the Egyptians never gave up their systems of "thing-writing" and restricted the new alphabet to the specific purpose of correspondence.

❦ FOLLOWING Warburton's reconstruction, I am now approaching the time when Moses "was brought up in all the wisdom and sciences of the Egyptians" (Acts 7:22). In his time, all four scripts were already in use. For Moses' purposes, the epistolic or alphabetic script was most appropriate. He only had to alter the shape of the letters in order to conform to the second commandment and to purge the letters of all iconic traces. The second commandment was directed against hieroglyphs because God had recognized that the use of hieroglyphic writing would necessarily lead to idolatry. This interpretation of the second commandment is one of the more brilliant moments of Warburton's otherwise rather long-winded argument.[65]

The second commandment prohibiting idol worship has two different implications.[66] It is mostly understood in the sense that God must not be represented because he is invisible and omnipresent.[67] But as Warburton correctly points out, the same commandment also prohibits the making of "any graven images, the similitude of any figure, the likeness of male or female, the likeness of any beast that is on the earth, the likeness of any winged fowl that flieth in the air, the likeness of anything that creepeth on the ground, the likeness of any fish that is in the waters beneath the earth" (Deuteronomy 4:15–18, Warburton's translation). Warburton's interpretation emphasizes the anti-Egyptian meaning of the prohibition of idolatry. It is the exact "normative inversion" of the very fundamental principles of Egyptian writing, thinking, and speaking: "Do not idolize the created world by [hieroglyphic] reproduction." The second commandment is the rejection of hieroglyphic knowledge and memory because it amounts to an illicit magical idolization of the world.

According to Warburton, idolatry is an outgrowth of hieroglyphic writing and thinking. It is a specifically Egyptian phenomenon because Egypt is the only civilization that retained the pictorial character of its

writing and resisted the usual tendency toward abstraction. The proof
of this is to be seen in the fact that "brute-worship," the worst form of
idolatry, occurs only in Egypt. Warburton goes on to delineate different stages in the development of idolatry. In the first stage, the figures
of animals are just signs which stand for some tutelary gods or deified
hero-kings. "This truth Herodotus seems to hint at in Euterpe, where
he says, the Egyptians erected the first altars, images, and temples to
the gods, and carved the figures of animals on stones."[68] The second
stage is reached when these figures are worshipped on their own instead
of being simply "read" as signs for the various gods. This stage was
reached during Moses' time, and that is the reason why the second
commandment prohibits the making of images, not the worship of the
things themselves. The worship was still directed toward the image. For
the same reason the Hebrews made the Golden Calf as a substitute for
Moses when they believed him dead.

Only later did the Egyptians begin to worship the beasts themselves.
This is the last stage of "idolitis." The priests welcomed and fostered
this development because it very efficiently protected the gods from
being found out. The priests, at least those who had passed the most
advanced initiations, knew the truth about the gods—that they were
only deified kings and lawgivers—and they had every reason to hide
this origin of the gods and to keep it a secret. The representation of
these deified mortals in the form of animals was a first step toward
making their origin invisible. The secret became even safer when the
people began to worship the representations instead of the represented. But absolute invisibility was reached when the animals themselves came to be worshipped. The animals were the perfect
concealment for the gods.

According to Warburton this is the meaning of a fable which Diodorus and Ovid tell about Typhon. Typhon is seen as the personification of inquisitiveness and impious curiosity, the very character that is
so dangerous for the pseudo-gods. The fable tells how the gods fled to
Egypt before Typhon and hid there in the shape of animals. Typhon
is the Greek equivalent of the Egyptian god Seth, who is actually
represented in the Egyptian texts as threatening the gods with the
sacrilegious discovery of their secrets. According to the Egyptians, the
secret of the gods is not the Euhemeristic concept of their mortal past,
but something not totally unrelated to the idea of mortality. The

paradigmatic secret, in Egypt, is the corpse of Osiris, which must by all means be protected against the assaults of Seth. The role of Seth as the potential discoverer and violator of the corpse of Osiris was transmuted in the Late Period into a general menace threatening all the secrets of all the gods. There was generally an enormous increase of secrecy in the Egyptian cults during the Late Period. This is quite natural under the conditions of foreign rule. Since this was the Egypt which the Greeks experienced and described, the emphasis laid on secrecy and the fear of inquisitiveness becomes quite understandable.

Warburton deduces two Egyptian specialties from their writing system. One is "brute-worship"; the other is the interpretation of dreams. According to Artemidorus there are two kinds of dreams: "speculative" *(theorematikos)* dreams and "allegorical" ones. The "speculative" dreams are just images of what they signify. They correspond to the "curiological" hieroglyphs. By contrast, the allegorical dreams need to be deciphered. The Egyptians were the first interpreters of dreams because they were accustomed to the methods of decipherment and could "read" the dreams while others guessed and puzzled. But the art of oneiromancy could only develop when hieroglyphics became sacred "and were made the cloudy vehicle of their theology."[69] This must have happened, however, before the time of Joseph. It is typical of Warburton's way of argumentation that he forms this brilliant insight into the relation between oneiromancy and hieroglyphic writing (which will become important in the work of Sigmund Freud) in the context of a chronological demonstration, thus forgoing the obvious possibility of establishing connections between the dream-book of Artemidoros and the hieroglyphic theories of Hellenism.

With these chronological clues, the secrecy function of writing, according to which writing serves to hide a certain knowledge rather than communicate it (the "grammatology of mystery"), can be historically reconstructed. The development of symbolic hieroglyphics as a sacred cryptography had to have occurred in Joseph's time because oneiromancy, a subdiscipline of cryptography and decipherment, was then already being practiced. Four hundred years later, in Moses' time, the use of hieroglyphs had already given rise to a general idolization of "things" to such a degree that God had to explicitly prohibit the use of hieroglyphs in the second commandment. But it is also clear that the Egyptians had not yet reached the stage of brute-worship because the

Hebrews made the Golden Calf instead of worshipping a living bull when they fell back on Egyptian customs.

🐚 LET ME close this section with an Egyptological remark. The Renaissance grammatology of immediate signification which Warburton was still using in his interpretation of Egyptian hieroglyphics was based on a misunderstanding as far as the relation between writing and language is concerned. Since 1822, the date of Champollion's publication of his decipherment of hieroglyphics, we have known that hieroglyphs refer both to the concepts and to the sounds of language. But the grammatology of immediate signification did justice to a property of Egyptian hieroglyphs that is notoriously left unexplained by modern Egyptology: the systematic iconicity of hieroglyphs. Why did Egyptian hieroglyphs keep their pictorial character? Warburton's answer is: because they referred to things and formed a virtually complete inventory of all the "figures" that constitute the created world. This concept of the hieroglyphic font as an *orbis pictus* comes very close to the way in which Egyptian word lists, or "onomastica," define this knowledge as containing

> what Ptah has created and Thoth has written down,
> the heaven with its constellations,
> the earth and what it contains,
> what the mountains spew out,
> what the inundation moistens,
> what the sun illuminates,
> and what grows upon the back of the earth.[70]

Ptah, the Egyptian creator, is the god of plastic arts, of image-making. Now hieroglyphs, in contrast to normal, that is, cursive writing, were considered by the Egyptians to be a genre of art rather than writing.[71] Warburton was perfectly right in basing his theory of hieroglyphs on the assumption of polygraphy. But digraphy, the distinction between hieroglyphs and hieratic, is completely sufficient. Hieroglyphics is the monumental script and is strictly iconic. Hieratic is the cursive script, which has lost its iconic reference to "things." Hieratic is the normal kind of writing which the Egyptian scribes learned and practiced. Hieroglyphs were related to arts and were learned and practiced by artists and craftsmen. Thoth was the god of writing, but Ptah was the god of hieroglyphs. He did not write, but he invented the hiero-glyphs by inventing the shapes and names of everything. Thoth, the god of writing, did not *invent*; he merely found the script: thus in the *Onomasticon of Anememope* the notion of "every word" is expressed as "everything which Ptah has created and which Thoth has written down." Writing only embodies what is already implicit in the structure of reality, and it is based on a general "readability of the world."[72]

This structure is "hieroglyphic." It is a kind of Platonism. Plato interprets the visible world as the infinite material reproduction of a finite set of immaterial ideas. The Egyptians interpreted the visible world as a kind of infinitely ongoing production which very faithfully follows an original finite set of types or models. And this same set is also represented by the hieroglyphic system. The hieroglyphs reproduce the world of things, and the world of things can be viewed as a world/word of signs. To the hieroglyphic mind, things and signs are interchange-able. It was this way of world-making that made Egyptian wisdom so attractive to the Neoplatonists of Late Antiquity and early modernity.

Thus the Biblical concept of idolatry seems inseparably linked to a concept of Egyptian hieroglyphs which not only reproduced and idol-ized the created world, but even imitated the activity of the creator himself.[73] The Egyptian scribes, artists, and magicians continued the work of their divine patrons Ptah and Thoth by constantly continuing the process of creation. These magic and mystical aspects of Egyptian cosmotheism remained connected to the vague notions of hieroglyphic writing that survived in European memory. In the Hermetic tradition, hieroglyphs were associated with cabalistic and alchemistic notions of a magical control of cosmic energies. The second commandment is the normative inversion of this principle.

Jehovah *sive* Isis: Karl Leonhard Reinhold

The philosopher Karl Leonhard Reinhold (1757–1825) is still well known as one of the earliest and most influential adherents and propa-gators of Kantian philosophy.[74] He taught at Jena and Kiel from 1787 until 1825. In 1788, Reinhold published a masonic treatise under the pseudonym Br(uder) Decius that dealt with the same subject as

Spencer's and Warburton's works: *Die Hebräischen Mysterien oder die älteste religiöse Freymaurerey (The Hebrew Mysteries, or the Oldest Religious Freemasonry)*.[75] Reinhold wrote this book not as a philosopher, but as a mason addressing his fellow masons. Reinhold was first a Jesuit (Pater Don Pius Reinhold) and joined the order of the Illuminates (where his pseudonym was Decius). In 1783, at the age of twenty-six, he became a member of the masonic lodge Zur Wahren Eintracht (True Concord) and passed all of the three degrees in only five months. Mozart, himself a member of Zur Wohltätigkeit (Beneficience), a sister lodge, and Haydn frequented this lodge.[76] Ignaz von Born, one of the leading figures of the Austrian Enlightenment and like Reinhold an Illuminist, was Grand Master.[77] In November 1783, Reinhold fled from Vienna and from the order of the Jesuits to Leipzig, where he continued his studies of philosophy. He met Christoph Martin Wieland in 1784, became his partner in editing the journal *Teutscher Merkur*, and became Wieland's son-in-law in 1785, when he married his daughter Sophie.

Wieland was in close contact with the Vienna lodge for some years before he himself became a Freemason. It was through the good offices of von Born and Josef von Sonnenfels that Reinhold was able to approach Wieland. Reinhold was converted to Protestantism by Superintendent Johann Gottfried Herder, a fellow Illuminist and mason, in 1785. In 1787 he was appointed professor extraordinarius of philosophy at the University of Jena, where he became a friend and colleague of Schiller (who taught history there). He wrote his essay on the Hebrew mysteries for von Born and his *Journal für Freymaurer*, where it appeared in two issues in 1786. Von Born had inaugurated this journal with a book-length treatise on the Egyptian mysteries. Reinhold continued the series with a contribution on the "mysteries of the Cabires" *(Die kabirischen Mysterien)* which is a manifest confession of pantheism in the Spinozistic form of *deus sive natura*.[78] The study on the Hebrew mysteries continued the series on ancient mysteries and appeared in parts one and three of the 1786 issue. In the same year, however, the Vienna lodge Zur wahren Eintracht was closed and the journal lost most of its readership. Reinhold, who wanted to reach a larger audience with this text (which he justly held in high esteem),[79] sought another place to publish his work, and found the well-known publishing house Göschen, in Leipzig. My main interest in Reinhold's small book lies in the fact that it forms the missing link between Spencer and Freud. It is based on a careful reading of Spencer and Warburton, and it had been not only used, but paraphrased—one could almost say plagiarized—by Friedrich Schiller in his famous essay *Die Sendung Moses*. Schiller's essay had a great influence on Sigmund Freud.

Reinhold held the same thesis as Spencer in postulating the Egyptian origin of the Mosaic Law. But he constructed this historical depend- ence and derivation without any reference to antagonistic concepts such as normative inversion or anti-idolatric therapy. For him, the Mosaic legislation is a faithful copy or translation of what he calls "the Egyptian mysteries." The concept of "mysteries," which was lacking in Spencer's reconstruction of Egyptian religion, is the decisive innovation that accounts for the vast difference between Spencer's Egyptophobia and Reinhold's Egyptophilia. With the concept of mystery, which he took from Warburton, a different perspective on Egyptian religion became possible, with a foreground and a background. The notorious problems of idolatry, superstition, animal worship, and magic, which were of such a great importance for Spencer, could now be interpreted as mere foreground or surface phenomena. These problems belonged to, or were based upon, a kind of exoteric political theology as opposed to an esoteric natural or cosmic theology that was monotheistic. Up to this point Reinhold was strictly following Warburton. But Reinhold differs from Warburton in the next step, in which he equates Egyptian esoteric monotheism and Mosaic revealed monotheism. Reinhold does not see any difference between the Egyptian, or Hermetic, idea of the One and Biblical monotheism. He thinks that Moses believed in God as the One-and-All and instituted a new mystery religion which can be inter- preted as the oldest form of Freemasonry.

Concerning Moses' theology, Reinhold follows Toland in making Moses a Spinozist *avant la lettre*,[80] relying mostly on Strabo's account. But unlike Strabo and Toland, Reinhold shows this religion to be not a counter-religion but a secret religion. The element of negation which made Strabo's Moses turn his back on Egypt and found a new religion in another country is replaced by concealment. But Reinhold's and Warburton's concept of a mystery cult retains the characteristics of a counter-religion, in that the secret teachings consist not only in the belief in the One, but also in the refutation of polytheism. Initiation is delusion. By passing the threshold from the lesser to the greater mys- teries, the initiate is supposed to abjure his former beliefs, to recognize their erroneous and fictitious nature, and "to see things as they are."[81] All this had already been said by Warburton.

Reinhold's personal and most important contribution to this discourse is his explanation of the Tetragrammaton. This passage is based on Voltaire's account of the "rites égyptiens." But whereas Voltaire maintains that the Egyptians called the Supreme Being by a similar or even the same name as did the Jews, namely, "I-ha-ho" or "Iao," Reinhold bases his equation not on the sound, but on the meaning.[82] He accepts the Hebrew etymology from *hayah* and translates the name quite traditionally as "I am who I am," but equates this formula with the inscription on the veiled statue at Sais: "I am all that is." This equation is the climax of his demonstration. He stages it as a mystical performance and revelation, appearing as a hierophant:

> Brethren! Who among us does not know the ancient Egyptian inscriptions: the one on the pyramid at Sais: "I am all that is, was, and shall be, and no mortal has ever lifted my veil," and that other on the statue of Isis: "I am all that is?" Who among us does not understand the meaning of these words, as well as in those days of the Egyptian initiate, and who does not know that they express the essential Being, the meaning of the name Jehovah?[83]

Plutarch tells the story of the veiled image in Sais in the ninth chapter of his treatise *On Isis and Osiris*. He wants to show that the Egyptians were acting upon the principle that the truth can only be indirectly transmitted by means of riddles and symbols and illustrates this point with three examples. The first is the custom of putting sphinxes at the doorways of the temples in order to insinuate that Egyptian theology contained enigmatic wisdom. The second is the veiled statue at Sais. The third example is the name of Amun, the Egyptians' highest god, meaning "the hidden one." At Sais, Plutarch writes, "the seated statue of Athena, whom they consider to be Isis also bore the following inscription: 'I am all that has been and is and shall be; and no mortal has ever lifted my mantle.'"[84] Nowhere does he speak of a pyramid, or of another inscription. I do not know where Voltaire, whom Reinhold is quoting in this passage, could have found the shorter inscription "I am all that is."

Proclus quotes the same inscription in different words. He places it in the *adytum* of the temple, calls the garment of the goddess a chiton instead of a peplos, replaces Plutarch's "no mortal" with "no one" (which includes the gods), and adds a sentence which gives the motif quite a different turn: "the fruit of my womb is the sun."[85]

Here, the statement that "no one lifted her garment" refers to the fact that the goddess bore the sun without male interference. Proclus' version cannot be taken from Plutarch; there must be a common and possibly Egyptian source. The additional sentence corresponds precisely to Saite theology because Neith was believed to be both female and male and to have given birth to the sun. It is very improbable that in Egypt there ever was such a thing as a veiled statue because the Egyptian cult images were hidden in wooden shrines, and were only allowed to be seen by the priest who opened the shrine during the daily ritual. It is equally improbable that the concept of a statue not to be seen by any mortal eye could arise in the context of an Egyptian cult. The rite "to see the god" has to be performed daily by the priest on duty. But it is very possible that a statue in a hall or courtyard that was open to visitors bore a hieroglyphic inscription that could be interpreted in that way. If retranslated into Egyptian, the last part of the Saitic formula may read something like *nn kjj wp ḥr.j*, which can be translated in two different ways. The correct translation is "there is nobody except me." This is a monotheistic formula that occurs twice in Akhenaten's hymns and that would be perfectly fitting in the context of a phrase like "I am all that was, is, and shall be" (which, in Egyptian, would be something like "I am yesterday, I am today, I am tomorrow," for which there can be quoted several parallels).[86] But a priest or dragoman who was not absolutely fluent in the Classical language could understand the words *wp ḥr* (which mean "except") in their literal meaning "open the face" and render the whole phrase as "there is nobody who opened [or: uncovered] my face." Very possibly, the priests were Neoplatonists themselves and discovered the other reading as a secret meaning.[87]

It is easy to relate Plutarch's and Proclus' renderings of the Saite inscription to authentic Egyptian texts and theology. But it seems far more difficult to equate the inscription with Yahweh's name and self-representation *æhyæh asher æhyæh*, "I am who I am / shall be." Reinhold does not even mention the obvious difference between the two propositions "I am *all that is*" and "I am *who I am*." In the first case, the deity points to the visible world or "nature" in a gesture of identification; in the second case God points to nothing outside himself and thus withdraws the foundation of all cosmic identification or "cosmotheism." The Hebrew formula *æhyæh asher æhyæh* is the negation and refusal of every cosmic referentiality. It draws the distinction between immanence and transcendence, or, to use the terms of the time, of "nature" and "Scripture."[88] Reinhold takes the Saitic formula to be the exact paraphrase of the Hebrew name. He may be right, and I think he is, in interpreting both propositions not as the revelation, but as the withholding, of a name, as the *revelation of anonymity*. The essence of the deity is too all-encompassing to be referred to by a name, and this kind of anonymity forms the common denominator of both formulas. For this idea of a *deus anomymus* he refers to Lactantius, who had quoted Hermes Trismegistus: "He [Trismegistus] wrote books—many, indeed, pertaining to the knowledge of divine things—in which he vouches for the majesty of the supreme and single God and he calls him by the same names which we use: Lord and Father. Lest anyone should seek His name, he says that He is 'without a name,' since He does not need the proper signification of a name because of His very unity, so to speak. These words are his: 'God is one; the one, however, does not need a name'; 'he is the One without a name'. God, therefore, has no name because He is the only one and there is no need of particular designation except when a multitude requires distinction so that you may designate each one character by his own mark and appellation. For God, though, because He is always One, the proper name is God."[89] This is the anonymous god who will be so important for Schiller and Goethe and to whom I will return later.

Yet the Hebrew "name" had already been understood in antiquity in the same way as Reinhold interprets it. Reinhold was, in fact, following an antique tradition based on the Septuagint, which renders the Hebrew formula "I am who I am" *(æhyæh asher æhyæh)* as *Egō eimi ho ōn*, "I am the being one."[90] In one of the so-called Sibyllinian Oracles this self-presentation of the Biblical God is interpreted in the sense of the universal God, *le dieu cosmique*: "I am the being one *[eimì d'égō-ge ho ōn]*, recognize this in your spirit: I donned heaven as my garment, I clothed myself with the ocean, the earth is the ground for my feet, air covers me as my body, and the stars revolve around me."[91] In identifying Yahweh and "the cosmic god"—*deus sive natura*—Reinhold is following an ancient tradition.

The closest parallel to Reinhold's interpretation of the Tetragrammaton and its equation with the Hermetic idea of God's anonymity occurs in a text which was written more than two hundred years before the publication of Spinoza's *Ethica* (1677) and even some years before Marsilio Ficino's translation of the *Corpus Hermeticum* (1471): *De Docta Ignorantia* by Nicholas of Cusa.[92] "It is obvious," Cusanus writes,

> that no name can be appropriate to the Greatest one, because nothing can be distinguished from him. All names are imposed by distinguishing one from the other. Where all is one, there cannot be a proper name. Therefore, Hermes Trismegistus is right in saying: "because God is the totality of things [*universitas rerum*], he has no proper name, otherwise he should be called by every name or everything should bear his name. For he comprises in his simplicity the totality of all things. Conforming with his proper name—which for us is deemed ineffable and which is the Tetragrammaton . . .—his name should be interpreted as 'one and all' or 'all in one,' which is even better [*'unus et omnia' sive 'omnia uniter', quod melius est*]."[93]

In this text, we find an early equation of the Hebrew Tetragrammaton with Hermes Trismegistus' anonymous god, who is *unus et ommnia*, "One-and-All," or *Hen kai pan*, as the expression used by Lessing.

There is a hint that Warburton knew this text. Speaking of the Hermetic concept of God's anonymity, he quotes Zechariah 14:9: "in that day shall there be one lord, and his name one." Hermes Trismegistus said: God is One; therefore he does not need a name *(ho de theos heis; ho de heis onomatos ou prodeitai; esti gar ho ōn anonymos)*; Zecharyah said: God shall be one and his name shall be one (or: "One")[94] *(adonay æḥād ve šemō æḥād)*. This appears as a real stroke of genius in the context of Warburton's rather pedestrian argumentation. The parallel is striking. But it had already been drawn by Nicholas of Cusa: "Yet even more appropriate than '*omnia uniter*' is the name '*unitas*' ['Oneness']. Therefore, the prophet says: 'on that day, God will be 'One' and his name will be 'One.'"[95] Here, the Zechariah quote appears in its appropriate context and it is probably here that Warburton found it.

❀ By EQUATING "who I am" and "what is," Yahweh and Isis, or Nature, Reinhold turned Warburton's argument on its head. Whereas Warburton wanted to draw a sharp distinction between the Mosaic initiation as a divine institution on the one hand, and the pagan mystery cults as human institutions on the other, Reinhold shows that both the Egyptian and the Mosaic initiation are human institutions, and that no side is in possession of absolute truth. But he also shows that God is observed on both sides because God is always and everywhere the same deity *(das wesentliche Daseyn)*, essential Being, or Nature (equivalent to Isis) that forms the object of initiation and worship.

Warburton took great pains to work out the distinction between the God of the mysteries and the God of the philosophers. He wanted to show that the mysteries, especially in their original Egyptian form, worshipped the One in a theistic, personal, and spiritual form, whereas the Greek philosophers systematized this concept of the One into a materialistic concept of nature. Being a philosopher and a mason, Reinhold could dispense with these rather artificial and sophisticated distinctions, which were necessary for an Anglican bishop, who could not contravene orthodoxy, however enlightened, if he wanted to keep his see. Reinhold did not even think it necessary to contradict Warburton; on the contrary, he showed complete agreement by quoting him as a source for his cause. He silently eliminated the distinctions which Warburton had erected and equated the God of the mysteries, the God of Moses, and the God of the philosophers. All the following refer to the same concept of God:

1. The Hebrew name of God.
2. The hymn of initiation, transmitted by Eusebius and Clement of Alexandria.
3. The inscriptions on the statue at Sais, which Reinhold reproduces, one on the statue, another on the pyramid. He is following Voltaire in this respect[96] and in his turn will be followed by Schiller.

All three sources refer to a god who is distinguished not by a name but by the withholding of a name, by anonymity.

It is moving to learn that Beethoven copied sentences (2) and (3) from Schiller, who was his favorite poet (Figure 1).[97] He kept them under glass on his working table until the end of his life.[98] These

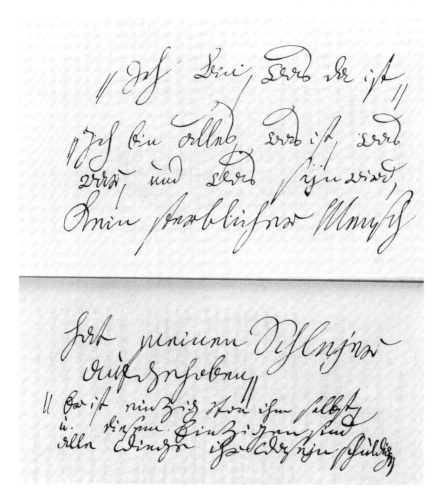

Figure 1. "I am all that is": Beethoven's Deist manifesto. Beethoven put these sentences, which he copied from Schiller's *Die Sendung Moses* and thought expressed ancient Egyptian wisdom and theology, in a frame that sat on his desk during the last years of his life.

sentences were commonly believed not only to be derived from ancient Egyptian arcane theology, but also to be the most adequate expression of the religiosity of the modern, enlightened mind.

According to Reinhold, the Sinai revelation was nothing other than the open-air performance of an Egyptian initiation ritual, meant not for a select few, but for a whole people. But there was a problem, and this problem forms the starting point for Reinhold's ingenious explanation of the ritual laws of Moses. The truth had to be revealed to a people unable to grasp it. Moses, not being able to appeal to their understanding, had to appeal to their senses. He had to rely on blind belief and adherence, that is, on miracles and bodily discipline. And since he could not possibly perform miracles every day, he had to transform his new religion into a matter of the body instead of the soul. In this task, he could rely on his Egyptian culture. He translated the "hieroglyphic" surface, the outside structure, of the Egyptian mysteries into ritual prescriptions. The ritual Law of the Hebrews is the Mosaic equivalent of the Egyptian "lesser" mysteries. Faith or belief, on the one hand, and bodily ("carnal") discipline or *halakha*, on the other, are nothing but indispensable substitutes for reason and understanding. The Egyptian (and other pagan) mystery religions had no need of faith and renunciation or ascesis because they were based on secrecy and revealed the truth only to those very few who were able to understand it. They appealed to the senses and did not have to depend on prescriptions and blind obedience.

Moses had to pay an extremely high price for making the secrets of the greater mysteries public. This included declaring the nonexistence of the known gods and the uniqueness and Oneness of an unknown God, Being as such. The abolition of idolatry was accomplished only by force of the most brutal sort: by executing one half of the people without really convincing and converting the other remaining half. He was not able to reconvert blind belief into rational cognition. He was forced to reduce the idea of his God to a deity the people could grasp, a national tutelary deity, and to turn recognition into obedience. Truth had to be enforced by secular power and religion had to assume the duties of a political entity. The mystery cult of Egypt had to be turned into a theocracy: "The sanctuary of Mosaic religion was at the same time the cabinet of the state . . . Religion and politics here shared the same secrets and consequently the same keys, which were held by the heads of the state and handed down to their successors."[99]

Reinhold's analysis of the ritual laws and institutions focuses on the ark and its decoration, the Cherubim and the curtain in the temple. It is a close paraphrase of Spencer's interpretation. As Spencer had already shown, all of the details are taken from Egypt. According to Clement of Alexandria, the curtain is the equivalent of what in Egypt is called the "adyton" of the temple.[100] Reinhold, however, dispenses with Spencer's concept of condescension and accommodation. Jehovah did not accommodate his truth to the erroneous customs and concepts of the time. The truth was already known by the Egyptians. The truth is on both sides of the borderline, and revelation dissolves into translation. The prevalent opposition of revelation and reason is immaterial, just a contest about words without any substantial reference. We must not forget that we are reading a masonic tract. Reinhold directs his argument to two contesting parties within Freemasonry, the "Hebraists" and the "Egyptianizers," or the "orthodox" and the "free-thinkers." The dispute between them is immaterial because God himself did not shun the Egyptian mysteries, but received and translated them into his religion.

Nature and the Sublime: Friedrich Schiller

As we have seen, Reinhold's contribution to the Moses discourse consisted of the equation of Jehovah and Isis (alias Nature). According to Clement of Alexandria, the last and highest initiation led to a point where all teaching ends, discursive instruction stops, and immediate vision takes over. "The doctrines delivered in the Greater Mysteries concern the universe. Here all instruction ends. Things are seen as they are; and Nature, and the workings of Nature, are to be seen and comprehended."[101] This is how Ignaz von Born, the Grand Master of True Concord, Vienna's most important lodge (of which Reinhold was a member in 1783–84) summarized the ultimate aim of the Egyptian mysteries: "The knowledge of nature is the ultimate purpose of our application. We worship this progenitor, nourisher, and preserver of all creation in the image of Isis. Only he who knows the whole extent of her power and force will be able to uncover her veil without punishment."[102]

In the last phase of initiation the adept is speechlessly confronted by Nature. But this stage was to be reached only by the very few who, by strength of reason, learning, and virtue, could stand the truth they were to behold. This was not experience for weak minds and it was certainly not anything that could be expected from an entire people like the Hebrews, uncultured, coarse, and primitive as they were after four hundred years of suppression and forced labor. Moses had to turn the deistic deity, the almost inaccessible truth of the mysteries, into a theistic, personal, and "national" god in order to make him the object of blind belief and obedience, and all he could save of his philosophical concept of God was the idea of unity. He declared his national god to be the only god and, consequently, his people as the chosen people.

At this point, the Moses discourse had definitely outgrown the frame of theology and it is little wonder that one of the most lucid minds of the German Enlightenment, the poet, playwright, historian, and essayist Friedrich Schiller, immediately grasped the enormous consequences of Reinhold's interpretation.[103] It was by mere coincidence that Reinhold's small book, published under a pseudonym and meant to circulate exclusively among Freemasons, became known outside these esoteric circles. Friedrich Schiller knew Reinhold as a colleague at the University of Jena, and he was acquainted with Christoph Martin Wieland and his daughter Sophie, Reinhold's future wife.[104] He met frequently with both and mentions them in his letters. Reinhold's book inspired Schiller in the writing of both his famous ballad *Das verschleierte Bild zu Sais* (1795) and his essay *Die Sendung Moses (The Legation of Moses;* 1790). For Schiller, the decisive discovery was the identification of the god of the philosophers, that is, the god of reason and enlightenment, with the deepest and most sublime secret of the Egyptian mysteries and the demonstration that it was this sublime and abstract God that Moses had come to accept in the course of his Egyptian initiation and that he had dared—at least partly—to reveal this God to his people.

Schiller's essay closely paraphrases Reinhold's book. He adds nothing to Reinhold's arguments, merely highlighting those points which to his mind were most important. One of these is the concept of Nature as the sublime deity of the mysteries: abstract, anonymous, impersonal, invisible, and almost beyond the reach of human reason—in Kant's words, "the sublimest thought ever expressed."[105] It is this idea that Moses had to transform and, in a way, distort in order to make it the engine of Hebrew ethnogenesis, the foundation of a political constitution and the object of public religion. Between Spencer and Schiller, the object of accommodation had changed. Spencer tried to explain certain peculiarities or even deficiencies of the ritual Law as concessions and allowances which God in his endless benevolence had made with regard to the "genius of the time" and the limitations of human understanding (*propter duritiem cordis,* Matthew 19:8) Warburton explained the same deficiencies as surface phenomena, constituting only the exterior of the "lesser mysteries." Schiller, however, does not speak at all of God as an actor in history, and he is not interested in the problem of the ritual Law. He is not concerned with the deficiencies of the Law, but with those of God, or rather of Moses' concept of God. Schiller tries to explain this concept of god as a device of historical accommodation in the same way as Spencer tried to explain the Law as historically conditioned.

Schiller's essay begins with a recapitulation of the historical facts concerning the sojourn of the tribes of Israel in Egypt. Closely following the model set forth in Reinhold's book, Schiller's reconstruction is based more on pagan than on Biblical sources. But Schiller highlights the motif of illness and dwells upon questions of public hygiene. He holds that because of suppression and neglect, leprosy became a hereditary epidemic among the Egyptian Hebrews and that this was the reason for both their concentration and their extreme oppression in Egypt. This also accounts for the great attention paid to the diagnosis and treatment of leprosy in the Law. Once again, the motif of illness comes to the fore, but now in a completely unsymbolic and naturalistic form. In characterizing the miserable situation of the Hebrews, Schiller anticipates Max Weber's famous comparison with the Hindu Pariah.[106]

Like the Moses of Reinhold, Warburton, and Spencer, Schiller's Moses is ethnically Hebrew and culturally Egyptian, initiated in all the mysteries of the Egyptians. Warburton and Reinhold stressed the political inevitability of both polytheism and secrecy. The people had to be kept in awe in order to be governed. The institutions of the state, of the mysteries, and of an official polytheistic cult, along with a belief in the immortality of the soul and a hereafter, were codependent, correlative, and contemporary achievements. Schiller held a somewhat different view. For him, the mysteries were a later development. First came the state, and ancient Egypt was the first society in the history of humankind to build a state. The state brought about a division of labor and fostered a group of professional priests whose exclusive task was "the attention paid to things divine" *(die Sorge für die göttlichen Dinge)*.[107] It is only in this context that "the first idea of the unity of the supreme being could be formed in a human brain." But this "soul-elevating idea" had to remain the exclusive property of a small group of initiates. It was impossible to communicate it to the people because polytheism had long since become the prevailing tradition, the state was based on its institutions, and nobody knew whether the new religion could support the political order. Like Warburton and Reinhold, Schiller emphasized the antagonistic relationship between official religion and mystery cults. He explained polytheism not as a strategic fiction, necessary for civil society and political order, but as a consequence of natural depravation. In Schiller's opinion, secrecy was a later development, which was necessary to protect the political order from a possibly dangerous truth and to protect the truth from vulgar abuse and misunderstanding. For this reason hieroglyphs were invented. Schiller thus reverts to the old misconception concerning the hieroglyphic writing which Warburton had taken such great pains to refute. Hieroglyphic writing and a complex ritual of cultic ceremonies and prescriptions were invented to form the exoteric aspect of the mysteries. They were devised so as to create a "sensual solemnity" *(sinnliche Feierlichkeit)* and through emotional arousal to prepare the soul of the initiate to receive the truth.

The truth that was to be revealed to the initiate only at the climax of a very long period of instruction and preparation consisted in the recognition of the "single supreme cause of all things" *(Die einzige höchste Ursache aller Dinge)*. Like Reinhold, Schiller took the Saitic formula "I am all that is, that was, and that shall be" to be the negation of a name and the proclamation of an anonymous god. He followed Reinhold in identifying the anonymous god of the mysteries with the God of Moses.[108] Moses went through all the stages of initiation (which Schiller estimates took some twenty years) until he was brought to contemplate anonymous Nature in its ineffable sublimity.

At this point Schiller introduces the notion of the "sublime," which was a key concept of the time: "Nothing is more sublime than the simple grandeur with which the sages spoke of the creator. In order to distinguish him in a truly defining form, they refrained from giving him a name at all."[109] In transcending the realm of human cognition, this unknowable deity would become increasingly identified with the sublimity of "Nature."[110] In the same year (1790) Kant's *Kritik der Urteilskraft* appeared. In it, he mentions in a footnote the veiled image at Sais and its inscription as the highest expression of the sublime:

Vielleicht ist nie etwas Erhabeneres gesagt oder ein Gedanke erhabener ausgedrückt worden als in jener Aufschrift über dem Tempel der Isis (der Mutter Natur): "Ich bin alles was da ist, was da war und was da sein wird, und meinen Schleier hat kein

Sterblicher aufgedeckt." Segner benutzte diese Idee, durch eine sinnreiche, seiner Naturlehre vorgesetzte Vignette, um seinen Lehrling, den er in diesen Tempel einzuführen bereit war, vorher mit dem heiligen Schauer zu erfüllen, der das Gemüth zu feierlicher Aufmerksamkeit stimmen soll.

Perhaps nothing more sublime was ever said or no sublimer thought ever expressed than the famous inscription on the temple of Isis (mother nature): "I am all that is and that shall be, and no mortal has lifted my veil." Segner availed himself of this idea in a suggestive vignette prefixed to his Natural Philosophy, in order to inspire beforehand the apprentice whom he was about to lead into the temple with a holy awe, which should dispose his mind to serious attention.[111]

Reinhold had doubtless sent his book to Kant, whom he admired.[112] Kant uses Schiller's language of initiation in describing Johann Andreas von Segner's vignette: *heiliger Schauer* ("sacred awe"), *feierliche Aufmerksamkeit* ("solemn attention"). This is especially striking since the illustration Kant is referring to shows nothing of the sort. Pierre Hadot has devoted an excellent study to the iconography of the "veiled image" and its relationship to the idea of the "secrets of Nature."[113] In Segner's vignette (Figure 2), we see not a statue, but a broken vase on a base, and no inscription, but a geometrical drawing. On the front of the base, Isis is striding, accompanied by three putti, who seem to measure her footsteps and movement with geometrical instruments. She wears a mantle, and her head is partly covered. The putti personify the natural sciences. But the veiled image of Sais was obviously not what the artist had in mind in creating this illustration.[114] The vignette conveys the idea that Nature/Isis cannot be looked directly in the face, but can only be studied a posteriori. The footsteps of Nature are mentioned in an Orphic hymn on Nature:

> Thy feet's still traces in a circling course,
> By thee are turn'd, with unremitting force.[115]

One of the images in Michael Maier's *Atalanta Fugiens* illustrates the same motif. Nature is represented as a young woman, not with a veil covering her face but wearing a veil that is dragging behind like a sail

Figure 2. *The Sciences, Measuring the Footprints of Nature.* Frontispiece to Andreas von Segner, *Einleitung in die Naturlehre* (1770).

to convey the swiftness of her motion.[116] A philosopher with a lantern is studying her footprints from afar.[117]

Kant is, however, right insofar as the motif of the veiled image and its unveiling does in fact appear often on the title pages of scientific and alchemistic books such as that of Segner. The most famous example, though much later than Segner's, is Thorwaldsen's engraving in Alexander von Humboldt's *Geographie der Pflanzen* with a dedication to Goethe, dating from 1806 (see Figure 3).[118] Early examples are the frontispieces to Gerard Blasius, *Anatome Animalium* (1681) (see Figure 4),[119] and

Figure 3. *The Genius of Poetry unveils the secrets of Nature.* Dedication to Goethe with an engraving by Bertel Thorwaldsen, in Alexander von Humboldt, *Ideen zu einer Geographie der Pflanzen* (1806).

J. J. Kunkelius, *Der Curieusen Kunst- und Werck-Schul Erster und Anderer Theil* (1705) (see Figure 5),[120] where we see not only the unveiling of the veiled Isis, but also the sun as the fruit of her womb, as in Proclus' version of the Saitic inscription.

Kant's main point is to emphasize the initiatory function of the sublime.[121] The holy awe and terror which the sublime inspires in a man serve to prepare his soul and mind for the apprehension of a truth that can only be grasped in a state of emotional arousal. The revelation of the ultimate secrets requires a sublime scenario. The same association of the sublime with the concepts of wisdom, mystery, and initiation appears again and again in the literature on the Egyptian mysteries, as for example in the following description of the "Hermetic cave" at Thebes, where the Egyptian initiates were supposed to have been

AMSTELODAMI. Apud Viduam Joannis a Someren Henricum et Viduam Theod. Boom. 1681

Figure 4. *Zoology Unveils Nature*. Frontispiece to Gerhard Blasius, *Anatome Animalium* (1681).

taught the doctrines of Hermes Trismegistus as inscribed on the pillars of wisdom:

> The strange solemnity of the place must strike everyone, that enters it, with a religious horror; and is the most proper to work you up into that frame of mind, in which you will receive, with the most awful reverence and assent, whatever the priest, who attends you, is pleased to reveal. . .

Figure 5. *Alchemy Unveils Nature.* Frontispiece to J. J. Kunkelius, *Der Curieusen Kunst und Werck-Schul Erster und Anderer Theil* (1705). This engraving is an obvious reworking of the frontispiece to Blasius, *Anatome Animalium* (see Figure 4).

Towards the farther end of the cave, or within the innermost recess of some prodigious caverns, that run beyond it, you hear, as it were a great way off, a noise resembling the distant roarings of the sea, and sometimes like the fall of waters, dashing against rocks with great impetuosity. The noise is supposed to be so stunning and frightful, if you approach it, that few, they say, are inquisitive enough, into those mysterious sportings of nature. . . .

> Surrounded with these pillars of lamps are each of those vener-
> able columns, which I am now to speak of, inscribed with the
> hieroglyphical letters with the primeval mysteries of the Egyptian
> learning. . . . From these pillars, and the sacred books, they main-
> tain, that all the philosophy and learning of the world has been
> derived.[122]

This is an appropriate scenario for the repository and transmission of secret wisdom. The more well-to-do among the Freemasons of the time even tried to construct such an ambiance in their parks and gardens. The scenic instructions for the trial by fire and water in the finale of the second act of Mozart's *Magic Flute* prescribe a cave where water gushes out with a deafening roar and fire spurts forth with devouring tongues. It is modeled not only upon Abbé Jean Terrasson's description of Sethos' subterranean trials and initiation, but also upon masonic garden architecture, such as the grotto in the park at Aigen near Salzburg owned by a mason who was a friend of Mozart.[123] The idea of the sublime, which was very important for the aesthetics of the time, and for the interpretation of ancient Egyptian art and architecture has to be viewed in close conjunction with the notions of mystery and initiation.

Of particular interest in this context is the extraordinary frontispiece that the Swiss-English artist of the sublime Henry Fuseli provided for Erasmus Darwin's poem *The Temple of Nature* (1808) (see Figure 6). It shows the unveiling of a statue of Isis (in the shape of the Ephesian Diana multimammia) by a priestess-hierophant with her face averted, and a female initiate, seen from the back, who kneels before the statue with gestures of rapture and terror. This engraving tries to capture the moment of the last stage of initiation when the initiate is confronted with Nature herself. Darwin's poem is largely based on Warburton's interpretation of the ancient mystery cults as forms of esoteric and monotheistic nature worship.[124]

🌀 THE ASSOCIATION of "nature" with "the sublime" goes back to Edmund Burke, who published his ground-breaking essay on the sublime in 1759.[125] The beautiful inspires pleasure, the sublime terror. The inspiration of terror is "the prerogative of nature only." Typical terror-inspiring phenomena of the sublime are obscurity, vacuity, darkness, solitude,

Figure 6. Henry Fuseli, frontispiece to Erasmus Darwin, *The Temple of Nature; or, The Origin of Society: A Poem* (1808), depicting the last stage of initiation into the greater mysteries of Nature: "Here all instruction ends. Things are seen as they are; and Nature, and the workings of Nature, are to be seen and comprehended" (Clement of Alexandria).

and silence—experiences which the *Magic Flute* (1791) and other works, such as Abbé Terrasson's *Séthos* (1731) and Ignaz von Born's essay on the Egyptian mysteries, linked with the Egyptian mysteries and initiation. Burke viewed the Egyptian temples as architectural realizations of the sublime and this association soon became commonplace.[126]

🕸 ACCORDING to Schiller, the sublimity of the veiled Isis lies in her anonymity. She is beyond language, unapproachable by invocations. All names are equally (in)appropriate. This concept of the anonymity of God is part of that kind of religious cosmopolitanism and its belief in the translatability of religious ideas and denominations which flourished in the Roman Empire that I mentioned earlier. In the eighteenth century this convivtion of religious translatability was called "cosmotheism" and it flourished in the circles of enlightened Freemasonry, appearing frequently in its literary works. One of Mozart's masonic hymns, the cantata K. 619, opens with lines that echo the ancient custom of praising God "with the names of the nations":

> *Die Ihr des unermesslichen Weltalls Schöpfer ehrt,*
> *Jehova nennt ihn,*
> *oder Gott—*
> *Fu nennt ihn,*
> *oder Brahman—*
> *Hört, hört Worte aus der Posaune des Allherrschers!*
> *Laut tönt von Erde, Monden, Sonnen*
> *ihr ewger Schall.*

> You who revere the
> Creator of the boundless universe,
> Call him Jehova or God,
> Call him Fu, or Brahma.
> Hark! Hark to the words
> Of the Almighty's trumpet call!
> Ringing out through earth, moon, sun,
> Its sound is everlasting.[127]

It is this nameless god Faust is speaking of when he answers Gretchen's famous question about his religion:

> *Wer darf ihn nennen*
> *Und wer bekennen:*
> *Ich glaub Ihn!*
> *Wer empfinden*
> *Und sich unterwinden*
> *Zu sagen: ich glaub ihn nicht!*
> *Der Allumfasser,*

Der Allerhalter,
Fasst und erhält er nicht
Dich, mich, sich selbst?
Wölbt sich der Himmel nicht dadroben?
Liegt die Erde nicht hierunten fest?
Und steigen freundlich blickend
Ewige Sterne nicht herauf?
Schau ich nicht Aug in Auge dir,
Und drängt nicht alles
nach Haupt und Herzen dir
Und weht in ewigem Geheimnis
Unsichtbar-sichtbar neben dir?
Erfüll davon dein Herz, so gross es ist,
Und wenn du ganz in dem Gefühle selig bist,
Nenn es dann, wie du willst:
Nenns Glück! Herz! Liebe! Gott!
Ich habe keinen Namen
Dafür! Gefühl ist alles;
Name ist Schall und Rauch,
Umnebelnd Himmelsglut.

For who can say that name
And claim
A very certain faith?
Or where is he with feeling
Of some revealing
Who dares to say it is a wraith?
He that's upholding,
All and enfolding,
Holds he not
You, me, himself?
Towers not the vault of heaven above us?
Does not the earth's fabric bear us bravely up?
Do not the friendly eyes of timeless stars
Still gleam upon our sight?
Gaze we for naught in one another's eyes?
Is not life teeming
Around the head and heart of you,
Weaving eternal mysteries,

Seen and unseen, even at your side?
Oh let them fill your heart, your generous heart,
And when you lose your being in that bliss,
Give it what name you will—
Your joy, love, heart, your God.
For me, I have no name
To give it: feeling's surely all.
Names are but noise and smoke,
Obscuring heavenly light.[128]

Asked about his religion, Faust points to the world that surrounds him and to his innermost self, his feeling heart.[129] It is the same gesture with which Isis points to all that was, is, and shall be. The deepest secret is the most evident, the most public one. "Heilig öffentlich Geheimnis," "sacred public secret," as Goethe puts it in another poem.

Müsset im Naturbetrachten
Immer eins wie alles achten;
Nichts ist drinnen, nichts ist draussen:
Denn was innen, das ist aussen.
So ergreifet ohne Säumnis
Heilig öffentlich Geheimnis.[130]

According to Reinhold and Schiller, this sublime idea of Nature as Supreme Being was the god in whose mysteries Moses was initiated in the course of his Egyptian education. But this god of Moses was not the god he revealed to his people. In the school of the Egyptian mysteries, Moses not only learned to contemplate the truth, but also "collected a treasure of hieroglyphs, mystical symbols, and ceremonies" with which to construct a religion and to mask the truth under the protective guise of cultic institutions and prescriptions, *sub cortice legis,* as Spencer had already formulated it. Yet according to Schiller, Moses was not an impostor, just an "accommodator."[131] "His enlightened mind and his sincere and noble heart" revolted against the idea of giving his people a false and fabulous god. But the truth, the religion of reason and nature, was equally impossible to reveal. The only solution was to proclaim the truth in a fabulous way and to endow the true god with some fictitious properties and qualities that the people would be able to grasp and to believe in. God had to be transformed from an object of pure reason and cognition into an object of blind belief and obedience. Thus Moses couched his vision of truth in the form of a national god and a national cult with all the hieroglyphic symbolism of lustrations, sacrifices, processions, oracles, and so forth. Schiller took the notion of polytheism as a necessary illusion from Warburton (via Reinhold) and applied it to theistic religion in general. Schiller replaced Maimonides' and Spencer's idea of God's accommodation of the Law with the idea of Moses' accommodation of God. Religion and revelation are only forms of accommodation. The enlightened mind, which has learned to immediately contemplate the truth, as Moses did in Egypt, can do away with both. With Schiller, we are approaching the point where religion will be defined as the "opium of the people" (Karl Marx) and as an "illusion" (Sigmund Freud).

Hen kai Pan: The Return of Egyptian Cosmotheism

On August 15, 1780, Gotthold Ephraim Lessing wrote the words *Hen kai pan* ("One-and-All") in Greek characters on the wallpaper of Gleim's garden house near Halberstadt, which was used as a guest-book.[132] Five years later, after Lessing's death in 1781, Friedrich Heinrich Jacobi revealed the secret of this motto when he published his conversations with Lessing in a booklet called *On the Doctrine of Spinoza, Exposed in the Form of Letters Addressed to Moses Mendelssohn* (1785).[133] The secret meaning of the motto was *deus sive natura*; it was a declaration of Spinozism.

Jacobi had visited Lessing, a fellow Freemason,[134] for the first time in 1780. In the course of a conversation on Goethe's (then unpublished) poem *Prometheus*, Lessing exclaimed: "The orthodox concepts of the divine are no longer for me. I cannot stand them. *Hen kai pan!* I know naught else." Jacobi: "Then you would indeed be more or less in agreement with Spinoza." Lessing: "If I am to call myself by anybody's name, then I know none better."[135]

The news of Lessing's Spinozism exploded like a bomb. Even Lessing's closest friends, including Moses Mendelssohn, did not know about it. Even in the seventeenth century, when the discourse on Moses and Egypt started to become an axial issue for the European Enlightenment, the figure of Spinoza had been lurking in the background. Spencer and Cudworth wrote their books just after the publication of

Ethica (1677) and *Tractatus Politico-Theologicus* (1670). With Lessing's *Hen kai pan*, the reaction to Spinoza entered a new phase. These words and Jacobi's publication triggered "one of the most significant debates for the emergence of a modern view of the world and one that considerably shook the self-confidence of the German Enlightenment."[136] It is important to realize that Reinhold and Schiller wrote their essays on Moses and Egypt in the immediate context of this debate. Reinhold even took an active part in it.[137] *Hen kai pan*, or the "One-and-All" immediately became a common motto, appearing in the writings of Herder, Hamann, Hölderlin, Goethe, Schelling, and others (many of them, Freemasons).[138]

As far as I can see, none of the numerous authors who wrote on the famous pantheism controversy seems ever to have asked the question of where Lessing got his formula *Hen kai pan*. Why did he not say "deus sive natura" if he wanted to refer to Spinoza?[139] Or why did Jacobi immediately think of Spinoza when he heard Lessing utter these Greek words? If we look for a source, we are led to Cudworth, thus to Egypt and to Hermes Trismegistus. In a study on *Empedokles und Hölderlin*, Uvo Hölscher had already pointed to Ralph Cudworth as the most plausible source for Hölderlin's *Hen kai pan*. Cudworth's *True Intellectual System of the Universe* went through several editions in the eighteenth century, one of them published in Germany.[140] There is not the slightest doubt that this book was still accessible and well known in Lessing's time. Yet to link the names of Gotthold Ephraim Lessing and Hermes Trismegistus is very strange. Was Lessing aware of the "trismegistick" connotations of the formula as Cudworth had spelled them out in his *Intellectual System?*

As I pointed out earlier, Cudworth had carefully collected all the occurrences of this formula. It never appears exactly as *Hen kai pan*, but only occurs in more or less close approximations, such as *Hen to Pan*, *To hen kai to Pan*, and so on. The formula plays a very prominent role in Greek texts that were written in Egypt: the texts that constitute the *Corpus Hermeticum*, the magical incantations and ceremonies known as *papyri Graecae Magicae*,[141] and the texts of the alchemical tradition.[142] Plotinus, the most prominent exponent of Neoplatonism, whose teaching is most closely associated with the notion of All-Oneness, was an Egyptian and a native of Assiut (Lykopolis).[143] Thus as a result of his investigations, Cudworth had demonstrated the formula to be the quintessential expression of Egyptian "arcane theology."

❦ CUDWORTH was convinced that the idea of the "One-and-All" was the most important part of Moses' Egyptian education. But Cudworth's subject was not the transmission of Egyptian wisdom to the Hebrews. He was interested in its transmission to the Greeks. In this respect, Orpheus played precisely the same role of mediator as Moses did in the Biblical tradition. Orpheus was generally believed to have been initiated into the "Greater" Egyptian mysteries.[144] Egypt was thus connected to Europe in a two ways: to Jerusalem via Moses and to Athens via Orpheus. The "Moses connection" informed European theology and religion, whereas the "Orpheus connection" influenced European philosophy.[145] Orpheus brought the idea of *Hen kai pan* to Greece, where it influenced the philosophies of Pythagoras, Herakleitus, Parmenides, Plato, the Stoics, and others. *Hen kai pan*—the conviction that one is all and all is one—was believed to be the nucleus of a great tradition that began in Egypt and was handed down to modernity. There were, however, some who lamented what they saw as the decline of that tradition. Thomas Taylor wrote in the preface to his translation of the *Hymns of Orpheus*, which appeared in 1787:

> Thus wisdom, the object of all true philosophy, considered as exploring the causes and principles of things, flourished in high perfection among the Egyptians first, and afterwards in Greece. Polite literature was the pursuit of the Romans; and experimental enquiries, increased without end, and accumulated without order, are the employment of modern philosophy. Hence we may justly conclude, that the age of true philosophy is no more.[146]

This is a fairly representative statement of the way Egypt was viewed by those who where thinking along the lines of Neoplatonism and "the Great Chain of Being" at the end of the eighteenth century. Taylor's view of history as a process of decline and depravation corresponds closely to the historical theory of Adam Weishaupt, the founder of Illuminism. There was only one cure for the maladies of the age, that is, "superstition" and "atheism": reorientation to the origins—to Egypt.

❦ JACOBI denounced this tradition as "atheism," because it seemed to deny the existence of God outside and independent of the world. He also considered accepting, but finally rejected, the term "cosmotheism," which to his mind merely blurred the necessary distinction between what he considered to be true and false. The term "cosmotheism" had been coined by Lamoignon de Malesherbes with reference to the antique, especially Stoic worship of the *cosmos* or *mundus* as Supreme Being. In his edition of Pliny the Elder's *Natural History* (1782), he commented on one of the most typical passages of this religion—*mundum, et hoc quodcumque nomine alio coelum appellare libuit, cujus circumflexu teguntur cuncta, numen esse credi par est*—by calling Pliny "non un Athée, mais un *Cosmo-théiste*, c'est à dire quelqu'un qui croit que l'univers est Dieu."[147] Malesherbes could not have found a better term for what seems to be the common denominator of Egyptian religion, Alexandrinian (Neoplatonic, Stoic, Hermetic) philosophy, and Spinozism, including the medieval traditions such as alchemy and the cabala that might have served as intermediaries.[148]

However, casting the idea of cosmotheism into the formula *Hen kai pan* meant tracing it back to its Egyptian origin. Spinoza did not use the phrase. It was Cudworth who had pointed out its Egyptian origin. Berkeley even translated it as "Osiris *[to Hen]* and Isis *[to Pan]*."[149] The *kai* in the Greek formula has the same meaning as Spinoza's *sive*. It amounts not to an addition, but to an equation. In its most common form, the formula occurs as *Hen to pan*, "All *Is* One," the world *is* God. This is what "cosmotheism" means. Cudworth had shown that cosmotheism originated in Egypt, "from whence it was derived through Orpheus into Greece."[150]

With the worship of *Hen kai pan*, the cosmotheism of Late Antiquity reappears in the German Romanticism of the 1780s. This early Romanticism expresses the conviction or "feeling" that all divine names are but "noise and smoke" (Goethe), as long as the all-embracing and all-sustaining unity and divinity of cosmic life is recognized. It is the same idea of God as Reinhold's and Schiller's notion of an anonymous god who does not need a name because he is the sole gold and every name is but a restriction on his all-encompassing unity. The "cosmotheism" of German pre-Romanticism as well as that of Late Antiquity could ignore or relativize the names because it was certain of its object, the divinely animated cosmos. So, we are back to Egypt again. Spinozism, pantheism, and all the other religious movements of the time look to Egypt for their origins. Egypt appears to be the homeland of cosmotheism.

Hen kai pan is the motto of a new "cosmotheism" which appeared to provide a way to escape the Mosaic distinction and its confrontations and implications—such as revealed or "positive" religion, error and truth, original sin and redemption, doubt and faith—and to arrive at a realm of evidence and innocence. The "cosmotheism" of early German Romanticism is a return of repressed paganism, the worship of the divinely animated cosmos. In a way, it is a return to Ancient Egypt. If the anonymous cosmic god or divine "nature" was given a name or a personification in the writings and engravings of the eighteenth and early nineteenth centuries, it was an Egyptian one: Isis.[151] *Deus sive natura sive Isis:* this is the way that Egypt returned in the religious climate of pre-Romantic Spinozism. Egypt was imagined to be the historical incorporation of this utopia,[152] the homeland of *religio prisca* or *religio naturalis*, "l'origine de tous le cultes."[153] In these years, European Egyptomania reached its climax. It is certainly not mere coincidence that in these same years Napoleon embarked on his Egyptian expedition, equipped with a staff of scholars, engineers, and artists, and that the results of this expedition led to the establishment of Egyptology as an academic discipline. But it is one of the ironies of history that this same discipline contributed more than anything else to a demystification of Egypt.

Egyptology was not the only discipline that forgot about the alleged Egyptian origin of *Hen kai pan*. With the "Aryan turn" of Classical studies in later Romanticism, so convincingly described by Martin Bernal and Maurice Olender, the Egyptian source of *Hen kai pan* was forgotten by both classicists and philosophers. Hegel, Schelling, Schopenhauer, Coleridge, and whoever else quoted this formula in the nineteenth century used it to refer to the Eleatic school and not to ancient Egypt.[154]

CHAPTER FIVE

Sigmund Freud: The Return of the Repressed

The Turning of the Kaleidoscope and the Genesis of Freud's Text

It is both moving and amusing to meet with the same set of quotations in such different books as those of Spencer, Cudworth, Toland, Warburton, and Reinhold. They base their arguments on exactly the same body of evidence. And Spencer is by no means the first to collect this evidence. He quotes scholars such as Samuel Bochart, John Selden, Hugo Grotius, Athanasius Kircher, Pierre-Daniel Huet, and Gerard Vossius who had already assembled the same data. This collection of classical, theological, and Rabbinic quotations is like a kaleidoscope to which every new scholar, living in a new age, belonging to a new generation, and confronting new controversies gives a different turn, so that the hundreds and thousands of pieces fall into a new pattern. This kind of intertextuality can be interpreted as a form of cultural memory that kept a certain body of knowledge accessible for more than two thousand years. Almost none of those taking part in the discourse on Moses and Egypt ever cared much about what the travelers to Egypt such as Richard Pococke or the antiquaries such as Bernhard de Montfaucon had to say.[1] Athanasius Kircher with his vast and insatiable curiosity is the only exception. Even Warburton's detailed and critical study of hieroglyphs can almost do without illustrations. The few illustrations that he does include are far from representative of the faithful reproductions of genuine Egyptian inscriptions that were available at the time. Spencer, Warburton, and Reinhold were working within a paradigm of memory, not of observation. But this paradigm vanishes with the rise of Egyptology, and all of the carefully collected and interpreted body of knowledge about Egypt fell into almost complete oblivion as soon as the primary sources began to speak. History took the place of memory. The chain of memory that was broken is the chain which links the past to the present and to the identity of the remembering subject, be it a group or an individual, so that only so much of the past is retained as is relevant for the present.

🕮 WHEN Sigmund Freud embarked on the subject in the 1930s he was operating outside the paradigm of memory.[2] He does not quote Spencer or Warburton, Reinhold or Schiller, let alone Herodotus or Strabo, Clement of Alexandria or Eusebius, Maimonides or Ibn Ezra. He knew of the Greek and Latin sources which described Moses as an Egyptian,[3] but he never mentions them in his book. He quotes Egyptologists such as Arthur Weigall and especially James Henry Breasted,[4] historians such as Eduard Meyer; Old Testament scholars like Ernst Sellin[5] and Elias Auerbach. Freud operates within the paradigms of history and psychoanalysis, seeking to unearth a truth that was never remembered, but instead repressed, and which only he is able to bring forth as a shocking opposite of everything consciously remembered and transmitted.

Regarding this radical break with tradition, one might even wonder whether I am justified in including Freud's Moses in my study of the Moses/Egypt discourse. Does he belong in the discourse, share the basic project, use the same intertextual kaleidoscope, giving it just another turn? Or is his book on "the Man Moses" totally unrelated to this tradition, in the same way as were all the other books on Moses and Exodus which were produced in the spirit of historical criticism in the nineteenth and twentieth centuries and which were characterized not only by the consideration of a new wealth of archaeological material, but also by the complete omission of the kaleidoscopic tradition and its issues?

There is no simple answer to this question. Certainly, the distance between Freud and the eighteenth century is immense. Not only did he base his work on archaeological discoveries instead of Classical authors and other second-hand sources about Egypt, but he thought in terms of a totally new paradigm: psychoanalysis. The old paradigm sought and accounted for similarities between cultures such as Israel and Egypt on the basis of diffusionism. The only problem was to determine the source of diffusion: was Israel or Egypt the origin? Psychoanalysis provided a new model, which is basically universalist. The conflicted father-son relationship is independent of cultural determination and is ubiquitous, manifesting itself on the individual level in the form of the Oedipus complex, and on the collective level in the form of religion, which Freud held to be a collective compulsive neurosis.[6]

The difference between the two models could not be greater. Yet in rereading Freud's book after having read Spencer, Warburton, Reinhold, and Schiller, one gets a much stronger impression of continuity than of discontinuity. In the first two "essays" of Freud's book, the impression of continuity is even overwhelming. Not only does Freud turn into a diffusionist himself, he uses words in praise of Egyptian and Mosaic monotheism which, coming from his pen, are astounding. It seems to me quite evident that in these parts, the only ones he originally intended to publish, Freud is, consciously and/or subconsciously, continuing the Moses/Egypt discourse, which seems to have been a subject of endless fascination for him. The sources of this fascination are easy to explain, and I will come back to them soon. These two chapters of Freud's book shake up the old intertextual kaleidoscope and give it a new turn. Tradition, or memory, is replaced by history, but the issue, the hidden agenda, is still the same.

The third part of Freud's study, which he withheld from publication until after his flight to London to escape the Nazi occupation of Vienna, exploits the "facts" his first two parts had expounded to support his psychoanalytic theory of religion. This, of course, is a new paradigm, asking new questions and devising new answers. But I think that this part also continues to address some of the crucial anthropological, historical, and theological issues that inform and identify the Moses/Egypt discourse. Freud's book on Moses seems to me much more closely related to Schiller's work than, for example, to Martin Buber's. Moreover, he was connected with Spencer in two, albeit indirect, ways. Schiller was among his favorite authors. As a Jew, he could not possibly have overlooked Schiller's essay on Moses.[7] And Schiller's essay was indirectly based on Spencer's *De Legibus*, this book being the most important source of Schiller's model, *Die Hebräischen Mysterien*, by Reinhold.[8] The other connection with Spencer was through W. Robertson Smith, Freud's favorite author in the field of religious studies. Smith championed Spencer and hailed him as the founder of the historical study of ritual.[9]

      APART from the essay on Michelangelo's Moses, with which I shall not be concerned here, Freud made four different attempts to write a book on Moses. The first attempt, which he neither finished nor published, dates to 1934. It is the fragment of a "historical novel" which Freud was moved to write after reading Thomas Mann's first and second Joseph novels, which had just appeared.[10] The second and third attempts are the two "essays" he published in the journal *Imago*, which he edited. The fourth attempt, the monograph entitled *Moses and Monotheism*, appeared in 1939, and begins with the two previously published essays.[11] This is an astonishing fact in itself. Instead of summing up his theory and method, Freud in his old age, when he was suffering from cancer and knew perfectly well that this was to be his last book, ventured into the controversial field of Biblical history and with utmost boldness wrote a very subjective book.

One reason readers are still fascinated by Freud's book is the unmistakable fact that it is itself written out of fascination, even obsession.[12] The several attempts and approaches, breaks and resumptions in Freud's dealing with the theme not only reflect the serious doubts and hesitations he had to overcome to publish his findings, but also the deep and irresistible fascination this theme exerted on him. He even ignored the urgent advice of some friends and specialists not to publish his manuscript in a time of persecution because it could prove detrimental to the Jewish cause.[13] Some of the reasons, for both his hesitation and his fascination, seem to me to be connected with his involvement in the discourse about Moses the Egyptian and its hidden agenda.

The agenda of the Moses/Egypt discourse was to deconstruct "counter-religion" and its implications of intolerance by blurring the basic distinctions as they were symbolized by the antagonistic constellation of Israel and Egypt. "Revelation" had to be (re)turned into "translation." Freud became involved not simply because he shared this agenda,[14] but also because he felt he could contribute the final and the decisive proof by availing himself of the discoveries of archaeology and history that had been inaccessible to his predecessors, from Manetho to Schiller.

Freud knew what all the others did not know: that there really was a monotheistic and iconoclastic counter-religion in ancient Egypt. He was able to fill the gap that so many had tried to fill with fanciful reconstructions. If the history of this discourse, from the early oral beginnings after the breakdown of the Amarna revolution until modernity, can be reconstructed as a story of remembering and forgetting, Sigmund Freud is the one who restored the suppressed evidence, who was able to retrieve lost memories and to finally complete and rectify the picture of Egypt. With his book, the Moses/Egypt discourse seemed to come to a conclusion. If we look at *Moses and Monotheism* not from the viewpoint of Freud's oeuvre but from that of the Moses/Egypt discourse, we realize that this book had to be written. The rediscovery of Akhenaten simply could not pass unnoticed by those who looked for Egyptian origins. The case of Moses had to be reopened.

The discovery of Akhenaten and his religious revolution was a sensation in itself. But it must have gained even more importance in the eyes of an *Aufklärer* thinking along the lines of the Moses/Egypt discourse. Akhenaten must have appeared to him as the ultimate solution to the riddle. Freud's Moses oscillates strangely between being a figure of memory and being a figure of history. This accounts for many of the obstacles Freud encountered in writing his book. He began writing a historical novel and ended up by using almost juridical forms of authentification to present his historical evidence.[15] As a figure of history, Freud's Moses lacks "proofs." The testimony of Scripture is dismissed as merely the voice of memory, which counts for nothing in the "tribunalistic situation" of history. Instead, Freud is looking for historical traces and clues and is all too aware of their scarcity. He speaks of the "feet of clay" on which he must erect a "statue of bronze." The "feet of clay" refers to the figure of history, the "bronze statue" to the figure of memory.[16] As a figure of memory, Freud's Moses is linked to the present. A figure of memory has a crucial, defining importance for the one who remembers; a figure of history is at best interesting. Despite his historical attitude, Freud consistently and consciously insists on speaking with regard to Moses and his time of "Jews" instead of "Hebrews" or "Israelites," which would be the historically correct designation. Freud views Moses (in the same way as Maimonides and Spencer did) as the creator and the timeless symbol of "interminable" Jewishness as it persists to the present. This conscious anachronism is the unmistakable sign that we are moving in the space of memory rather than history. Therefore, Freud's Moses is within the scope of mnemo-historical research.

☘☘ FREUD originally considered the title *Moses und der Monotheismus*, which (in English) is the title of the English translation, but then changed it to *Der Mann Moses und die monotheistische Religion*. I cannot find in the literature any reference to the fact that Freud's final version of the title contains a Biblical quotation. "The Man Moses" is a trans-lation of Exodus 11:3. It is the only place in the Pentateuch where Moses is referred to in such a distancing manner, and that phrasing is especially conspicuous because it occurs after the reader has already become totally familiar with the figure of Moses.[17] Even more significant, it is the only verse in the Hebrew Bible that alludes to Moses' important Egyptian position: *gm h-'iš Mšh gdwl m'd b-'rṣ mṣrym*, "and moreover, the Man Moses was exceedingly important in the land of Egypt." The other verse alluding to Moses' Egyptian status occurs not in the Hebrew Bible, but in the New Testament: "And Moses was learned in all the wisdom of the Egyptians, and was mighty in words and deeds" (Acts 7:22), a description which corresponds to Philo's image of Moses. Freud does not comment on his formulation of the title nor does he quote Exodus 11:3. Nevertheless, "the Man Moses" is a clear allusion to the *Egyptian* Moses and to the only trace he left in the Hebrew Bible.

Yosef Yerushalmi interprets the shift as a means of emphasizing Judaism: "The shift is emblematic. On the one hand, the title does not specifically proclaim this to be a Jewish book. Yet 'The Monotheistic Religion,' with its emphatic specificity, is, in effect, Judaism."[18] I see it rather the other way round. "The Man Moses," translating *ha-'ish Mosheh*, is the specific element and "The Monotheistic Religion" is the general term. Monotheism is the crucial issue of the Moses/Egypt discourse, and notwithstanding Christianity's not being recognized as a monotheistic religion by Judaism, Christianity considers itself to be so, and reflects its monotheistic character in the Moses/Egypt discourse. Freud, in joining the discourse, inherits and must continue to deal with this issue.[19] The whole point of the Moses/Egypt discourse is that it is neither Jewish nor Christian, but aiming at a point beyond these distinctions. Freud's contribution is certainly not an exception in this respect.

Moses the Egyptian and the Origin of Monotheism

Freud begins his first article, "Moses: An Egyptian" with a discussion of the name of Mose, which, as many before him had observed, is almost certainly Egyptian, meaning "child." It is a short form of some theophorous[20] name such as Thut-mose, Ah-mose, Ra-mose, Ptah-mose, Amun-mose.[21] He asks the obvious question: Why did nobody among those who identified the Egyptian etymology of the name consider the possibility that Moses was an Egyptian? He tries to substantiate the truth of this hypothesis with a new argument.

As Otto Rank has shown, the story of Moses' childhood closely follows the archetypal pattern of "the birth of the hero." A child of noble or even royal birth is abandoned—frequently in a chest floating in a river—and found and raised by a family of low standing. But in the case of Moses there is an important "narrative inversion." Here, the abandoning family is low class and the finding and raising family is royal. The motive behind the normal pattern is clear: to glorify the hero. What could be the motive behind the inverted pattern? Freud's explanation is that the story served not to glorify a hero but to "Judify" an Egyptian.

Freud's ingenious observation links up perfectly well with the relationship between the Biblical account of the Exodus and what has to be considered the historical evidence for it. The historical evidence for a longer sojourn of Syro-Palestinian Semites in Egypt is the Hyksos occupation, when the foreign invaders reigned as kings over Egypt, eventually to be expelled by an Egyptian dynasty. These events came by narrative inversion to be shaped into the story of slaves that were able to escape slavery and were elected by God to become a people and even have kings of their own.

Freud, however, closes his fascinating and brilliantly written article with a strange note of resignation. "An objective proof for the exact date of Moses' life and the Exodus from Egypt was not to be found. Therefore, the publication of all further conclusions that could be drawn from the fact that he was an Egyptian has to stop."

Some months later, Freud breaks his vow. Has the "objective proof" he was looking for turned up? No, but, strangely enough, a memory has returned. Only now does he seem to realize that Moses' being an Egyptian could have something to do with "Ikhnaton" and his mono-theistic revolution. This could be explained if Freud had learned about these events only after completing his historical studies. But Freud knew about Akhenaten as early as 1912, when he suggested this subject to Karl Abraham and published Abraham's important article on Akhen-aten in the first volume of his newly founded journal, *Imago*.[22] In this article, Abraham drew a portrait of Akhenaten and his religion which closely anticipates the one that Freud himself would postulate. But Freud never mentions Abraham in the book.[23] Is it possible that Freud was devising his "historischen Roman" as a serialized novel, breaking off at the point of highest suspense so that he could continue in the following issue? Did he consciously postpone the obvious conclusion that Moses, if he was an Egyptian, must have been an Atenist, saving it for another article? I do not think so. The remembrance of Akhenaten and the discovery that Moses was an Atenist must have struck him like a revelation between the first and second issues of *Imago*, volume 23 (1937).

Yet Freud, in taking up this theme where he left it and before presenting his new findings, again warns his readers: "It is not going to be the whole and not even the most important part of it." He starts with an account of the greatest obstacle to the thesis that Moses was an Egyptian: the antagonism between Egyptian and Biblical religion. He even goes so far as to suspect that the one was consciously opposing the other, thinking along the lines of "normative inversion": *die eine ver-dammt, was in der anderen aufs Üppigste wuchert* ("the one is condemning what is luxuriantly flourishing in the other"). In discussing the antago-nism between the two religions he focuses on five points:

1. The condemnation of magic.
2. The condemnation of images.
3. The negation of a hereafter and of immortality.
4. The negation of a plurality of deities and the affirmation that there is only one God.
5. The emphasis on ethical as opposed to ritual purity.

Freud concludes that this antagonism makes it extremely improbable that Moses, being an Egyptian, could have brought his own religion to "the Jews." Of course, this is nothing new. No one ever argued that

Moses could possibly have taught the Hebrews the tenets of Egyptian official religion or popular polytheism. The antagonism between this religion and what Moses taught has always been clear and has formed the very core of the Moses/Egypt discourse. But this was never deemed a serious obstacle to believing that Moses was an Egyptian (in the ethnic or cultural sense) and that his teaching was (partly or entirely) derived from Egyptian wisdom. The traditional explanation of this antagonism was based on the distinction between popular official religion and the mystery cult. The mystery cult opposes the popular religion in the same way that Biblical religion opposes Egyptian idolatry, and Moses merely translates and makes public what the mystery cults preserved under the cover of the hieroglyphs. This distinction is based on a sociological differentiation. The truth can only be grasped by a few. The unequal distribution of knowledge among human beings leads quite naturally to a hierarchical structure. Freud does away with this social topology of knowledge, only to replace it with a psychic topology. As we shall see, he replaces "mystery" with "latency." But he did not take this step until "the most important" part of his study, which he was still intending to withhold from publication while he wrote his second article on Moses the Egyptian. In this article, he replaces the traditional construction of Egyptian "mysteries" with the historical evidence on Akhenaten and his revolutionary monotheism.

Like Thomas Mann, who treated this very topic during those same years, Freud traced the origins of Akhenaten's revolutionary ideas back to Heliopolis and its ancient cult of the sun god. Both based their accounts on Breasted's impressive and influential books entitled *History of Egypt* (1906), *The Development of Religion and Thought* (1912), and *The Dawn of Conscience* (1934). Breasted was among the very first to recognize the immense importance of the newly discovered Akhenaten and his religion for the history of religion and the development of Biblical monotheism. His Berlin dissertation of 1894, written in Latin, is the first appraisal of the Amarna hymns and their religious content.[24] The concept of a universal god as the religious counterpart of political imperialism originated in Heliopolis. The pharaohs of the Eighteenth Dynasty transcended not only the political borders but also the mental boundaries of the Egyptian world. While ruling over a multinational empire which they deemed universal, they formed the concept of a universal deity as the creator and preserver of all. While the Egyptian

armies were conquering the world, the Heliopolitan priests were drawing the concomitant theological conclusions. Breasted's correlation of
monotheism and imperialism echoes the political theology of Eusebius
of Caesarea, who pointed out to Constantine the correspondence between terrestrial and celestial monarchy, that is, the Roman Empire and
Christian monotheism.[25] Akhenaten inherited the Heliopolitan concept of a universal god (whom we easily recognize as the god of the
mysteries), but he turned a local cult into a general religion and gave it
the character of an intolerant monotheism. This notion is also quite
familiar. Reinhold and Schiller applied it to their image of Moses.
Whereas the Heliopolitan priests worshipped the sun god as the highest god and the creator of all, Akhenaten proclaimed him to be the one
and only god: "you sole god beside whom there is no other."[26] There
is only one possible conclusion to draw: "If Moses was an Egyptian and
if he communicated his own religion to the Jews, it must have been
Akhenaten's, the Aten religion."[27]

By exercising common sense, Freud fortunately forgoes what he calls
"the short way of proving our thesis" by relying solely on the alleged
assonance of the divine names "Aton" and "Adonai."[28] Instead, he takes
the "long way" of comparing the religions involved and shows quite
convincingly that Akhenaten's revolutionary religion meets all of the
requirements of Biblical anti-Egyptianism:

1. It is a strict monotheism, showing the most intransigent intolerance toward traditional polytheism.
2. It excludes magical rites and ceremonies.
3. It is aniconic.
4. It stresses ethical requirements.
5. It eschews any concept of a hereafter and of human immortality.

It is only on the last point that Freud's view of Amarna religion
differs from the traditional view of Egyptian mystery religion.[29] It is
also a point which was of great importance for Spinozism and Deism.
A religion that lacks the ideas of an immortal soul and a future life
cannot be true, they held. By contrast, Warburton tried to show that
Biblical monotheism differed on this point from all pagan religions and
that this is precisely what shows its divine origin.

In Freud's reconstruction, the whole body of ritual Law is reduced

to one single prescription: "the sign of circumcision." But this particular law becomes the cornerstone of his argumentation, the decisive
proof that Moses did in fact bring an Egyptian religion to the "Jews."
First, it is striking that Freud calls circumcision "a sign." This is a
Pauline formula *(to sēmeion tēs peritomēs)* referring to Genesis 17:11,
where circumcision is called "a sign *[ōt]* of the covenant." Spencer
devoted a long chapter to "the sign of circumcision" *(signum circumci-
sionis)* and reactivated the whole apparatus of Augustinian semiotics to
interpret it. Spencer also adduced a large collection of Classical quotations in order to determine its antiquity and distribution. The Classical
sources agree that circumcision originated with the Egyptians and
Ethiopians and then spread to other areas of the Near East and as far
as Kolchis on the Black Sea. But the Bible makes circumcision the sign
of the Abrahamitic covenant. Spencer left the question open as to who
borrowed the custom from whom. This indeterminateness was rather
bold. Of course, Freud was free of any such scruples regarding the
orthodox view. He concluded that it was Moses who brought this
Egyptian custom to the Jews because he saw a sign of superiority, of
purity, and distinction in it and he did not want his new people to fall
behind the Egyptians in this respect.[30] This Egyptian origin of circumcision was later concealed along with everything else regarding the
Egyptian identity of Moses and his religion by the attribution of the rite
to Abraham.

     According to Freud, the reason for Moses' leaving his country and
choosing the Jews as a people in order to realize a new kind of polity
based on a new religion and constitution was the failure of the Aton
religion. Like Toland at the beginning of the eighteenth century, Freud
saw in Moses a princely figure, close to the throne, perhaps the governor of a province such as Goshen, where the Jews settled. Moses was
also convinced of the truth of Atonism and too proud to return to
orthodoxy. He made the decision not only to emigrate but to found a
new nation. For this purpose, he chose the Jews. The situation was
favorable for their emigration because the kingdom went through a
state of anarchy after Akhenaten's death.[31] Moses led the Jewish tribes
out of Egypt, taught them his monotheistic creed (which might have
assumed an even more strict and radical form with him than that which
Akhenaten had introduced),[32] and gave them laws. The Bible still retains a trace of his foreign descent in that it speaks of his "heavy tongue"

and his dependence on his brother Aaron. As an Egyptian, Moses did not speak Hebrew and had to rely on an interpreter. Strangely enough, Freud breaks off at this point. "Now, however, or so it seems, our work has reached a provisional end. For the moment, we can draw no further conclusions from our hypothesis that Moses was an Egyptian, whether it has been proved or not."[33] He then proceeds to the discussion of Eduard Meyer's completely different reconstruction.

The Two Moseses and Jewish Dualism

Meyer's Moses is a Midianite and a worshipper of Yahweh, "an uncanny, bloodthirsty demon who wanders at night and shuns daylight." According to Meyer, the connection with the Exodus story is only secondary. As will soon become evident, Freud could not wish for a stronger confirmation of his own thesis. Yet he breaks off again: In view of these unsurmountable contradictions "we shall have to admit that the thread which we tried to spin from our hypothesis that Moses was an Egyptian has broken for the second time. And this time, as it seems, with no hope of mending."[34] But in section 5 he takes up the abandoned thread: "Unexpectedly, here once more a way of escape presents itself."[35] His own Moses the Egyptian and Meyer's Moses the Midianite were two different persons! The first was slain by his people, who could not bear the demands of his exacting monotheism. The second one, who lived some generations later, was the one who persisted in the traditional memory. The idea that Moses was murdered by his rebellious followers is based on an ingenious theory by the Old Testament scholar Ernst Sellin. He interpreted the traditions about the suffering slave of God (*'ebed Yahweh*) in the prophets not only as a foreshadowing of the Messiah, but also as the distorted memory of the murder of Moses. I shall discuss the importance of the murder theory for Freud's theory of religion in the next section. Here, I will concentrate on another aspect of this motif which is related to a traditional issue of the discourse: the issue of "accommodation."

Freud's precursors in the history of the Moses/Egypt discourse tried to explain why God or Moses did not reveal the true religion, the timeless truth, to the people instead of revealing a mixture of truth and absurdity. Maimonides called this the "cunning of God." It was necessary for the time and the people. Closely following Maimonides,

Spencer explained that God was benevolent and condescending enough not to confront his unprepared people with the truth, but to accommodate the truth to the limitations of their understanding *(propter duritiem cordis)* and to the "spirit of the time" *(genius secoli)*. Reinhold and Schiller attributed the same policy not to God but to Moses, who had to found a nation and not an esoteric sect of initiates. As a result, he had to transmit the truth in a system functioning on the principle of "blind belief" instead of on insight and knowledge. The Law was not perfect, but was instead a compromise between divine truth and the limitations of human understanding.[36] These were the issues at stake in the Moses/Egypt discourse. Where and in what form do they reappear in Freud's text?

Freud's Egyptian Moses (M_1) did not make any compromises or "accommodations." Therefore, "the wild Semites took their fate into their own hands and did away with the tyrant."[37] Freud's expression "wild Semites" echoes the traditional descriptions of the "coarseness" of the people to whom Moses taught his religion and his laws. In the tradition of the discourse, the opposition between truth and history was resolved by the conception of accommodation. In Freud's reconstruction, it led to violent confrontation and murder. There was no "cunning" on the side of Moses the Egyptian, but intransigent demands backed up by brutal force and tyranny, for which (according to Freud) he had to pay with his life. In Freud's reconstruction, the cunning and the compromises came later, after the violent death of the Egyptian Moses. Freud explains the "imperfections" of the Law by introducing distinctions. On the human plane, he distinguishes between the Egyptian and the Midianite Moses (M_1 and M_2), while on the divine plane, he distinguishes between Aton, M_1's god of Akhenaten, and Yahweh, M_2's volcanic demon of the Midianites (A and Y). He is thus able to attribute those traits which were formerly attributed to the true and perfect religion to M_1 and A, and all the imperfections of the Biblical god and his Law to M_2 and Y or to the compromises that were negotiated between the followers of M_1 and those of M_2.

Freud's ingenious distinction between M_1 and M_2 not only accounts for the "imperfections" of the Law, but also captures something of the antagonistic force inherent in monotheism. These were the central issues of the Moses/Egypt discourse. No one writing within the discourse ever went so far as to speak of a "deception," as did the infamous treatise *De Tribus Impostoribus*, but some did speak of an "imposition" mitigated by accommodation. In eliminating the idea of accommodation, Freud stressed the aspect of imposition, of apodictic laws and unreasoned demands, and of the intransigent confrontation inherent in monotheism. We must not forget that Freud wrote his book in times of persecution, of violent confrontation and murderous hatred. One of his goals was to discover the sources of this hatred. His analysis of monotheism and violence is certainly one of the more important contributions of *Moses* to the theory of religion.

According to Freud, this primordial dualism reproduced itself structurally in the course of Jewish history in the same way as the distinction between Roman-ruled Germany and free Germany reappeared after more than a thousand years during the Reformation, when the areas once ruled by the Romans stayed Catholic and the free areas became Protestant. "History is fond of reinstatements as this."[38] The Jewish dualism reappeared in the form of the two names of God, Elohim and Yahweh; the two kingdoms, Israel and Judah; and the conflict between prophetic and official religion. By transforming the idea of accommodation into historical phenomena such as conflict and compromise between different groups, Freud was able to reconstruct the course of Jewish history as a process of the slow reemergence and final dominance of a suppressed tradition. At the end, it is A who wins, "the idea of a single deity, embracing the whole world, who was not less all-loving as all-powerful, who was averse to all ceremonial and magic, and set before humans as their highest aim a life in truth and justice."[39]

With this sublime idea of a Supreme Being, we are back to the God of the Enlightenment. This is the God Strabo attributed to Moses, the God of Cudworth and of Schiller, of the Deists, the free-thinkers, and the Freemasons, the God whose gospel forms the subtext of the Moses/Egypt discourse. Seemingly, a circle closes. Freud brings home from his "Egyptian dig"[40] a god such as Schiller and Strabo claimed him to be. Freud's characterization of Akhenaten's god is strongly informed by the ideas of God fostered by Spinozism, Deism, cosmotheism, and pantheism underlying the various versions of the Moses/Egypt discourse. Among those traditional traits which Freud's Aton inherited from the God of Warburton, Reinhold, and Schiller, I would count:

- The stress on spirituality.
- The aniconicity of worship.
- The negation of magic and ceremony.
- The stress on the ethical.
- The negation of a hereafter and the immortality of the soul.

All these traits play a crucial role in the Moses/Egypt discourse and a very small role, if at all, in the Amarna texts. It is true, however, that Freud found they had already been stressed in Breasted's several publications.[41]

The only problem with Freud's God was that he did not believe in him. This god was not a theological or philosophical truth, but an archaeological discovery. Had Freud still believed in this "one single all-encompassing" God or nature as Toland, Reinhold, and Schiller did, his book would perhaps have ended here. He would have contented himself with his findings:

- Moses was an Egyptian.
- He brought an Egyptian religion to the Hebrews.
- This religion was a revolutionary monotheistic counter-religion.
- Moses did not make any "accommodations," but instead intensified the spiritual and intellectual demands of this religion.
- He was murdered because of his intransigency.
- Another leader took his place: a man of different stature and beliefs, a worshipper of a volcanic demon called Yahweh.
- The ensuing compromises with the Egyptian emigrants may account for many tensions and contradictions in the Biblical texts.
- The duality of the Moses figures accounted for the dualism of exclusivity and universalism inherent in the Jewish tradition.
- The truth, however, could not be concealed or "accommodated" forever and in the end it was the Egyptian god who gained predominance.

All these points are on the agenda of the Moses/Egypt discourse, which Freud treated up to this juncture in a successful, surprising, and entertaining way.

But Freud no longer believed in this god as the ultimate truth. Rather, he saw him as a historical idea linked with Egyptian imperialism and universalism. He felt dissatisfied with his results and began a completely new chapter, apparently leaving the confines of the Moses/Egypt discourse.

Repetition and Repression: Patricide and the Origin of Religion

I think that the reasons for Freud's insisting on Moses' Egyptian identity have very much to do with the traditional project of the Moses/Egypt discourse and its hidden agenda. The Egyptian Moses explained the origin of monotheism. In this, Freud proved a faithful continuer of the discourse. The historical construction of "Moses the creator of a nation" and of his Egyptian background meant the theological deconstruction of "Moses the prophet" and of his transcendent mission. This was precisely the concern of the discourse on Moses and Egypt. But Freud's strange insistence on Moses' violent death, even after Sellin had given up his theory, cannot be explained by reference to the discourse.[42] Concerning this theory, Yerushalmi has made a point which in my opinion is decisive. The question is not whether Moses was really murdered, but rather whether the murder, if it ever occurred, would have been repressed or concealed in an account that dwells in such detail on the misdeeds and rebellions of the wilderness generation. Would this narrative repress a fact that so completely fits into the overall semantics of the tale? The same applies to the whole of the Biblical tradition, which relentlessly recorded every sin of Israel's disobedience.[43] The idea of concealing a fact such as Moses' violent death at the hands of his people runs not only against the letter but also against the spirit of the Biblical account. Why was it so important for Freud?

The *slain Moses* is inseparable from Freud's theory concerning the origin and essence of religion. Freud's theory as propounded in *Totem and Taboo* and in *Moses and Monotheism* is too well known to need detailed recapitulation. I confine myself to the basics. In the primal horde, the father reigned in a completely tyrannical way over his sons, whom he threatened with death and castration if they dared to become rivals in his claim on the females of the horde. Eventually the father was killed by his sons.[44] This archetypal event oscillates strangely between singularity and repetition. "We do not believe," Freud wrote, "that one great god exists today, but that in primeval times there was one single person who at that time had to appear gigantic." One single person? According to Freud, the killing of the primeval father was repeated over and over again. Only by this repetition of the primal crime could the deed leave indissoluble traces in the human psyche, forming its "archaic heritage."[45] In the hidden depths of these traces, "men have always known that they once possessed a primal father and that they killed him."[46] The decisive forces that turned an archaic experience into a lasting anthropological trait were repetition and repression. By repetition, the experience became engraved on the human psyche in a (biologically) hereditary way. By repression, the engraving or "archaic heritage" became "encrypted,"[47] that is, inaccessible to conscious reflection and "working through." By its very inaccessibility, it became compulsory.

The kind of history Freud is referring to is psychohistory. The deified father is a figure of memory, not of history. It is only by virtue of having been slain that the father "returned to the memory of the people" and was "elevated to the rank of a deity." The cult he inspired also performed the function of burying or "encrypting" the memory of the deed. According to Freud, this is the founding act of culture or civilization (Freud does not make any distinction between them). Internecine rivalry between the males of the horde stopped. Killing was now perceived as sin, reminiscent of the primordial sin which led to the origin of culture. The memory of the primeval patricide was repressed and transformed into a strong feeling of guilt that infused the nascent religion with myriad precautions and anxieties such as taboos, restrictions, abstinences, self-castigations, and cruel sacrifices.

According to Freud, the same thing happened in the case of Moses and monotheism. Moses' monotheism was itself a repetition. Moses' teaching, the Egyptian ideas of Akhenaten's revolutionary monotheism, revitalized the primeval monotheism of original religion: "When Moses brought to his people the conception of a single god, it was nothing new, but it signified the resuscitating of an experience out of the primeval times of the human family that had long ago disappeared from the conscious memory of the people." Moses' monotheism was the return of the father.[48] The murder of Moses was an even more powerful repetition that revived encrypted memories. "Neither conscious nor unconscious denial of the deed could eliminate the presence in the psyche of the act or guilt, but would merely intensify the unconscious store of guilt and anxiety; indeed Freud maintains that the obsession with this unrecognized remorse drove the perpetrators and their heirs to compensate for their sin and that of their primeval forefathers by becoming increasingly more devoted to god and the religion of Moses."[49]

By becoming repressed in their turn, the slain Moses (M_1) and his religion of undiluted monotheism became encrypted as well. A natural death would not have been sufficient to work such powerful effects on the collective psyche. The experience had to be traumatic in order to persist. In Freud's words, it had to "undergo the fate of repression" in order to "force the masses under its spell." The murder of Moses reenacted the fate of the primeval father. The paradoxical point of Freud's argument is that only by virtue of having been murdered and through the subsequent repression of the deed did Moses become what he is: a "statue of bronze," the "creator of the Jewish nation," a figure of lasting and endless memory.

This argument can only be understood in the light of Freud's theory of repression. According to Freud, the distinction between forgetting and repression is that the first is a form of abandonment whereas the second is a form of retention and stabilization. Not only do repressed memories persist, but they acquire an often dangerous power over the personality. Unlike conscious memories, which are accessible and can be edited and "worked through," repressed memories work from within or "below" and keep the consciousness under their spell.

In *Moses and Monotheism*, Freud transfers this theory from the plane of individual psychology to that of collective psychology. The distinction between conscious memory and repressed memory appears on the plane of collective psychology as the distinction between tradition and memory. "A tradition that was based only on [direct] communication could not lead to the compulsive character that attaches to religious phenomena. It would be listened to, judged, and perhaps dismissed, like any other piece of information from outside, but would never attain the privilege of being liberated from the coercion of logical thinking. It must first have undergone the fate of being repressed, the condition of lingering in the unconscious, before it is able to display such powerful effects on its return and force the masses under its spell."[50] This is how Moses the Egyptian (M_1) and his monotheism (A) "returned to the memory of his people" and became—as a figure of repressed and returned memory—the "creator of the Jewish people." The Jews did away with the person of Moses but eventually embraced his monotheism. The "tame Egyptians waited until fate had removed the sanctified person of their Pharaoh"[51] but eventually did away with his monotheism. As a figure of history, Akhenaten became so totally "encrypted" that he never "returned to the memory of his people" except in the guise of Moses.

This is how Freud explains the coercive power that religion has over the masses. The most forceful element of this coercing power is guilt. The notion of guilt is Freud's most interesting contribution to the semantics of religious antagonism.

> Ambivalence is a part of the essence of the relation to the father: in the course of time the hostility too could not fail to stir, which had once driven the sons into killing their admired and dreaded father. There was no place in the framework of the religion of Moses for a direct expression of the murderous hatred of the father. All that could come to light was a mighty reaction against it—a sense of guilt on account of that hostility, a bad conscience for having sinned against God and for not ceasing to sin.[52]

Freud's theories, outdated and problematic as they may seem, have the incontestable merit of having assured memory its place in the history of religion and of having convincingly exposed as reductive any unilinear reconstructions based on evolution and tradition.

Sensus Historicus: Freud's Version of Euhemerism

Let me preface this section with two lines from Schiller's poem *Die Götter Griechenlands (The Gods of Greece)* which must have been on Freud's mind when he was writing *Moses and Monotheism:*[53]

> Da die Götter menschlicher noch waren,
> waren Menschen göttlicher[54]

These lines help to restore to the idea of mortal gods the radiance which seems somewhat obscured by the dry and overrationalistic concept of Euhemerism.

🏵 ACCORDING to Spencer, everything in the Egyptian mysteries had three different meanings: a moral, a mystical, and a historical one. Moses adopted this principle of threefold signification for his laws. In his masonic treatise *On the Egyptian Mysteries*, Ignaz von Born took up this idea and complained that all that was left to us of the Egyptian mysteries was their historical meaning.[55] There seems to be more implied in this resignation than von Born might have intended. The discourse on Moses and Egypt is generally characterized by a strong tendency toward historicization. This tendency forms the most striking continuity, linking even Freud's psychoanalytic theory of religion to the Moses/Egypt discourse. I am thinking of what could be called "the historical turn" and what Freud described as the shift from "material truth" to "historical truth."[56]

Freud's historical turn is reminiscent of a concept that is commonly associated with the name of Euhemerus, but this kind of "Euhemerism" is much more general than the rather specific method of mythological exegesis practiced by Euhemerus might suggest.[57] The idea that the gods were mortals—kings, culture-bringers, lawgivers, saviors—who had been deified by their grateful posterity because of their outstanding deeds was an assumption common to all of the authors from John Spencer to Friedrich Schiller who wrote along the thematic lines of the discourse. It is a basic assumption of the ancient and modern Enlightenment. The Moses/Egypt discourse in its later stages extended the method of historicization to revelation itself. Revelation became historically interpreted as translation or transference from Egypt to Israel. But it was only Freud who dared to make the ultimate extension and to historicize even the One, the creator and preserver of all.

The concept of the great man as the historical origin of deification and religion is as central to the discourse as it is central to Freud's construction of Moses. Therefore, Freud insists on his historical personality, calling him "the *man* Moses." Few would contest that there might be a kernel of historical truth in the traditions about Moses and that there might have existed a person with this or a similar name who was the starting point of a legendary tradition. But Freud does much more than just maintain the historical existence of Moses. Whereas the Biblical texts insist on attributing the deed of liberation to God "which have brought thee out of Egypt," Freud attributes to Moses not only the liberation from Egypt but also the "creation of the Jewish nation."

Freud insists on this point just as strongly as he insists on Moses' being an Egyptian and on his having been killed by his people. It is a "fact" of the same basic importance for Freud.

It is important to realize the boldness and historical improbability of this construction in order to better understand Freud's intentions. One man the creator of a whole nation? Normally, one would conceive of the "creation of a nation" as a typical process of "longue durée" and apply Freud's notion of "inscription by repetition" to this process. Seen this way, the creation of the Jewish nation was brought about by a chain of recurring events such as the destruction of the first temple, the Babylonian exile, the Maccabean wars, the destruction of the second temple, and the diaspora that turned Israel, to use Mary Douglas' terms,[58] from an "individualistic culture" into a "hierarchic culture" and then into an "enclave culture." It is the historical experience and the social structure of an enclave culture that informed the final redaction of the Biblical texts, the literary creation of the figure of Moses and the "creation of the Jewish nation." This is the way the "creation of a nation" normally occurs. Freud's radical method of historical per-sonification compresses a process of centuries into the figure of "the great man."

Freud's construction of Moses as the creator of his nation goes against all historical probability. No nation has ever been created. Some "great men" might have had a bigger share in the social construction of reality than others, but there certainly never was anyone whose share in this construction amounted to the creation of a nation. Why was it necessary for Freud to have recourse to such extreme assumptions? Freud was aware of the problem and provided an interesting answer. It was not the "living" or "historical Moses" alone to whom he attributed the creation of the Jewish nation, but the living and the dead, the historical, the repressed, and the remembered Moses taken together. The return of the repressed was also for Freud a process of "longue durée." It was this process which resulted in the creation of the nation. The same applies to the primeval father. The return of the repressed and the development of religion "took place slowly and certainly not spontaneously but under the influence of all the changes in conditions of life which fill the history of human civilization."[59] Yet all of this took place on the plane of history. Freud's theory is a compelling (if not convincing) new version of Euhemerism. The amplification of Moses follows logically from the historicization of God. Moses had to take the place of the primal father, who had to take the place of God. This is the "sensus historicus" of the religious traditions. Therefore, Moses "had to appear gigantic" in the same way as the primeval father.

It is precisely this construction of Moses as the creator of a nation that forms the strongest link between Freud's text and the Moses/Egypt discourse. The orthodox Jewish tradition tends to play down Moses' role in the Exodus. In the Passover Haggadah, the annual reenactment of the Exodus from Egypt in the form of a family liturgy, Moses is not even mentioned. It is not a particularly Jewish project to make Moses the creator of the Jewish nation. Rather, it is one of the presuppositions of the discourse on Moses and Egypt that is shared by all the participants, including the ancient sources. It is not "Moses the prophet" but "Moses the lawgiver" who forms the thematic focus of the discourse. For Moses the prophet, an Egyptian background is unimportant. Indeed, he will have to forget what he learned from his Egyptian masters in order to become a faithful medium of God's messages. It is Moses the lawgiver and political creator who needs his Egyptian education.

Freud, we should note, with his model of a psychic topology and its transference from the individual to the collective level, is able to avoid the notorious flatness of Euhemerism. God is turned from a material truth into a fact of history, but it is a different kind of history which Freud is referring to. On the plane of psychohistory, God stays inaccessibly and uncontrollably remote and powerful. Religion works its coercive power from within and from below, from the immeasurable depth of the human psyche and its "archaic heritage."

❀ IF WE LOOK back at the various versions of the discourse, we make a surprising discovery. All those who turned the kaleidoscope and contributed a new variation on the story of Moses wrote a different text than what they intended to write. All of them were writing about Egyptian cosmotheism and its modern avatars in the guise of Spinozism, Deism, and pantheism, and all were read and received as propagators of this "natural religion," even those who consciously intended the exact opposite, as Spencer, Cudworth, Warburton, and Jacobi explicitly did. It is as if someone else was guiding their pen and writing his subtext when they wrote theirs. This applies even to Freud, whose text makes an extremely polyphonic impression. It is as if the story of Moses the Egyptian had a life of its own, incorporating itself in different versions: passing through the media and the conceptual frameworks of theology, Freemasonry, philosophy, history, literature, and psychoanalysis. The discourse seems to have a dynamics and a semantics of its own. It is the embodiment of a dream: the dream dreamt by Biblical monotheism of its own counterpart. In this dream, the counter-religious institution of Moses' monotheistic revelation is revoked. It is a dream of reconciliation. In this general respect, even the third part of Freud's Moses book pertains to this dream because he identifies (counter-)religion, in the sense of Mosaic monotheism, as a neurotic compulsion centered on a complex of guilt. He offers a therapy for this religious neurosis by analyzing its underlying guilt complex. What else is this therapy than a quest for reconciliation?

In dealing with religion, Freud continues to use the language of illness. But he is the first one to do so literally as a doctor of medicine and not just metaphorically. He translates Holbach's and Heine's idea of religion as a sickness originating in Egypt and thence contracted and disseminated by other peoples into the terminology of psychopathology. His contribution to the phenomenology of religious antagonism is "compulsion." The influence that religion exerts on the masses is explicable only as a deep-rooted psychic dynamism not only comparable but absolutely analogous to compulsory neurosis.

Religion as compulsory neurosis—what a strange idea. Was Freud aware of the fact that he was continuing the eighteenth-century struggle against fanaticism and enthusiasm? Was he aware of the fact that he was haunted to a considerable degree by the issues of the Moses/Egypt discourse, the issues of nature, tolerance, and reason, of an "education of the human genre" (Origen/Lessing), or "Fortschritt in der Geistigkeit" (progress in spirituality/intellectuality) as Freud called it?[60]

What Freud put in pathological terms, Schiller and Reinhold had expressed in political terms: the element of compulsion inherent in Mosaic monotheism. They spoke of blind belief brought about by brutal force and miracles as the means Moses had to resort to because of the "brutishness of the people" and the heart's stubbornness, *propter duritiem cordis.* Freud's concept of monotheism intensified the element of compulsion. His most important contribution to the Moses discourse is the discovery of the central role of guilt. This concept transcends the *sensus historicus* of religion and restores its *sensus moralis*. "Freud thought that ethics originated with 'consciousness of guilt due to the hostility to God.' Exalted, overt devotion to God concealed the roots of the devotee's enormous unconscious guilt about both the murder of the father (be he the primeval one or Moses) and their enormous hostility that culminated in patricide. Thus, heinous, violent acts can serve as a source not only of spirituality and intellectual achievement, but also of ethical codes for a just and virtuous life."[61] But the reverse is also true. Spiritual and intellectual achievement in the pursuit of monotheism could always provoke hostility and heinous, violent acts in a repetition of the primal crime.

Freud wanted to discover the roots of anti-Semitism. Strikingly enough, his question was not how the Gentiles, or the Christians, or the Germans came to hate the Jews, but "how the Jew had become what he is and why he has attracted this undying hatred." Freud traced this "undying hatred" back to the "hostility" inherent in monotheism as a religion of the father. Not the Jew but monotheism had attracted this undying hatred. By making Moses an Egyptian, he deemed himself able to shift the sources of negativity and intolerance out of Judaism and back to Egypt, and to show that the defining fundamentals of Jewish monotheism and mentality came from outside it. But this time the source of intolerance is enlightenment itself. Akhenaten is shown to be a figure both of enlightenment and of intolerant despotism, forcing his universalist monotheism onto his people with violence and persecution. Freud concentrates all the counter-religious force of Biblical monotheism in Akhenaten's revolution from above. This was the origin of it all. Freud stresses (quite correctly) the fact that he is dealing with the absolutely first monotheistic, counter-religious, and exclusivistically intolerant movement of this sort in human history. The similarity of this interpretation to Manetho's is evident. It is this hatred brought about by Akhenaten's revolution that informs the Judeophobic texts of antiquity.

CHAPTER SIX

Conceiving the One in Ancient Egyptian Traditions

The story of Moses the Egyptian is a story of religious confrontation and the overcoming of it. The name of Moses is associated with a counter-religion that defined its identity in contradistinction to Egyptian "idolatry." Making Moses an Egyptian amounts to abolishing this defining opposition. Tracing Moses and his message back to Egypt means leaving the realm of "revealed" or "positive" religion and entering the realm of *lumen naturale:* experience, reason, tradition, and wisdom. Starting in Hellenism and continuing through modernity up to Freud, the Mosaic project was interpreted as the claim for unity: there is but one God, the invisible source of all. The counter-religious antagonism was always constructed in terms of unity and plurality. Moses and the One against Egypt and the Many. The discourse on Moses the Egyptian aimed at dismantling this barrier. It traced the idea of unity back to Egypt.

Two men stand out among those who spoke of Egyptian monotheism in the frame of this discourse. One is Ralph Cudworth, who reconstructed this monotheism as *Hen kai pan:* the "grand arcanum, that God is all things." The other is Sigmund Freud, who was the first to introduce the newly retrieved memory of an authentic Egyptian monotheism into the debate and who made Moses an adherent of this monotheistic movement. But neither of them had a first-hand knowledge of Egyptian sources. Cudworth wrote in a time when the hieroglyphs were still undeciphered and when any attempt to form an idea of ancient Egyptian religion was totally dependent on Greek and Latin (and in this respect second-hand) sources. Freud relied on a few Egyptologists without being able to distinguish between first-rate scholars such as Breasted and phantasts such as Weigall. Moreover, he never went so far as to read carefully through the texts that were available in translation in his time, and his interest in Amarna religion was rather limited.

Therefore, two things remain for an Egyptologist to do. He should complement Freud's passing and superficial remarks on Akhenaten's religious revolution with a close reading of at least the most important text and discuss the contributions Egyptology can make concerning the counter-religious character of that monotheism. Second, he should assist Cudworth in his quest for any pre-"Trismegistick" testimonies of Egyptian theology and, however briefly, show what might be learnt in this respect from the original texts. Let me then give the last word in this debate to the Egyptians themselves.

A Counter-Religion of Nature: The Revolutionary Monotheism of Akhenaten

King Amenophis IV, who changed his name to Akhenaten or Akhanyati[1] ("Beneficial for the Aten") and ruled Egypt for seventeen years in the middle of the fourteenth century B.C.E., is the first founder of a monotheistic counter-religion in human history.[2] Freud was correct in stressing this point.[3]

It seems evident that all founded or, to use the eighteenth-century term, "positive" religions are counter-religions. This is so because all of them had to confront and to reject a tradition. None of them was founded within a religious void. Therefore, they may be termed "secondary religions" because they always presuppose the preceding and/or parallel existence of "primary religions."[4] We have no evidence of evolutionary steps leading from primary to secondary religions. Wherever secondary religions occur, they always seem to have been established by foundational acts such as revolution and revelation. Such positive acts often have their negative complements in rejection and persecution. "Positive" religions imply negated traditions.

The Amarna religion has many characteristics of later secondary religions, in particular some similarities to Biblical monotheism in its later stages. It is not merely antipolytheistic, but also rationalistic. I agree with Freud that the Amarna religion exhibits tendencies toward what Max Weber called the "disenchantment of the world"[5] in its rejection of magical practices, sacramental symbolism ("idolatry"),[6] and mythological imagery.[7]

Secondary or counter-religions are determined and defined by the distinction they draw between themselves and primary religions. If the Amarna religion is in fact a secondary religion, it is imperative to determine the particular "defining difference" which it established between itself and the primary Egyptian religion. So far I have dealt only with the Mosaic distinction, which was expressed as the difference between Israel and Egypt. How is the distinction to be interpreted that Akhenaten drew between his new religion and the traditional one?

For the study of this defining difference we are, unfortunately, in a much less favorable situation than is the case with later secondary religions. The reason for this difficulty is that there seems to exist a necessary link between counter-religions and canonization. All counter-religions base themselves on large bodies of canonical texts. First of all, counter-religions, or secondary religions, appear in textual space, that is, in the form of textual articulation and scriptural tradition, as a specific kind of collective memory based on richly structured textual architectures, inherited and kept alive by means of elaborate techniques and institutions of interpretation. Secondary religions live in and by textual memory, which they must create and cultivate.[8] The distinction between primary and secondary religions appears always as the distinction between nature and Scripture. Owing to its episodic character, the Amarna religion did not have time to construct such a memory. It died out with its first generation and fell into complete oblivion. Its discovery is a feat of archaeology, not of memory. We are thus reduced to a handful of hymns, actually only two hymns on which all the others depend, addressed to the new god and composed almost certainly by the king himself. They are conventionally called the "Great Hymn"[9] and the "Shorter Hymn."[10]

But interpretation of the Amarna religion as a counter-religion does not rest solely on these few texts. The defining difference between the old and the new, "tradition" and "truth," is created not so much by verbal means as by practical means. The latter were indeed drastic. I have already shown how deep, and even traumatic, an impression these practical means of negation and destruction must have made on the minds of the people living at that time. The traditional cults and feasts were discontinued, the temples were closed, the names and images of the gods (above all those of Amun) were destroyed,[11] the capital was

transferred, a new style was introduced into language and repre-
sentational art, and so forth. These radical measures of persecution and
innovation show beyond any doubt that the Amarna movement viewed
itself as a new religion that was absolutely incompatible with the continuation of traditional forms of religious life.

In the extant texts, the difference between the old and the new is
more difficult to grasp. There is no attempt at explicit refutation of
traditional concepts. This would have required mentioning them, and
even that would have been deemed unacceptable. The term "gods,"
let alone the names of specific gods, does not appear in the Amarna
texts.[12] Even a phrase like "there are no gods besides the sun disk" is
inadmissible.[13] There are no traces of "normative inversion" or other
forms of explicit rejection in the extant texts. The difference is therefore only negatively marked, by not mentioning, intentionally avoid-
ing, or replacing what traditional religion would have had to say. The
difference can only be brought out by negative reasoning. This method
requires a detailed knowledge of traditional religion and its forms of
expression. The more precisely we know what to expect, the more
accurate will be our identification of what is absent. This explains why
any new insight into the essence of Amarna religion is to be gained
not so much from excavations at Amarna, which until now have failed
to unearth any new textual material, but from a better understanding
of traditional religion.

The discovery of new texts at Thebes has led to the distinction
between two antipolytheistic movements: the "New Solar Theology"
starting some decades before Amarna and continuing after its fall well
into the Late Period, and the "Amarna Theology," which is a radicali-
zation of the first and found no continuation after the abandonment of
the new capital. If there ever was a "school of Heliopolis" as Sigmund
Freud and Thomas Mann (drawing upon contemporary Egyptology)
imagined it, it must have been the transmitter of these new ideas.

It has become clear that the Amarna revolution is the peak of a
much broader movement which was certainly related, as Sigmund
Freud assumed, to the broadening of the Egyptian world in the course
of the political events of the New Kingdom and the rise of an empire.
This movement led to a "crisis of polytheism" that persisted after
Amarna; far from being a mere "return to orthodoxy," it was instead
a quite new form of pantheistic "summodeism," which I will briefly

consider in the second part of this chapter.[14] Further, the study of Theban hymns has led to a new appraisal of the Amarna texts as well, especially of the "Great Hymn." It may, therefore, be of interest to take a closer look at this fundamental text and thereby to gain a more detailed idea of the contents of Akhenaten's counter-religion.[15] The following analysis focuses on the points of contrast between Akhenaten's view and traditional theology. It is therefore inevitable that the reader will be confronted with much specialized Egyptological material. But since I am dealing here with the very first occurrence of a counter-religion and the construction of religious otherness, this excursus into Egyptology is justified.

The Text of the "Great Hymn"

FIRST SONG: THE DAILY CIRCUIT [TAGESZEITENLIED]

First Stanza: Morning—Beauty

1   Beautifully you rise
2   In heaven's lightland,
3   O living Aten, who allots life!
4   You have dawned on the eastern horizon
5   And have filled every land with your beauty.

Second Stanza: Noon—Dominion

6   You are beauteous, great, radiant,
7   High over every land;

8   Your rays embrace the lands to the limit of all you have made.
9   Being Re, you reach their limits
10 And bend them down for the son whom you love.

11 Though you are far, your rays are on earth;
12 Though one sees you, your strides are hidden.

Third Stanza: Night—Chaos

13 When you set in the western lightland,
14 Earth is in darkness
15 In the condition of death.

16 The sleepers are in [their] chambers,

17 Heads covered, one eye does not see the other,

18 Were they robbed of their goods under their heads, they don't notice it.

19 Every lion comes from its den,

20 All the serpents bite.

21 Darkness is a grave,

22 Earth is in silence:

23 Their creator has set in his lightland.

Fourth Stanza: Morning—Rebirth

24 At dawn you have risen in the lightland

25 And are radiant as the sundisk of daytime.

26 You dispel the dark, you cast your rays,

27 The Two Lands are in festivity daily.

28 Humans awake, they stand on their feet, you have roused them.

29 They wash and dress,

30 Their arms in adoration of your appearance.

31 The entire land sets out to work.

32 All beasts browse on their herbs,

33 Trees, herbs are sprouting;

34 Birds fly from their nests,

35 Their wings raised in adoration of your ka.

36 All flocks frisk on their feet,

37 All that fly up and alight,

38 They live when you dawn for them.

39 Ships fare north,

40 Fare south as well,

41 Every road lies open when you rise.

42 The fish in the river

43 Dart before you—

44 Your rays are in the midst of the sea.

SECOND SONG: CREATION

First Stanza: The Creation of Life in the Womb

(a) The Child

45   [You] who make seed grow in women,
46   Who make water into men;
47   Who vivify the son in his mother's womb,
48   Who soothe him to still his tears,
49   You nurse in the womb!
50   You giver of breath,
51   To nourish all that he made.
52   When he comes from the womb
53   To breathe, on the day of his birth,
54   You open wide his mouth and supply his needs.

(b) The Chicken in the Egg

55   The chicken in the egg,
56   It speaks in the shell;
57   You give it breath within to sustain it.
58   You have fixed a term for it
59   To break out from the egg;
60   When it comes out from the egg,
61   To speak at its term,
62   It already walks on its legs when it comes forth from it.

Second Stanza: Cosmic Creation—Multitude and Diversity

63   How many are your deeds,
64   Though hidden from sight,
65   O Sole God beside whom there is none!

66   You made the earth following your heart when you were
       alone,
67   With people, herds, and flocks;
68   All upon earth that walks on legs,
69   All on high that fly on wings,
70   The foreign lands of Syria and Nubia,
71   The land of Egypt.

72 You set every man in his place, you supply his needs;
73 Everyone has his food, his lifetime is counted.

74 Their tongues differ in speech,
75 Their characters likewise;
76 Their skins are distinct, for you distinguished the people.

Third Stanza: The Two Niles

77 You made the Nile in the netherworld,
78 You bring him when you will,
79 To nourish the people, for you made them for yourself.
80 Lord of all, who toils for them,
81 Lord of all lands who shines for them,
82 Sundisk of daytime, great in glory!

83 All distant lands, you keep them alive:
84 You made a heavenly Nile descend for them;
85 He makes waves on the mountains like the sea,
86 To drench their fields with what they need.

87 How efficient are your plans, O Lord of eternity!
88 A Nile from heaven for foreign peoples
89 And for the creatures in the desert that walk on legs,
90 But for Egypt the Nile who comes from the netherworld.

THIRD SONG: TRANSFORMATIONS [KHEPERU]—GOD, NATURE, AND THE KING.

First Stanza: Light—Seeing and Knowing

(a) The Seasons

91 Your rays nurse all fields,
92 When you shine, they live and grow for you.
93 You made the seasons to foster all that you made,
94 Winter, to cool them,
95 Summer, that they taste you.

(b) Kheperu in Heaven and on Earth

96   You made the *sky* far to shine therein,
97   To *see* all that you make, while you are *One*,
98   Risen in your *form* [*kheperu*] of the living *sundisk*,
99   Shining and radiant,
100 Far and near.

101 You make millions of *forms* [*kheperu*] from yourself *alone*,
102 Towns, villages, fields,
103 Road and river.
104 All eyes *behold* you upon them,
105 When you are above the *earth* as the *disk* of daytime.

(c) The king, the unique knower

106 When you are gone there is no eye (whose eyesight you have created
107 in order not to *look* upon yourself as the *sole* one of your creatures),
108 But even then you are in my heart, there is no other who knows you,
109 *Only* your son, *Nefer-kheperu-Re Sole-one-of-Re*,
110 Whom you have taught your ways and your might.

Second Stanza: Time—Acting and Ruling

111 The earth comes into being by your hand as you made it,
112 When you *dawn*, they live,
113 When you *set* they die;
114 You yourself are lifetime, one lives by you.

115 All eyes are on beauty until you *set*,
116 All labor ceases when you *rest* in the west;
117 But the *rising* one makes firm [every arm] for the king,
118 And every leg moves since you founded the earth.

119 You rouse them for your son who came from your body,
120 The king who lives by Ma'at, the lord of the two lands,
121 *Nefer-kheperu-Re, Sole-one of Re*,
122 The Son of Re who lives by Ma'at,

123   The lord of crowns, *Akhenaten*, great in his lifetime,
124   And the great Queen whom he loves,
125   The lady of the Two Lands *Nefertiti*,
126   Who lives and rejuvenates
127   For ever, eternally.[16]

I propose a division of this long text into three parts of approximately equal length. Beneath its surface structure as a hymn I discern the outlines of three treatises, the first on visibility, the second on creation, and the third on energy.

Visibility

The first part is a transformation of that section of a traditional hymn to the sun god that describes the daily solar circuit in its three phases of morning, noon, and evening/night *(Tageszeitenlied)*.

Before analyzing this first part, let me describe how this subject is treated in a traditional solar hymn. The subject is not, as one might assume, simply the sun god, his theology or mythology, but a very complex cosmic drama (wherein the sun god simply plays the central role). The Egyptians traditionally conceived of the world not in terms of spatial structure, but in terms of action and process. In their view, the cosmos is a cyclic process.[17] Its order and structure unfolds over time: in the regularity of cyclical repetition and in the vigor of reasserted cosmic life. Every morning, indeed every moment, life triumphs over the counteracting forces of death, dissolution, and cessation. The imagery of Egyptian cosmological conceptualization dramatically unfolds into images of motion, conflict, and triumph. The cosmic drama is interpreted in biological, ethical, and political terms: it is viewed as a process of life triumphant over death and rule and justice triumphant over rebellion. Life, rule, and justice, as well as death, rebellion, and injustice, are constantly associated. The cosmic drama is interpreted by this analogical imagination in a way that reflects the fundamentals of human life: social justice and harmony, political order and authority, and individual hopes for health, prosperity, and—above all—life after death. It is this interpenetration of the cosmic, the sociopolitical, and the individual that lends this world-view and interpretation of reality the character of truth, and of natural evidence.[18]

In the traditional hymns to the sun, the cosmic process is represented in a form which I have called, in German, *Tageszeitenlied*, the "song of the three times of day."[19] The traditional morning stanza focuses on "life." The sun is praised as a living being, reborn, and at the same time spontaneously reemerging within the constellations of birth-giving and life-sustaining deities.

Turning to the Amarna texts, we find that these mythical images of regenerating life have been transformed into concepts of transitive-active life-giving.[20] The sun is the god of life who, from his own inexhaustible plenitude of life, assigns a portion to everything in existence. The term has a specifically temporal meaning. It refers to a temporally defined portion of life.[21] The "Shorter Hymn to the Aten" is a bit more explicit about this concept of an allocation of individual lives out of the One source of cosmic life:

> You are the One yet a million lives are in you,
> To make them live. The sight of your rays
> Is breath of life to their noses.[22]

The abstract notion of time is conceived of in the concrete terms of light and air.[23] From the rays of the rising sun life is absorbed every day by all creatures. The traditional imagery of the living god—reliving and rejuvenating his life daily within the constellations of the divine world— is transformed into the concept of the life-giving god who is neither included nor embedded in divine interaction, but who confronts the world from high above and sends from there his life-giving rays into the world.[24] The same transformation from constellational intransitivity to confrontational transitivity applies to the second stanza, devoted to the second phase of the circuit: noon. This stanza traditionally focuses on the topic of rule. The motion of the sun over the sky is interpreted as the exercise of rule and justice. In the traditional, "constellational" view of the solar circuit, this phase assumes the form of a triumphant victory of the sun god and his companions over Apophis, a water dragon and the personification of evil on the cosmic plane. In a typically Egyptian way, this conflict is more characteristic of a lawsuit than of a physical combat.[25]

In Akhenaten's hymn this mythical image is transformed: the rays of the sun embrace all lands and bend them to the submission of the king, a change which obviously translates an imperialistic concept of universal rule into cosmic imagery. The political significance of the noon phase is retained. But again, instead of a relationship between heavenly and earthly, and cosmic and political action, we have the direct transitive subject-object relation between the god and the earthly political sphere. This is not just a variation on a theme, but a fundamental change which affects the central Egyptian concepts of kingship, state, and political action.

The elimination of the cosmic foe turns the traditional dualistic world-view into a monistic one. Traditionally, both the cosmic and the political processes are based upon, and shaped by, the idea of a conflict between good and evil, rule and rebellion, motion and arrest, continuity and rupture, coherence and dissolution, light and darkness, justice and injustice, and also life and death. It is a whole universe of meaning which is discarded with the elimination of the cosmic foe. The "lands" which the sun "embraces" and "bends to submission" for the king are, of course, not enemies in a political sense—they have lost their political meaning. In the light of the sun, all political boundaries disappear because the sun shines over Egyptians and non-Egyptians alike, as well as over good and evil. The abolition of the cosmic foe amounts to a depolarization of the cosmos, which is reflected in the human sphere by a depoliticalization of society.[26]

The third stanza, devoted to the night, is perhaps the most revolutionary of all. Here, we meet with one of those negations which had a crucial importance for Freud: the negation of the netherworld, the realm of Osiris and of the dead. Traditionally, sunset and night are interpreted as the descent of the sun god into the netherworld to give life to the dead and to provide for their well-being.[27] Just as the idea of political welfare rests on the myth of the triumph over Apophis, the hopes for life after death rest upon the myth of the nocturnal overcoming of death. In the Amarna hymns there is scarcely any mention of the netherworldly realm of the death.[28] In Akhenaten's world, reality is restructured from the point of view of the human eye. In the traditional representations of the cosmic process, the observing eye was systematically excluded. The cosmic process was conveyed by the traditional mythical imagery, not from "far below," but from "within." The texts depict divine actions and constellations, and the topography of that world which no human eye has ever seen. They describe not visible reality but its inner mythical meaning. It is not just the visible, but the intelligible world that counts as reality.[29] In Amarna, by contrast, reality is reduced to the visible, to the here and now of a human observer. Seen from this point of view, the night appears simply as darkness. Darkness means the absence of light, of divine presence and of life. In the night, when the sun withholds its emission of life, the world relapses into death and chaos: robbers rob, lions rove, serpents bite. There is no Egyptian text, outside Amarna, that depicts the night as divine absence.[30] The closest parallel to this vision of the night is found in a Biblical text, Psalm 104:20–23, where we read:

> Thou makest darkness and it is night;
> When all the beasts of the forest do creep forth,
> The young lions roar after their prey
> And seek their food from God.
> The sun rises, they shrink away and lay them down in their dens.
> Man goes forth to his work and to his labour until the eve-
>   ning.[31]

The fourth stanza depicts the reawakened life in the morning in no less than twenty-one lines. Obviously, the restriction to the visible world is to be felt not as a limitation, but as an enormous amplification and enrichment. What is striking about this stanza is its fondness for detail and its enraptured contemplation of visible reality. After four introductory lines, four more are devoted to the awakening of human beings who rise, wash, dress, and go to work. The following seven lines refer to the beasts of the earth and the sky and another six lines refer to aquatic creatures and the ships that appear alongside the fish. The same allocation of ships and fishes—as inhabitants of the sea—occurs in Psalm 104:26:

> So is this great and wide sea, wherein are creeping things
> Innumerable, both small and great beasts;
> There go the ships, there are the dolphins,
> Whom thou hast made to play therein.

Behind the minuteness of detail and the enraptured tone of devoted description one senses a peculiar theological concern. What could be the theological significance of the requickening of nature in the morning? Lines 30 and 35, which are closely parallel, give a hint. The birds greet the light with their wings as do the men with their hands. The revival of nature is one song of praise. The praise of God is no exclusive

human privilege; it is shared with all other creatures. In the corresponding stanza of the "Shorter Hymn," human beings are totally absent:

> All flowers exist, what lives and sprouts from the soil,
> Grows when you shine, drunken by your sight.
> All flocks jump on their feet,
> The birds in their nests fly up in joy,
> Their folded wings unfold in praise
> Of the living Aten, their maker.[32]

The returning presence of the divine, which again fills the world with
light and time, is greeted and answered by the sheer reawakening of
nature. Life and existence itself acquire religious meaning. To exist
means to adore, to acknowledge the creative workings of light and time.
The flowers which turn themselves toward the light[33] and adore God's
indwelling presence in sheer vegetative receptivity become the model
of piety and devotion.[34] There are texts, those of seventeenth-century
German Protestant mysticism, in which exactly the same concept of
vegetative religiosity is found. It is expressed in words which could be
translated from Amarna hymns; consider, for example, Gerhard Ter-
steegen's song "Die Gegenwärtigkeit Gottes in der Natur" ("The Presence of God in Nature") which starts with the proclamation "Gott ist
gegenwärtig!" ("God is present"). In this song we read

> Wie die zarten Blumen
> Willig sich entfalten
> Und der Sonne stille halten,
> Lass mich so,
> Still und froh,
> Deine Strahlen fassen
> Und dich wirken lassen.[35]

But what is only a symbol and a simile in the context of Christian
pietism is literally meant as reality in the context of Amarna religion.
God is not "like" the rays of the sun; he "is" the rays of the sun.

❀ LET ME summarize my analysis of the first part. Its most striking
feature is the complete or, rather, the iconoclastic abolition of mythical

imagery, in particular of the cosmic foe and the realm of the dead. The cosmic foe had given to the solar circuit the political meaning of power, rule, and justice while the *descensus* myth had given night the meaning of salvation, of life after death. Instead of meaning we are given the beauty and the richly detailed variety of the visible world as the effect of the divine light. Mythical imagery is replaced by visible reality; the mythical concept of meaning is replaced by a physical concept of function and causality.

Creation

The second part of Akhenaten's hymn is devoted to the theme of creation. Usually, this theme refers to what in traditional language is called "the first time" *(zp tpj)* which corresponds to the Hebrew *be-re-shit,* "in the beginning," the primordial time of origin. This reference is eliminated by Akhenaten, whose world-view is structured by the sensual apprehension of reality.

Visibility is in the dimension of light (or space), which the present is in the dimension of time. Past and future give way to eternal presence much in the same way as the mythical imagery of heaven and the underworld give way to the visible reality. There is no reference to primordial creation and cosmogony in the Amarna texts.[36] But how can the author speak of creation when he restricts himself to the present? Akhenaten's solution to this problem is as ingenious as it is innovative. Instead of cosmogony he deals with embryology. This is the subject of the first song of the second part. The second song celebrates what could be called the well-structured or well-arranged nature of the world in its present, apprehensible form.

The growth of the seed in the womb and of the chicken in the egg reveals "time" as the other aspect of that creative energy which flows from the sun into the world. The workings of time transcend the visible sphere; they are "hidden from sight" (l. 64) and closer to air than to light. Thus the notions of breath, air, and time are closely linked in this embryology.

🍥 THE IDEA of a divine breath of life vivifying the embryo in the womb occurs as early as in the "Coffin Texts" of the Middle Kingdom, where it is said of Shu, the god of the air, that "he knows how to vivify the one who is in the egg."[37] The hymn of Suty and Hor, the most important text of pre-Amarna "New Solar Theology," calls the sun god "Khnum and Amun of mankind."[38] According to traditional beliefs, Khnum is the god who forms the child in the womb, and Amun is the one who endows the child with the breath of life.[39] In an older hymn, Amun appears as "the one who gives air to him who is in the egg."[40] This traditional formula of emblematic concinnity is transformed in the "Great Hymn" into a whole treatise on embryology. In two stanzas it demonstrates the growth of the child in the womb and of the chicken in the egg, correlating the two parts by the symmetrically arranged key words "to vivify" (ll. 47 and 57) and "to come forth" (ll. 52 and 60). They refer to "breath" and "time" as the two forms in which the creative energy of the sun manifests itself beyond the realm of visibility.[41]

🌸 The second song passes from micro- to macrocosmos and praises the well-arranged nature of the world, whose inhabitants are carefully divided into separate kinds living in the air, in the water, and upon the earth. Humankind is also divided into different peoples, who are set apart in respect of language, character, and color.[42] Every kind is plentifully provided for, by the sun which shines upon them all and by the water which the sun brings forth from the earth for Egypt in the form of the Nile and for distant countries from the sky in the form of rain.[43]

In its cosmopolitan and universalistic scope, this view of the world corresponds to the political experience of the Late Bronze Age, as had been noted by Breasted and rightly stressed by his attentive readers, such as Thomas Mann and Sigmund Freud. Now, for the first time in history, there evolved the idea of an ecumene, a world inhabited by many different nations stretching to the end of the earth and interconnected by political and commercial ties.[44] The very possibility of something like international law forced Egypt to give up its traditional self-image as an ordered universe surrounded by chaos and to extend the notion of a divinely ordered creation to the limits of the ecumene.

🌸 Multiplicity and order characterized the divine wisdom of creation. Two exclamations—"how many!" and "how excellent!" (or "sophisticated")—convey these two characteristics. They recur in Psalm 104 as

> How manifold are thy works!
> In wisdom hast thou made them all.

If we ask for what is significantly absent—or rejected and negated—in this second part of the hymn, we find the concept of primordial time. In the same way as the first part abolishes the mythical imagery of the not-here, that is, the images of heaven and the underworld, the second part abolishes the images of the not-now: that method of mythical ontology which Kenneth Burke called "the temporizing of essence."[45] Not-here and not-now are the two dimensions of mythical imagination or image-making through which *homo interpres* bestows meaning to the universe. Again, function replaces meaning, and explanation replaces interpretation, reducing the multiplicity of visible reality to one under-lying principle of cosmic energy. The mythical theme of creation is transformed into a physiological treatise on embryology and ecology, that is, an appraisal of the creative energies of the sun in its micro- and macrocosmic functions.

Kheperu: Creative and Transformative Energy

The third part of the hymn is centered on one Egyptian word, *ḫpr*, "to become." It is a theory of becoming. At the same time it is a treatise on the relationship between God and world. The visible world is shown to be nothing but a "becoming": a transformation[46] of God himself. The relation between God and the world is neither that of the traditional Egyptian hymns mirroring divine order and social order, nor that of Hebrew monotheism drawing a sharp distinction between creator and creation. In Amarna, God and the world are much more intimately interlocked by God's being identified as the source of energy which maintains the world by "becoming" the world, in a process of constant self-transformation.[47]

In the Egyptian language, *ḫpr* "to become, to come into being, to develop" is the antonym of *wnn*, "to exist, to persist." *Hpr* is associated with the god Khepre, the morning sun, the principle of autogenetic energy. By contrast, *wnn* is associated with the god *Wnn-nfr*, "who exists in completion," Osiris, the god of the dead, the principle of unalterable duration. We are confronting here the famous dichotomy of *nḥḥ* and *dt*, time happening and time persisting, cyclical and linear time, "imperfective" and "perfective" time.[48] It is quite consistent with the hymn's equation of the visible world with *ḫprw* that the god himself is called *Nḥḥ* in the Amarna texts. God is time *(Nḥḥ)*, and everything unfolding, "developing" in time *(ḫpr)* is a transformation *(ḫprw)* of his essence or energy.

Lines 96–100 deal with the celestial transformation of God, the sun, while lines 101–105 deal with his terrestrial transformations.[49] These appear to be nothing other than the millionfold reality of the visible world itself: towns and villages, fields, roads, and rivers, the world of habitation and traffic. The two parts of this bipartite world are inter-connected not only by the notion of "becoming"—everything, includ-ing the sun itself, emanates from God—but also by the notion of *seeing*. In the form of the sun, God *sees* millions of his earthly transformations, and he has made the sky high in order to overlook the whole earth.[50] In the same way, he can be seen by all living creatures at the same time and at an equal distance. "Every eye sees you in front of itself."[51] From line 121 we learn that God creates the eyes in order that they might look on him as he looks on them, and that his look might be returned and that light might assume a communicative meaning, uniting every-thing existing in a common space of intervision. God and men com-mune in light.[52] This interpretation of the world as a sphere not just of visibility, but of intervision, gives it a communicative character that includes a relation of response and reciprocity.

❀ By SEEING the light, that is, God, the eye is created; therefore seeing is the sense of divine communication. The light creates every-thing, but in addition to this general creation it "creates eyes for every creature":

Your light makes eyes for everything that you create.[53]

In his *Farbenlehre*, Goethe expresses a strikingly similar thought. "The eye," he writes, "owes its existence to the light": "Das Auge hat sein Dasein dem Licht zu danken. Aus gleichgiltigen tierischen Hilfsor-ganen ruft sich das Licht ein Organ hervor, das seinesgleichen werde, damit das innere Licht dem äusseren entgegentrete."[54] In this context Goethe quotes his famous verse version of a passage from Plotinus, who had taken up Plato's parable of the cave and his idea of the "sunlike" eye *(helio-eides)*.[55]

The first song of this third part deals with the "becomings" of God in their spatial dimension of light: heaven and earth, sun and eye, connected by intervision. The second song deals with their temporal dimension. As time, the divine energy operates in the rhythm of night and day, thus in an interrupted, discontinuous mode, and exposes the creatures in their absolute dependence on light and time to an equally discontinuous mode of existence. In these verses the hymn reaches its apex of clarity and radicality:

> The world becomes on your hand as you make them;
> When you dawn, they live,
> When you set, they die.
> You yourself are lifetime; one lives by you.[56]

The time which the sun produces by its rising and setting forms as close a link as the light between God and world. God and world commune in time as they commune in light. Time is divine cosmic energy *and* individual lifetime.[57] The lifetime of the individual is created by the motion of the sun just as the light is created by its radiation. But motion and radiation, and with it light, time, and life, stop during the night. The night is an interval of death.

But the theme of the third part is not the relation of God and the world; this is rather the subject of the first two parts. Here, a third entity is introduced, by which the bipolar structure of reality is extended into a tripolar one: the king.

The king is already implied in the semantics of the word *ḫprw*, "becoming." Almost every king of the Eighteenth Dynasty, among them Akhenaten himself, chooses as his throne name a statement about the *ḫprw* of the sun god. These names are statements about the visible reality which the king proclaims to be a manifestation of Re, and to be "great," "firm," "beautiful," and so on. They are statements about the god who constantly creates the world by "becoming" the world, about the world, which constantly unfolds the divine energies, and about the king, who rules over the world in its sun-created entirety. God, world, and king are the conceptual triad on which this third part of the hymn is based.

Explicitly, the king appears first in the third song (ll. 106–110) in a sentence which is so difficult that most translators have given up trying to render it at all.[58] But I think the sense conveyed is of a striking simplicity. I translate it in the following way:

> When you have gone and there is no eye, whose eyesight you
>   have created
> In order not to be compelled to look at your[self as] the sole
>   one of creation,
> you are in my heart.
> There is no other who knows you,
> Only your son Nefer-kheperu-Ra Sole-one-of-Ra,
> Whom you have taught your ways and your might.[59]

These lines draw a sharp distinction between seeing and knowing. Seeing is exposed to the rhythm of night and day; knowledge establishes a permanent relationship. In a world constantly alternating between life and death, presence and absence of divine energy, the heart of the king is the only point of permanence and stability.

THE DISSOCIATION of seeing and knowing had already occurred in the first part of the hymn, where it is said:

> Though you are far, your rays are on earth;
> Though one sees you, nobody knows your "going."[60]

"Going" has the connotation of "departing" or "passing away"[61] and refers not only to the hiddenness of the ways of the sun to mortal eyes, but also to its disappearance from human sight during the night. Knowledge, which is limited to seeing, ceases at night. In a very fragmentary early text on a *"talatat"* from Karnak, Donald Redford has been able to decipher the following traces:

> [(Aten) . . . who himself gave birth] to himself,
> and no one knows the mystery of [. . .]

he [go]es where he pleases, and they know not [his] g[oing . . .]
[. . .] to him [?] by [?] night,
but I approach [. . .][62]

The text is tantalizingly mutilated, but one thing is clear: we are dealing here with the same idea of god being hidden to mortal understanding, but accessible to the king, even at night. This dissociation of seeing and knowing makes it perfectly clear that there is no meaning to visible reality. God is revealed to the eye, but concealed to the heart, except to the heart of the king.

This is the exact inversion of traditional convictions. The religion of the New Kingdom develops the notion of "taking God into one's heart" as a central idea.[63] This means knowledge of God, which is required of everybody. But *seeing* God is the privilege only of the dead, who are believed to meet the gods face to face in the hereafter. In Amarna, knowledge of God becomes the monopoly of the king, whereas the ability to see God is extended to everybody. Only the understanding heart of the king is also able to see, in the emission of light and time, an emission of meaning. Only for him does cosmic energy assume personal traits and does emission come to mean revelation: "you taught him your ways and your might."[64]

WE ARE now able to reconstruct the initial insight or "revelation" which induced Akhenaten to abolish traditional polytheism and to found a new religion based on the idea of divine unity and uniqueness. It was the discovery that not only light, but also time is to be explained as manifestations of solar energy.[65] With this discovery, *everything* could be explained as workings, "emanations," or "becomings" of the sun. In this system, the concept of "One" has not a theological but a physical meaning: the One is the source of cosmic existence. There are no other sources besides this One, and everything can be reduced and related to it.

But a new concept of God, and a new religion, can never emerge as the result of *explanation*. What Akhenaten actually discovered, what he was probably the first to discover, and what he certainly experienced himself as a revelation, was a concept of *nature*.[66] With regard to the Divine, his message is essentially negative: God is *nothing else than* the sun, and he is also nature.

Let me here interrupt this line of argument for a moment to consider an objection that naturally arises. Is it really true that Akhenaten's "nature" is void of meaning? The hymn has an unmistakably anthropocentric ring in its attribution of a benevolent intention to the workings of light and time, which even assume the character of loving labor:

> Their Lord of all, who toils for them;
> Lord of all lands, who shines for them.[67]

Where there is intention, there is also meaning. The cosmic process is stripped of its anthropomorphic significance, but is nevertheless not indifferent to man. To the contrary: the less anthropo*morphic* its interpretation, the more anthropo*centric* its meaning. Man is *intended or "meant"* by that cosmic performance and he may read the signs of parental love in the cosmos. "You are the mother and father of all that you make."[68]

It is true that the Amarna hymns are obsessively repetitive in stating that all the sun does it does "for them,"[69] but at the end of the "Great Hymn" all this is related to the king as the ultimate goal of creation, so that the anthropocentric perspective is transformed into a pharaocentric one in the end. It is true that the sun rises to vivify the world, but it is for the sake of the king that the sun vivifies it. The king is the one who is ultimately "meant" by the cosmic process and he is the only one for whom it has meaning. Meaning, in this world, is something between God and king, not anything shared by the people.

Yet meaning is a social phenomenon; so is religion, and so is God. Saying that meaning is only accessible to the understanding heart of the king amounts to saying that there is no meaning at all. Explanation replaces interpretation. The more there is that can be explained, the less there is to interpret. Thus we may perhaps say that, instead of founding a new religion, Akhenaten was the first to find a way out of religion. His negative revelation went far beyond the disillusionment which Warburton, Reinhold, and Schiller attributed to the last stage of initiation. He rejected not only the polytheistic pantheon but even the theistic idea of a personal god. There is nothing but nature.

Akhenaten's explanation of the world as nature is above all an act of iconoclastic destruction: of negating its religious significance. The negativity of Akhenaten's revelation becomes clear when it is viewed against the background of traditional Egyptian religion. The traditional world is not "nature" because it is not natural. It is not natural because:

1. It cannot be left alone. Its "natural" tendency is toward chaos, entropy, dissolution, and cessation. It has to be constantly maintained by cultural efforts.

2. It is dualistic in character. Or rather, it is ambiguous and has to be constantly disambiguated by the imposition of moral distinctions. Only in the light of this moral distinction between good and evil, good and bad, just and unjust, truth and falsehood does the world become habitable and meaningful.[70]

3. The moral sphere which gods and men cooperate to institute and maintain prevails over "natural" distinctions. Justice may overcome death. The forces of order which vanquish darkness, dissolution, and arrest are able to defeat illness, suffering, and death.[71]

4. In the light of religious interpretation the world is structured not only by intervision, but also by interlocution. The gods listen and can be spoken to. The sun god looks down from the sky, but he also hears the cries of the oppressed:

> who hears the supplications of the oppressed,
> whose heart inclines toward him who calls unto him,
> who rescues the fearful from the hand of the violent,
> who judges between the poor and the rich.[72]

Language and interlocution construct the world as moral space.[73] Nature itself is amoral. Freud was astonishingly blind to this amoral aspect of Amarna religion. Instead, he stressed its strongly ethical character, which he based on an epithet of the king who called himself "living on truth/justice." But it is very important to recognize that, in the context of Amarna religion, this traditional epithet of the sun god is transferred to the king. "Living on truth" relates not to the god-man relationship, but to the king-subject relationship. The epithet is transferred from the realm of religion to the realm of loyalism. God is no longer the embodiment of ethical demands because this idea cannot be reconciled with Akhenaten's strictly natural and heliomorphic concept.

Only by eliminating these dimensions of signification, by means of a radical demystification, demythologization, dedivinization, depolarization, depoliticalization, and demoralization is Akhenaten able to demonstrate the "natural" character of reality. It is therefore essentially negative. But it is precisely this "natural," dedivinized, and desemioticized character of the world which made Akhenaten's depiction of it—at least in some aspects—acceptable for a Biblical psalm. It remains a mystery as to how Sigmund Freud could have overlooked the fact that parts of Akhenaten's hymn found their way into Psalm 104, since this had been stressed both by Arthur Weigall and James Henry Breasted, his two Egyptological sources, and would have lent much support to his own thesis.[74]

The negativity of Akhenaten's revelation finds its most poignant expression at the beginning of the last stanza in lines 111–114:

> The world becomes on your hand, as you made them;
> When you dawn, they live,
> When you set, they die;
> You yourself are lifetime, one lives by you.

The gist of this passage is the idea of the world's absolute dependence on the sun. It has no life of its own. All life comes from the sun. This is what Akhenaten's antipolytheism means. Further, it means denying the world its own sources of life, meaning, power, and order, which means for the Egyptians the world's own divinity. In this view, the world becomes disenchanted, it becomes mere "nature."

In Psalm 104:29–30 the same idea of the world's dependency on God's periodic introjection of life is reformulated as:

> Thou hidest thy face: they are troubled;
> Thou takest away "their" [read: thy][75] breath: they die and return to their dust;

Thou sendest forth thy breath: they are created
And thou renewest the face of the earth.

In this case, there might be the possibility of reconstructing the way
in which a passage from Akhenaten's hymn could have found its way
into a Biblical psalm. In a letter which the king of Tyre, Abumilki,
wrote to Akhenaten, he politely refers to the sun god, the king's father,
in words which William Moran, relying on an article by Comelia
Grave,[76] renders as:

. . . qui accorde la vie par son doux souffle
et revient avec son vent du nord.[77]

It seems evident to me that the idea of God's intermittent introjection of life into the world is common both to the psalm and to the
Egyptian hymn. The "sweet breath," which appears in the Bible as
ruach, is a common Egyptian metaphor for both time and light. "The
sight of your rays," we read in the "Shorter Hymn," "is the breath of
life in their noses."[78]

Transplanted into a Biblical context, Akhenaten's concept of nature
again becomes charged with religious significance. Here, God is not
reduced to cosmic energy and meaning, is not focused in a pharaocentric perspective. Pharaoh's absence makes nature again readable,
namely in a theocentric light. Reading nature leads to the knowledge
of the Lord and to the recognition of his glory.[79]

The World as Creation and as Manifestation of God

In this section I answer the questions Ralph Cudworth addressed to
Ancient Egypt three hundred years ago.[80] In his day, Egypt was not yet
able to answer these questions in its own voice because the knowledge
of the hieroglyphic script had been forgotten. Cudworth had to rely on
interpreters of more or less dubious credibility. In our time, when the
Egyptian texts have begun to be readable, Cudworth's questions have
fallen into oblivion. What was it that he wanted to know about Egypt?
My reconstruction of the discourse on Moses and Egypt has attempted
to retrieve the memory and the relevance of these questions. Let me

now turn to the Egyptian sources and look for any passages that could have satisfied Cudworth's quest for *Hen kai pan*.

Hen kai pan is a statement about the relation between God and the world. It amounts to an equation in the same sense as Spinoza's *deus sive natura*. Statements about the relation between God and the world abound in Egyptian texts. I shall focus on those that speak of God as the "One" and shall analyze the form of relationship which they establish between the One and the world. In the seventeenth century, there were two ways of conceiving this relationship. The one which conceived of this relation in terms of creation, generation, or origination was generally deemed acceptable to orthodox Jewish or Christian theology. The other, which conceived of this relation in terms of manifestation, transformation, or emanation, was deemed heretical and was associated with terms such as pantheism, materialism, and even atheism. My thesis is that this same duality had already been present in Ramesside Egypt. It was only during the preparation of this book that I became aware that some terms which I believed I had coined to characterize the specificity of Ramesside theology, such as "cosmotheism"[81] or *die Weltwerdung Gottes* ("the cosmogenesis of God"),[82] had in fact been used in the seventeenth and eighteenth centuries. In Egypt, however, this duality was not antagonistic or controversial, because there was neither orthodoxy nor heresy. The two paradigms interacted and interfused in various ways without any signs of confrontation or conflict.

Time and again the Egyptian sources predicate the oneness/singleness/uniqueness of a god. Amun-Re in particular is regarded as a solar deity who develops his all-embracing creative and life-giving efficacy in the form of the sun. In the context of traditional Amun-Re religion this unifying and centralizing view focuses on the problems of life. Further, it answers the question of where all life comes from and which forces are effective in the emergence, preservation, and continuation of life. In this tradition, the postulate of the oneness of god does not exclude the existence of other gods. In contrast to the Amarna texts, the texts referring to Amun-Re constantly mention the gods. They appear not as individuals with their own names, but collectively. As a result, they do not enter a constellation with the "one god." Instead, they are his counterparts, along with other living creatures, such as humans, animals, and even plants. In all contexts that mention the oneness of god, the *one* god transcends the constellations and spheres of the divine world. This phenomenon might have been responsible for the Classical idea that the polytheistic structure of Egyptian religion is a sort of façade concealing a basic monotheism.

The oneness of Amun, which by no means denies the existence of the other gods, is based on the fact that he is

1. the primeval god, who existed before the entire world;
2. the creator, who transformed the world from the primeval condition into the cosmos;
3. the life god, who gives life and spirit to the world in the form of the three life-giving elements;
4. the sun god, who completes his journey alone and illuminates and guards the world with his eyes;
5. the ruler god, who exercises rule over his creation and is represented by the king on earth;
6. the ethical authority, who watches over right and wrong, the "vizier of the poor,"[83] the judge and savior, the lord of time, "favor,"[84] and fate;
7. the hidden god, whose symbols, images, and names are the many gods.

It is this last aspect of Amun's Oneness that is of particular interest here because it is so closely related to the idea of esoteric monotheism and the "god of the mysteries." It plays a very prominent role in the "paradigm of manifestation." Yet the concept of hiddenness is also important in the "paradigm of creation." There, it is associated with the "self-generated" primeval god (1), who has no parents or other witnesses of his birth that know his name. The "anonymity" of this god is certainly the oldest and most prominent characteristic of his hiddenness.[85] He appears in the "Pyramid Texts" (ca. 2500 B.C.E.) as "the great god, whose name is not known."[86] The well-known myth of the Cunning of Isis, which has survived in the form of a magical spell, lends this idea of the creator and sun god as an "anonymous" primeval god the inconsistent and somewhat burlesque form typical of Egyptian stories.[87] This concept of an anonymous god, rooted in a beginning not witnessed by anyone, was adopted from solar theology by Amun-Re theology in the Ramesside period. One reason is undoubtedly the word play between the name of Amun *Jmn* (Amun = the Hidden One) and the epithet of the sun god *Jmn rn.f* ("Hidden of Name"). But the main reason is that this concept of hiddenness, unlike all the others, is associated with the concept of oneness by definition:

> The one who initiated the emergence at the beginning,
> Amun, who emerged at the beginning, whose origin is not known,
> Who was not preceded by any god.
> There was no other god with him, who could say what he
>   looked like.
> He had no mother who created his name.
> He had no father to beget him or to say, "He is my flesh and
>   blood."88
> Who formed his own egg,
> Power of secret birth, who created his beauty.
> Most divine god, who came into being alone,
> Every god came into being after he had begun himself.89

> You have no father who created you,90
> You were not sent into the body of a woman.
> No Khnum formed [your body].
> Neither your form nor nature is known.
> Hearts long to know you,
> People drill [into the depth], stretch [into the height] and grow
>   weary [in seeking you in vain]—
> You are [too] great and exalted,
> Firm and wide-ranging,
> Strong and powerful.91

The concept of a god "whose birth is secret";92 "whose place of origin is not known";93 whose birth is not witnessed, but (and this is crucial) who keeps the secret of his nature concealed from all who are born after him: "who formed himself and kept himself hidden from gods and humans"94—this concept became a central theme of Ramesside theology. In the context of Amun-Re theology, which developed and privileged the paradigm of manifestation, the idea of the hiddenness and oneness of the primeval god underwent a change of meaning. The temporal relationship between preexistence and existence was transformed into an ontological one.95 In the paradigm of manifestation, the Hidden One inhabits an ontological Beyond, but not a temporal Beyond. This concept of divine transcendence is most clearly expressed in Hymn 200 of the "Leiden Amun Hymn":

> Secret of transformations and sparkling of appearances,
> Marvelous god, rich in forms!
> All gods boast of him
> To make themselves greater with his beauty to the extent of his
>   divinity.
>
> Re himself is united with his body.
> He is the Great One in Heliopolis.
> He is called Tatenen/Amun, who comes out of the primeval wa-
>   ters to lead the "faces."
>
> Another of his forms is the Ogdoad.
> Primeval one of the primeval ones, begetter of Re.
> He completed himself as Atum, being of one body with him.
> He is Universal Lord, who initiated that which exists.
>
> His *ba*, it is said, is the one who is in heaven;
> It is he, the one who is in the underworld, who rules the east.
> His *ba* is in heaven, his body in the west,
> His image is in southern Heliopolis and wears his diadem.
>
> One is Amun, who keeps himself concealed from them,
> Who hides himself from the gods, no one knowing his nature.
> He is more remote than heaven,
> He is deeper than the underworld.
>
> None of the gods knows his true form;
> His image is not unfolded in books;
> Nothing certain is testified about him.
>
> He is too secretive for his majesty to be revealed;
> He is too great to be inquired after,
> Too powerful to be known.
>
> People fall down immediately for fear

That his name will be uttered knowingly or unknowingly.
There is no god able to call him by it.
He is *ba*-like, hidden of name like his secrecy.[96]

The form of this magnificent hymn is comparable to that of a sonnet: its bipartite division into two unequal halves (8/8 and 7/7) is based on an antithesis of thought, a change of aspect. The first part is a piece of "affirmative theology" which describes how the god is manifested on earth in the other gods. The second part is a piece of "negative theology" which reads like a revocation of all the theological scholarship displayed and developed in the first part. The subject of this first part was not the One, but the many gods who reflect his nature in the world. Amun of Thebes also belongs there. Not only is the "one Amun" hidden "from them," he is absolutely hidden. No statement about him is possible. He is still beyond heaven and the underworld, the holy and the otherworldly regions of the world. He is hidden from the gods, who reflect his unfathomable nature in this remote sphere. He is even more hidden from humans. The scriptures give no information about him. He cannot be explained by any theory. The final stanza clearly expresses the concept of the Ineffable God and associates it with the two significant epithets "having the quality of *ba*" and "he who keeps his name hidden." The two epithets belong together. The god is called *ba* because there is no name for him. His hidden all-embracing abundance of essence cannot be apprehended. "Amun" is merely a pseudonym used to refer to the god in the cosmic sphere of manifestation. Basically, every divine name is a name of the hidden one, but the term *ba* is used when the hidden one behind the multitude of manifestations is meant. *Ba* is the key concept of the "paradigm of manifestation" as opposed to the "paradigm of creation." We translate the Egyptian term *ba* conventionally as "soul." This yields the idea that for the Egyptians the visible world has a "soul" that animates and moves it, just as it did for the Neoplatonists, who believed in the *anima mundi*. The parallel is not altogether artificial. I think that there are strong connections between the Egyptian and Platonic concepts of a cosmic "soul."

In the paradigm of manifestation, the relationship between the one and the many is "detemporalized." In "becoming" the world, God is still God. This is also what the hymn contends. The one is not regarded as the primeval god *before* the many, whose unity becomes plurality in creation, but as the one *in* the many, a hidden power called *ba*, which assumes form in the many gods and makes them into gods. But far from being a sort of "mana" or abstract principle, it is a personal nature that transcends all knowledge and speculation.

A hymn of Ramesses III to Amun-Re does not address the god by name, but begins as follows:

> I will begin to say his greatness as lord of the gods,
> As *ba* with secret faces, great of majesty;
> Who hides his name and conceals his image,
> Whose form was not known at the beginning.[97]

In the verses that follow, the hymn develops the theory of the life-giving elements, such as "light," "air," and "water," in which the god materializes in the world. This text praises Amun as a cosmic god *whose body is the world.* By praising this god as *ba* rather than with his usual name, the hymn refers to god as the *ba* of the world, the "vital principle" of the cosmos which gives life to the cosmos in the same way that the human *ba* ("soul") gives life to the individual human being.

Ba, however, is a bifocal term. It may refer not only to the invisible life-giving principle in and behind the visible world, but also to its visible manifestations. The visible world, in some of its aspects, can also be called *ba*. Thus the life-giving elements can be called God's *ba*s and these can be experienced in the cosmos as the ways in which god works. Thus we read in a text:

> The *ba* of Re [= the light of the sun] is throughout the entire land.[98]

And in another text, known as "The Teaching of Ani," we read:

> The god of this land is the sun in heaven.
> He gives his *ba*s in millions of forms.[99]

Ramesside Amun-Re theology went even further by regarding not only the light but also the totality of the energies that perform a life-giving function in the world as manifestations, or *ba*s, of Amun. This idea is clearly opposed to the tenets of Amarna religion, where the concept *ba* does not occur and the corresponding category is *kheperu:* the visible world is the *kheperu* of god, that is, it proceeds from him, but is not itself divine.

But the idea of the world being the *kheperu* of god seems closer to the paradigm of manifestation than to that of creation. It means that the world is a transformation of God. Some passages in the Amarna hymns which oppose the "One" source of life to the "millions" of transformations seem to closely anticipate Ramesside pantheism:

> You create millions of forms [*kheperu*] from yourself, the One,
> Cities and towns
> Fields, paths, and river[100]

The million *kheperu* refer obviously to the visible world in its aspect of a space made habitable by light and constituted as a cosmos. Yet the "Shorter Hymn" opposes the One and the Millions as aspects of God himself:

> You made heaven remote to rise in it
> To see all that you created, you being alone
> But there being millions of lives in you [for you] to make them
>   live.[101]

Both passages implicitly reject the idea of primordial creation and replace it with the idea of continuous creation. Yet it seems evident that they clearly distinguish between creator and creation, however closely the two are related. Aten does not create form "within" but from "above"; there is a clear notion of confrontation implied in this solar symbolism of heaven and earth. In the Amarna texts the term *ba* is completely missing with reference to Aten. This confirms my belief that the paradigm of manifestation is alien to Amarna theology. It is the great innovation of post-Amarna theology.

The paradigm of manifestation and Ramesside *ba* theology reach their high point in the theory of the ten *ba*s of Amun, developed in a tremendous hymn. Unfortunately, of the ten cantos, each one devoted to a specific *ba*, only the first three have been preserved. But an introductory hymn names all ten of them so that the system as such is recognizable.[102]

In the first five *ba*s we once again find the life-giving elements. The first pair of *ba*s are the sun and the moon, which can also be explained as the right and the left eyes of the cosmic god. Then come the *ba*s of Shu and Osiris for air and water. The fifth *ba* is not that of Geb for earth, as one might expect, but that of Tefnut, the goddess of the flaming uraeus snake. The theological interpretation is given in the hymn. Sun and moon represent not light, but time, which also appears here as a cosmic life-giving energy. Light is attributed to the *ba* of Tefnut. The life-giving elements here are thus time, air, water, and light. When they are represented in human form, all five *ba*s wear the insignia of their cosmic manifestation on their heads: sun, moon, sail, three water bowls, and torch, respectively. Up to this point we find ourselves on familiar ground, even if this pentad is otherwise not attested.[103]

The second group of five *ba*s takes us into theologically new territory. They represent five classes of living creatures. Hence, this theology distinguishes between cosmic and animal life. The five life-giving cosmic elements are paired with five classes of life-endowed animate creatures: human beings, quadrupeds, birds, creatures of the water, and creatures of the earth, such as snakes, scarabs, and the dead. The *ba* of human beings has human form and is called "royal ka"; the *ba* of quadrupeds is lion-headed and is called "ram of the rams"; the *ba* for birds has a human form and is called Harakhty; the *ba* of aquatic creatures has a crocodile head and is called "*ba* of those in the water"; the *ba* of terrestrial creatures has the head of a snake and is called Nehebka. The system is illustrated in the following table:

First Pentad		
Ba	"In his name"	Function
Ba in the right eye	Re of every day	Time
Ba in the left eye	Full moon	Time
Ba of Shu	Remaining in all things	Air, wind
Ba of Osiris	Eldest Nun	Water
Ba of Tefnut	The one who awakes whole	Light

Second Pentad		
Symbol	Class	"In his name"
Human	Human beings	Royal-ka
Lion	Quadrupeds	Falcon
Falcon	Birds	Harakhty
Crocodiles	Aquatic creatures	*Ba* of those in the water
Snakes	Terrestrial creatures	Nehebkau

This theology understands the *ba*s of God not as the visible world in itself, but as a decad of mediating powers that animate and sustain the world. Perhaps the most puzzling feature of this theology is the place assigned to the king. The king belongs to the ten *ba*s; he is one of the ten worldly manifestations in the form of which the god gives life to, animates, and organizes the world. The king is indeed the divine energy responsible for human beings—not the king himself, of course, but the royal *ka* as the divine institutional principle of kingship, embodied in each king and identical with Horus.[104] Kingship is a cosmic energy, like light and air: the power of god that animates, takes care of, and orders the human world is manifested in it.

Not only is this theology given linguistic expression in a hymn, but it is also translated into a cult activity in the form of a ritual. This ritual is known to us from the Taharqa building next to the sacred lake in Karnak, where the wall reliefs are unfortunately very badly damaged, and from the Opet Temple in Karnak, in whose crypts a well-preserved variant has been discovered by Claude Traunecker.[105] The fact that the cult was performed in a crypt might indicate that it was some kind of secret cult. The hymn is also surrounded by indications of secrecy. In the Hibis temple version it bears the title "Book of the Secrets of Amun Written Down on Boards of *Nbs*-Wood."[106] Here, we find ourselves on the threshold of Hermeticism and the Greco-Egyptian magical papyri, which to some extent develop a similarly complex theo-cosmology.[107]

A magical text from about the same time period as the ritual of the ten *ba*s of Amun counts seven *ba*-manifestations of Amun:

The "Bes" with seven heads . . .
He is [embodies] the *ba*s of Amun-Re, lord of Karnak, chief of
    Ipet-Sut,
The ram with sublime face, who dwells in Thebes.
The great lion who generated by himself,
The Great god of the beginning,
The ruler of lands and the king of gods,
The lord of heaven, earth, underworld, water, and mountains
Who conceals his name from the gods,
The giant of millions of cubits,
The strong . . . who fixed the sky on his head,
Of whose nose the air comes forth,
In order to animate all noses,
Who rises as sun, in order to illuminate the earth,
Of whose bodily secretions the Nile flows forth in order to
    nourish every mouth . . .

This text accompanies and explains a vignette showing a strange being
with seven different heads. Bes is a familiar figure in Egyptian magic. He
is the god of the bed chamber who wards off the evil demons by means of
his monstrous exterior. In this form, with his seven heads, he appears
even more monstrous. In any event, he seems worlds apart from the sublime concept of a Supreme Being as postulated by Ramesside theology.
Nevertheless, he is presented here as a universal deity embodying the
seven *ba*s of Amun. We have to understand both the text and the picture
on two levels. What the picture shows is the level of immanence, of the
seven *ba*s, a combination of all the different manifestations in which the
cosmogonic energy of the creator is present and operative in the world.
What the text refers to is the level of transcendence, the ineffable and
hidden universal god, whom, of course, no image can represent. All the
epithets which the text uses refer to Amun-Re, not to Bes. Bes is
identified as the combined *ba*s of the Supreme God. It is Bes who is
shown in the image, but it is the supreme god who is referred to in the
text. And the textual passage, again, is a remarkable piece of theology.

Another vignette in this same papyrus shows a similar figure, but with
nine heads instead of seven. It stands upon an oval, encircled by a snake
biting its tail (*sd m r3*, Greek *ouroboros*) and containing several beasts
that incorporate or symbolize evil powers: lion, hippopotamus, croco-

dile, snake, scorpion, turtle, and dog. The accompanying text describes
the picture, but without giving a theological interpretation.

> With nine faces on a single neck,
> a face of Bes, a face of a ram,
> a face of a hawk, a face of a crocodile,
> a face of a hippopotamus, a face of a lion, a face of a bull,
> a face of a monkey, and a face of a cat.[108]

This figure reappears on magical stelae such as the famous Metternich
stela and becomes in fact quite common during the Late Period. It is
the same figure which in the Greco-Egyptian magical papyri is called
enneamorphos, the one with nine forms.[109] We may be sure that this is
just another rendering of the same idea: a visualization of the different
forms in which the cosmogonic energy of the supreme and transcendent God is present in the world. The Egyptian pantheon is a composite form of this divine immanence. The seven *ba*s, the nine shapes or
the million beings are variant expressions of the same idea that God is
one *and* many, one *and* all, *Hen kai pan*, as the Greek formula runs.

In the present context, the main interest of this strange figures lies in
the fact that it provides the "missing link" between Ramesside theology
and Greco-Egyptian religious beliefs and practices. Magic served as the
most important means of transmission and continuity. The magical
purpose for which this highly theological concept of God is brought to
function in the two vignettes of the magical Brooklyn papyrus is as
general and all-encompassing as God himself. The papyrus is designed
as a general and unspecific protection against every possible form of
danger. "Pantheism" proved a magically successful theory of the world.

In the Greco-Egyptian magical papyri, many theological passages
display very much the same concept of a supreme god as that which we
have met with in the Brooklyn papyrus, the concept of a hidden and
universal supreme Being whose visible manifestation is the world:

> Come to me, you from the four winds,
> God, ruler of all,
> Who has breathed spirits into men for life,
> Master of the good things in the world.
> Hear me, lord, whose name is ineffable.

The demons, hearing it, are terrified—
The name BARBAREICH ARSEMPHEMPHROOTHOU—
And because of hearing it the sun, the earth, are overturned;
Hades, hearing, is shaken; rivers, sea, lakes, springs, hearing,
    are frozen;
Rocks, hearing it, are split.
Heaven is your head;
Ether, body;
Earth, feet;
And the water around you, ocean,
O Agathos Daimon.
You are lord, the begetter and nourisher and increaser of all.[110]

Let me now turn to what I claim is the Egyptian equivalent of the
Greek formula that so intrigued Cudworth, Lessing, and the German
pre-Romantics: *Hen kai pan*. A Ramesside magical papyrus contains a
short version of one of the most important Amun-Re hymns. Consequently, the hymn can be dated to the Nineteenth Dynasty, though the
earliest complete surviving version occurs in the Hibis temple from the
Persian period. The short version is as follows:

Hail, the One who makes himself into millions,
    Whose length and breadth are limitless![111]
Power in readiness, who gave birth to himself,
    Uraeus with great flame;
Great of magic with secret form,
    Secret *ba*, to whom respect is shown.

King Amun-Re may he live, be powerful and healthy, who
    came into being himself,
    Akhty, Horus of the east,
The rising one whose radiance illuminates,
    The light that is more luminous than the gods.
You have hidden yourself as Amun the great;
You have withdrawn in your transformation as the sun disk.[112]
Tatenen, who raises himself above the gods.

The Old Man forever young, traveling through Time,

Amun, who remains in possession of all things,
This god who established the earth by his providence.

The first stanza deals with an aspect of the god that is of particular interest to us (as it would have been for Ralph Cudworth). This is the aspect of the hidden nameless power, for whom neither the divine name Amun(-Re) nor the description *ntr* (usually translated as "god") appear sufficient. For this reason, circumlocutions are used such as "power," "uraeus," "great of magic" and, finally, what has to be regarded as the *nomen ipsum* of this concept of God, "hidden *ba*." This stanza is quite different from the second one, which not only names the hidden god, but also emphasizes this name with cartouches and titles. There can scarcely be a clearer expression of the fact that the name too is only an aspect of the god which he uses when he exercises his rule over the world. As a nameless and secret *ba* the god is unlimited and omnipresent. The forms in which his power manifests itself are the millionfold totality.

The hymn uses a formula that appears very frequently with reference to this hidden, universal creator: "the One who makes himself into millions." The problems presented by the interpretation of this formula can be summarized as follows:

1. "The One": Does the predication of "oneness" refer to the "aloneness" of the primeval god *before* creation or to the all-oneness of God as manifested *in* creation?
2. "Who transforms himself": Does this refer to the creation at the beginning or to the continuous stream of the all from the one?
3. "Into millions": Does this refer to the millions of gods or the totality of living creation or a concept of everything (Greek *pan* / Latin *omnia*)?[113]

Erik Hornung has interpreted the formula in a temporal sense. He regards (1) "oneness" as the condition of the god before creation; (2) the verbs describing the creation or emergence of the many from the one as a description of primeval creation; and (3) the "millions" as the polytheistic divine world that represents existing reality.[114]

By and large, these views are supported by the texts, almost all of which refer to creation. Occasionally, the temporal relationship between oneness and allness is also expressly emphasized by the additional statement that all gods emerged *after* the one. Therefore it is not a matter of disputing Hornung's interpretation, but of asking whether the formula, apart from its undeniable reference to creation (which introduces nothing new in Egyptian religious history), also implies a "manifestational" concept of God like that expressed by the Latin formula *una quae es omnia*. The hymn quoted above deals with the concept of God as a "hidden power" and as the source of the millionfold plurality in which he unfolds and extends into the "boundlessness."[115] This boundlessness is not predicated of the world, but of God, to whom the hymn is addressed. Accordingly, God *is* the million into which he has transformed himself: *unus qui est omnia*. In other texts, "million" is said to be his body,[116] his limbs,[117] his transformation[118] and even his name: "'million of millions' is his name."[119] By transforming himself into the millionfold reality, God has not ceased to be one. He *is* the many in that mysterious way, hidden and present at the same time, which this theology is trying to grasp by means of the *ba* concept. A common text even goes so far as to describe God as the *ba* (and not the creator) of gods and humans (that is, "the millions"):[120]

> The One Alone who created what is,
> The illustrious *ba* of gods and humans.[121]

The unity of God becomes a problem only when it has to be made to harmonize with the idea (realized in polytheism) of the divinity of the world without being reduced to the before/after solution of creation theology. That is the situation in Ramesside theology. The unity of God is realized as neither preexistence nor a (counter-religious) monotheistic concept, but as latency, as a "hidden unity," in which all living plurality on earth has its origin and whose inscrutable nature can be experienced and stated only in its manifestations, the "colorful reflection" of the polytheistic divine world.

The predication "the One who makes himself into millions" means that God, by creating the world, transformed himself into (or manifested himself as) the totality of divine forces which are operative in the creation and maintenance of the world and that all of the gods are comprised in the One. It is more than probable that the corresponding predication of Isis as "the one who is all" translates and continues this form of predication. She is called *una quae es omnia* in that inscription from Capua which was so important for Cudworth,[122] or *moune su ei hapasai*,[123] meaning that all the other goddesses are absorbed or united in her divine being. She is also called *myrionyma*, "with innumerable names," which means that all divine names are hers and that all other deities are merely aspects of her all-encompassing nature. This idea occurs also in the *Corpus Hermeticum:* all names are those of one god.[124] Giordano Bruno refers to a cabalistic tradition according to which there is an ineffable name as the first principle, "from which, second, there proceed four names, which afterwards are converted into twelve, in a straight line change into seventy-two, and obliquely and in a straight line into one hundred forty-four, and farther on are unfolded by fours and by twelves into names as innumerable as species. And likewise, according to each name (inasmuch as it befits their own language), they name one god, one angel, one intelligence, one power, who presides over one species. From this we will see that all Deity reduces itself to one source, just as all light is reduced to the first and self-illuminated source and images that are in mirrors as diverse and numerous as there are particular subjects are reduced to their source, the one formal and ideal principle."[125] I cannot help believing that this kind of speculation would have appealed very much to an Egyptian priest thinking within the paradigm of manifestation.

As Ralph Cudworth had shown, the famous proclamation "One-and-All," the manifesto of Hermeticism, has the same origin as the Isis formula *una quae es omnia*. Alchemistic and Hermetic manuscripts transmit this device through the Middle Ages into the pantheist revival in the eighteenth century.

CHAPTER SEVEN

Abolishing the Mosaic Distinction: Religious Antagonism and Its Overcoming

The discourse on Moses and Egypt started, or at least became intense and prominent, at the end of the seventeenth century. It was part of the project of the Enlightenment and formed what could be termed "the Protestant Enlightenment." Most of those who took a prominent part in this debate were Protestant Biblical scholars like Spencer, Marsham, and Cudworth or even bishops like Warburton, Berkeley, and Stillingfleet. Reinhold started as a Jesuit and was converted to Protestantism by Superintendent Herder, whose book *God* is an answer to Jacobi's concept of Spinozism. The authors who wrote within the frame of the Moses/Egypt discourse confronted the constellation of Israel and Egypt as a powerful figure of memory and approached Egypt within this constellation. By doing so, they practiced cultural *Erinnerungsarbeit* in the Freudian sense. This distinguishes them from other authors who wrote about Egypt, especially the Hermeticists, who were not primarily concerned with Moses and monotheism and did not view Egypt as the subtext of the Bible. But the constellation of Israel and Egypt has proved very powerful and influential as a figure of cultural memory. This is shown by the simple fact that two of the leading minds on the twentieth-century intellectual scene, Thomas Mann and Sigmund Freud, made painstaking efforts to reconstruct and analyze this same constellation.

The meaning of the Biblical image of Egypt and the target of this discourse can easily be defined in retrospect. The Biblical image of Egypt means "idolatry." It symbolizes what "the Mosaic distinction" excluded as the opposite of truth in religion. By drawing this distinction, "Moses" cut the umbilical cord which connected his people and his religious ideas to their cultural and natural context. The Egypt of the Bible symbolizes what is rejected, discarded, and abandoned. Egypt is not just a historical context; it is inscribed in the fundamental semantics of monotheism. It appears explicitly in the first commandment and implicitly in the second. Its role in the Exodus story must be sharply distinguished from the roles that Assyria, Babylonia, the Philistines, and other Iron Age powers including Late Period Egypt itself play in the historical and prophetic books of the Bible. Egypt's role in the Exodus story is not historical but mythical: it helps define the very identity of those who tell the story. Egypt is the womb from which the chosen people emerged, but the umbilical cord was cut once and for all by the Mosaic distinction.

To this idea of definite separation, Spencer, Cudworth, Marsham, and others opposed the idea of translation. This shift of paradigm might perhaps become clear by means of a metaphor. A counter-religion can be compared to a palimpsest, a reused papyrus or parchment. The old text is erased, and the new text is written on the cleaned surface. The more care has been taken to clean the surface, the less of the old text is visible. But some faint trace of the old text usually remains. It is viewed with hatred and abomination. This is the old paradigm. The new paradigm focuses on the old text which is still visible under the new inscription. But instead of seeing in it traces of what has to be rejected and discarded, the paradigm looks upon it as a kind of "golden ground" as that was used in Sienese paintings of the Trecento. It was the restoration of the golden ground which ultimately amounted to the revision of Exodus and revelation and to the cancellation of the Mosaic distinction. This project was part of the general humanist quest for overarching ideas that would help to destroy the boundaries between nations, confessions, religions, and classes and to "deconstruct" ideological distinctions characterized by hatred, incomprehension, and persecution.

The problem of antagonism, and the attempt to dissolve and overcome it form the engine, the driving force, of the Moses/Egypt discourse. It begins with Spencer, who is still arguing within the extremely antagonistic framework of normative inversion, and ends with Freud, who dissolves the antagonism by psychoanalyzing the negativity of revelation as the return of a repressed event in the "archaic heritage" common to all humankind.

The project of deconstructing the Biblical image of Egypt proceeded in stages that correspond to different forms of religious antagonism.

Revolution; or, The Old and the New

Amarna

The Amarna religion has to be counted among the revolutionary forms of monotheism. It opposed tradition in the most violent forms of negation, intolerance, and persecution. But the rejected tradition is never mentioned in the texts. We are thus unable to grasp its conceptual construction. This is one of the fundamental differences between Amarna religion and Biblical monotheism. I attribute this fact partly to the lack of tradition and partly to the "cosmotheistic" character of Amarna religion. We cannot exclude the possibility that Amarna monotheism, had it persisted long enough to create a body of normative texts and interpretations, could have developed an antagonistic construction of the discarded tradition. The occurrence of a revolutionary counter-religion in the fourteenth century B.C.E. is as unique as the fact that such a phenomenon lasted for twenty years at most and that we have only the first, original sources, without any later reworkings, interpretations, or apologetics. Therefore, we cannot tell whether the construction of antagonistic conceptions such as "paganism" or "idolatry" would be inside or outside the range of possibilities of the Amarna religion.

One point is certain: the Amarna revolution was based not on revelation but on evidence. This is the other fundamental difference between Amarna and Biblical monotheism. The Amarna religion is cosmotheistic. Aton is a cosmic god. He is not invisible; he is the creator of light and visibility. He is neither spiritual nor ethical; he is strictly heliomorphic. Freud did not understand this. A "natural" religion based on evidence is obviously less dependent on contradistinctive self-definition than a "positive" religion based on revelation.

It is characteristic of the Moses/Egypt discourse that it tends to blur this distinction and also to turn Moses into a cosmotheist. The God of Moses then becomes not the liberator from Egypt, but the creator of heaven and earth and the one source of all that is. As Yehoshua Amir has convincingly shown in a brilliant article, this confusion began in Hellenistic times and corresponds to the aims of Jewish and Christian apologists, who were eager to prove that Moses' teachings did not differ from those of the greatest philosophers of later times, who, they thought, all borrowed from him.[1] The God of the Exodus is very different. He is much closer to Pharaoh than to Aton or Amun, let alone Aristotle's unmoved mover, in being a primarily political figure. Neither is he a "volcanic demon." His "wrath" and "jealousy" are political affects, befitting a king who has entered into a treaty with a vassal.[2] In the last phase, even the distinction between God and world, or creator and creation, is blurred. Toland was the first to openly call Moses a "Spinozist." But he did so by explicitly ignoring the Biblical record and by relying exclusively on Strabo. Reinhold and Schiller achieved the same without excluding the Bible.

"Moses"

The monotheistic movement that is especially associated with the name of Moses within the overall context of Biblical history and theology presents itself in the book of Exodus as an anti-Egyptian revolution. Again, I am concerned here not with the historical Moses and his personal thoughts and intentions, but with the semantics of the Biblical text that bears the name of Moses. In striking contrast to the Amarna religion, this monotheism derives its crucial semantic elements from a construction of the rejected other, and these semantics have continued to exert their influence to the present day.[3] Mosaic monotheism is an explicit counter-religion which depends on the preservation of what it opposes for its own definition. For this reason, the Bible has preserved an image of Egypt as its own counter-image. The central term here is idolatry. This term is defined not on the lexemic level, but on the level of a model narrative, a "primal scene." The primal scene of idolatry is the story of the Golden Calf. It serves as a terminological definition in answering the question "what is idolatry?" As such, it is the exact counterpart to the Egyptian story about the "lepers." The two stories define by way of narrative demonstration a mutual repudiation. The "idolators" abhor the "iconoclasts" and vice versa.

The Golden Calf is an Egyptian image, the image of Apis. This fact might not have been realized by the original authors of the story, and might only have been read into it by Rabbinic and Christian commentators. However, this point is immaterial in the context of mnemohistory. The "original author(s)" might also not have been aware of the fact that they were writing a "primal scene," a story of absolutely crucial, defining importance. It is only in the course of a long history of reception and canonization that a tradition achieves such a central position. The story of the Golden Calf has certainly achieved such status because it forms the liturgical reading on the Day of Atonement. Can the wrath of God once again be averted, the covenant continued, life go on for another year? It is a question of life and death, to be or not to be, and it is connected with Egyptian idolatry.

Secrecy; or, The Revealed and the Concealed

There is no doubt that secrecy is an indispensable element in any religion. There is hardly any religion that could do completely without secrecy, and the further we go back in time the more central the element of secrecy becomes. There is thus on first sight nothing special about the strong concept of secrecy which the Moses/Egypt discourse propounds as a major factor in religious history. There is, however, a fundamental difference between its secrecy and that of other religions. In the frame of the Moses/Egypt discourse, secrecy becomes a figure of religious antagonism. The general concept of secrecy in religion draws a distinction between general knowledge and special knowledge. General knowledge is open to, and to a degree even obligatory for, everybody. It is in no respect devalued by special knowledge. Special knowledge builds upon general knowledge and goes some steps further into regions that are simply too difficult and dangerous to be accessible to everybody. But the concept of secrecy that is constructed in the context of the Moses/Egypt discourse draws a completely different distinction. It opposes open and secret knowledge in terms of the Mosaic distinction implying the most radical contradiction. The two bodies of knowledge are completely incompatible: one is the negation of the other.

This rather schizophrenic idea of a split religion is one of the most eccentric concepts in religious history. There may have been actual secret societies that held views about God and the world that would completely overturn the institutions of church, state, and society if made public. But these societies would have advocated virtual revolution, not a "structural" concept of secrecy.[4] There is scarcely any historical evidence for the thesis that this is the way society and religion work and that secret societies of this sort are structurally indispensable. Yet this is precisely what was entailed by the concept of secrecy that was brought up in the course of the Moses/Egypt discourse, especially by Warburton. There is no state that can do without secrecy of this type. Pagan religion is a political institution that is structurally opposed to the truth. Moses was the only one who dared to build a society without secrecy because he could rely on "extraordinary providence." Again, we must not forget that we are investigating the workings of cultural memory and not the "facts" of actual history. Historically, this concept of secrecy is certainly as mistaken as rationalistic concepts can be. But notwithstanding its historical absurdity, it was a powerful and extremely influential concept that informed not only the reconstruction of the past, but also beliefs about the present and the future.

The concept of split religion occurs in a nonantagonistic, a moderately antagonistic, and a radically antagonistic form. The nonantagonistic form is represented by most of the classical theories about Egyptian religion, such as those of Philo, Plutarch, Clement of Alexandria, and Iamblichus. It corresponds to the Stoic and Neoplatonic sociology of knowledge and can be subsumed under the notion of accommodation. Since human beings are differently equipped for grasping the truth, the distribution of knowledge within a society has to accommodate itself to these differences. There is one truth which fits Tamino and another one that fits Papageno. Virtually all Classical sources agree that the famous wisdom which the Egyptian priests kept secret in the adyta of the temples was of this sort. It was a knowledge that was inaccessible to the common mind, but not subversive of the maintenance of public order. The latter idea was not included in the ancient model of Egyptian religion.

THE MODERATE form of split religion that Warburton propounded goes back to the Greek rationalism of the fifth century B.C.E. The *locus classicus* that is constantly referred to in this context is the famous fragment of Critias which reconstructs human history in three stages:

1. The natural state of savagery: a state without reward and punishment where virtues remained unrewarded and crimes were

not punished. It was a state of disorder and internecine competition.

2. The institution of justice, which helped create and uphold order, but only to a certain degree. Much crime and violence continued secretly and remained unpunished because it remained undetected.

3. The invention of religion and of the ideas of divine omniscience and a future state of rewards and punishments, which served the purpose of discouraging secret criminality as long as its artificial and strategic character remained undetected. The placebo effect of religion could work only if the truth was not discovered. But the purpose of the invention is good; therefore it is not a fraud, but an indispensable institution for the welfare of humanity.[5]

This extremely improbable theory about ancient Egyptian religion found its strongest support in the traditions about hieroglyphic writing, which was commonly interpreted as a cryptographic system devised to transmit the esoteric monotheism of the priests in a form that would protect the truth from vulgarization and spare the uninitiated the shock of disillusionment.

The radical form of the concept of split religion is the theory of imposture. This theory, which was very common in the seventeenth and eighteenth centuries, is particularly associated with Bernard Fontenelle[6] and his notion of a "trahison de clercs." Fontenelle's *Histoire des oracles* (1686) replaced the "devil" or the demons who, according to the traditional view, worked pagan oracles and miracles with shrewd priests, and explained the miracles as very human, behind-the-scenes machinations and manipulations. This is perhaps the crudest distortion of Egyptian polytheism. It remains a mystery how such an absurd view of ancient Egyptian religion could have persisted for so long among the most advanced minds of European scholarship. How could a religion ever survive the complete negation or "disillusionment" of its truth? The Mosaic distinction between truth and falsehood may function in the relation between two religions or cultural systems, but how can it function within one and the same system? But the authors who propounded the radical model of split religion with regard to ancient Egypt were not really interested in discovering the Egyptian subtext of Biblical and Christian memory and self-definition. They constructed an Egypt of their own in order to speak about the present without risking persecution. The model of the treacherous Egyptian priests was meant to act as a mirror of contemporary clerical institutions. In the context of this study, which concentrates on reconstructions of the past, we can dispense with the imposture theory because it is historically uninteresting. It was not really concerned with Egypt.

Latency; or, The Forgotten and the Remembered

In the long history of the discourse on Moses and Egypt, from Hecataeus to Freud, a displacement of antagonism can be ascertained which proceeds from the outer to the inner. We start with revolution and expulsion, then proceed to secrecy and mystery, in which the antagonism takes place within one society, and end up with latency, where the antagonism resides in the individual as well as the collective soul. Latency as a third model of religious antagonism and tension is the discovery of Sigmund Freud and constitutes his most important contribution to the discourse on Moses and Egypt. Freud's great discovery and lasting contribution to this discourse is the role which he attributed to the dynamics of memory and the return of the repressed. I have to confess that I cannot make much of Freud's theories about primal patricide or of the close analogy he draws between individual and collective memory, which his generalization of the Oedipus complex requires in order to work as a theory of culture. But I think that even if one does not believe in these particular tenets of Freudian theory, one should acknowledge that the concepts of latency and the return of the repressed are indispensable for any adequate theory of cultural memory. They need, however, to be redefined in cultural terms. Freud reminded us of the fact that there is such a thing as "cultural forgetting" or even "cultural repression." Since Freud, no theory of culture can afford not to take these concepts into consideration. The old concept of tradition has proved insufficient.

What is "cultural forgetting"? According to current theories, forgetting occurs in societies which lack writing in the form of "structural amnesia."[7] The cultural memory is constantly reworked in oral tradition. Those elements of knowledge about the past that no longer meaningfully correspond to actual concerns are discarded and in the long run they are forgotten. Oral society does not possess any means of storing discarded knowledge. It equally does not know any techniques of forgetting. These develop only with the scripturalization of cultural memory. The simplest and commonest technique of forgetting is the destruction of memory in its cultural objectifications such as inscriptions and iconic representations. This is what happened to the monotheistic revolution of Akhenaten, and the destruction was thorough enough to keep this event completely unretrievable until its archaeological rediscovery in the course of the nineteenth century. I think that my study of the legends about the "lepers" and the Exodus circulating in Egypt in the Late Period has sufficiently shown in what sense it is possible to speak not only of forgetting, but also of repression. The Amarna episode came to be completely forgotten within about eighty years, but the experience was traumatic enough to produce legendary traditions which—because of their unlocatability in the official cultural memory—became free-floating and thus susceptible to being associated with a variety of semantically related experiences. They formed a "crypt" in the cultural memory of Egypt.

Another technique of forgetting is silence. This technique was practiced by the Amarna texts, which never speak of what they implicitly reject. The exact opposite of this technique is normative inversion. Here, the rejected is remembered: not for its own sake, but as the counter-image of one's own identity. Normative inversion is structurally related to conversion, where there is a strong obligation of anamnesis in order to avoid relapse. Every convert lives his story of conversion.[8] We have met with the motif of normative inversion in the earliest texts relating to Moses the Egyptian and have studied its full exposition in the writings of Maimonides and John Spencer. Normative inversion keeps a memory of the other alive because this image is needed for contradistinctive self-definition. The "Sabians" would certainly never have been remembered were it not for Maimonides, who elevated them to the status of a counter-image of monotheism. It is impressive that we meet with the term "Sabiism" or "Sabianism" in texts from as late as the nineteenth century. But this memory is not an image of the other religion; it is only a counter-image of one's own. Thus it destroys whatever might have survived of authentic memories and traditions and supplants them with a polemical counter-construction.

In the Jewish and Christian tradition, this strategy of forgetting worked so well that we are still far from a full understanding of "polytheism." Normative inversion is the construction of cultural abomination. The rejected and "forgotten" culture survives in the form of abomination. Thus Egypt is turned into a nightmare and a fatal disease. The Israel-and-Egypt constellation is the model of mutual abomination. But the discourse concerning this constellation is ambivalent if not openly sympathetic to Egypt, though it never went so far in terms of Egyptophilia as the Hermetic discourse. There is always an antiregressive drive in these texts which forbids a return to Egypt, and this tendency becomes most marked in Freud. Nobody taking part in this discourse ever went so far as to intone "praise of polytheism." This remained for postmodern philosophy to formulate.[9]

With cosmotheism, however, the situation is different. The power and influence of cosmotheistic movements such as Neoplatonism, Hermeticism, alchemy, cabala, Spinozism, Deism, and pantheism—many of which developed pronounced forms of Egyptophilia—might be explained as a return of the repressed. It is only necessary to (re)translate some of Freud's categories from the psychical topology into the social, cultural, and political one in order to bring his insights to bear on a cultural theory of memory. In cultural terms, "latency" can assume many different forms:

1. *The nonrepresentable traumatic.* Collective or cultural repression, such as Freud was thinking of, occurs under traumatic conditions. The Holocaust is an example. In spite of an immense number of works and the intensity of the scientific historiography devoted to that period in Germany, there are only a few futile attempts at cultural commemoration. Cultural memory still seems paralyzed in Germany.

2. *The implicit.* There are other forms of latency as well. Among those forms I would consider what Michael Polanyi called "the tacit dimension," or implicit knowledge which is too self-evident to become part of explicit communication and social consciousness.

3. *The marginalized.* A third form of latency is, quite simply, marginalization. Cultural knowledge is always embodied in human minds and circulates in groups and channels of communication. As soon as it ceases to circulate it becomes marginalized, either because the carrier group is persecuted or loses its influence, or because the knowledge is

superseded by a new paradigm, a shift of interest. It may, however, remain stored in books and thus "return" at a later time. History is full of forgotten knowledge that returned in the discovery of a book, from legendary discoveries such as the unearthing of the book of Deuteronomy during restoration work in the temple of Jerusalem and the discovery of the works of Confucius in a private house in China to the reemergence of the Hermetic writings and the book of Horapollo in the Renaissance and the discovery of the libraries of Qumran and Nag Hammadi in our time. Cultural memory is rich in crypts and dark spaces. Discoveries and reemergences are always possible and prevent intellectual history from proceeding on a simple path of unilinear evolution. The return of Egypt and its cosmotheism as the suppressed counter-religion of Biblical monotheism may perhaps be considered one of the supreme examples of this phenomenon—at least in the West—to judge by its past and potential consequences for the development of thought, society, and moral institutions.

Notes

1. Mnemohistory and the Construction of Egypt

1. George Spencer Brown, *Laws of Form* (New York: The Julian Press, 1972), 3.

2. Peter Artzi, "The Birth of the Middle East," *Proceedings of the Fifth World Congress of Jewish Studies*, Jerusalem: Magnes Press, 1969), 120–124.

3. See Moshe Halbertal and Avishai Margalit, *Idolatry* (Cambridge, Mass.: Harvard UP, 1993).

4. Aleida Assmann drew my attention to *Wisdom of Solomon* as a particularly anti-idolatric text; Julia Annas pointed out to me the importance of Philo in this context.

5. See Pier Cesare Bori, *L'estasi del profeta ed altri saggi tra Ebraismo e Cristianismo* (Bologna: Il Molino, 1989), 237–258. I owe this reference to the kindness of Mauro Pesce.

6. Ilse Gubrich-Simitis, *Freuds Moses-Studie als Tagtraum: ein bibliographischer Essay*. Die Sigmund-Freud-Vorlesungen, vol. 3 (Weinheim: Verlag Internationale Psychoanalyse, 1991).

7. For a response by Biblical scholarship see especially Bori, *L'estasi del profeta*, and "Moses, the Great Stranger" in Pier Cesare Bori, *From Hermeneutics to Ethical Consensus among Cultures* (Atlanta: Scholars Press, University of South Florida, 1994), 155–164. For Egyptology see Abraham Rosenvasser, *Egipto e Israel y el monoteismo Hebreo: A proposito del libro Moisés y la religión monoteista de Sigmund Freud*, 2nd. ed., (Buenos Aires: University of Buenos Aires Faculty of Philosophy and Letters, Institute of Ancient Near Eastern History, 1982).

8. Arthur D. Nock, *Conversion: The Old and the New in Religion from Alexander the Great to Augustine of Hippo* (1933; repr. Oxford: Oxford UP, 1963).

9. See Thomas Luckmann, "Kanon und Konversion," in *Kanon und Zensur*, ed. A. and J. Assmann (Munich: Fink, 1987), 38–46.

10. For a good summary of reception theory see Martyn P. Thompson, "Reception Theory and the Interpretation of Historical Meaning," *History and Theory* 32 (1993): 248–272.

11. See Dan L. Schacter, J. T. Coyle, G. D. Fischbach, M. M. Mesulam, and L. E. Sullivan, ed., *Memory Distortion* (Cambridge, Mass.: Harvard UP, 1995). See

also the ongoing discussion on memory and on memory distortions by Frederick Crews and others in the *New York Review of Books* 1994, issues 19 and 20, 1995, issue 2 (with bibliography).

12. See Jacob Taubes, *Die politische Theologie des Paulus* (Munich: Fink, 1993).

13. Counter-memory opposes both a different construction of the past and a different construction of the present. It strives at keeping present in the world of today an image of yesterday that contradicts it. The term has been used in this sense by Aleida Assmann, "The Sun at Midnight: The Concept of Counter-Memory and Its Changes," in *Commitment in Reflection. Essays in Literature and Moral Philosophy*, ed. Leona Toker (New York, 1994), 223–243.

14. Amos Funkenstein, *Perceptions of Jewish History* (Berkeley: U of California P, 1993), 32–49; David Biale, *Gershom Scholem: Kabbala and Counterhistory* (Cambridge, Mass.: Harvard UP, 1979).

15. The modern historical discussions of the Egyptian background of the figure of Moses which I find most intriguing are Ernst Axel Knauf, *Midian: Untersuchungen zur Geschichte Palästinas und Nordarabiens am Ende des 2. Jt. v. Chr.* (Wiesbaden: Harrassowitz, 1988), 97–149, and Donald B. Redford, *Egypt, Canaan, and Israel in Ancient Times* (Princeton: Princeton UP, 1992), 408–422. These two scholars however, do not agree with each other. Knauf identifies Moses with Bay alias Ramosekhayemnetjeru, a Syrian who ascended to the throne of Egypt after having occupied the extremely high position of Chief Treasurer of the Entire Land. Bay met with violent opposition and civil war, which ended in the expulsion of both him and his party. Redford sees reminiscences of the Hyksos' occupation of and later expulsion from Egypt in the Exodus tradition and views Moses as an entirely legendary figure. For the problem of the historical Moses see the brilliant survey by Rudolf Smend, "Moses als geschichtliche Gestalt," *Historische Zeitschrift* 260 (1995): 1–19. I owe this reference to Elke Blumenthal.

16. Martin Bernal, *Black Athena: The Afroasiatic Roots of Classical Civilization* (vol. 1: *The Fabrication of Ancient Greece, 1785–1985;* vol. 2: *The Archaeological and Documentary Evidence*) (New Brunswick: Rutgers UP, 1987–1991).

17. See my review "Sentimental Journey zu den Wurzeln Europas: Zu Martin Bernals *Black Athena*," *Merkur* 522 (1992): 921–931. I do not mean to say that there are no "proofs" in history and archaeology. I only want to emphasize that the images of retrospective self-modeling have a truth of their own, and that the investigation of this truth requires a different methodology, which is mnemohistory. Archaeological evidence can never prove such a model to be true or false. Its truth lies elsewhere. But it can, of course, be highly interesting to confront such models with archaeological evidence, as long as one keeps the different methodologies separated.

18. See François Hartog, *Mémoire d'Ulisse: Récits sur la frontière en Grèce ancienne* (Paris: Gallimard 1996), 73–75.

19. Jacques-Bénigne Bossuet, *Discours sur l'histoire universelle à Monseigneur le Dauphin: pour expliquer la suite de la religion et les changements des empires: Première partie: Depuis le commencement du monde jusqu'à l'empire de Charlemagne* (1681; repr. Paris, 1744).

20. *Athenian Letters or, the Epistolary Correspondence of an Agent of the King of Persia, Residing at Athens during the Peloponnesian War. Containing the History of the Times, in Dispatches to the Ministers of State at the Persian Court. Besides Letters on*

Various Subjects between Him and His Friends, 4 vols. (London: James Bettenham 1741–1743). I owe this reference to Carlo Ginzburg.

21. Ignaz von Born, "Über die Mysterien der Aegyptier," *Journal für Freymaurer* 1 (1784): 17–132.

22. Instead of being the opposite of myth, "history" (as Michel de Certeau has observed) "is probably our myth. It combines what can be thought, the 'thinkable,' and the origin, in conformity with the way in which a society can understand its own working"; see Michel de Certeau, *The Writing of History* (French ed. 1975), trans. Tom Conley (New York: Columbia UP, 1988), 21.

23. See Maurice Halbwachs, *La topographie legendaire des évangiles en Terre Sainte* (1941; 2nd ed. Paris: Presses Universitaires de France, 1971), *Les cadres sociaux de la mémoire* (Paris: F. Alcan, 1925), and *La mémoire collective* (Paris: Presses Universitaires de France, 1950). On Halbwachs see Gérard Namer, *Mémoire et société* (Paris: Meridiens Klincksieck, 1987).

24. Michael S. Roth, "We Are What We Remember (and Forget)," *Tikkun* 9.6 (1994): 41–42, 91.

25. Oliver Sacks, *The Man Who Mistook His Wife for a Hat and Other Clinical Tales* (New York: Summit Books, 1985), 110, quoted from Funkenstein, *Perceptions*, 33. See also Dan McAdams, *The Stories We Live By: Personal Myths and the Making of the Self* (New York: Morrow, 1993). Many of the "stories we live by" belong not to individual memory, but to collective and cultural memory. This point was made particularly clear by Thomas Mann in several of his novels (e.g., *Joseph und seine Brüder, Doktor Faustus)* and essays (esp. "Freud und die Zukunft," 1936); see my essay "Zitathaftes Leben: Thomas Mann und die Phänomenologie der kulturellen Erinnerung," *Thomas Mann Jahrbuch*, vol. 6, ed. E. Heftrich and H. Wysling (1994), 133–158. Eric Berne's concept of "script" also is relevant in this context; see Berne, *Beyond Games and Scripts* (New York: Grove Press, 1976). See also Donald P. Spence, *Narrative Truth and Historical Truth: Meaning and Interpretation in Psychoanalysis* (New York: Norton, 1982).

26. The notion of the "mythomoteur" was originated by Ramon d'Abadal i de Vinyals, "A propos du Legs Visigothique en Espagne," *Settimane di Studio del Centro Italiano di Studi Sull' Alt. Medioevo* 2 (1958): 541–585, and developed by J. Armstrong, *Nations before Nationalism* (Chapel Hill: U of North Carolina P, 1983), and Anthony D. Smith, *The Ethnic Origins of Nations* (Oxford: Blackwell, 1986). See my article "Frühe Formen politischer Mythomotorik: Fundierende, kontrapräsentische und revolutionäre Mythen," in *Revolution und Mythos*, ed. Dietrich Harth and Jan Assmann (Frankfurt: Fischer, 1992), 39–61.

27. See the particularly clear account of Foucault's concept of "discourse" by Christopher Tilley in Tilley, ed., *Reading Material Culture* (Oxford: Blackwell, 1990), 290–304. I owe this reference to Louise A. Hitchcock.

28. Siegfried Morenz, *Die Zauberflöte: Eine Studie zum Lebenszusammenhang Ägypten-Antike-Abendland* (Cologne and Münster: Böhlau, 1952).

29. Frances A. Yates, *Giordano Bruno and the Hermetic Tradition* (Chicago: U of Chicago P, 1964). Erik Iversen, *The Myth of Egypt and Its Hieroglyphs in the European Tradition* (1961; 2nd ed. Princeton: Princeton UP, 1993); Liselotte Dieckmann, *Hieroglyphics: The History of a Literary Symbol* (St. Louis: Washington UP, 1970). The treatise by Horapollo was discovered in 1419 on the island of Andros and was printed as early as 1505 in a Latin translation. The *Corpus Hermeticum* had been

brought to Italy by an agent of Cosimo de Medici in 1460. In 1463, it was translated into Latin by Marsilio Ficino, who interrupted his translation of Plato's works to do it.

30. See Yates, *Giordano Bruno.*

31. See Ingrid Merkel and Allen G. Debus, ed., *Hermeticism and the Renaissance: Intellectual History and the Occult in Early Modern Europe* (Washington, D.C.: Folger Books, 1988); A. Faivre, ed., *Présence d'Hermès Trismégiste,* Cahiers de l'Hermétisme (Paris: Albin Michel, 1988).

32. See besides Erik Iversen's magisterial survey the classic studies by Karl Giehlow, *Die Hieroglyphenkunde des Humanismus in der Allegorie der Renaissance, besonders der Ehrenpforte Kaisers Maximilian I.,* Jahrbuch der kunsthistorischen Sammlungen 32 (1915), vol. 1; Ludwig Volkmann, *Bilderschriften der Renaissance: Hieroglyphik und Emblematik in ihren Beziehungen und Fortwirkungen* (Leipzig, 1923); and Arthur Henkel and Albrecht Schöne, *Emblemata: Handbuch zur Sinnbildkunst des 16. und 17. Jahrhunderts* (Stuttgart: J. B. Metzler, 1967).

33. See Paolo Rossi, *The Great Abyss of Time: The History of the Earth and the History of Nations from Hooke to Vico,* trans. Lydia G. Cochrane (Chicago: U of Chicago P, 1985).

34. Isaac Casaubon, *De Rebus Sacris et Ecclesiasticis Exercitationes XVI: Ad Cardinalis Baronii Prolegomena in Annales* (London, 1614), 70ff. See Yates, *Giordano Bruno,* 398–403; A. Grafton, "Protestant versus Prophet: Isaac Casaubon on Hermes Trismegistos," *Journal of the Warburg and Courtauld Institutes* 46 (1983): 78–93.

35. James Stevens Curl, *The Egyptian Revival: An Introductory Study of a Recurring Theme in the History of Taste* (London: Allen & Unwin, 1982); Dirk Syndram, *Ägypten-Faszinationen: Untersuchungen zum Ägyptenbild im europäischen Klassizismus bis 1800* (Frankfurt: P. Lang, 1990).

36. For this tradition, see esp. Margaret C. Jacob, *The Radical Enlightenment: Pantheists, Freemasons, and Republicans* (London: Allen & Unwin, 1981).

37. An early instance of the interpretation of Ancient Egyptian religion as monotheistic worship of "Nature" is to be found in Henry Reynolds, *Mythomystes* (1633): "those old wise Aegyptian priests beganne to search out the Misteries of Nature (which was at first the whole world's divinity)" and devised "certain marks and characters of things," namely, the hieroglyphics, to hide and transmit their knowledge. Moses learned the art of concealing his true wisdom in allegorical language from his Egyptian teachers (quoted from Dieckmann, *Hieroglyphics,* 96f.).

38. Spiegel merit mention here because of his tremendous and in many respects even monstrous magnum opus *Das Werden der Altaegyptischen Hochkultur* (Heidelberg: Kerle, 1953), which embodies in the most extreme way the reorientation of German Egyptology after World War II and its quest for a spiritual Egypt.

39. *Ägypten: Der Weg des Pharaonenreichs* (Stuttgart: Kohlhammer, 1954).

40. *Altägyptische Erziehung* (Wiesbaden: Harrassowitz, 1956).

41. *Ägyptische Religion* (Stuttgart: Kohlhammer, 1960). *Gott und Mensch im alten Ägypten* (Leipzig: Koehler & Amelang, 1965); *Die Begegnung Europas mit Ägypten* (Berlin: Akademie-Verlag, 1968).

42. *Kulturgeschichte des alten Ägypten* (Stuttgart: A. Kroener, 1962).

2. Suppressed History, Repressed Memory

1. On the history of the discovery of the Amarna religion see Erik Hornung, "The Rediscovery of Akhenaten and His Place in Religion," *Journal of the American Research Center in Egypt* 29 (1992): 43–49.

2. They were not, of course. But Freud was strongly influenced by Weigall's suggestions.

3. Philippe Aziz, *Moise et Akhenaton, les énigmes de l'univers* (Paris: Editions Robert Laffront, 1980); Ahmed Osman, *Moses, Pharaoh of Egypt: The Mystery of Akhenaten Resolved* (London: Grafton Books, 1990).

4. Aleida Assmann, "Stabilizers of Memory—Affect, Symbol, Trauma," unpublished lecture at the Getty Center for the History of Art and the Humanities, March 23, 1995.

5. See my article "Das ägyptische Prozessionsfest," in *Das Fest und das Heilige: Religiöse Kontrapunkte zur Alltagswelt*, Studien zum Verstehen fremder Religionen 1, ed. Jan Assmann and Theo Sundermeier (Gütersloh: Bertelsmann, 1991), 105–122.

6. See my article "Ocular Desire in a Time of Darkness: Urban Festivals and Divine Visibility in Ancient Egypt," *Torat ha-Adam*, Yearbook of Religious Anthropology 1, ed. A. Agus and J. Assmann (Berlin: Akademie-Verlag 1994), 13–29.

7. Wolfgang Helck, *Urkunden IV: Urkunden der 18. Dynastie*, vol. 22 (Berlin: Akademie Verlag, 1958), 2025ff. This work is hereafter cited as Urk.

8. See Hans Goedicke, "The 'Canaanite Illness,'" *Studien zur Altägyptischen Kultur* 11 (1984): 91–105; id., "The End of the Hyksos in Egypt," *Egyptological Studies in Honor of Richard A. Parker*, ed. Leonard H. Lesko (Hanover and London: UP of New England, 1986), 37–47. I owe these references to Thomas Schneider.

9. About the possible encounter with the Persians: The Achaemenids were adherents of Zoroastrism, and the attribution by later Egyptian sources to Cambyses of the destruction of Egyptian temples and the killing of the Apis bull may not be completely without foundation.

10. Papyrus Sallier I, 1.2–3 = Alan H. Gardiner, *Late-Egyptian Stories*, Bibliotheca Aegyptiaca 1 (Brussels: Editions de la Fondation Egyptologique Reine Elizabeth, 1932), 85; Hans Goedicke, *The Quarrel of Apophis and Seqenenre* (San Antonio: Van Sicklen, 1986), 10f.

11. Eduard Meyer, *Aegyptische Chronologie*, Abhandlungen der Preussischen Akademie der Wissenschaften (Leipzig: Hinrichs, 1904), 92–95.

12. Rolf Krauss, *Das Ende der Amarnazeit* (Hildesheim: Gerstenberg, 1978); Donald B. Redford, "The Hyksos Invasion in History and Tradition," *Orientalia* 39 (1970): 1–51, traces the story of the lepers back to the Amarna age; this piece also appears in *Pharaonic King Lists, Annals, and Day-Books: A Contribution to the Study of the Egyptian Sense of History* (Mississauga: Benben Publications, 1986), 293. Redford even goes so far as to correlate certain details of the legend with concrete events of the Amarna period, such as the compulsory labor in the quarries and the excessive building activity of Amenophis III and IV; the concentration camp in the desert and the secession of the court to Amarna; the thirteen years that the lepers are purported to have ruled Egypt and the thirteen years that Akhenaten probably spent in his new capital; the pestilence that broke out at the end of the Amarna period and raged for twenty years in several countries of the Ancient Near East; and

the epidemic mentioned in several versions of the legend. Finally there is the issue of dating the whole story to the reign of Amenophis III. Redford arrives at the same conclusion that I think inevitable: "what the tale proves is that the Amarna debacle, with all its characters and events, had not been lost to the collective memory of Egypt, but had survived in some form" (*King Lists* 294).

13. See Jan Assmann, *Monotheismus und Kosmotheismus: Ägyptische Formen eines "Denkens des Einen" und ihre europäische Rezeptionsgeschichte*, Sitzungs/berichte der Heidelberger Akademie der Wissenschaften 1993.2 (Heidelberg, 1993).

14. See Raymond Weill, *La fin du Moyen Empire égyptien: Etude sur les monuments et l'histoire de la période comprise entre la xiie et la xviiie dynastie* (Paris: A. Picard, 1918), 95–145.

15. See Pier Cesare Bori, "Immagini e stereotipi del popolo ebraico nel mondo antico: asino d'oro, vitelle d'oro," in *L'estasi del profeta*, 131–150 (with a rich bibliography; I owe this reference to Mauro Pesce, who drew my attention to this important book). For the polemical impact of this tradition see esp. Peter Schäfer, *Judaeophobia: The Attitude Towards the Jews in the Ancient World* (Cambridge, Mass.: Harvard UP, 1997).

16. I am using the edition by W. G. Waddell, ed. and trans., *Manetho*, Loeb Classical Library (Cambridge, Mass.: Harvard UP, 1940).

17. King "Thumosis"; Ptolemy of Mendes has "Amosis" as the king of the Exodus (poreia) of the Jews from Egypt under Moses, which can only refer to Ahmose, the liberator from the Hyksos; *apud* Tatianus, *Oratio ad Graecos*, 38 = Menachem Stern, *Greek and Latin Authors on Jews and Judaism*, 3 vols. (Jerusalem: Israel Academy of Sciences and Humanities, Magnes Press, 1974–1984), vol. 1, no.157a/b, 380f. Apion refers to Ptolemy, who dates the Exodus to the reign of Ahmose.

18. Stern, *Greek and Latin Authors*, vol. 1, no. 21, 78–86; Eduard Meyer, *Geschichte des Altertums* (repr. Darmstadt: Wissenschaftliche Buchgesellschaft, 1953), vol. 2, p. 1, 420–426; Redford, *King Lists*, 282f.; D. Mendels, "The Polemical Character of Manetho's Aegyptiaca," in *Purposes of History*, ed. H. Verdin, G. Schepens, and E. de Keyser, *Studia Hellenistica* 30 (1990) 91–110. I owe this reference to T. Schneider.

19. The name is commonly explained as "Osiris-Sepa." Chaeremon uses the form "Peteseph," which can only be explained as *P3dj-Sp3*, "Given by Sepa." Sepa is a minor deity and lord of a small town south of Cairo which the Greeks called Babylon. To Thomas Mann we owe the attractive interpretation of the name as "Osiris Joseph," i.e., "Joseph in the netherworld." The interpretation of the first element as "Osiris" had already occurred in Josephus, *Contra Apionem*, 250 *(apò tou en Helioupólei theou Osireos)*. See Krauss, *Amarnazeit*, 213, n. 1.

20. Mary Douglas, *In the Wilderness: The Doctrine of Defilement in the Book of Numbers* (Sheffield: Sheffield Academic Press, 1993).

21. Funkenstein, *Perceptions* 36.

22. There is general consent that the mention of Moses in Manetho's text must be regarded as a later addition; see John G. Gager, *Moses in Greco-Roman Paganism* (New York: Abingdon Press, 1972), 117. But it is equally possible that Manetho wrote the gloss himself in order to make his account conform with Hecataeus' version, which he probably knew.

23. See Raymond Weill, *La fin*, 22–68, 76–83, 111–145, 605–623.

24. Hecataeos of Abdera, *Aigyptiaka,* excerpts in Diodorus, *Bibliotheca Historica,* 40.3 = *Diodorus of Sicily,* ed. and trans. F. R. Walton, Loeb Classical Library (Cambridge, Mass.: Harvard UP, 1967), 281; Redford, *King Lists* 281f.

25. Martin Bernal, who builds his theories about the Egyptian derivation of Greek culture largely on this passage and similar passages in Diodorus (1.28.1–29.5; cf. 1.55.5 and 1.94.1ff.), does not seem to be aware of the legendary character of this tradition.

26. See Hartog, *Mémoire d'Ulisse,* 72–75.

27. See Stern, *Greek and Latin Authors,* vol. 1, no. 11, 20–44. Tacitus also characterizes the Jewish concept of God as monotheistic and aniconic: "Aegyptii pleraque animalia effigiesque compositas venerantur, Iudaei mente sola unumque numen intellegunt: profanos, qui deum imagines mortalibus materiis in species hominum effingant; summum illud et aternum neque imitabile neque interiturum" (*Historiae,* 5.5.4; see Stern, *Greek and Latin Authors,* vol. 2, no. 281, 19 and 26).

28. E.g., Lysimachos, *Aegyptiaca,* excerpt in Josephus, *Contra Apionem,* 1.304–311 = Stern, *Greek and Latin Authors,* vol. 1, no. 158, 383–386, and Tacitus.

29. E.g., Manetho and Chaeremon. Bocchoris belongs to the Twenty-fourth Dynasty and is purported to have been executed by the Ethiopian king Shabaka. He might have been regarded as the last legitimite Egyptian pharaoh before the Assyrian conquest and the rule of the Ethiopians. However, Amenophis refers to Amenophis III. He is the last king before the religious revolution of Akhenaten. Both kings may have been connected with serious crises in collective memory. Further they share a common connection with some "messianic" oracles. Amenophis III appears in a Greek text, known as the "Oracle of a Potter" which predicts a long period of distress when Egypt will fall into the hands of the *zonophoroi,* or "girdle-bearers" (a reference to the Macedonians). After this, a king will rise who will be chosen by the sun god and enthroned by Isis; see Laszlo Kakosy, *Acta Orientalia* 19 (1966): 345; Ludwig Koenen, *Zeitschrift für Papyruskunde und Epigraphik* 2 (1968): 178ff.; John W. B. Barns, *Orientalia* 46 (1977): 31ff.; Redford, *King Lists,* 284–286. Bocchoris appears in a demotic text known as the "Oracle of the Lamb," predicting the liberation of Egypt and the return of the stolen images of the gods after nine hundred years of suppression; see Kakosy, *Acta Orientalia* 19, 344f., and Redford, *King Lists,* 286 (with bibliography). Both oracles seem to belong to the same kind of nativistic tradition which spread under the experience of foreign domination and which formed the context of the Egyptian "Exodus" stories.

30. John G. Gager, *The Origins of Anti-Semitism* (New York: Oxford UP, 1983). Jerry L. Daniel, "Anti-Semitism in the Hellenistic Period," *Journal of Biblical Literature* 98 (1979): 45–65; Arieh Kasher, *The Jews in Hellenistic and Roman Egypt: The Struggle for Equal Rights* (Tübingen: Mohr, 1985); Schäfer, *Judaeophobia.*

31. See Apollonius Molon, *apud* Josephus *Contra Apionem* 2.148 *(hōs atheous kai misanthrōpous),* and Diodorus, *Bibl. Hist.,* 34–35, where he says of Moses that he gave the Jews their "misanthropic and unlawful rules" *(ta misanthrōpa kai paranoma ēthē):* Stern, *Greek and Latin Authors,* vol. 1, no. 63, 182.

32. Chaeremon, *Aegyptiaca Historia, apud* Josephus, *Contra Apionem,* 1.288–292, Stern, *Greek and Latin Authors,* vol. 1, no. 178, 419–421; Redford, *King Lists,* 287f. For Chaeremon see P. W. van der Horst, *Chaeremon. Egyptian Priest and Stoic Philosopher* (Leiden: Brill, 1984), esp. 8f. and 49f.

33. Quoted from Gager, *Moses,* 49.

34. See Arthur J. Droge, *Homer or Moses? Early Christian Interpretations of the History of Culture* (Tübingen: Mohr, 1989), 25–35.

35. See P. M. Fraser, *Ptolemaic Alexandria*, 3 vols. (Oxford: Clarendon, 1972), vol. 1, 704–706.

36. Stern, *Greek and Latin Authors*, vol. 2, no. 281, 17–63. A. M. A. Hospers-Jansen, *Tacitus over de Joden* (Groningen: J. B. Wolter, 1949); Redford, *King Lists*, 289.

37. "Aegyptii pleraque animalia effigiesque compositas venerantur, Iudaei mente sola unumque numen intellegunt: profanos, qui deum imagines mortalibus materiis in species hominum effingant; summum illud et aeternum neque imitabile neque interiturum"; *Historiae*, 5.5.4 = Stern, *Greek and Latin Authors*, vol. 2, no. 281, 19 and 26.

38. *De Iside et Osiride*, 31.9.363C-D = Plutarch's *Moralia*, 5, ed. and trans. Frank Cole Babbitt, Loeb Classical Library (Cambridge, Mass.: Harvard UP, 1962), 76f.; John G. Griffiths, *Plutarch's "De Iside et Osiride"* (Cardiff:, U of Wales P, 1970), 418f.

39. See Gager, *Moses*, 30–31.

40. See Stern, *Greek and Latin Authors*, vol. 1, 97–98.

41. Stern, *Greek and Latin Authors*, vol. 1, no. 164, 392–395.

42. John Toland, *Origines Judaicae* (London, 1709), 118–119; see Rossi, *The Dark Abyss of Time*, 128. William Warburton, *The Divine Legation of Moses Demonstrated on the Principles of a Religious Deist, from the Omission of the Doctrine of a Future State of Reward and Punishment in the Jewish Dispensation* (1738–1741; 2nd ed. London, 1778), 117.

43. Strabo is arguing along the line of Stoic theology, according to which the cosmos is (the true and only temple of) god, who must not be enshrined within walls and ceilings (a theology which Cicero also attributes to the Zoroastrian Persians). It is needless to stress the completely un-Biblical character of this argument against idolatry. The Biblical god explicitly "wants to dwell in darkness." The coincidence in the refusal of images is purely formal. In the Biblical sense of idolatry, the worship of images is apostasy, turning to other gods instead of Yahweh. In the sense of Greek philosophy, the worship of images is an inadequate reduction of the All-Encompassing and Intelligible to a material object. See Yehoshua Amir, "Die Begegnung des biblischen und des philosophischen Monotheismus als Grundthema des jüdischen Hellenismus," *Evangelische Theologie* 38 (1978): 2–19, esp. 7, and Gager, *Moses*, 40–41.

44. Strabo, *Geographica*, 16.2.35; Stern, *Greek and Latin Authors*, vol. 1, no. 11, 261—351, esp. 294f.

45. See Gregor Ahn, "'Monotheismus'—'Polytheismus.' Grenzen und Möglichkeiten einer Klassifikation von Gottesvorstellungen," *Mesopotamica—Ugaritica —Biblica: Festschrift für Kurt Bergerhof*, ed. M. Dietrich and O. Loretz (Kevelaer-Neukirchen: Neukirchner Verlag, 1993), 1–24, esp. 5–12.

46. Nicolas Abraham and Maria Torok, *L'écorce et le noyau* (Paris: Aubier, 1978).

47. See Aleida Assmann, "Affect, Symbol, Trauma," with reference to J. F. Lyotard.

48. Donald B. Redford, *Egypt, Canaan, and Israel in Ancient Times* (Princeton: Princeton UP, 1992), 419.

49. Emma Brunner-Traut, *Altägyptische Tiergeschichte und Fabel, Gestalt und Strahlkraft* (Darmstadt: Wissenschaftliche Buchgesellschaft, 1984).

50. Douglas, *In the Wilderness*, 148.

51. For ancient theories on icons and the divine presence see Moshe Barasch, *Icon: Studies in the History of an Idea* (New York: New York UP, 1992), 23–48.

52. Papyrus CPJ 520, quoted from David Frankfurter, *Elijah in Upper Egypt: The Apocalypse of Elijah and Early Christianity* (Minneapolis: Fortress Press, 1993), 189–191.

53. See Heinz Heinen, "Ägyptische Grundlagen des antiken Antijudaismus," *Trierer Theologische Zeitschrift* 101 (1992): 124–149, 128–132.

54. Gager, *Origins of Anti-Semitism*, and esp. Schäfer, *Judaeophobia*.

55. Carlo Ginzburg, *Ecstasies: Deciphering the Witches' Sabbath*, trans. Raymond Rosenthal (New York: Pantheon Books, 1991) chap. 1: "Lepers, Jews, Muslims," pp. 33–62.

56. The revival of interest in Josephus Flavius' work during the Middle Ages may also have contributed to the revival of this association. Ginzburg refers to H. Schreckenberg, *Die Flavius-Josephus-Tradition in Antike und Mittelalter* (Leiden, 1972). Quotations from Josephus in medieval texts refer, however, only to *Bellum Judaicum* and *Antiquitates Judaicae* and never to *Contra Apionem*, where the ancient traditions about Jews and lepers are recorded. But the story occurs also in other texts which were read during the Middle Ages, such as those by Tacitus and Orosius.

57. Ginzburg, *Ecstasies*, 63–86.

58. Benno Landsberger, R. Hallock, Thorkild Jacobsen, and Adam Falkenstein, *Materialien zum Sumerischen Lexikon (MSL) IV: Introduction. Part I: Emesal Vocabulary* (Rome: Pontificate Institute Press, 1956), 4–10.

59. Robert L. Litke, "A Reconstruction of the Assyro-Babylonian God Lists An: Anum, Anu ša Ameli," diss., Yale University, 1958. I owe this reference and much pertinent information to the kindness of Karlheinz Deller of Heidelberg, to whom I express my sincere gratitude. I would also like to thank my research assistant in Santa Monica, Louise A. Hitchcock, who contributed much information concerning Mesopotamia.

60. British Museum, tablet K 2100 = British Museum. Department of Egyptian and Assyrian Antiquities, *Cuneiform Texts from Babylonian tablets, &c., in the British Museum*, vol. 25 (London: British Museum, 1909), 18.

61. Nock, *Conversion*, 138.

62. John Gwyn Griffiths, *Apuleius of Madauros: The Isis-Book (Metamorphoses, Book XI)*, Etudes Préliminaires des Religions Orientales 39 (Leiden: Brill, 1975), 70f., 114ff.

63. The fact that Apuleius reckons with two instead of only one chosen people, namely, the Ethiopians and Egyptians, finds an easy explanation in the fact that the most important temple of Isis was situated on the island of Philae on the border between Egypt and Lower Nubia (= Ethiopia).

64. In the ancient cult place of the Egyptian goddess of the harvest, Renenutet or (Th)Ermutis, King Ptolemy Soter II built a temple to Isis-Thermutis.

65. Thiouis = e.g., *t3 wʿt* Copt. TIOYI, "the one"; see A. Vogliano, *Primo rapporto degli scavi condotti dalla missione archeologica d' Egitto della R. universita di Milano nella zona di Madinet Madi* (Milan, 1936), 27–51, esp. p. 34. Cf. the Hebrew *æchad* as a divine name and see Cyrus H. Gordon, "His Name Is 'One,'" *Journal of Near Eastern Studies* 29 (1970): 198ff.

66. Vera F. Vanderlip, *The Four Greek Hymns of Isidorus and the Cult of Isis*, American Studies in Papyrology 12 (Toronto: A. M. Hakkert, 1972), 18f.; Etienne Bernand, *Inscriptions métriques de l'Egypte gréco-romaine* (Paris: Belles Lettres, 1969), no. 175, 632ff.; Maria Totti, *Ausgewählte Texte der Isis-Serapis-Religion*, Subsidia Epigrapha 12 (Hildesheim and New York: G. Olms, 1985), 76–82; Françoise Dunand, "Le syncrétisme isiaque à la fin de l'époque hellénistique," in *Les syncrétismes dans les religions grecque et romaine*, Colloque de Strasbourg, Bibliothèque des Centres d'Études Supérieures spécialisés, ed. F. Dunand and P. Levêque (Paris: Presses Universitaires de France, 1973), 79–93. On Isidorus see Han J. W. Drijvers, *Vox Theologica* 32 (1962): 139–150.

67. B. P. Grenfell and A. S. Hunt, *The Oxyrhynchus Papyri*, vol. 11 (London, 1915), 196–202, no. 1380; see B. A. van Groningen, "De papyro Oxyrhynchita 1380," diss., University of Groningen, 1921; Nock, *Conversion*, 150ff.

68. On *Hypsistos* see Martin Nilsson, *Harvard Theological Review* 56 (1963): 101–120. For *Hypsistos* as a designation of the god of the Jews, translating Hebrew *El Elyon*, see Elias Bickerman, *The Jews in the Greek Age* (Cambridge, Mass.: Harvard UP, 1988), 263f.; Martin Hengel, *Judentum und Hellenismus*, 3rd ed. (Tübingen: Mohr, 1988), 545f.; Carsten Colpe, "Hypsistos," in *Der Kleine Pauly*, vol. 2 (Munich, 1979), 1292f.

69. Erik Peterson, *Heîs Theós: Epigraphische, formgeschichtliche und religions-geschichtliche Untersuchungen*, Forschungen zur Religion und Literatur des Alten und Neuen Testaments NF 24 (Göttingen: Vandenhoeck & Ruprecht, 1926); Otto Weinreich, *Neue Urkunden zur Sarapis-Religion* (Tübingen: J. C. B. Mohr, 1928).

70. Martin Nilsson, *Grundriss der Griechischen Religionsgeschichte*, 2nd ed. (Munich: C. H. Beck, 1974) vol. II, 573f.

71. Ps. Just. *Cohortatio ad Graecos*, 15 = *Orphicorum Fragmenta*, 239. Macrobius, *Saturnalia*, 1.18.17, quotes the first verse.

72. Macrobius, *Saturnalia*, 1.18, 20; see Peterson, *Heîs Theós*, 243f.; Hengel, *Judentum*, 476f. See also the inscription *Heîs Zeùs Sérapis Iaó* (*CIL*, 2, suppl. 5665 = F. Dunand, "Les syncrétismes dans la religion de l'Egypte gréco-romaine," *Les syncrétismes dans les religions de l'antiquité*, ed. F. Dunand and P. Leveque, Etudes Préliminaires des Religions Orientales 46 (Leiden: Brill, 1975), 170.

73. E. Peterson, *Monotheismus als politisches Problem* (Leipzig: Hegner, 1935); id., *Theologische Traktate* (Munich: Kösel, 1951), 45–147; Alfred Schindler, ed., *Monotheismus als politisches Problem: Erik Peterson und die Kritik der politischen Theologie*, Studien zur evangelischen Ethik 14 (Gütersloh: Gütersloher Verlagshaus, 1978). See also Arnaldo Momigliano, "The Disadvantages of Monotheism for a Universal State," in *On Pagans, Jews, and Christians* (Middletown, Conn: Weselyan UP, 1987), 142–158. See also Dunand, "Les syncrétismes," 152–185, 173ff., on the political dimension of syncretism. For Late Antiquity see Garth Fowden, *Empire to Commonwealth: Consequences of Monotheism in Late Antiquity* (Princeton: Princeton UP, 1993).

74. See Reinhold Merkelbach and Maria Totti, *Abrasax: Ausgewählte Papyri religiösen und magischen Inhalts 1: Gebete*, Abhandlungen der rheinisch-westfälischen Akademie der Wissenschaften, Sonderreihe Papyrologica Colonensia, vol. 17.1 (Opladen: Westfälischer Verlag, 1990), 166f. See also Peterson, *Heîs Theós*, 254, for more parallels.

75. K. Preisendanz et. al., ed., *Papyri Graeca Magicae: Die Griechischen Zauber-papyri*, 2nd ed. (Stuttgart: Teubner, 1973), vol. 2, 109, 119.

76. Hippolytus, *Refutatio Omnium Haeresium*, 5.9, 7–11, quoted from W. Foerster, *Die Gnosis*, vol. 1: *Zeugnisse der Kirchenväter* (Zurich: Artemis, 1969), 358f.

77. Karl Leonhard Reinhold, *Die Hebräischen Mysterien oder die älteste religiöse Freymaurerey* (Leipzig: Göschen, 1788), 35; Warburton, *Divine Legation*, vol. 2, 524.

78. "An Outlandish Medley to a Marble Statue of Liber Pater in My Country House, Having the Attributes of All Gods."

79. See H. G. E. White, ed. and trans., *Ausonius*, 2 vols. (Cambridge, Mass.: Harvard UP, 1985), 186f.

80. According to White, this refers to the Thebans, the sons of Ogyges, the mythical founder of the city.

81. This refers to Ausonius' estate.

82. "Omne hoc quod vides, quo divina atque humana conclusa sunt, unum est: membra sumus corporis magni." Seneca, *Ad Lucilium Epistulae Morales*, ed. and trans. Manfred Rosenbach, in *Seneca: Philosophische Schriften*, vol. 4, (Darmstadt: Wissenschaftliche Buchgesellschaft 1995), 492–495.

83. Eduard Norden, *Agnostos Theos* (Leipzig: Teubner, 1912), 61.

84. Augustine *De Consensu Evangelist.* 1.22.30 and 23.31 *PL*, 34, 1005f. = Varro, fr. 1, 58b; see Hengel, *Judentum und Hellenismus*, 472.

85. *Letter to Anebo*, quoted by Iamblichus, *De Mysteriis Aegyptiorum*, 7.5, ed. and trans. Edouard Des Places, 2nd ed. (Paris: Les Belles Lettres, 1989) 193.

86. Origen *Contra Celsum*, 1.24, 5.41 (45); see Hengel, *Judentum*, 476.

87. Plutarch, *De Iside et Osiride*, chap. 67, pp. 377ff., trans. Griffiths, in *Plutarch's "De Iside and Osiride,"* 223f.

3. Before the Law

1. Another trace might be seen in Exod. 11:3: "and moreover, the man Moses was very great in the land of Egypt," a strange mention because it speaks of Moses, with whom the reader is already perfectly familiar, as if he were a newcomer to the story: "the man Moses." Note that Freud took precisely this contextually strange trace of the "Egyptian" Moses as a title for his book. See Knauf, *Midian*, 129.

2. By "Hebraists" I mean those scholars of the sixteenth and seventeenth centuries who not only knew Hebrew and were able to read the Bible in the original language, but also studied the Rabbinic and cabalistic traditions in the sources available to them. My own acquaintance with this literature is admittedly limited, but judging from Spencer and his references to fellow Hebraists the level of these studies seems to have been somewhat higher than what is usually seen in contemporary Old Testament studies. For Christian Hebraists, especially those of the seventeenth century, see Frank E. Manuel, *The Broken Staff: Judaism through Christian Eyes* (Cambridge, Mass.: Harvard UP, 1992), and Aaron L. Katchen, *Christian Hebraists and Dutch Rabbis: Seventeenth Century Apologetics and the Study of Maimonides' "Mishneh Torah"* (Cambridge, Mass.: Harvard UP, 1984).

3. Cambridge, 1685; frequently reprinted, e.g. The Hague, 1686; Leipzig: Zeitler, 1705; Cambridge, 1727; and Tübingen: Cotta, 1732. My quotations are from the 1686 edition and my deepest gratitude goes to my student Florian Ebeling, who procured for me a microfilm and a photocopy of the book.

4. Philo Judaeus, *Vita Mosis*, 1.5.23.

5. See also Selden's distinction between *ius naturale* (the Noahidic laws) and *disciplina Hebraeorum:* John Selden, *De Iure Naturali et Gentium Iuxta Disciplinam Hebraeorum Libri Septem* (London, 1640); Friedrich Niewöhner, *Veritas sive Varietas: Lessings Toleranzparabel und das Buch von den drei Betrügern* (Heidelberg: Lambert Schneider, 1988), 333–336. The discovery of the "natural law" of nations is the object of Vico's "new science." Vico mentions Hugo Grotius, John Selden, and Samuel Pufendorf as the leading theorists of natural law. See Leon Pompa, ed. and trans., *Vico: Selected Writings* (Cambridge: Cambridge UP, 1982), 81–89.

6. Several of the immediate predecessors and contemporaries of Spencer, such as Samuel Bochart (1599–1667), Pierre-Daniel Huet (1630–1721), Edward Stillingfleet (1635–1699), and Theophile Gale (1628–1678), engaged in the project of reestablishing the priority of Biblical wisdom and theology over the Renaissance concept of *prisca theologia*, which attributed highest authority to figures like Hermes Trismegistus and Zoroaster. When they speak of translation, derivation, borrowing, and the like, they invariably make Biblical tradition the giver and pagan traditions the receiver. Moreover, they interpret reception as degeneration or even perversion.

7. Shlomo Pines, trans., Moses Maimonides, *The Guide of the Perplexed (Dalalat al-ha'irin)* (Chicago: U of Chicago P, 1963). Spencer mostly quotes Maimonides in Hebrew, only occasionally giving the original Arabic.

8. Pines, *Guide*, introduction, cxxiii.

9. Koran 2:59; cf. 5:73 and 22:17.

10. In 1662, Edward Stillingsfleet identified the Sabians with the "Eastern Chaldaeans," by which term he denoted the Zoroastrians: "Concerning these Zabii, Maimonides tells us, that the understanding of their rites would give a great deal of light to several passages of Scripture which now lie in obscurity: but little is supposed to be yet further known of them than what Scaliger hath said, that they were the more Eastern Chaldaeans." According to Stillingfleet, Zoroaster was both "the author of the Zabbi" and "the founder of the Persian worship, or rather a promoter of it among the Persians." He saw the common denominator of Zabiism and Persian worship in "their agreement in the chief point of idolatry, the worship of the sun": *Origines sacrae, or a Rational Account of the Grounds of Christian Faith, as to the Truth and Divine Authority of the Scriptures, and the Matters Therein Contained* (London, 1662: 3rd ed. London, 1666; 4th ed. Oxford, 1797), vol. 1, 49–51 (4th ed.) Theophile Gale held that "the Rites of the Zabii are the same with those of the Chaldaeans and Persians, who all agreed in this worship of the Sun, and of Fire, &c."; see *The Court of the Gentiles*. 2 vols. (Oxford, 1669–1671), vol. 2, 73. According to Gale, Abraham transmitted the original wisdom to the Chaldaeans, in whose hands the tradition soon degenerated into "that Black Art (deservedly so called because of Hell) of Judicial Astrologie, or Divination." Later, this "Black Art" gave rise to "Zabiisme." A later development of this tradition was Zoroastrianism, for "Soroaster, who is reputed the Founder of the Persick Philosophie, and Worship, was indeed but the Promoter of it: for the main of the Persian Rites, and Wisdom, wherein their Magi were instructed, were traduced from the Zabii, or Chaldean Philosophers." On the Sabians or Zabii see also Theophile Gale, *Philosophia Generalis in Duas Partes Determinata* (London, 1676), 139–140. Thomas Hyde, *Historia Religionis Veterum Persarum, Eorumque Magorum* (1700; 2nd ed. Oxford, 1760), 122–138, inverts the sequence and sees in Zabiism a later degeneration of Zoroas-

trianism. Thomas Stanley devoted the last volume of his monumental *History of Philosophy*, 3 vols. (London, 1665–1672; London, 1687 = New York and London, 1978), to the "History of the Chaldaick Philosophy" which deals with the "Sabeans" on pp. 1062–1067. I am indebted to Michael Stansberg for much information; see his forthcoming book *Faszination Zara/Austra: Zoraster und die Europäische Religionsgeschichte*.

11. See D. Chwolsohn, *Die Ssabier und der Ssabismus*, 2 vols. (St. Petersburg, 1856).

12. Funkenstein, *Perceptions*, 144.

13. Walter Scott, ed. and trans., *Hermetica: The Ancient Greek and Latin Writings Which Contain Religious or Philosophic Teachings Ascribed to Hermes Trismegistus* (1929; repr. Boston: Shambhala, 1993), 97–108.

14. The most important among them was Thabit ibn Qurra (835–901) who wrote among many others a book called *De Religione Sabiorum*. See Scott, *Hermetica*, 103–105.

15. Pines, *Guide*, cxxiii–cxxiv.

16. Umberto Eco, "An Ars Oblivionalis? Forget It!" *PMLA* 103 (1988): 254–261.

17. *Talattuf alallah waḥakhmatah*, "the cunning (or 'practical reason') of God and his wisdom," is an expression which Funkenstein very interestingly links with Hegel's concept of "the cunning of reason"; see *Perceptions*, 141–144, with the important footnote 38 on p. 143 referring to Maimonides, *Moreh Nebukhim*, 3.32, and G. W. F. Hegel, *Philosophie der Geschichte* (Stuttgart: Reclam, 1961), 78ff. Spencer speaks of God's using "honest fallacies and tortuous steps," *methodis honeste fallacibus et sinuosis gradibus*, quoted from Gotthard Victor Lechler, *Geschichte des englischen Deismus* (Tübingen, 1841; repr. Hildesheim: Olms, 1965), 138. See also S. D. Benin, "The Cunning of God and Divine Accommodation," *Journal of the History of Ideas* 45 (1984): 179–191.

18. "Ut omnes isti cultus aut ritus, qui fiebant in gratiam imaginum, fierent in honorem Dei," Spencer's translation of Rabbi Shem Tov ben Joseph ibn Shem Tov's commentary on Maimonides' *Guide for the Perplexed*.

19. Spencer, *De Legibus*, vol. 2, 213. As Pines points out in his introduction, this corresponds to the Arabic use of the term, where "the appellation Sabians came to be applicable to all pagans." But, he adds, "no example of this linguistic usage ever occurs in the Guide" (*Guide*, cxxiv).

20. See Francis Schmidt, "Des inepties tolérables: La raison des rites de John Spencer (1685) à W. Robertson Smith (1889)," *Archive de Science Sociale des Religions* 85 (1994): 121–136.

21. Maimonides' main work on idolatry is his commentary on the Mishna tractate *Hilkhot Avodah Zarah* in book 1 of his *Mishneh Torah*. This commentary was frequently translated into Latin and formed one of the basic texts of Christian apologetic literature of the seventeenth century; see Katchen, *Christian Hebraists*. Gerard Vossius published as an appendix to his much-quoted *Theologia Gentili* a work by his son Dionysius Voss (1612–1633): *Maimonides, "De Idolatria," cum Interpretatione Latina et Notis*. See Gerardus Joannis Vossius, *De Theologia Gentili et Physiologia Christiana: sive de Origine ac Progressu Idololatriae, ad Veterum Gesta, ac Rerum Naturam, Reductae; deque Naturae Mirandis, Quibus Homo Adducitur ad Deum* (Amsterdam, 1641; 2nd ed. Frankfurt, 1668; repr. New York and London, 1976).

22. Funkenstein, *Perceptions*, 17. I am grateful to Gesine Palmer for some important clarifications. In a letter dated May 5, 1995, she pointed out to me that *halakhic* thinking attempts to keep valid a historical law under conditions that differ from its original historical circumstances. Seen this way, historical interpretation amounts not to abolition, but to preservation. The distinction between the historical case, A, and the present case, B, is made in order to discover a common metahistorical denominator, C, which becomes established as the meaning of the law.

23. See, however, Funkenstein, *Perceptions*, 16–18, who sees a source of historical consciousness in legal reasoning.

24. Spencer, *De Legibus*, vol. 3, 12.

25. *Moreh Nebukhim*, 3.46, Pines, *Guide*, vol. 2, 581–582.

26. For the following history see esp. Bezalel Porten, *Archives from Elephantine: The Life of an Ancient Jewish Military Colony* (Los Angeles: U of California P, 1968).

27. Porten, *Archives*, 105–150.

28. Porten, *Archives*, 133–150.

29. Porten, *Archives*, 173–179.

30. Porten, *Archives*, 290f.

31. Herodotus, *Hist.*, 3.27–29.

32. Georges Posener, *La première domination perse en Egypte: Recueil d'inscriptions hiéroglyphiques* (Cairo: Imprimerie de l'Institut Français d'Archéologie Orientale, 1936); Friedrich Karl Kienitz, *Die politische Geschichte Ägyptens vom 7. bis zum 4.Jahrhundert vor der Zeitwende* (Berlin: Akademie Verlag, 1953), 55–60.

33. Diodorus, *Bibl. Hist.*, 1.94f.; Kienitz, *Politische Geschichte Ägyptens*, 61–66.

34. Porten, *Archives*, 292f.

35. I am basing my account on Porten, *Archives*, and on the still immensely readable book by Eduard Meyer, *Der Papyrusfund von Elephantine: Dokumente einer jüdischen Gemeinde aus der Perserzeit und das älteste erhaltene Buch der Weltliteratur*, 3rd ed. (Leipzig: Hinrichs, 1912).

36. Spencer, *De Legibus*, vol. 2, 231.

37. "Non itaque sine causa creditur, Deum, in Deorum Aegyptiacorum, comtemptum, arietem et bovem, in solemni Paschatis festo, immolari voluisse."

38. "Deus ea animalia quae Veteres Aegyptii maximi fecerunt, in Lege sua studiose vilificare et maxima cum contumelia tractare videatur."

39. Pace Funkenstein, *Perceptions*, 37.

40. Vol. 2, chap. 3, pp. 223–229.

41. Spencer uses the term "zoolatry" in Greek transcription.

42. Funkenstein, *Perceptions*, 37. He means it ironically. The historian of religion who saluted Spencer as the founder of the discipline two hundred years in advance of his age was William Robertson Smith; see Francis Schmidt, "Des inepties tolérables." I am grateful to Guy Stroumsa for putting me in touch with Francis Schmidt and to Schmidt for having sent me the above-mentioned article.

43. Exod. 23:19, 34:26; Deut. 14:21; see vol. 2, chap. 8, sect. 1, pp. 270–279.

44. Deut. 26:13, 14 see vol. 2, chap. 24, sect. 1, pp. 420–424.

45. Othmar Keel, *Das Böcklein in der Milch seiner Mutter und Verwandtes: im Lichte eines altorientalischen Bildmotivs*. Orbis Biblicus et Orientalis 33 (Fribourg: Presses Universitaires, 1980). Keel gives an excellent survey of the various traditions

of interpretation, rejecting those based on "normative inversion" as speculative and anachronistic.

46. But the Jewish application of this law extends the notion of "kid" to any kind of meat and the notion of milk to any kind of dairy product. Cooking meat in milk is typical of Arabic cuisine. In Lebanon there even exists a famous lamb dish called *laban 'ummu*, "the milk of its mother"; see H. G. Fischer, "'Milk in Everything Cooked' (Sinuhe B 91–92)," in *Egyptian Studies, I: Varia* (New York: The Metropolitan Museum of Art, 1976), 97–99.

47. The credit for this discovery is Bochart's (*Hierozoicon*, 1, 639f.); see Keel, *Böcklein*, 33.

48. Menachem, *'adah le-derekh*, fol. 83, col. 2; Spencer, *De Legibus*, vol. 2, 276, gives the Hebrew text and his latin translation.

49. I am alluding to David Lowenthal, *The Past Is a Foreign Country* (Cambridge: Cambridge UP, 1985), but the techniques of estrangement by historicization are more specifically dealt with by Anthony Kemp, *The Estrangement of the Past: A Study in the Origins of Modern Historical Consciousness* (New York and Oxford: Oxford UP, 1991).

50. *Epist.* book 2, ep. 1 (in Spencer's orthography):

> Agricolae prisci, fortes, parvoque beati,
> Condita post frumenta, levantes tempore festo
> Corpus, & ipsum animum spe finis dura ferentem,
> Cum sociis operum, & pueris, & conjuge fida,
> Tellurem porco, Sylvanum lacte piabant.

51. Spencer, *De Legibus*, vol. 2, 273–274.

52. Diodorus, *Bibl. Hist.*, 1.14.2 = C. H. Oldfather, trans., *Diodorus of Sicily*, vol. 1 (Cambridge, Mass.: Harvard UP, 1933), 49.

53. *De Error. Prophan. Relig.*, 2, 3; see Theodor Hopfner, *Fontes Historiae Religionis Aegyptiacae, IV* (Bonn: Markus and Weber, 1924), 519.

54. Papyrus Salt 825, 1, 1–6 = Philippe Derchain, *Le Papyrus Salt 825—rituel pour la conservation de la vie en Egypte* (Brussels: Académie Royale de Belgique, 1965); F.-R. Herbin, "Les premieres pages du pap. Salt 825," *Bulletin de l'Institut Français d'Archéologie Orientale* 88 (1988): 95–112.

55. Papyrus Louvre I, 3079 = Jean Claude Goyon, "Le ceremonial de glorification d'Osiris du pap. Louvre I 3079," *Bulletin de l'Institut Francais d'Archéologie Orientale* 65 (1967): 96f.

56. *Praep. Evang.*, book 1, chap. 9.

57. Book 21, p.m. 221; book 19, p.m. 134.

58. *De Dea Syria*, 1058.

59. See Douglas, *In the Wilderness*, 24.

60. Spencer deals at large with the ancient traditions about the "unknown god" (*agnostos theos*).

61. Isidor Pelusiota, book 2, ep. 133 = *PC*, vol. 78, 575–576.

62. Spencer, *De Legibus*, vol. 1, 14.

63. On the chronological debates about Egypt's place in history see Rossi, *The Dark Abyss of Time*. The debate became most heated after the publication of La Peyrères book on the "Preadamites," which Spencer does not quote. His calm and

circumspect method of exposition does not give the impression that he feels himself moving on "mined terrain" (Rossi, *Abyss*, 139). In England, the terrain seems to have become "mined" only after the publication of John Marsham's, *Canon Chronicus Aegyptiacus, Hebraicus, Graecus* (London: 1672).

64. Pierre-Daniel Huet, *Demonstratio Evangelica* (Paris, 1679); see Schmidt, "Des inepties tolérables," 127; 129; A. Dupront, *Pierre-Daniel Huet et l'exégèse comparatiste au xviie siècle* (Paris, 1930).

65. A very similar picture of the Israelites in Egypt as "assimilated Jews" was drawn by Abraham S. Yahuda, *Die Sprache des Pentateuch in ihren Beziehungen zum Ägyptischen* (Berlin: W. de Gruyter, 1929), one of the few books quoted by Freud in his Moses book (51, n. 30).

66. Eusebius, *Praep. Evang.*, book 7, chap. 8.

67. Rabbi Juda, *In Pirq. Eliez.*, chap7 47.

68. These are the sources which Spencer quotes and to which he adds, among the moderns, Samuel Bochart, *De Animalibus Sacris* (= *Hierozoicon* [London, 1663]); Athanasius Kircher, *Oedipus Aegyptiacus*, 3 vols. (Rome, 1652–1654); and John Selden, *De Dis Syris Syntagmata II. Adversaria Nempe de Numinibus Commentijs in Veteri Instrumento Memoratis. Accedunt Fere Quae Sunt Reliqua Syrorum. Prisca Porro Arabum, Aegyptiorum, Persarum, Afrorum, Europaeorum Item Theologia, Subinde Illustratur* (London, 1617).

69. Spencer, *De Legibus*, vol. 3, 255, with reference to Clement of Alexandria, *Stromata*, book 5. In the same sense, Plutarch interpreted Pythagorean prohibitions such as "do not eat upon a stool" and "do not lop off the shoots of a palm-tree" as hieroglyphs, which Pythagoras copied from the "symbolism and occult teachings" of the Egyptian priests (*De Iside:* see Dieckmann, *Hieroglyphics*, 8).

70. See Exod. 28:30–35:

> And thou shalt put in the breastplate of judgment the Urim and the Thummim; and they shall be upon Aaron's heart, when he goeth in before the LORD: and Aaron shall bear the judgment of the children of Israel upon his heart before the LORD continually.
>
> And thou shalt make the robe of the ephod all of blue.
>
> And there shall be an hole in the top of it, in the midst thereof: it shall have a binding of woven work round about the hole of it, as it were the hole of an habergeon, that it be not rent.
>
> And beneath upon the hem of it thou shalt make pomegranates of blue, and of purple, and of scarlet, round about the hem thereof; and bells of gold between them round about:
>
> A golden bell and a pomegranate, a golden bell and a pomegranate, upon the hem of the robe round about.
>
> And it shall be upon Aaron to minister: and his sound shall be heard when he goeth in unto the holy place before the LORD, and when he cometh out, that he die not.

71. *De Legibus*, vol. 3, p. 220.

72. It is precisely for this emphasis on "visible religion" that he is praised by W. Robertson Smith as a precursor; see Schmidt, "Inepties tolérables."

73. *De Legibus*, vol. 3, p. 223.

74. Aelianus, *Hist. Var.*, 1.14, cap. 34; see Hopfner, *Fontes*, vol. 3, 429; Diodorus, *Bibl. Hist.*, 1.75.5; see *Fontes*, vol. 1, 123. Spencer, *De Legibus*, vol. 3, 388f. On p. 389 Spencer quotes Grotius and J. Scheffer, who also noticed the correspondence between the function and meaning of Thummim and the Egyptian tradition as reported by Aelianus and Diodorus. But they reconstructed the line of dependence and derivation inversely: Egypt borrowed this custom from the Hebrews.

75. Reinhold, *Die Hebräischen Mysterien*, paraphrases Spencer's dissertation on pp. 175–180.

76. Some eighty years later, the atheist Paul Henri Thiry, baron d' Holbach, in his book *La contagion sacrée, ou, Histoire naturelle de la superstition* (Amsterdam, 1768; Paris, 1797), would use the same language in characterizing religion in general; see Frank E. Manuel, *The Eighteenth Century Confronts the Gods* (Cambridge, Mass.: Harvard UP, 1959), chap. 2, sect. 3, "A Psychopathology of Enthusiasm," pp. 70–81.

77. For an early Jewish text representing "pagan" religion in this way see the *Wisdom of Solomon* in the *Apocrypha*; the earliest important Christian text is Tertullian, *De Idololatria*; see Barasch, *Icon*, 110–123.

78. Yosef Hayim Yerushalmi, *Freud's Moses: Judaism Terminable and Interminable* (New Haven: Yale UP, 1991), p. 31f.

79. The concept of a withdrawal program gets an even clearer expression in the writings of Christopher Castro, who speaks of "weaning" *(ablactare);* see Reinhold, *Hebräische Mysterien*, 175, footnote.

80. Spencer's term is "ethnicismus" or, in the second book, "Zabiismus."

81. See Moshe Halbertal and Avishai Margalit, *Idolatry* (Cambridge, Mass.: Harvard UP, 1982), 9–36.

82. George Boas, *The Hieroglyphics of Horapollo*, Bollingen Series 23 (New York: Pantheon Books, 1950); Iversen, *The Myth of Egypt*, 47–49.

83. On Athanasius Kircher see Iversen, *Myth*, 92–100.

84. "Primaria erat, ut Lex ea medium esset Ordinarium, quo Deus, ad idololatriam abolendam, & Israelitas in Ipsius fide cultuque retinendos, uteretur; Secundaria erat, ut Legis illius ritus & instituta mysteriis quibusdam adumbrandis inservirent" (*De Legibus*, vol. 1, 153).

85. Spencer, *De Legibus*, vol. 1, 154f., with reference to Maimonides and to the Babylonian Talmud, tractate *Berakhot*, chap. 5.

86. Spencer's dislike of allegorizing corresponds to "a general movement to de-allegorize, to perceive the ordinary where previous generations had sought occult connotations" typical of the late seventeenth century and especially of Pierre Bayle, whose *Dictionnaire historique et critique* appeared in 1697; see Manuel, *The Eighteenth Century Confronts the Gods*, 24–33 (the quotation is from p. 26).

87. Plutarch, *De Iside et Osiride*, 8.353e.

88. "Judaeorum plebem quidem, ritibus omnibus quomodo Legum ipsarum verbis concepti erant, Moses obstrictam, teneri iussit. Caeteros autem, quorum mens esset virtusque firmior, cùm eo cortice liberatos esse, tum ad diviniorem aliquam et hominum vulgo superiorem Philosophiam assuescere, & in altiorem Legum earum sensum mentis oculo penetrare, voluit." *Praep. Evang.*, book 7, chap. 10, p.m. 378. Spencer, vol. 1, 156.

89. Spencer, vol. 1, 157: "Deum voluisse ut Moses mystica rerum sublimiorum

simulacra scriberet, eo quod huiusmodi scribendi ratio, literaturae, qua Moses institutus erat, hieroglyphicae non parùm conveniret."

90. *Contra Celsum*, book 1, p. 11 (PG, vol. 11, 677–678).

91. Clement of Alexandria, *Stromata* book 5, p.m. 556 (= book 5, chap. 4, 21.4).

92. Spencer, *De Legibus*, vol. 1, 157: "aequum est opinari, Deum religionem, carnalem quidem in frontispicio, sed divinam et mirandam in penetrali, Judaeis tradidisse, ut instituta sua ad seculi gustum et usum accommodaret, nec quicquam sapientiae nomine commendatum, Legi vel cultui suo deesse videretur."

93. Spencer combines two distant passages from Clement's *Stromata* book 5: chap. 3, 19.3, and chap. 6, 41.2; see Clemens Alexandrinus, *Stromata Buch I–VI*, ed. Otto Stählin, 4th ed. (Berlin: Akademie Verlag, 1985), 338 and 354; Reinhold, *Hebräische Mysterien*, 83, quotes the same sentences, obviously after Spencer, *De Legibus*.

94. *The True Intellectual System of the Universe: The First Part, Wherein All the Reason and Philosophy of Atheism Is Confuted and Its Impossibility Demonstrated* (1st ed. London, 1678; 2nd ed. London, 1743).

95. Cudworth explicitly rejects Robert Fludd's identification of Moses' philosophy with the mystical pantheism of Jacob Boehme *(Philosophia Mosaica)* as "grossly fanatick." But he nevertheless asserts that "Moses was as well instructed in this hieroglyphick learning and metaphysical theology of theirs [the Egyptians'] as in their mathematicks" *(True Intellectual System*, 317).

96. For the notion of "Pantheism" and the pantheist tradition, see Thomas McFarland, *Coleridge and the Pantheist Tradition* (Oxford: Clarendon Press, 1969), esp. 53–106.

97. Edward, Lord Herbert of Cherbury, *De Veritate* (Paris, 1624).

98. Let me quote one of the pertinent passages at some length in order to give an idea of Cudworth's witty and lively rhetoric: "But whatever these *Atheists* deny in words, it is notwithstanding evident, that even themselves have an *Idea* or *Conception* in their Minds answering to the *Word, God*, when they deny his Existence, because otherwise they should deny the existence of *Nothing*. Nor can it be at all doubted, but they have also the same *Idea of God* with *Theists*, they denying the Existence of no other thing than what these assert. And as in all other Controversies, when men dispute together, the one Affirming the other Denying, both parties must needs have the same *Idea* in their Minds of what they dispute about, or otherwise their whole Disputation would be but a kind of *Babel*-language and Confusion; so must it be likewise in this present Controversie, betwixt *Theists* and *Atheists*. Neither indeed would there be any Controversie at all between them, did they not both by *God*, mean one and the same thing; nor would the *Atheists* be any longer *Atheists*, did they not deny the Existence of that very same Thing, which the *Theists* affirm, but of something else." *(True Intellectual System*, 194). The form of argument might be illustrated by an anecdote repeated by Yerushalmi *(Freud's Moses*, 55) which culminates in the immortal sentence "There is only one God—and we do not believe in him!"

99. Cudworth, 195.

100. Cudworth, 208–209.

101. Cudworth, 209.

102. Cudworth, 223.

103. Cudworth, sect. 17, 294–308.

104. Cudworth, 308.

105. Cudworth, 308–355.

106. Cudworth, 312.

107. Cudworth, 314.

108. "Die Einheit des Menschengeistes," in Thomas Mann, *Gesammelte Werke*, 16 vols. (Frankfurt: Fischer, 1974), vol. 10, 751–756, esp. 752.

109. *Contra Celsum*, book 1, chap. 12 = *PG*, vol. 11, 677–678; Cudworth, *True Intellectual System*, 314–315.

110. *Stromata*, book 5, p. 508 (= book 5, chap. 7, 41.1) = Cudworth, *True Intellectual System*, 314.

111. *De Iside et Osiride*, 354 (chap. 8). Cudworth adds Clement of Alexandria, *Stromata*, (= book 5, chap. 5, *Stromata*, 31.5): "*Therefore do the Egyptians place* Sphinges *before their Temples, to declare thereby, that the Doctrine concerning God is Enigmatical and Obscure. . . . But perhaps the meaning of those Egyptian* Sphinges *might be also to signifie, that the Deity ought both to be Loved and Feared; to be loved as benigne and propitious to the Holy, but to be Feared as inexorably just to the Impious, the* Sphinx *being made up of the Image both of a Man and a Lion.*"

112. Cudworth, 316; cf. Plutarch, *De Iside*, chap. 68.

113. Cudworth, 316.

114. Cudworth, 317.

115. Cudworth, 317.

116. *De Rebus Sacris et Ecclesiasticis Exercitationes XVI. Ad Cardinalis Baronii Prolegomena in Annales* (London, 1614), 70ff. See Yates, *Giordano Bruno*, 398–403; Anthony Grafton, "Protestant versus Prophet: Isaac Casaubon on Hermes Trismegistos," *Journal of the Warburg and Courtauld Institutes* 46 (1983): 78–93.

117. Yates, *Giordano Bruno* 398.

118. "Wherefore the Learned Casaubon seems not have [sic] reckoned or concluded well, when from the detection of forgery in two or three of those Trismegistick books at most, he pronounces of them all universally, that they were nothing but Christian Cheats and Impostures. And probably he was lead into this mistake, by reason of his too securely following that vulgar Error (which yet had been confuted by *Patricius*) that all that was published by *Ficinus* under the name of *Hermes Trismegist*, was but one and the same Book Poemander, consisting of *several chapters*, whereas they are all indeed so many Distinct and Independent Books, whereof Poemander is only placed First" (Cudworth, 320–321).

119. Cudworth, 320.

120. Cudworth, 320.

121. Cudworth, 334.

122. Cudworth, 334f.

123. *Praep. Evang.* book 3, chap. 11, p. 115 (= 3.11.45–46).

124. Cudworth, 337; cf. Damascius, *De Principiis* (Paris, 1991), vol. 3, 167.

125. Cudworth, 339.

126. Cudworth, 341.

127. Cudworth, 341.

128. Cudworth, 343.

129. Cudworth, 344–346; cf. *De Defectu Oracul.*, 419.

130. George Berkeley, *Siris: A Chain of Philosophical Reflexions and Inquiries con-*

cerning the Virtues of Tar Water, 2nd. ed. (London. 1744), 144. I am grateful to Dana M. Reemes for drawing my attention to this book.

131. Cudworth, 349, misprinted as "409" in the first edition.

132. First or second century C.E.: *CIL*, 10, 3800 = Dessau, *ILS*, 4362; L. Vidman, *Sylloge Inscriptionum Religionis Isiacae et Sarapidae* (Berlin, 1969), no. 502.; Dunand, "Le syncrétisme isiaque," 82, n. 1. See *moyna sy ei hapasai*, "being one, you are all" (Isidorus hymn); see Dunand, "Le syncrétisme isiaque," 79ff..

133. Cudworth, 351 (misprinted as 411).

134. Macrobius, *Saturnalia*, 1.20.17; Hopfner, *Fontes*, 1.2.597f.

135. *Re und Amun: Die Krise des polytheistischen Weltbilds im Ägypten der 18.-20.Dynastie*, Orbis Biblicus et Orientalis 51 (Fribourg and Göttingen: Freiburger Universitättsverlag and Vandenhoeck & Ruprecht, 1979), 242–246; *Egyptian Solar Religion*, 174–178.

136. Iamblichus, *De Mysteriis Aegyptiorum*, 8.265.

137. *Siris*, 144f.

4. The Moses Discourse in the Eighteenth Century

1. John Marsham, *Canon Chronicus*.

2. John Toland, *Christianity Not Mysterious* (London: 1702), *Letters to Serena* (London, 1704), *Origines Judaicae* (London, 1709). On Toland see Robert Rees Evas, *Pantheisticon: The Career of John Toland* (New York: Peter Lang, 1991), and Gesine Palmer, *Ein Freispruch für Paulus. John Tolands Theorie des Judenchristentums* (Berlin, 1996).

3. Matthew Tindal, *Christianity as Old as the Creation; or, The Gospel, a Republication of the Religon of Nature* (London, 1732).

4. See Rossi, *The Dark Abyss of Time*, 155f.

5. I have used with profit Peter Gay, *Deism: An Anthology* (Princeton: Van Nostrand, 1968); John Orr, *English Deism: Its Roots and Its Fruits* (Grand Rapids: Eerdmans, 1934); Lechler, *Geschichte des Englischen Deismus*. The period of Deism proper is usually dated from 1696 (the date of the publication of John Toland's *Christianity Not Mysterious)* through the end of the 1740s.

6. *Adeisidaemon sive Titus Livius a Superstione Vindicatus . . . Annexae Sunt . . . Origines Judaicae ut Religio Propaganda Etiam, Quae Est Juncta cum Cognitionae Naturae; Sic Superstitionis Stirpes Omnes Ejicendae Annexae Sunt Origines Judaicae sive, Strabonis, de Moyse et Religione Judaica Historia, Breviter Illustrata* (The Hague: Thomas Johnson, 1709), 99–199.

7. See Margaret C. Jacob, *The Radical Enlightenment: Pantheists, Freemasons, and Republicans* (London: Allen & Unwin, 1981).

8. See Silvia Berti, *Trattato dei tre impostori: La vita e lo spirito del Signor Benedetto de Spinoza* (Turin: Einaudi, 1994). For Toland's involvement in the distribution and possible co-authorship of this text see Jacob, *Radical Enlightenment*, 22–26, 215–255.

9. Bilingual editions: Wolfgang Gericke, *Das Buch "De Tribus Impostoribus"* (Berlin: Evangelische Verlagsanstalt, 1982); Gerhard Bartsch and Rolf Walther, ed., *De Tribus Impostoribus Anno MDCIIC: Von den drei Betrügern 1598 (Moses, Jesus, Mohammed)*. (Berlin: Akademie Verlag, 1960). This Latin text, usually identified by its incipit "Deum esse," could well go back to the sixteenth century.

10. According to this text, the lawgivers "ont tous suivi la même Route dans l'établissement de leurs Loyx. Pour obliger le Peuple à s'y soumettre de lui même, ils lui ont persuadé, à la faveur de l'ignorance qui lui est naturelle, qu'ils les avoient reçues, ou d'un dieu, ou d'une déesse" (Berti, *Trattato*, 110).

11. "Si sacerdos itaque Moses, bene potuisset esse nomarcha," *Origines Judaicae*, 150.

12. *Origines Judaicae*, 150ff., with reference to Gen. 47:27.

13. *Origines Judaicae*, 117ff., with reference to Cicero, *De Natura Deorum* book 2.

14. *Origines Judaicae*, 157.

15. Toland adduces several other passages from the prophets that oppose the cult in the name of nature (properly speaking in the name of justice, but this does not seem important for Toland).

16. "Totam de diis immortalibus opinionem fictam esse ab hominibus sapientibus Rei publicae causa." The political function of religion is the theme of *Adeisidaemon*, which was published together with *Origines Judaicae*.

17. The immediate target of Warburton's attack on the Deists is Thomas Morgan, who for precisely these reasons advocated total exclusion of the Old Testament; see his works *The Moral Philosopher*, 3 vols. (London, 1738–1740; repr. 1969, ed. G. Gawlick), and *Physico-Theology; or, A Philosophical-Moral Disquisition Concerning Human Nature, Free Agency, Moral Government and Divine Providence* (London 1741).

18. For instance, The Divine Legation of Moses Demonstrated on the Principles of a Religious Deist, from the Omission of the Doctrine of a Future State of Reward and Punishment in the Jewish Dispensation (London, 1738–1741; 2nd ed. London, 1778), vol. 1, 201–204, the famous hymn to the "One who originated by himself and to whom all things owe their being" transmitted by Eusebius and Clement of Alexandria.

19. *Divine Legation*, vol. 1, 173.

20. *Divine Legation*, vol. 1, 190, quoting Clement of Alexandria.

21. *Divine Legation*, vol. 1, 202, quoting Clement of Alexandria, *Admonitio ad Gentes*, ed. Sylburgh, p. 36B; (= *Protreptikos* 74, 4f.); *Stromata*, 5.12.78.4, and Eusebius, *Praep. Evang.*, 13.12.5, ed. Mras, vol. 2, 191f. Heimo Erbse, *Fragmente griechischer Theosophien*, Hamburger Arbeiten zur Altertumswissenschaft 4 (Hamburg, 1941), 15ff. and 180ff. Orphicorum, fr. 245, 246, 247 Kern. The capitalization is Warburton's.

22. *Divine Legation*, vol. 1, 223, and passim; see esp. 201.

23. Clement of Alexandria, *Stromata*, book 5, 11, 71.1; see *Divine Legation*, vol. 1, 191. The Greek text reads: *"metà taûta d'estì tà mikrà mustêria didaskalías tina hupóthesin ékhonta prò paraskeuês tôn mellónton, tà dè megála perì tôn sumpánton, hoû manthánein [ouk] éti hupoleípetai, epopteúein dè kaì perinoeîn te phúsin kaì tà prágmata."*

24. Warburton quotes Eusebius first, who shows "that the Hebrews were the only people whose object, in their *public and national worship*, was THE GOD OF THE UNIVERSE, he suits his whole expression, by one continued metaphor, to the usages of the *Mysteries*. 'For the Hebrew people alone (says he) was reserved the honor of being INITIATED into the knowledge of God the Creator of all things, and of being instructed in the practice of true piety towards him'" (*Divine Legation*, vol. 1, 193).

The quote is from Eusebius, *Praepr. Evang.*, 1.9.15, in *Eusebius Werke*, vol. 8, ed. Karl Mras, *Die Praeparatio Evangelica*, vol. 1, 2nd ed. (Berlin: Akademie Verlag, 1982), 38.

25. *Divine Legation*, vol. 1, 192–193. Warburton is highlighting the mystical terminology with italics and capitals.

26. The question as to whether Spinoza's famous equation of God and nature was derived from cabalistic sources, especially from Herrera's *Porta Coelestis*, was much debated during the eighteenth century: see Gershom Scholem, "Abraham Cohen Herrera—Leben, Werk und Wirkung," in Rabbi Abraham Cohen Herrera the Portugese, *Das Buch Schaar ha-Schamajim oder Pforte des Himmels in welchem Die kabbalistischen Lehren philosophisch dargestellt und mit der Platonischen Philosophie verglichen werden*, trans. Friedrich Häussermann, Frankfurt 1974, 7–67 (I owe this to Moshe Barasch); see also Scholem, "Die Wachtersche Kontroverse über den Spinozismus und ihre Folgen," *Spinoza in der Frühzeit seiner religiösen Wirkung*, Wolfenbütteler Studien zur Aufklärung 12, ed. Karlfried Gründer and Wilhelm Schmidt-Biggemann (Heidelberg: Lambert Schneider, 1984), 15–25. On other possible Jewish sources of Spinoza's famous equation *deus sive natura* (based on the numeric equivalence of the Hebrew words *elohim*, "God," and *teva'*, "nature"), see Moshe Idel, "Deus sive natura—les métamorphoses d'une formule de Maimonide à Spinoza," in Idel, *Maimonide et la mystique juive*, trans. Ch. Kopsik (Paris: Editions du Cerf, 1991), 105–136. Closer to Spinoza is Giulio Cesare Vanini, who wrote in his *De Admirandis Naturae Reginae Deaeque Mortalium Arcanis*, dialogue 50, *De Deo*, ed. L. Corvaglia, *Le opere di Giulio Cesare Vanini e le loro fonti* (Milan, 1934), vol. 2, 276: "Man should live according to natural Law alone, because nature, which is God (because it is the principle of movement), has engraved this law in the hearts of all men *(In unica Naturae Lege, quam ipsa Natura, quae Deus est (est enim principium motus) in omnium gentium animis inscripsit)*;" quoted from Berti, *Trattato*, 272; see Jacob, *Radical Enlightenment*, 39. In the older treatise *De Tribus Impostoribus* (beginning with the words "Deum esse"), we read "hoc Ens . . . alii naturam vocant, alii Deum"; see Wolfgang Gericke, *Das Buch "De Tribus Impostoribus,"* 61, sect. 7. See also Giordano Bruno, *The Expulsion of the Triumphant Beast*, ed. and trans. Arthur D. Imerti (Lincoln and London: U of Nebraska P, 1964), 240: "So, then, that God, as absolute, has nothing to do with us except insofar as he communicates with the effects of Nature and is more intimate with them than Nature herself. Therefore, if he is not Nature herself, he is certainly the nature of Nature, and is the soul of the Soul of the world, if he is not the Soul herself." A similar idea that has, as far as I can see, not yet been taken into account is the Renaissance theory of art as an imitation of "nature, that is, God," which, as Jan Bialostocki has pointed out, occurs already in Alberti; see "The Renaissance Concept of Nature and Antiquity," in Jan Bialostocki, *The Message of Images: Studies in the History of Art* (Vienna: IRSA Verlag, 1988), 64–68, esp. 68 with nn. 51–54.

27. Pierre-Adam d'Origny, *L'Egypte ancienne ou mémoires historiques et critiques sur les objects les plus importantes de l'histoire du grand empire des Egyptiens*, 2 vols. (Paris, 1762). Some thirty years earlier, George Berkeley had already identified Isis with *natura naturata* and Osiris with *natura naturans* (*Siris*, 144).

28. D'Origny, *L'Egypte ancienne*, vol. 2, 148f., quoted from Dirk Syndram, *Ägypten-Faszinationen. Untersuchungen zum Ägyptenbild im europäischen Klassizismus bis 1800* (Frankfurt: Peter Lang, 1990), 61.

29. D'Origny, *L'Egypte ancienne*, vol. 2, 195, quoted from Syndram, *Ägypten-Faszinationen* 322, n. 179.

30. The theory of religion as a *pia fraus* is ancient and is particularly associated with Lucretius. The idea is that religion is a political fiction, instituted by wise men and legislators in order to inspire people with respect for justice and the state. Cicero discusses the theory at length in *De Natura Deorum*. Equally important for the Deists was Livy's account of Numa Pompilius' establishing the fundamental institutions of ancient Rome; see esp. John Toland, *Adeisidaemon sive Titus Livius a Superstitione Vindicatus* (The Hague, 1709). The most influential advocate of the fraud theory of religion was Fontenelle, see Manuel, *The Eighteenth Century Confronts the Gods*, chap. 2 ("The Grand Subterfuge").

31. Critias, fr. 43F19 Snell; Warburton, *Divine Legation*, vol. 2, 149ff. See Dana Sutton, "Critias and Atheism," *Classical Quarterly* 31 (1981): 33–38, with bibliography. I owe this reference to Julia Annas.

32. See Karl F. H. Frick, *Licht und Finsternis*, part 2 (Graz: Akademische Druck- und Verlagsanastalt, 1978); Rolf Christian Zimmermann, *Das Weltbild des jungen Goethe: Studien zur hermetischen Tradition des deutschen 18.Jahrhunderts*, 2 vols. (Munich: Fink, 1969–1979); P. Chr. Ludz, ed., *Geheime Gesellschaften*, Wolfenbütteler Studien zur Aufklärung, vol. 5/1 (Heidelberg: Lambert Schneider, 1979).

33. See Aleida Assmann, *Die Legitimität der Fiktion* (Munich: Fink, 1980). Thomas Green refers to the same distinction as "conjunctive" vs. "disjunctive" semiotics.

34. Ignace J. Gelb, *A Study of Writing: the Foundations of Grammatology* (Chicago: U of Chicago P, 1952).

35. Jacques Derrida, *De la grammatologie* (Paris: Editions de Minuit, 1967).

36. See Hugh Ormsby-Lennon, "Rosicrucian Linguistics: Twilight of a Renaissance Tradition," in *Hermeticism*, ed. Merkel and Debus, 311–341. (In a footnote to this essay, Ormsby-Lennon mentions a monograph he is preparing on the same subject which I have not been able to find: *Nature's Mystick Book: Magical Linguistics, Modern Science, and English Poetry from Spenser to Coleridge.*) See also Ernst H. Gombrich, *Icones Symbolicae: Studies in the Art of the Renaissance*, vol. 2, (Oxford: Phaidon, 1972).

37. Johann Georg Wachter, *Naturae et Scripturae Concordia. Commentatio de Literis ac Numeris Primaevis, Aliisque Rebus Memorabilibus, cum Ortu Literarum Coniunctis, Illustrata, et Tabulis Aeneis Depicta* (Leipzig and Copenhagen, 1752).

38. See A. Assmann, *Die Legitimität der Fiktion*.

39. Notwithstanding Swift's famous ridicule of such a "natural language" in his description of the inhabitants of Laputa and their strange system of communicating through things they carried along: Jonathan Swift, *Gulliver's Travels*, ed. Peter Dixon and John Chalker (1727; Harmondsworth: Penguin, 1967), 227–231, see A. C. Howell, *"Res et Verba:* Words and Things," *ELH*, 13 (1946): 131–142.

40. See Umberto Eco, *La ricerca della lingua perfetta nella cultura europea* (Rome and Bari: Laterza, 1993). See Aleida Assmann, "Die Weisheit Adams," in *Weisheit*, ed. Aleida Assmann (Munich: Fink, 1991), 305–324.

41. *True Intellectual System*, 316.

42. Plotinus, *Enneades*, 5.8.5, 19 and 5.8, 6, 11, quoted from Barash, *Icon*, 74f. See A. H. Armstrong, "Platonic Mirrors," in *Eranos*, vol. 55 (Frankfurt: Insel, 1988), 147–182. On Plotinus' concept of nondiscursive thinking see Richard Sorabji, *Time*,

Creation, and the Continuum: Theories in Antiquity and in the Early Middle Ages (Ithaca: Cornell UP, 1983), 152f. (I owe this reference to Julia Annas).

43. Marsilio Ficino, *In Plotinum*, 5.8 = P. O. Kristeller, *Supplementum Ficinianum. Marsilii Ficini Florentini Philosophi Platonici Opuscula Inedita et Dispersa*, 2 vols. (Florence: Olschki, 1937–1945; repr. 1973), 1768, quoted from Dieckmann, *Hieroglyphics*, 37. See Edgar Wind, *Pagan Mysteries in the Renaissance* (New Haven: Yale UP, 1958), 169ff.; Barasch, *Icon*, 75.

44. Sir Thomas Browne, *Pseudodoxia Epidemica*, vol. 3, 148, quoted from Dieckmann, *Hieroglyphics*, 113.

45. *Divine Legation*, book 4, sect. 4, vol. 2, 387–491. This section appeared separately in a French translation by Léonard des Malpeines, *Essai sur les hiéroglyphes des Egyptiens, où l'on voit l'origine et le progrès du langage et de l'écriture, l'antiquité des sciences en Egypte et l'origine du culte des animaux. Traduit de l'anglais de M. Warburton. Avec des observations sur l'antiquité des hiéroglyphes scientifiques et des remarques sur la chronologie et sur la première écriture des Chinois*, 2 vols. (Paris, 1744). A reissue of this publication appeared in 1978: *Essai sur les hiéroglyphes des Egyptiens . . .*, trans. Léonard des Malpeines, with notes by Patrick Tort, preceded by *"Scribble" (pouvoir/écrire)* by Jacques Derrida and *"Transfigurations" (archéologie du symbolique)* by Patrick Tort. (Paris: Flammarion, 1978). Peter Krumme translated and edited an abbreviated German version of this French reissue: *Versuch über die Hieroglyphen der Ägypter*, (Frankfurt: Ullstein, 1980).

Warburton's sources are Horapollo and other Greek references to hieroglyphs. On these see P. Marestaing, *Les écritures égyptiennes et l'antiquité classique* (Paris, 1913); P. W. van der Horst, "The Secret Hieroglyphs in Classical Literature," in *Actus: Studies in Honor of H. L. W. Nelson*, eds. J. den Boeft and A. H. M. Kessels (Utrecht: Instituut voor Klassieke Talen, 1982), 115–123; id., "Hieroglifen in de ogen van Grieken en Romeinen," *Phoenix ex Oriente Lux* 30 (1984): 44–53; Erich Winter, "Hieroglyphen," *Reallexikon für Antike und Christentum*, vol. 15 (Stuttgart: Hiersemann, 1991), 83–103, esp. 89ff.

46. Cudworth, *True Intellectual System*, 316.

47. Manuel, *The Eighteenth Century Confronts the Gods*, 65–69.

48. Warburton, *Divine Legation*, vol. 2, 398, with reference to Martino Martini, *Sinicae Historiae Decas Prima, Res a Gentis Origine ad Christum Natum in Extrema Asia, sive Magno Sinarum Imperio Gestas Complexae* (Munich, 1658).

49. A perfectly correct description of the hieroglyph *ḥ3*, "combat."

50. The distinction between "curiological" and "tropical" hieroglyphs is taken from Clement of Alexandria. "Curiological," from *kyrios*, "lord," means "nonfigurative," in contrast to *tropical*, "figurative," and *symbolic*, "enigmatic."

51. This example is from Clement of Alexandria (1.5).

52. Warburton, *Divine Legation*, vol. 2, 399.

53. Warburton, *Divine Legation*, vol. 2, n [X].

54. See Iversen, *The Myth of Egypt*, 48: "The relations between sign and meaning were according to Horapollo always of an allegorical nature, and it was always established by means of exactly the same sort of 'philosophical' reasoning which we find later in the Physiologus and the bestiaries of the Middle Ages."

55. Warburton, *Divine Legation*, vol. 2, p. 403.

56. See Pierre Hadot, *Zur Idee des Naturgeheimnisses: Beim Betrachten des Widmungsblattes in den Humboldtschen "Ideen zu einer Geographie der Pflanzen,"* Abhan-

dlungen der Akademie der Wissenschaften und der Literatur Mainz, geistes- und sozialwissenschaftliche Klasse Abhandlung, 8 (Wiesbaden: Steiner, 1982).

57. Serge Sauneron, *L'écriture figurative dans les textes d'Esna* (Cairo: Imprimerie de l'Institut Français d'Archéologie Orientale, 1982), 47ff.

58. See van der Horst, "The Secret Hieroglyphs in Classical Literature," and "Hierogliefen in de ogen van Grieken en Romeinen"; Winter, "Hieroglyphen"; Iversen, *The Myth of Egypt.*

59. For the terminology see A. Assmann, *Die Legitimität der Fiktion.*

60. *Phaedrus*, 274c–275d. See Jean Pierre Vernant, "Le travail et la pensée technique," in J. P. Vernant, *Mythe et pensée chez les Grecs: Etudes de psychologie historique* (Paris: F. Maspéro, 1971) 16–43. See Plato, *Philebus*, 18b-d, where the "letters" of Theuth resemble those of the Greek alphabet and refer to sounds, thus being phonographic instead of hieroglyphic.

61. On hieroglyphics and memory see Francis Bacon, *Advancement of Learning* (London, 1605), 2.14.3: "Embleme deduceth Conceptions Intellectuall to images sensible, and that which is sensible, more forcibly strikes the memory, and is more easily imprinted, than that which is Intellectuall" (quoted from Dieckmann, *Hieroglyphics*, 102).

62. Warburton, *Divine Legation*, vol. 2, 428.

63. Giordano Bruno, *De Magia* (*Opera Latina*, vol. 3, 411–412), quoted from Yates, *Giordano Bruno*, 263. The connection between hieroglyphics and magic is provided by the church historian Rufinus, who reports that the temple at Canopus was destroyed by the Christians because there existed there a school teaching magic arts under the pretext of teaching the "sacerdotal" writing of the Egyptians (*ubi praetextu sacerdotalium litterarum [ita etenim appellant antiquas Aegyptiorum litteras] magicae artis erat paene publica schola*; Rufinus, *Hist. Eccles*, 11.26).

64. See Iamblichus, *De Mysteriis Aegyptiorum*, 7.5.

65. Warburton, *Divine Legation*, vol. 2, 437.

66. See Barasch, *Icon.*

67. See Halbertal and Margalit, *Idolatry*, 37–66 ("Idolatry and Representation").

68. Herodotus, *Hist.*, 2.4; see Alan B. Lloyd, *Herodotus, Book II: Commentary 1–98* (Leiden: Brill, 1976), 29–33. Warburton interprets the word "zoa," which means "figure, image" (Liddell-Scott-Jones, *Greek-English Dictionary*, p. 760, s.v. zoon II) as "animals."

69. Warburton, *Divine Legation*, vol. 2, 458.

70. Alan H. Gardiner, *Ancient Egyptian Onomastica*, 3 vols. (Oxford: Clarendon Press, 1947) vol. 1, *1.

71. Henry G. Fischer, *L'écriture et l'art dans l'Egypte ancienne: Quatre leçons sur la paléographie et l'épigraphie pharaonique*, Collège de France, essais et conférences (Paris: Presses Universitaires de France, 1986).

72. Hans Blumenberg, *Die Lesbarkeit der Welt* (Frankfurt: Suhrkamp, 1981); A. Assmann, *Die Legitimität der Fiktion.*

73. See Iamblichus, *De Mysteriis Aegyptiorum*, 8.1: "The Egyptians imitate the nature of the universe and the 'demiurgy' of the gods in producing images of the mystical, invisible and secret notions by means of symbols, in the same way as nature is expressing the invisible logoi into visible forms in a symbolical manner, and the divine 'demiurgy' is writing down the truth of the ideas by visible images."

74. See A. Klemmt, *Karl Leonhard Reinholds Elementarphilosophie: Eine Studie über den Ursprung des spekulativen deutschen Idealismus* (Hamburg, 1958); Gerhard W. Fuchs, *Karl Leonhard Reinhold—Illuminat und Philosoph, Eine Studie über den Zusammenhang seines Engagements als Freimaurer und Illuminat mit seinem Leben und philosophischen Wirken* (Frankfurt: P. Lang, 1994), and Yun Ku Kim, *Religion, Moral und Aufklärung: Reinholds philosophischer Werdegang* (Frankfurt: P. Lang, 1996). I owe the last reference to Florian Ebeling.

75. Neither Klemmt nor Fuchs mentions this important book by Reinhold. It is to this book and not to the *Kabirische Mysterien* (as Fuchs believes) that Schiller refers at the end of *Die Sendung Moses*. See also Christine Harrauer, "'Ich bin was da ist . . .' Die Göttin von Sais und ihre Deutung von Plutarch bis in die Goethezeit," in *Sphairos*; Wiener Studien, Zeitschrift für Klassische Philologie und Patristik 107–108 (Vienna: Verlag der Österreichischen Akademie der Wissenschaften, 1994–95), 337–355. I thank Elisabeth Staehelin for drawing my attention to this important article, which did not appear until after I had completed my manuscript.

76. On Mozart's Freemasonry see Maynard Solomon, *Mozart: A Life* (New York: HarperCollins, 1995), 321–335.

77. Helmut Reinalter, "Ignaz von Born als Freimaurer und Illuminat," in *Die Aufklärung in Österreich: Ignaz von Born und seine Zeit*, ed. H. Reinalter (Frankfurt: P. Lang, 1991). Ignaz von Born is the author of a book-length article, "Über die Mysterien der Ägypter," *Journal für Freymaurer* 1 (1784): 17–132. Von Born's article is one of the masonic sources of Mozart's and Schikaneder's *Magic Flute*.

78. "Über die kabirischen Mysterien," *Journal für Freymaurer* 3 (1785). See Fuchs, *Reinhold*, 39f. Since Fuchs took this article to be Schiller's source, he overlooked the *Hebräischen Mysterien*.

79. See the letter of March 23, 1787, to the publisher Nicolai in Reinhard Lauth et al., ed., *Karl Leonhard Reinhold: Korrepondenzausgabe der Österreichischen Akademie der Wissenschaften*. vol. 1: *Korrepondenz, 1773–1788* (Stuttgart: Fromman-Holzboog, 1983), 197–198. I owe this reference to Florian Ebeling.

80. "This, indeed, is the rankest Spinozism," Warburton exclaims with regard to Strabo's account of Moses' theology (*Divine Legation*, book 3, sect. 4, vol. 2, 117).

81. Warburton, *Divine Legation*, vol. 1, 190, quoting Clement of Alexandria.

82. *Essay sur le moeurs des peuples*, sect. 22, "Des rites égyptiens," ed. M. Beuchot, *Oeuvres de Voltaire* (Paris, 1829), vol. 15, 102–106; cf. p. 103: "Le nom même le lus sacré parmi les Egyptiens était celui que les Hébreux adoptèrent, I ha ho. On le prononce diversement: mais Clément d'Alexandrie assure dans les Stromates, que ceux qui entraient dans le temple de Sérapis étaient obligés de porter sur eux le nom de I ha ho, ou bien de I ha hou, qui signifie le Dieu éternel."

83. Reinhold, *Die Hebräischen Mysterien*, 54. The passage is almost a translation of Voltaire, *Essay sur le moeurs*, 103.

84. "Egó eimi pân tò gegonòs kaì òn kaì esómenon kaì tòn emòn péplon oudeís pō thnētòs apekálupsen"—Plutarch, *De Iside et Osiride*, chap. 9 (354c), 9–10 = Griffiths, *Plutarch's "De Iside et Osiride,"* 130f., 283f. See Jean Hani, *La religion égyptienne dans la pensée de Plutarque* (Paris: Les Belles Lettres, 1976), 244f; Harrauer, "'Ich bin,'" 337–339.

85. Proclos, *In Tim.*, 30, in A.-J. Festugière, ed. and trans., *Proclus, Commentaire sur le "Timée,"* vol. 1 (Paris: Budé, 1966), 140; Griffiths, *Plutarch, "De Iside,"* 283. Proclus quotes the image at Sais and its inscription in his commentary on

Timaeus and in the context of Solon's visit to the priests of Sais. Harrauer, "'Ich bin,'" 339.

86. Papyrus Turin 1993 [10], vso. 2 = J. F. Borghouts, *Ancient Egyptian Magical Texts*, Nisaba 9 (Leiden: Brill, 1978), no. 102, 74.

87. In a Greco-Egyptian magical text Isis is summoned to lift her sacred cloth: Preisendanz, *Papyrus Graecae Magicae*, no. 57, 16–18 = Hans Dieter Betz, ed., *The Greek Magical Papyri in Translation* (Chicago: U of Chicago P, 1986), 284. In *Le culte de Neith à Sais* (Paris, 1888), Dominique Mallet suggested that a passage from pLouvre 3148 was the Egyptian prototype of Plutarch's and Proclus' inscription. This is an invocation of the mother-goddess personifying the realm of the dead: "Oh great goddess whose mummy-clothes can not be loosened, whose bandages are not to be loosened." The identification of Plutarch's veiled image of Sais with the deity of death as a mother-goddess is interesting, but certainly does not correspond to what Plutarch had in mind.

88. Concerning Exod. 3:14 see Oskar Grether, *Name und Wort Gottes im A. T.* (Giessen: A. Töpelmann, 1934), 3ff.; Michel Allard, "Note sur la formule 'Ehyeh ašer ehyeh,'" *Recherches de Science Religieuse* 44 (1957): 79–86; Wolfram von Soden, *Bibel und Alter Orient* (Berlin: De Gruyter, 1985), 78–88; Georg Fohrer, *Geschichte der israelitischen Religion* (Berlin: De Gruyter, 1969), 63ff.; Johannes C. de Moor, *The Rise of Yahwism* (Louvain: Leuven UP Uitgeverij Peeters, 1990), 175; 237ff. See also the brilliant analysis of the Tetragrammaton by Michel de Certeau, *The Writing of History*, 341: "the Tetragrammaton YHWY, 'Yahweh,' inscribes what is being withdrawn. It is not the sacrament of a being who is there, nor does it signify something else which might be hidden behind it, but it is the trace of an evanescence. It *is not pronounced*. It is the *written figure* of a loss, the very operation of being erased. It cannot be voice (a sign of the body that comes and speaks), but solely a *graph*." What de Certaeau is saying about "voice" versus "graph" corresponds to the distinction between "nature" and "scripture" which the revelation of the name in Exod. 3:14 is drawing and which the eighteenth century sought to overcome. See, e.g., Johann Georg Wachter, *Naturae et Scripturae Concordia*.

89. Lactantius, *The Divine Institutes*, trans. Sister Mary Francis McDonald, O.P. (Washington D.C.: The Catholic U of America P, 1964), 32. Lactantius paraphrases the Hermetic text Pseudo-Apuleius, *Asclepius*, chap. 20, ed. A. D. Nock and A.-J. Festugière, *Corpus Hermeticum*, vol. 2, 320f. Reinhold, *Die Hebräischen Mysterien*, 54, retranslates Lactantius' Greek into Latin (instead of quoting the Latin original): "Hic [Trismegistus] scripsit libros, in quibus majestatem summi ac singularis Dei asserit, iisdemque nominibus appellat, quibus nos Deum ст patrem, ac ne quis NOMEN ejus requireret, ANONYMON esse dixit, eo quod Nominis proprietate non egeat, ob ipsam scilicet UNITATEM. Ipsius verba sunt: Deo igitur *Nomen non est, quia solus est:* nec opus est proprio vocabulo nisi cum discrimen exigit MULTITUDO, ut unamquamque personam sua nota et appellatione designes" (1.6). Capitals and Italics are Reinhold's. Reinhold found the quote from Lactantius in Warburton, *Divine Legation*, vol. 2, 568–569. But there is a world of difference between Reinhold's interpretation of this passage and Warburton's pedestrian argument. Warburton wants to show that the Hebrews were so used to Egyptian idolatry that they forgot about the unity of God and asked for his name. "Out of indulgence therefore to this weakness, God was pleased to give himself a name."

90. See Wolfgang Beierwaltes, "Reuchlin und Pico della Mirandola," *Tijdschrift voor Filosofie* 56 (1994): 313–336, esp. 330–334.

91. Reinhold Merkelbach and Maria Totti, *Abrasax: Ausgewählte Papyri religiösen und magischen Inhalts*, vol. 2, *Gebete*, Abhandlungen der rheinisch-westfälischen Akademie der Wississenschaften, Sonderreihe Papyrologica Coloniensia (Opladen: Westdeutscher Verlag, 1991), 131.

92. Aleida Assmann drew my attention to this important text.

93. Nicolaus Cusanus, *De Docta Ignorantia*, 1.4, ed. H. G. Senger, Philosophische Bibliothek 264a (1440; Hamburg: Felix Meiner, 1993), 96–97.

94. See Gordon, "His Name is 'One.'"

95. *De Docta Ignorantia*, 98–99.

96. "Des rites Egyptiens," 103: "Il se serait fondé sur l'ancienne inscription de la statue d'Isis, 'Je suis ce qui est'; et cette autre, 'Je suis tout ce qui a été et qui sera; nul mortel ne pourra lever mon voile.'" Is Voltaire the author of this curious duplication of the Saitic inscription?

97. Beethoven knew Schiller's essay *Die Sendung Moses;* in a conversation book from 1825 there is an entry by Matthias Artaria: "Have you read 'Ueber die Sendung Moses' by Schiller?" See Maynard Solomon, *Beethoven Essays* (Cambridge Mass.: Harvard UP, 1988), 347, n. 24.

98. This text combined the two Saitic formulas and the Orphic hymn. See Anton F. Schindler, *The Life of Beethoven*, trans. and ed. Ignaz Moscheles (1841; Mattapan, 1966), vol. 2, 163.

> If my observation entitles me to form an opinion on the subject, I should say he (scil. Beethoven) inclined to Deism; in so far as that term might be understood to imply natural religion. He had written with his own hand two inscriptions, said to be taken from a temple of Isis. These inscriptions, which were framed, and for many years constantly lay before him on his writing table, were as follows:—
> I. I AM THAT WHICH IS:—I AM ALL THAT IS; ALL THAT WAS; AND ALL THAT SHALL BE.—NO MORTAL HATH MY VEIL UPLIFTED!
> II. HE IS ONE; SELF-EXISTENT; AND TO THAT ONE ALL THINGS OWE THEIR EXISTENCE.

Beethoven's German text is shown in facsimile and reads:

> Ich bin, was da ist //
> // Ich bin alles, was ist, was war, und was seyn wird, kein sterblicher Mensch hat meinen Schleyer aufgehoben //
> // Er ist einzig von ihm selbst, u. diesem Einzigen sind alle Dinge ihr Daseyn schuldig//

The sentences are separated from each other by double slashes. The third seems to have been added later; the writing is smaller and more developed. Beethoven was not a mason but he had close friends in masonic circles, especially among the Illuminists, who included both Reinhold and Beethoven's teacher Neefe. Solomon also very justly points out that these sentences "were known to most educated persons in Beethoven's time and even found their way into the ritual of

Freemasonry." I owe the reference to Solomon's book to Annette Richards. See also Erhart Graefe, "Beethoven und die ägyptische Weisheit," *Göttinger Miszellen* 2 (1972): 19–21.

99. Reinhold, *Die Hebräischen Mysterien*, 130.

100. See above, p. 79.

101. Clement of Alexandria, *Stromata*, book 5, 11, 71.1; Warburton, *Divine Legation*, vol. 1, 191.

102. Von Born, "Über die Mysterien der Aegyptier," 22. He quotes Plutarch as his source.

103. Friedrich von Schiller, *Die Sendung Moses*, ed. H. Koopmann, *Sämtliche Werke IV: Historische Schriften*. (Munich: Winkler, 1968), 737–757. Schiller's dependence on Reinhold is rightly stressed by Harrauer, "'Ich bin,'" 344–349.

104. Schiller was not a mason, but was extremely interested in the phenomenon of secret societies, as his novel *Der Geisterseher* (1787–1789) shows. Through the good offices of Theodor Körner, his closest friend and a mason, he frequented masonic circles. Wieland did not become a mason until 1808, but he shared the ideas of enlightened masonry and had good relations with prominent masons, especially with members of the Vienna lodge True Concord (von Sonnenfels, van Swieten, Tobias Ph. v. Gebler). See Britta Rupp-Eisenreich, "Wieland, l'histoire du genre humain et l'Egypte," *D'un Orient l'autre* (Paris: Editions du CNRS, 1991), 107–132, esp. 127–128, n. 33; Ludz, ed., *Geheime Gesellschaften*.

105. Kant's *Kritik der Urteilskraft* appeared in the same year as Schiller's essay (1790).

106. Schiller, *Die Sendung Moses*, 741.

107. *Die Sendung Moses*, 743.

108. He omits, however, Reinhold's ingenious equation, which related this formula to the Biblical "I am who I am."

109. "Nichts ist erhabener, als die einfache Grösse, mit der sie von dem Weltschöpfer sprachen. Um ihn auf eine recht entscheidende Art auszuzeichnen, gaben sie ihm gar keinen Namen": *Die Sendung Moses*, 745.

110. On Isis as a personification of "Mother Nature," see Pierre Hadot, *Zur Idee des Naturgeheimnisses: Beim Betrachten des Widmungsblattes in den Humboldtschen "Ideen zu einer Geographie der Pflanzen,"* Abhandlungen der Akadmie der Wissenschaften und der Literatur Mainz, geistes- und sozialwissenschaftliche Klasse Abh. 8 (Wiesbaden: F. Steiner, 1982). In the iconological tradition of the eighteenth century, the Sphinx came to denote the same idea of "the secrets of nature"; see Syndram, *Ägypten-Faszinationen*, 216–219. For this reason, the Sphinx was often used to decorate gardens. The comte de Caylus gives an ingenious explanation: the Sphinx, being a combination of a virgin and a lion, symbolizes the two signs of the Zodiac that are in the ascendent during the annual inundation of the Nile (Syndram, *Ägypten-Faszinationen*, 217, with n. 873).

111. Trans. after J. H. Bernard, trans., *Kant: Critique of Judgment* (New York: Hafner Press, 1951), with slight alterations.

112. In his aforementioned letter to Nicolai of March 23, 1787, Reinhold speaks of his book circulating in manuscript form among a small circle of friends even before its publication by Göschen in 1788.

113. Hadot, *Zur Idee des Naturgeheimnisses*.

114. Johann Andreas von Segner, *Einleitung in die Natur*, 3rd ed. (Göttingen:

Lehre, 1770); see Adolf Weis, *Die Madonna Platytera: Entwurf für ein Christentum als Bildoffenbarung anhand der Geschichte eines Madonnenthemas* (Königstein: Langewiesche, 1985), 9–10, and Hadot, *Zur Idee des Naturgeheimnisses,* 9–10.

115. Trans. T. Taylor, "The Hymns to Orpheus" = Kathleen Raine and George Mills Harper, ed., *Thomas Taylor the Platonist,* Bollingen Series 88 (Princeton: Princeton UP, 1969), 222.

116. This form of veil is called *aura velificans* ("veil-forming breeze") in Roman art.

117. Frances A. Yates, *The Rosicrucian Enlightenment* (London: Routledge and Kegan Paul, 1972), 82, fig. 23, facing p. 96. Yates refers in a footnote to G. Bruno, *Articuli Adversus Mathematicos* (Prague, 1588), preface, and to her book *Giordano Bruno,* 314–315 for the history of this motif.

118. *Ideen zu einer Geographie der Pflanzen* (1817), with the subtitle *Der Genius der Poesie entschleiert das Bild der Natur—*"the genius of poetry unveils the image of nature." Nothing could have been more unpalatable to Goethe, who in fact did not like the dedication; see Hadot, *Zur Idee des Naturgeheimnisses.*

119. Amsterdam; see Hadot, *Zur Idee des Naturgeheimnisses,* fig. 2.

120. Nuremberg; see Weis, *Madonna Platytera,* 12, fig. 3. Kunkelius' frontispiece varies only slightly from that of Blasius.

121. I am speaking here only of the footnote quoted above that mentions the veiled image of Isis. Kant devotes a long section of his third critique to what he calls an "analytic of the sublime." The sublime is the absolutely overpowering principle which human nature is nevertheless able to withstand. Without using the term "initiation," Kant comes very close to initiatory concepts. Only the strongest minds are able to confront "Nature." Kant's examples for the experience of the sublime are not exclusively mountains and thunderstorms. He also speaks of the Egyptian pyramids and of St. Peter's Cathedral (2nd ed., 1793, sect. 26, 88–89) as well as of the second commandment as instances of the sublime: "There is perhaps no more sublime passage in the law-code of the Jews than the commandment 'thou shalt not make unto thee any graven image'" (2nd ed., sect. 29, 125). The sublime resists human understanding, but a strong self resists the sublime. It is possible to think of God without reducing him to an image and likeness.

122. *Athenian Letters or, the Epistolary Correspondence of an Agent of the King of Persia, Residing at Athens during the Peloponnesian War. Containing the History of the Times, in Dispatches to the Ministers of State at the Persian Court. Besides Letters on Various Subjects between Him and His Friends,* 4 vols. (London: James Bettenham, 1741–1743), vol. 1, 95–100 (letter 25 by Orsames, from Thebes). Carlo Ginzburg drew my attention to this extraordinary history of the eastern Mediterranean at the end of the fifth century B.C.E. The letters by Orsames add up to a fair summary of the knowledge of the time concerning Ancient Egypt.

123. Magnus Olausson, "Freemasonry, Occultism, and the Picturesque Garden towards the End of the Eighteenth Century," *Art History* 8.4 (1985): 413–433. I owe this reference to Annette Richards, who shared with me some results of her study of "fantasia" as a musical genre and its parallels in eighteenth-century gardens. She also drew my attention to Olausson's fascinating article.

124. Irwin Primer, "Erasmus Darwin's *Temple of Nature:* Progress, Evolution, and the Eleusinian Mysteries," *Journal of the History of Ideas* 25.1 (1964): 58–76. I

owe this reference to Stuart Harten. Primer compares this engraving to the frontispiece to Peyrard's *De la nature et de ses lois* (Paris, 1793), where not a statue but
the Ephesian Diana herself is shown being unveiled by the sitting figure of a
bearded, elderly man, probably Chronos, the personification of time. This picture
seems to belong to the tradition of *veritas filia temporis:* the unveiling of secrets and
the development of learning and knowledge through the progress of time. On
personifications of time see Erwin Panofsky, "Father Time," *Studies in Iconology,*
(Oxford: Oxford UP, 1939), 69–94.

125. Edmund Burke, *A Philosophical Enquiry into the Origine of our Ideas on the
Sublime and the Beautiful* (London, 1759).

126. Syndram, *Ägypten-Faszinationen,* 104–108. Especially interesting is the interpretation of Egyptian temple architecture as an expression of the sublime by
Giuseppe del Rosso in *Ricerche sull'architettura Egiziana* (Florence, 1787); he refers
to Burke on pp. 104–108. See Syndram, 122–124.

127. Trans. Solomon, *Mozart,* 331. The text is by Franz Hermann Ziegenhagen
(1753–1806), a pietist, Spinozist, Freemason, and pedagogue who devised a new
program of adult education based on the study of nature and who commissioned
the cantata from Mozart for the inauguration ceremony of his institute in the
summer of 1791. In December 1784, when Mozart entered the masonic lodge
Beneficience (Zur Wohltätigkeit), Reinhold had already left Vienna.

128. Johann Wolfgang von Goethe, *Faust/Part One,* trans. Philip Wayne (Harmondsworth: Penguin, 1949), 152f.

129. Faust does not mention the element of awe and terror in this respect. But
it plays a central role in Goethe's concept of nature ("Das Schaudern ist der
Menschheit bestes Teil"); see Hadot, *Zur Idee des Naturgeheimnisses,* 32f.

130. Literally:

> In the observation of nature,
> Always consider the one as All;
> Nothing is inner, nothing is outer,
> Because what is inside is the same as what is outside.
> Thus, you should grasp without delay
> The sacred-public secret

Johann Wolfgang von Goethe, *Gesamtausgabe der Werke und Schriften,* vol. 18,
Schriften zu Natur und Erfahrung: Schriften zur Morphologie vol. 1, ed. Wilfried
Malsch (1820; Stuttgart: Cotta, n.d.), 26. See Aleida Assmann, "Zeichen—Alle-
gorie—Symbol," in *Die Erfindung des inneren Menschen,* ed. Jan Assmann (Güters-
loh: Gütersloher Verlagshaus, 1993), 28–50, esp. 41; Aleida Assmann, "Auge und
Ohr. Bemerkungen zur Kulturgeschichte der Sinne in der Neuzeit," *Torat ha-
Adam,* Jahrbuch für Religiöse Anthropologie 1 (Berlin: Akademie Verlag, 1994),
142–160, esp. 159f.

131. The anonymous treatise *De Tribus Impostoribus,* postulating that the three
religions of revelation, Judaism, Christianity, and Islam, owe their foundation to the
three arch-impostors Moses, Jesus, and Mohammed, was one of the most controversial books in the theological debates of the seventeenth and eighteenth centuries;
see Jacob, *The Radical Enlightenment;* Hugh B. Nisbet, "Spinoza und die Kontroverse *De Tribus Impostoribus,*" in *Spinoza in der Frühzeit seiner religiösen Wirkung,* ed.

K. Gründer and W. Schmidt-Biggemann (Heidelberg: L. Stiem, 1984), 227–244; Niewöhner, _Varietas:_ and especially Berti, _Trattato,_ n. 273.

132. The inscription, which is now lost, had been seen by Herder: see Erich Schmidt, _Lessing: Geschichte seines Lebens und seiner Schriften,_ 2 vols. (Berlin, 1884–1886), vol. 2, 804; _Gotthold Ephraim Lessings Sämtliche Schriften,_ ed. Karl Lachmann, 3rd ed. (Berlin: W. de Gruyter, 1915), vol. 22.1, p. ix; Hermann Timm, _Gott und die Freiheit, Bd.I: Die Spinoza-Renaissance_ (Frankfurt: Klostermann, 1974), 15ff.; Karl Christ, _Jacobi und Mendelssohn: Eine Analyse des Spinozastreits_ (Würzburg: Königshausen and Naumann, 1988), 59f. Peter Bachmeier, ed., _Briefwechsel Friedrich Heinrich Jacobi,_ vol. 3 (Stuttgart: Frommann-Holzboog, 1987), 279.

133. Heinrich Scholz, _Die Hauptschriften zum Pantheismusstreit zwischen Jacobi und Mendelssohn_ (Berlin: Reuther & Reichard, 1916); see Horst Folkers, "Das immanente Ensoph: Der kabbalistische Kern des Spinozismus bei Jacobi, Herder und Schelling," in _Kabbala und Romantik,_ ed. E. Goodman-Thau, G. Mattenklott, and Chr. Schulze (Tübingen: Niemeyer, 1994), 71–96. Alexander Altmann, "Lessing und Jacobi: Das Gespräch über den Spinozismus," _Lessing Yearbook_ 3 (1971): 25–70. In an interesting letter to Jacobi Hamann discusses the main issues of his book: _Briefe, ausgewählt, eingeleitet und mit Anmerkungen versehen von A. Henkel_ (Frankfurt: Insel, 1988), 130–133.

134. See K. Christ, _Jacobi und Mendelssohn: Eine Analyse des Spinozastreits_ (Würzburg: Königshausen & Neumann, 1988), 49–54.

135. Gérard Vallée, _The Spinoza Conversations between Lessing and Jacobi: Texts with Excerpts from the Ensuing Controversy_ (New York: UP of America, 1988), 85.

136. Vallée, _Spinoza Conversations,_ 2.

137. Fuchs, _Reinhold,_ 64–70.

138. See Paul Müller, _Untersuchungen zum Problem der Freimaurerei bei Lessing, Herder und Fichte_ (Bern: Franke, 1965).

139. On Spinoza's concept of All-Oneness see Konrad Cramer, "Gedanken über Spinozas Lehre von der All-Einheit," _All-Einheit: Wege eines Gedankens in Ost und West,_ ed. Dieter Henrich (Stuttgart: Clett/Cotta, 1985), 151–179.

140. Uvo Hölscher, _Empedokles und Hölderlin_ (Frankfurt: Suhrkamp, 1965), 49, n. 116, refers to Ralph Cudworth, _True Intellectual System._ A very comprehensive treatment of the Greek tradition is given by Eduard Norden in _Agnostos Theos: Untersuchungen zur Formengeschichte religiöser Rede_ (Leipzig: Teubner, 1912; repr. of the 4th ed., Darmstadt: Wissenschaftliche Buchgesellschaft, 1956), 240–250. The most important Greek references are Heraclitus, who postulated _hen panta einai_ (that all is one: fr. 50 Diels), and Xenophanes according to Simplicius, _Phys._, 22, 22ff., who postulated that "all is one" and that "this One and All, tò èn touto kaì pan, is God" (Hermann Diels, _Die Fragmente der Vorsokratiker,_ 11th ed., ed. Walther Kranz [Zurich and Berlin, 1964], 121), as well as the Stoic doctrine of divine All-Oneness according to Poseidonius, Cicero, and Seneca.

141. A book of magic with the title _The One and the All_ is quoted in Preisendanz, _Papyri Graecae Magicae,_ no. 13, 980, as vol. 5 of _Ptolemaika;_ see Merkelbach, _Abrasax,_ vol. 1, 202f. See also Norden, _Agnostos Theos,_ 248f.

142. _Collection des alchimistes grecs,_ ed. Berthelot-Ruelle, as quoted by Norden, _Agnostos Theos,_ 248–249. Norden used a vignette in the alchemist manuscript known as Codex Marcianus as a frontispiece for his book. It shows a serpent biting its tail (Uroboros) and encircling the inscription _Hen to Pan._

143. See Dana M. Reemes, "On the Name 'Plotinus,'" *Lingua Aegyptia* 5 (1995).

144. In his novel *Séthos* (Paris, 1731), Abbé Terrasson gave a romanesque account of Orpheus' initiation. After having successfully passed the tests of fire and of water, he failed the third test, involving the element of air (the test with the rings), but was nevertheless accepted into the circle of the initiates because of his extraordinary virtues.

145. This genealogy of philosophy goes back to Marsilio Ficino; see Yates, *Giordano Bruno*, 14f.

146. Raine and Harper, ed., *Thomas Taylor*, 163. It was Dana M. Reemes who drew my attention to Thomas Taylor and to this book.

147. Emmanuel J. Bauer, *Das Denken Spinozas und seine Interpretation durch Jacobi* (Frankfurt: P. Lang, 1989), 234ff.

148. Jacobi refers to Malesherbes as the inventor of the term. He rejects it as being an "insincere euphemism" for atheism; see Friedrich Heinrich Jacobi, *Über die Lehre des Spinoza in Briefen an Herrn Moses Mendelssohn*, ed. Fr. Roth and Fr. Köppen, *Werke* (repr. Darmstadt: Wissenschaftliche Buchgesellschaft, 1968), vol. 4/1, 1–253, 217–219. Hermann Timm, *Gott und die Freiheit, Bd. I: Die Spinoza-Renaissance* (Frankfurt: Klostermann, 1974), 226ff. But as early as 1699 Johann Georg Wachter used the somewhat similar term *vergötterte Welt* ("idolized world") with regard to Spinoza. See Scholem, "Die Wachtersche Kontroverse," 15–25, esp. 15.

149. *Siris*, 144.

150. Taylor, *Thomas Taylor the Platonist*, 178f., recapitulating Cudworth.

151. See Hadot, *Zur Idee des Naturgeheimnisses*.

152. On the idea of Egypt as the Golden Age of humanity see Syndram, *Ägypten-Faszinationen*, 54–61. Egypt was widely held to be the origin of civilization, of the arts and sciences as well as of legislation and political and social organization. According to Syndram, the most influential promotors of this extremely positive image of Egypt were Bossuet, de Goguet and the comte de Caylus. Bossuet published his *Discours sur l'histoire universelle. Premiere partie: Depuis le commencement du monde jusqu'à l'empire de Charlemagne*, in 1681. Antoine-Yves de Goguet's book *De l'origine des loix, des arts et des sciences et leur progrès chez les anciens peuples* appeared in Paris 1758 in three volumes. The 7 volumes by Anne Claude Philippe, comte de Caylus, *Recueil d'antiquités égyptiennes, étrusques, grecques et romaines*, appeared between 1752 and 1767 in Paris. Bossuet and d'Origny explicitly addressed their versions of Egyptian history and civilization to Louis XIV and Louis XV, respectively, as models of tolerant and enlightened absolutism (d'Origny: Syndram, *Ägypten-Faszinationen*, 58). This exaggerated praise of Egypt was strongly condemned by most of their contemporaries, especially admirers of the *Encyclopédie;* see Syndram, *Ägypten-Faszinationen*, 68–72. Ignaz von Born devised his "Egyptian Mysteries" (see n. 71), which were the basis of Mozart's and Schikaneder's opera *The Magic Flute*, as a model of enlightened statemanship for Emperor Joseph II, who was himself a mason. See Syndram, *Ägypten-Faszinationen*, 273–274.

153. Charles F. Dupuis, *Origine de tous les cultes, ou la religion universelle*, 12 vols. in 7 (Paris, 1795); see Jurgis Baltrusaitis, *La quête d'Isis: Essay sur la legende d'un mythe* (Paris: Flammarion, 1967) 21–40; Manuel, *The Eighteenth Century Confronts the Gods*, 269–270, 276–277; Bernal, *Black Athena*, vol. 1, 181–183.

154. See Thomas MacFarland, *Coleridge and the Pantheist Tradition* (Oxford: Clarendon Press, 1969).

5. Sigmund Freud

1. The more important results of the travels by Frederic Ludwig Norden (1755, Engl. 1757) and Carsten Niebuhr (1774 and 1779) appeared only after the publication of Warburton's three volumes of *The Divine Legation of Moses:* Frederic Ludwig Norden, *Voyage d'Egypte et de Nubic,* 2 vols. (Copenhagen, 1755), and Carsten Niebuhr, *Reisebeschreibung nach Arabien und anderen umliegenden Länden,* 2 vols. (Copenhagen, 1774–1778).

2. The literature on Freud's book on Moses is rapidly growing. See Brigitte Stemberger, "'Der Mann Moses' in Freuds Gesamtwerk," *Kairos* 16 (1974): 161–225; Marthe Robert, *D'Oedipe à Moise: Freud et la conscience juive* (Paris: Calmann-Levy, 1974); E. Amado Levy-Valensi, *Le Moise de Freud ou la référence occultée* (Monaco: Editions du Rocher, 1984); Pier Cesare Bori, "Il 'Mosè' di Freud: per una prima valutazione storico-critica," in Bori, *L'estasi* 179–222, esp. 179–184; Ilse Gubrich-Simitis, *Freuds Moses-Studie als Tagtraum,* Die Sigmund-Freud-Vorlesungen, vol. 3 (Weinheim: Verlag Internationale Psychoanalyse, 1991); Emanuel Rice, *Freud and Moses: The Long Journey Home* (New York: State U of New York P, 1990); Yosef Hayim Yerushalmi, *Freud's Moses: Judaism Terminable and Interminable* (New Haven: Yale UP, 1991); Bluma Goldstein, *Reinscribing Moses: Heine, Kafka, Freud, and Schoenberg in a European Wilderness* (Cambridge, Mass.: Harvard UP, 1992); Carl E. Schorske, "Freud's Egyptian Dig," *The New York Review of Books,* May 27, 1993, 35–40; Pier Cesare Bori, "Moses, the Great Stranger," in Bori, *From Hermeneutics to Ethical Consensus among Cultures* (Atlanta: Scholars Press, 1994), 155–164.

3. See Freud's letter to Arnold Zweig of June 8, 1936, and the reply of June 17, quoted from Bori, *L'estasi,* 198, n. 69.

4. See Carl E. Schorske's contribution to Wilfried Seipel, ed., *Egyptomania* (forthcoming).

5. Whom he insists on calling "Ed." Sellin. For the details see Yerushalmi's carefully researched and beautifully written study, *Freud's Moses.* For a competent critical evaluation of Freud's concept of Moses from an expert in Biblical scholarship see especially the contributions by Pier Cesare Bori.

6. Abraham Rosenvasser, *Egipto e Israel y el monoteismo Hebreo: A proposito del libro Moises y la religion monoteista de Sigmund Freud,* 2nd ed. (Buenos Aires: University of Buenos Aires, 1982), 8–11, gives a good summary of Freud's general theses concerning religion.

7. E. Blum, "Über Sigmund Freuds: Der Mann Moses und die monotheistische Religion," *Psyche* 10 (1956–57): 367–390, holds that Freud knew Schiller's text even though he did not mention it (p. 375). See Yerushalmi, *Freud's Moses,* 114, n. 17.

8. Bori, *L'estasi,* 203, mentions Spencer, along with other authors of the seventeenth and eighteenth centuries, such as P.-D. Huet, *Demonstratio Evangelica ad Serenissimo Delphinum* (Paris, 1679), John Marsham, *Canon Chronicus* (London, 1672), G. Voorbroek, *Origines Babylonicae et Aegyptiacae* (Liège, 1711) and William Warburton, *The Divine Legation of Moses* (London, 1741), as precursors of Freud, but does not regard Schiller as a possible intermediary.

9. See Schmidt, "Inepties tolérables."

10. Yerushalmi, *Freud's Moses,* 16; Bori, *L'estasi,* 237–258. See especially Michel de Certaux, who devotes the last and highly interesting chapter of his book *The*

Writing of History to Freud's *Moses and Monotheism*. I think that de Certeau somewhat overestimates Freud's fictional ambitions and intentions for his "historical novel." The connection with Thomas Mann's Joseph project has been pointed out by Marthe Robert, *D'Oedipe à Moïse*, 256.

11. Sigmund Freud, *Der Mann Moses und die monotheistische Religion, Gesammelte Werke*, vol. 16, ed. Anna Freud (1939; Frankfurt: Fischer, 1968); *Standard Edition of the Complete Psychological Works of Sigmund Freud*, trans. James Strachey (London: Hogarth, 1959), vol. 23. I am quoting the English translation from the *Standard Edition*; the German version is quoted from Sigmund Freud, *Der Mann Moses und die monotheistische Religion: Schriften über die Religion* (Frankfurt: Fischer Taschenbuch Verlag, 1975).

12. See the letters Freud wrote to Arnold Zweig during the years he worked on Moses: *The Letters of Sigmund Freud and Arnold Zweig*, ed. Ernst L. Freud, trans. Elaine Robson-Scott and William Robson-Scott (New York: Harcourt Brace & World, 1970).

13. See Yerushalmi, *Freud's Moses*, 2, with n. 5 on p. 113.

14. For Freud as a partisan of the Enlightenment see Peter Gay, *A Godless Jew: Freud, Atheism, and the Making of Psychoanalysis* (New Haven: Yale UP, 1987); for the deconstructive impulse behind Freud's Moses project see Robert, *D'Oedipe à Moïse*.

15. Freud's search for "proofs" in the field of history is related to the problems of evidence investigated by Carlo Ginzburg, *Der Richter und der Historiker* (Berlin: Wagenbach, 1991).

16. See Goldstein, *Reinscribing Moses*, 94f.

17. The only other verse which refers to Moses in a comparable way appears in both Exodus 32:1 and 32:23: "This Moses, the man who brought us up out of the land of Egypt, we do not know what became of him." This question occurs in the story of the Golden Calf and is put into the mouth of the rebels, who ask Aaron to make for them "*elohim* to walk in front of us." As a speech of the rebels, the verse shows how Moses should not be spoken of. He is not the one "who brought us out of the land of Egypt." But this is precisely Freud's image of "the man Moses."

18. See Yerushalmi, *Freud's Moses*, 55.

19. I find the emphasis which Yerushalmi and others have recently laid on Freud's Jewishness somewhat distorting with regard to his position as he constructs it in *Moses and Monotheism*. As far as *Moses and Monotheism* is concerned, I agree with Peter Gay in seeing Freud more on the side of the *philosophes* than on that of the Rabbis; see "The Last Philosophe: Our God Logos" in Gay, *A Godless Jew*, 33–68. It should also be remembered that the very terms "monotheism" and "polytheism" were coined in the larger context of the Moses/Egypt discourse, especially with reference to the Deists' idea of primitive monotheism. For Freud's Jewish background see especially Rice, *Freud and Moses*.

20. Theophorous names are names formed with a name of a god. The divine name was frequently dropped in Egyptian names, as in the use of Mahu for Amun-em-heb or Huya for Amun-em-hat. Such a short form would be particularly appropriate for Egyptians who had turned their back on traditional Egyptian polytheism, such as the followers of Akhenaten and the Egyptian Moses.

21. See J. Gwyn Griffiths, "The Egyptian Name of Moses," *Journal of Near Eastern Studies* 12 (1953): 225–231.

22. "Amenhotep IV (Ichnaton): Psychoanalytische Beiträge zum Verständnis seiner Persönlichkeit und des monotheistischen Atonkults," *Imago* 1 (1912): 334–360. This appears in English in *Clinical Papers and Essays on Psychoanalysis* (London: Hogarth, 1955), 162–190.

23. See Jacques Trilling, "Freud, Abraham, et le Pharaon," *Etudes freudiennes* 1–2 (1969): 219–226; de Certeau, *The Writing of History*, 353, n. 59; Bori, *L'estasi*, 186f. Lévy-Valensi, *Le Moise de Freud*, 11ff.

24. James Henry Breasted, *De Hymnis in Solem sub Rege Amenophide IV Conceptis* (Berlin, 1894). The first edition of the texts did not appear until 1884: Urbain Bouriant, *Mission archéologique française au Caire*, vol. 1 (Cairo: Imprimerie de l'Institut Français d'Archéologie Orientale, 1884), 2–5.

25. See Momigliano, *Pagans, Jews, and Christians*; Garth Fowden, *Empire to Commonwealth*.

26. Freud, *Standard Edition*, vol. 23, 22, with reference to James Henry Breasted, *History of Egypt* (New York: Scribner's, 1906), 374.

27. Freud, *Standard Edition*, vol. 23, 24.

28. Freud refers in a footnote to Arthur Weigall, who, being hieroglyphically almost illiterate, felt free to formulate the most adventurous hypotheses on the basis of the alleged assonance of the names Atum (the god of Heliopolis), Aton, and Adonis. Freud does not refute this as nonsense (which it is), but he does express some misgivings, probably because of Breasted's silence on this apparent coincidence. There is, in fact, no assonance at all. The name "Atum" sounded something like "Atúm" (cf. the Hebrew rendering of the local name Pithom = *pr-Jtm*, "the house of Atum") and the name "Aton" sounded something like "Yati" (cf. the cuneiform rendering of the name of Merit-Aton, *Mrjt-Jtn*, as Mayati). There was no assonance between them or with Adonis, let alone Adonay. This does not prevent some, such as Philippe Aziz, in *Moise et Akhenaton*, from pursuing this alleged assonance, which Freud at least did not dwell on. Aziz includes a chapter entitled "Ecoute Israel, notre dieu Aton est le dieu unique"; even this might be of some slight mnemohistorical interest, though I find it impossible to include this kind of literature in the present study.

29. Incidentally, it is a point on which he was historically mistaken. It is true that Akhenaten did away with Osiris and the Osirian netherworld, but not with the immortality of the "soul," or *ba*. The individual was believed to live on after death in the form of *ba* and to worhip the king and the sun, but in this world of life and light, not in another world of the dead. He was also mistaken concerning point (4), which to my mind is much more serious. But I will postpone the Egyptological details until the next chapter.

30. Cf. the Spencerian argument that God did not want his religion to be deficient in any respect as compared to Egyptian religion.

31. This can now be historically substantiated; see Krauss, *Das Ende der Amarnazeit*.

32. Moses, Freud seems to suggest, might have done away with the sun as an object of worship instead of with the creator of the sun, the lord of all. This distinction forms the theme of the famous conversation between Joseph and Akhnaton in Thomas Mann's *Joseph der Ernährer*.

33. *Standard Edition*, vol. 23, 33; "Nun aber, scheint es, ist unsere Arbeit zu

einem vorläufigen Ende gekommen. Aus unserer Annahme, dass Moses ein Ägypter war, können wir zunächst nichts weiter ableiten." (*Moses*, 46f.).

34. *Standard Edition*, vol. 23, 36.

35. *Standard Edition*, vol. 23, 36. "Unerwarteterweise findet sich auch hier ein Ausweg" (*Moses*, 49).

36. Of crucial importance in this debate was the twentieth chapter of Ezekiel, where God himself declares his Law not to be good. In striking anticipation of Christian historicization of the Law, the prophet makes God refute the timeless perfection of his legislation and explain its imperfections by referring to the obstinacy of the people, who twice rejected the perfect Law and thus finally had to be given an imperfect one.

37. Goldstein, *Reinscribing Moses*, 120.

38. *Standard Edition*, vol. 23, 38. "Die Geschichte liebt solche Wiederholungen"; *Moses*, 51.

39. *Standard Edition*, vol. 23, 50. "Die Idee einer einzigen, die ganze Welt umfassenden Gottheit, die nicht minder alliebend war als allmächtig, die, allem Zeremoniell und Zauber abhold, den Menschen ein Leben in Wahrheit und Gerechtigkeit zum höchsten Ziel setzte" (*Moses*, 61).

40. See Schorske, "Freud's Egyptian Dig."

41. Carl E. Schorske contributed a study on Breasted as a source for Freud to the Vienna conference on Egyptomania (November 1994) that will appear in a supplementary volume to the cataolgue, edited by Wilfried Seipel.

42. For a critical discussion of this thesis, see Bori, *L'estasi.*

43. See Yerushalmi, *Freud's Moses*, 84–86. See Odil Hannes Steck, *Israel und das gewaltsame Geschick der Propheten* (Neukirchen-Vluyn: Neukirchner Verlag, 1967).

44. See *Standard Edition*, vol. 23, 17; Goldstein, *Reinscribing Moses*, 101.

45. See the excellent summary by Goldstein, *Reinscribing Moses*, 117ff.

46. *Standard Edition*, vol. 23, 101. Goldstein, *Reinscribing Moses* 117.

47. This term was first used by Nicolas Abraham and Maria Torok; see *L'écorce et le noyau.* It was not used by Freud.

48. There is much to be said in support of Freud's description of monotheism as a "religion of the father." This seems to apply to Atenism. What Freud did not know, because Breasted and Weigall did not mention it, was that the name of Akhenaten's god ("Yati") sounded very much like the Egyptian word for "my father" ("yat-i") and that the texts constantly play on this assonance. The god even bears the royal title "my father." Akhenaten enacted his monotheism as a coregency between himself and the sun god, who acted as a senior partner in this theocracy. Akhenaten's Aton religion was very much a father-religion, except that the concept of fatherhood was related exclusively to the king, not to the people or to humankind at large.

49. Goldstein, *Reinscribing Moses*, 118.

50. *Standard Edition*, vol. 23, 101, quoted from Goldstein, *Reinscribing Moses*, 117, and Yerushalmi, *Freud's Moses*, 30.

51. *Standard Edition*, vol. 23, 47, quoted from Goldstein, *Reinscribing Moses*, 120.

52. *Standard Edition*, vol. 23, 134. German: "Zum Wesen des Vaterverhältnisses gehört die Ambivalenz: es konnte nicht ausbleiben, dass sich im Laufe der Zeiten auch jene Feindseligkeit regen wollte, die einst die Söhne angetrieben, den bewunderten und gefürchteten Vater zu töten. Im Rahmen der Moses-Religion war

für den direkten Ausdruck des mörderischen Vaterhasses kein Raum; nur eine mächtige Reaktion auf ihn konnte zum Vorschein kommen, das Schuldbewusstsein wegen dieser Feindseligkeit, das schlechte Gewissen, man habe sich gegen Gott versündigt und höre nicht auf, zu sündigen" (*Moses*, 131).

53. Freud quotes another couplet from this same poem, which is highly relevant for the concept of cultural memory. *Standard Edition*, vol. 23, 101: "Was unsterblich im Gesang soll leben, / Muss im Leben untergehn." Literally: "What is to be immortal in song must perish in life."

54. Literally, "When the gods were more human, humans were more divine."

55. Von Born, "Über die Mysterien der Aegyptier," 85–87.

56. Letter to Lou Andreas Salomé, January 6, 1935, *Briefwechsel*, 224; *Letters*, 205, quoted from Goldstein, *Reinscribing Moses*, 100; *Autobiographische Studie, Gesammelte Werke*, vol. 16, 33; *Standard Edition*, vol. 20, 72; Goldstein, *Reinscribing Moses*, 100f.

57. *Hierà Anagraphé, Die Fragmente der griechischen Historiker, 3 vols. in 15*, ed. F. Jacoby (Leiden: Brill, 1926–1958; repr. 1954–1960), 63.

58. Douglas, *In the Wilderness*.

59. *Standard Edition*, vol. 23, 133. German: "vollzieht sich langsam, gewiss nicht spontan, sondern unter dem Einfluss all der Änderungen in den Lebensbedingungen, welche die Kulturgeschichte der Menschen erfüllen" (*Moses*, 130).

60. For Freud's commitment to the issues of the Enlightenment, see especially the splendid chapter "The Last Philosophe: Our God Logos" in Gay, *A Godless Jew*, 33–68.

61. Goldstein, *Reinscribing Moses*, 120.

6. Conceiving the One in Ancient Egyptian Traditions

1. Gerhard Fecht, "Amarna-Probleme," *Zeitschrift für ägyptische Sprache und Altertumskunde* 85 (1960): 83–118, has shown this form to be the probable vocalization of the royal name.

2. For recent literature concerning Akhenaten and his age see Cyril Aldred, *Akhenaten, King of Egypt* (London: Thames & Hudson, 1988); Donald B. Redford, *Akhenaten, the Heretic King* (Princeton: Princeton UP, 1984); Hermann A. Schlögl, *Echnaton—Tutenchamun: Fakten und Texte*, 2nd ed. (Wiesbaden: Harrassowitz, 1985); Erik Hornung, *Echnaton: Die Religion des Lichtes* (Zurich: Artemis, 1995). For comparisons with Biblical monotheism See Othmar Keel, ed., *Monotheismus im Alten Israel und seiner Umwelt*, Biblische Beiträge 14 (Fribourg: Verlag Schweizerisches Katholisches Bibelwerk, 1980); Karl Rahner, ed., *Der eine Gott und der dreieine Gott: Das Gottesverständnis bei Christen, Juden und Muslimen*, (Freiburg: Katholische Akademie, 1983). Hornung contributed an article on Amarna religion to each of these collections. Johannes de Moor, *The Rise of Yahwism* (Louvain: Leuven UP, 1990), seems to be the first to search for "the roots of Israelite monotheism" not in Amarna but in the Ramesside worship of Amen-Re.

3. This section is based on my article "Akhanyati's Theology of Time and Light," *Israel Academy of Sciences and the Humanities Proceedings* 7 (1992); 143–176.

4. Theo Sundermeier, "Religion, Religionen" in *Lexikon missionstheologischer Grundbegriffe*, eds. K. Müller and Theo Sundermeier (Berlin: Reimer, 1987), 411–

423; Jan Assmann, *Ma'at: Gerechtigkeit und Unsterblichkeit im Alten Ägypten* (Munich: C. H. Beck, 1990), 17ff., 279ff.

5. Max Weber, "Die Protestantische Ethik und der Geist des Kapitalismus," in *Gesammelte Aufsätze zur Religionssoziologie*, 7th ed. (Tübingen: Mohr, 1978), 17–206; Marcel Gauchet, *Le désenchantement du monde* (Paris: Gallimard, 1985). Freud speaks of "progress in spirituality/intellectuality" (*Fortschritt in der Geistigkeit*; the German word *Geistigkeit* makes no distinction between spirit and intellect).

6. See my contribution "Semiosis and Interpretation in Ancient Egyptian Ritual," in *Interpretation in Religion*, ed. S. Biderstein and B.-A. Scharfstein, Philosophy and Religion, vol. 2 (Leiden: Brill, 1992), 87–110.

7. Because of its physical rationalism, James P. Allen, "The Natural Philosophy of Akhenaten," in *Religion and Philosophy in Ancient Egypt*, ed. W. K. Simpson, Yale Egyptological Studies 3 (New Haven: Yale UP, 1989), 89–101, denied the religious character of the Amarna movement altogether and spoke instead "of an intellectual movement." According to Allen, we are dealing with a "Natural philosophy," underpinning man's *understanding of* the universe, but not a religion, underpinning man's *relationship to* the universe. But this seems to imply a restricted notion of religion that is anachronistic with regard to ancient Egypt. Intellectual movements appear in the form of religious movements, and a religion always establishes not only a relationship to, but also an understanding of, the universe. There is no possibility, before the Greeks, of distinguishing between "philosophy" and "religion." For this reason Akhenaten was unable to tolerate traditional religion alongside his new "philosophy," but had to eradicate the old in order to introduce the new.

8. See Aleida Assmann and Jan Assmann, ed., *Kanon und Zensur* (Munich: Fink, 1987).

9. The French epigrapher Urbain Bouriant was the first to publish the text of the "Great Hymn," in *Mission Archéologique française au Caire*, vol. 1, 2–5; it appears also in Urbain Bouriant, George Legrain, and Gustave Jéquier, *Monuments du culte d'Atonou*, vol. 1 (Cairo: Imprimerie de l' Institut Français d'Archéologie Orientale, 1903), 30, and pl. 16; the authoritative edition is by Norman de Garis Davies, *The Rock Tombs of El-Amarna*, vol. 6 (London: Egypt Exploration Society, 1908) 29–31, and pls. 27, 41. Among the first translators and commentators is James H. Breasted, "De Hymnis in Solem sub Rege Amenophide IV Conceptis," diss., University of Berlin, 1894. For a recent English translation see Miriam Lichtheim, *Ancient Egyptian Literature*, vol. 2 (Berkeley: U of California P, 1976), 96–100.

10. Norman de Garis Davies, *The Rock Tombs of El-Amarna*, vol. 4 (London: Egypt Exploration Society, 1906), 26–29, and pls. 32–33; Lichtheim, *Ancient Egyptian Literature*, 90–92.

11. These images were destroyed as far south as Kawa, Soleb, and Faras in Nubia. See Robert Hari, "La religion amarnienne et la tradition polythéiste," *Studien zu Sprache und Religion Ägyptens*, ed. W. Westendorf, 2 vols. (Göttingen: F. Junge, 1994), 1039–1055. Ramadan Saad, "Les martelages de la *18ème* dynastie dans le temple d' Amon-Ré à Karnak," diss., University of Lyon, 1972 (not seen).

12. See Erik Hornung, *Der Eine und die Vielen* (Darmstadt: Wissenschaftliche Buchgesellschaft, 1971), trans. John Baines as *Conceptions of God in Ancient Egypt* (Ithaca: Cornell UP, 1982), 248f.

13. The phrase which comes closest to such a "monotheistic" statement is verse 64 of the "Great Hymn" *p3 nṯr wꜥ nn kjj wp ḥr.k*, "O sole god, beside whom there is

none!" Maj Sandman, *Texts from the time of Akhenaten* Bibliotheca Aegyptiaca 8 (Brussels: Fondation Reine Elizabeth, 1938), 94.17; see *nn kjj wp ḥr.f,* "there is no other except him," in Sandman, *Texts,* 7.7–8.

14. The term *summodeism* (the worship of a supreme god as head of a polytheistic pantheon) is borrowed from Eric Voegelin, *Order and History,* 4 vols. (Baton Rouge: U of Louisiana P, 1956–1974).

15. For a stylistic analysis of the "Great Hymn" (based on my translation in *Ägyptische Hymnen und Gebete,* ed. Jan Assmann [Zurich: Artemis, 1975]; hereafter cited as *ÄHG*), see Pierre Auffret, *Hymnes d'Egypte et d'Israel: Etude de structures littéraires* (Fribourg: Presses Universitaires, 1981), 229–277.

16. My structuring of the text is based on G. Fecht's reconstruction of Egyptian metrics; see his article "Prosodie" in *Lexikon der Ägyptologie,* vol. 4 (Wiesbaden: Harrassowitz, 1982), 1127–1154. My translation follows Lichtheim, *Ancient Egyptian Literature,* as closely as possible.

17. For the idea of the solar circuit as a temporal conception of the cosmos, see E. Hornung, "Verfall und Regeneration der Schöpfung," *Eranos* 46 (1977): 411–449; J. Assmann, *Ma'at,* 160–199.

18. For a reconstruction of this form of thought see Assmann, *Re und Amun,* 21–95 = *Egyptian Solar Religion,* 16–66.

19. See *ÄHG,* 47–63; *Re und Amun,* 54–95 = *Egyptian Solar Religion,* 38–66. For the phase structure of the solar circuit and its time span of twenty-four hours see my *Liturgische Lieder an den Sonnengott* (Berlin: Deutscher Kunstverlag, 1969), 333–342.

20. The decisive predication of the god—*p3 jtn ʿnḥ š3jw ʿnḥ*—has been notoriously misunderstood owing to a probable misreading by Bouriant. The passage is shown as destroyed in Davies, *Rock Tombs,* pl. 32, which is rendered after Bouriant. All the better preserved parallels of this divine epithet show *š3<jw>* instead of *š3<w>*: Sandman, *Texts,* 59.8, 100.7, and 111.1. Jan Quaegebeur, *Le dieu égyptien Shai dans la religion et l'onomastique* (Louvain: Leuven UP, 1975), 45f., quotes on p. 46 n. 1, my passage along with the three other ones as occurrences of *š3j ʿnḥ,* "qui détermine la vie." The common translation is "you living sun who first lived," reading *š3ʿ* as "to be the first in doing something." The true reading is *š3j,* "to allot," the verb from which the word *š3jj,* "destiny, fate," is derived.

21. Quaegebeur, *Shai.*

22. Sandman, *Texts,* 15.4–9; *ÄHG,* 91.54–56; Lichtheim, *Ancient Egyptian Literature,* vol. 2, 92.

23. For the association of "time" and "air" in Egyptian texts see *Liturgische Lieder,* 216, n. 137; *Zeit und Ewigkeit,* 40, n. 137; 56f.; 63, n. 74; *Ma'at,* 169f.

24. For the vertical division of the world into upper and lower, heaven and earth, see *Liturgische Lieder,* 302–306.

25. *Re und Amun,* 71–82 = *Egyptian Solar Religion,* 49–57; *Ma'at,* 160–199. The juridical aspects of the sun religion, in Egypt and Mesopotamia, have been dealt with in an extremely well-documented way by Bernd Janowski, *Rettungsgewissheit und Epiphanie des Heils: Das Motiv der Hilfe Gottes "am Morgen" im Alten Orient und im Alten Testament,* vol. 1, *Alter Orient* (Neukirchen-Vluyn: Neukirchner Verlag, 1989).

26. See my "State and Religion in the New Kingdom," *Religion and Philosophy in Ancient Egypt,* ed. W. K. Simpson, Yale Egyptological Studies 3 (New Haven; Yale UP, 1989), 55–89; *Ma'at,* 231–236.

27. *Re und Amun*, 83–94 = *Egyptian Solar Religion*, 57–66; Erik Hornung, *Die Nachtfahrt der Sonne* (Zurich: Artemis, 1990).

28. The sole exception occurs in a mortuary text, where the deceased *(Ay)* is addressed this way: "may you pass freely through the doors of the netherworld [*d3t*]" (Sandman, *Texts*, 101.16–17).

29. In the second chapter of *Re und Amun* I have collected the "icons" which form the basic elements of the traditional solar discourse and which lend themselves with equal ease to verbal and pictorial articulation.

30. The only exceptions are found in two pre-Amarna texts on the "New Solar Theology": the stela of Suti and Hor and the stela Leiden 5, 70; see *Re und Amun*, 143 = *Egyptian Solar Religion*, 100–101.

31. I am quoting the translation by Harold Fisch in the *Koren Bible* (Jerusalem: Magnes, 1983), 777.

32. Text: Sandman, *Texts*, 15; translation: Lichtheim, *Ancient Egyptian Literature*, vol. 2, 92.

33. The Egyptian word is *msnḥ* and it occurs exclusively in this context of "vegetal piety." For later texts see *ÄHG*, no. 132.14; no. 195, 159f., 236; no. 100; no. 49, 16.

34. See Paul Barguet, Le temple d'Amon Re à Karnak: Essay d'exégèse (Cairo: Imprimerie de l'Institut Français d'Archéologie Orientale, 1962), 238; Proclus, *perì tês hieratikês téchnē*s, from Theodor Hopfner, Griechisch-ägyptischer Offenbarungszauber, 2 vols. (Amsterdam: A. M. Hakkert, 1974–1990), vol. 1, 208–209, sect. 393.

35. As the tender flowers / willingly unfold / and quietly turn towards the sun, / thus let me, / quietly and gladly, / grasp thy rays and suffer thy influence (*Evangelisches Kirchengesangbuch*, no. 128).

36. The only exception I know of is an early inscription where Aten is referred to as "the noble god of the first time"; see H. Brunner, "Eine Inschrift aus der Frühzeit Amenophis IV," *Zeitschrift für ägyptische Sprache* 97 (1971): 12–18.

37. A. de Buck, ed., *The Egyptian Coffin Texts*, 7 vols. (Chicago: Oriental Institute Publications, 1938–1961), vol. 2, 33c; see Jan Zandee, "Sargtexte Spruch 80 (Coffin Texts II 27d-43)," *Zeitschrift Für Ägyptische Sprache* 101 (1974): 62–79, 70f.

38. *ÄHG* no. 89, 40; see *Re und Amun*, 119.

39. F. Daumas, *Les mammisis des temples égyptiens* (Paris: Belles Lettres, 1958) 412f.

40. Papyrus Cairo CG 58038 (= Papyrus Boulaq 17), 6, 5; *ÄHG*, no. 87E, 115. See *Re und Amun*, 353 (i) for Amun as an air god.

41. For the association of air and time see n. 23. For Egyptian embryology see Bruno Stricker, *De geboorte van Horus*, 5 vols. (Leiden: Brill, 1963–1982) (with some precautions).

42. See Serge Sauneron, "La différentiation des langages d'après la tradition égyptienne," *Bulletin de l'Institut Francais d'Archéologie Orientale* 60 (1960): 31–41.

43. For the provision of irrigation as an important aspect of the "well-arranged world," see also the first part of Psalm 104. For the motif of the heavenly Nile see *ÄHG*, no. 127B, 45f.; no. 195, 166; no. 143, 46, 100ff., 164f. (see p. 590 ad loc.); no. 144C, 39; no. 214, 29–32 (= *Book of the Dead*, chap. 183); no. 242, 7–8 (see Dirk v. d. Plaas, "De hymne aan de overstroming van de Nijl" diss., University of Utrecht, 1980, 16f. and 60–63); see Alain P. Zivie, "Regen," in *Lexikon der Ägyptologie*, vol. 4 (Wiesbaden: Harrassowitz, 1983), 202 and 204.

44. See Guy Kestemont, *Diplomatique et droit international en Asie occidentale (1600–1200 av. J.C.)*, (Louvain-la-neuve: Université Catholique de Louvain, Institut Orientaliste, 1974).

45. See Kenneth Burke, *Language as Symbolic Action* (Berkeley: U of California P, 1966), 380ff., and *A Grammar of Motives* (Berkeley: U of California P, 1969), 430–440.

46. See Winfried Barta, "Zur Semantik des Substantivs *ḫprw*," *Zeitschrift für Ägyptische Sprache* 109 (1982): 81–86, who stresses the meaning "manifestation." Strictly speaking, "manifestation" refers to something invisible becoming visible. The notion of invisibility or hiddenness, however, is precisely what is *not* meant in the Amarna texts. Therefore, the usual translation "transformation" is much to be preferred.

47. On Ancient Egyptian conceptions of genesis as creation-transformation see my article "Schöpfung," in *Lexikon der Ägyptologie*, vol. 5 (1984), 676–690, and James P. Allen, *Genesis in Egypt: The Philosophy of Ancient Egyptian Creation Accounts*, Yale Egyptological Studies 2 (New Haven: Yale UP, 1988).

48. See my *Zeit und Ewigkeit*.

49. Note the symmetrical arrangement of the key words "heaven" (l. 95) and "earth" (l. 104).

50. The motif of the creator seeing and supervising his creation in the form of the sun occurs first in the closing hymn of the *Teaching for Merikare*, which dates back to the Middle Kingdom: "He makes daylight for their sake, / He sails by to see them"; / (Miriam Lichtheim, *Ancient Egyptian Literature*, vol. 1 (Berkeley: U of California P, 1973), 106. The motif becomes very common in the context of the "New Solar Theology"; cf. my *Re und Amun*, 108 = *Egyptian Solar Religion*, 75, and esp. the references in *ÄHG*, 513, n. 39.

51. Cf. Theban Tomb 65, Assmann, *Sonnenhymnen*, text no. 83.8–11 (a hymn occurring also in the Saite tomb of Pedamenophis, Theban Tomb 33, ibid., text no. 36): "Who approaches the face though being far away, / every country being in front of him. / Men spend the day without getting satisfied of him." In the time of Amenophis II, on an ostracon representing one of the earliest examples of "Personal Piety," the "beautiful face of Amun" was praised as "being seen by the whole earth" (Papyrus Cairo 12202 vso.; see Georges Posener, "La piété personelle avant l'age Amarnien," *Revue d'Egyptologie* 27 [1975]: 202).

52. Cf. A. Schöne, *Goethes Farbentheologie* (Munich: C. H. Beck, 1987).

53. Sandman, *Texts*, 11.12–13 ("Shorter Hymn"); 23.4–5. Cf. ibid., 21: "who makes eyes for everything he creates." For later texts see Assmann, *Sonnenhymnen*, 266 (c).

54. J. W. von Goethe, "Entwurf einer Farbenlehre," *Goethes Werke*, vol. 13, 7th ed. (Munich: C. H. Beck, 1975), 323.

55. Goethe, "Entwurf einer Farbenlehre," 324 (cf. "Zahme Xenien," *Goethes Werke*, vol. 1, 367):

> Wär nicht das Auge sonnenhaft,
> Wie könnten wir das Licht erblicken?
> Läg nicht in uns des Gottes eigne Kraft,
> Wie könnt uns Göttliches entzücken?

The passage from Plotinus' *Enneads* which Goethe notes in his diary runs "neque vero oculus unquam videret solem, nisi factus solaris esset" (1.6). See W. Beierwaltes, "Die Metaphysik des Lichtes in der Philosophie Plotins," *Zeitschrift für Philosophische Forschung* 15 (1961): 223ff.

For Goethe, as for Plotinus and Plato, the "solarity" *(Sonnenhaftigkeit)* of the eye is evidence of the inward presence of the divine. Like the eye, the human mind is "light out of light" *(phôs èk photós)*. Seeing and knowing are one and the same. But this is exactly what the "Great Hymn" denies. Only the king is able to proceed from inward solarity to inward divinity and to speak of *Gottes eigner Kraft*, god's own power, within him:

> I am your son, who is beneficial for you,
> who displays your name and your might,
> with your force fixed in my heart

Sandman *Texts*, 14.13–16, 15.1–3.

56. Sandman, *Texts*, 95.17–18. See Assmann, *Zeit und Ewigkeit*, 55.

57. *Nḥḥ*, cosmic and cyclical time, is a common denomination of the sun god in Amarna (*Zeit und Ewigkeit*, 55–57). *Nḥḥ* is the inexhaustible and infinite plenitude out of which the sun allots individual portions of time—*'ḥ 'w*—to everything existing.

58. Allen, *Natural Philosophy*, 97, ventures a translation: "When you have gone, no eye exists, for you create their sight so as not to be seen [your]self." This makes good sense, but does not take into account the remaining *m w' n jrt.k*. Hornung, *Echnaton*, 92, translates:

> Wenn du gegangen bist, kein Auge nicht mehr da ist,
> das du um ihretwillen geschaffen hast,
> damit du nicht dich selber siehst als einziges was du geschaffen hast.

59. Sandman, *Texts*, 95.14–16.

60. Sandman, *Texts*, 93.16–17. This passage occurs almost verbatim in an important Theban text of the "New Solar Theology": Tomb 41 (6), Assmann, *Sonnenhymnen*, no. 54, 76–80, 78 n.(u):

> You are in front of us, but we do not know your 'going.'

Cf. also *Sonnenhymnen*, 355 n.(w) and text no. 253, 36f.:

> You cross the sky in front of them
> incessantly, but one does not know your "going."

61. See, for example, spell 213 of the "Pyramid Texts" (the best-known and most frequently copied spell from this corpus), which starts:

> O King, you have not departed dead,
> you have departed alive.

Kurt Sethe, *Die altägyptischen Pyramidentexte*, vol. 1 (Leipzig: Hinrichs, 1908), 80.

62. Donald B. Redford, "A Royal Speech from the Blocks of the Tenth Pylon,"

Bulletin of the Egyptological Seminar of New York 3 (1981): 87–102; Redford, *Akhenaten, the Heretic King*, 172f.

63. See my "Weisheit, Loyalismus und Frömmigkeit," in *Studien zu altägyptischen Lebenslehren*, ed. Erik Hornung and Othmar Keel, Orbis Biblicus et Orientalis 28 (Fribourg and Göttingen: Presses Universitaires de Fribourg, 1979), 12–72 passim.

64. The motif "god as teacher" occurs in texts expressing "Personal Piety"; see Assmann, "Weisheit," 16–19.

65. The most common epithet for the sun god as creator of time is *wpjw rnpt jrjw trw*, "who distinguishes [or: separates] the year and creates the seasons." This appears in a magical text of the Middle Kingdom (18th ccentury B.C.E.); see Papyrus Ramesseum IX, 3.7 = A. H. Gardiner, *Ramesseum Papyri* (Oxford: Clarendon Press, 1955), 42. In the context of "New Solar Theology," the motif is developed into a central theologumenon; see *Zeit und Ewigkeit*, 49–54.

66. See Allen, "Natural Philosophy," 89–101.

67. Sandman, *Texts*, 95.3–4.

68. Sandman, *Texts*, 12, 8–12 ("Shorter Hymn"). The following *jrtj.sn*, "their eyes," probably has to be connected with this sentence: "You are mother and father of all whose eyes you have made."

69. Assmann, "Aton," *Lexikon der Ägyptologie* 1 (1973): 526–540, esp. 532, 539, n. 109; *Liturgische Lieder*, 321f., 344.

70. See *Ma'at*, chap. 6.

71. For the typical correlation of "light" and "justice" in ancient oriental thought see Janowski, *Rettungsgewissheit*.

72. Papyrus Boulaq 17= Papyrus Cairo CG 58038, 4, 3–5; cf. *Re und Amun*, 176f. = *Egyptian Solar Religion*, 125. See also *Instruction for Merikare*, 130–138, and *Re und Amun*, 168f. = *Egyptian Solar Religion*, 119f.; *Ma'at* 234f.

73. See Charles Taylor, *Sources of the Self* (Cambridge Mass.: Harvard UP, 1989), 25ff. ("The Self in Moral Space").

74. The relationship between the "Great Hymn" and Psalm 104 has often been remarked upon. Among the more recent treatments of this question are by B. Celada, "El Salmo 104, el Himno de Amenofis IV y otros documentos egipcios," *Sefarad* 30 (1970): 305–324; K.-H. Bernhardt, "Amenophis IV und Psalm 104," *Mitteilungendes Instituts Für Orientforschung* 15 (1969): 193–206; and E. von Nordheim, "Der grosse Hymnus des Echnaton und Psalm 104," *Studien zur Altägyptischen Kultur* 7 (1979): 227–251. All of these scholars reject any direct influence of the Egyptian text on the Biblical text. After submitting the material to a very careful consideration, Christoph Uehlinger, "Leviathan und die Schiffe in Ps. 104, 25–26," *Biblica* 71 (1990): 499–526, arrives at the conclusion that a direct dependence of Psalm 104 on Akhenaten's hymn is impossible. He even considers the possibility that Akhenaten's text might be dependent on a Canaanite model. G. Nagel, "A propos des rapports du Psaume 104 avec les textes égyptiens," *Festschrift A. Bertholet* (Tübingen: Mohr, 1950), 395–440, esp. 395–403; Frank Crüsemann, *Studien zur Formgeschichte von Hymnus und Danklied in Israel*, Wissenschaftliche Monographien zum Alten und Neuen Testament 32 (Neukirchen-Vluyn: Neukirchner Verlag, 1969), 287f. with 287, n. 2; and P. Auffret, *Hymnes d'Egypte et d'Israel: Etudes des structures littéraires* (Fribourg: Editions Universitaires, 1981), all think a dependence of Psalm 104 on Akhenaten's hymn is possible.

75. Cf. M. Dahood, "Psalms III 101–150." in *The Anchor Bible* (New York: Macmillan, 1970), 46, who breaks the consonantal *rwḥm* down into *rwḥ* plus the enclitic *mem*, "which serves here as a stylistic surrogate for the pronominal suffix" (viz., "your"), in order "to eschew parallelistic monotony."

76. C. Grave, "Northwest Semitic Sapanu in a Break-up of an Egyptian Stereotype Phrase in EA 147," *Orientalia* n.s. 51 (1982): 161–182.

77. William L. Moran, *Les lettres d'El-Amarna* (Paris: Edition du Cerf, 1987), 378.

78. Sandman, *Texts*, 15, 6–9.

79. Ps. 104:31–35.

80. This section is based on chap. 5 of my book *Egyptian Solar Religion in the New Kingdom* (London: Kegan Paul International, 1995). I am grateful to Dr. Anthony Alcock for the English translation of that book.

81. See above, p. 142 with nn. 147–148 on p. 251.

82. The term has been used by Johann Georg Wachter (*Spinozismus im Juden-thümb*, 1699); see Scholem, "Abraham Cohen Herrera—Leben, Werk und Wirkung."

83. G. Posener, "Amon, juge du pauvre," in *Festschrift H. Ricke* (Wiesbaden: Steiner, 1971), 59–63.

84. *Zeit und Ewigkeit*, 60–64; "Weisheit, Loyalismus und Frömmigkeit," 31.

85. See the collection of pertinent passages in Jan Zandee, *Der Amunshymnus des Pap. Leiden I 344 vso*, 3 vols., (Leiden: Instituut voor het Nabije Oosten, 1992), 126–133. On *Jmn rn.f* see *Sonnenhymnen* (= STG) Texts 87(k) and 253(m), Zandee, *Amunshymnus*, 131–133.

86. Sethe, *Die altägyptischen Pyramidentexte*, vol. 1, sect. 276c (there are many occurrences in later texts).

87. A translation and references are in Emma Brunner-Traut, *Altägyptische Märchen* (Munich: Diderichs, 1976), 115–120.

88. In these words the father recognizes himself in his child and knows the child as his child; see *Liturgische Lieder*, 99, with n. 41.

89. Papyrus Leiden J 350, 4, 9–11; Jan Zandee, *De Hymnen aan Amon van Papyrus Leiden I 350* (Leiden: Brill, 1947), 71–75; *ÄHG*, no. 137.

90. Cf. Papyrus Leiden I, 344, vso. 1.4: "who created his father, begot his mother"; Zandee, *Amunshymnus*, 24–27.

91. Jaroslav Černý and Alan H. Gardiner, *Hieratic Ostraca* (Oxford: Clarendon Press, 1957), pl. 106.

92. "Whose birth is secret": cf. Papyrus Leiden I, 350, 4, 11; Zandee, *Hymnen*, 74; Papyrus Berlin 3049, 6, 7–8; *ÄHG*, no. 131, 10; *Sonnenhymnen*, text 42a(i). On "holy of birth" see Papyrus Leiden I, 344, 1.1, Zandee, ed., *Amunshymnus*, 17–18; see also Horemheb BM 551 = *ÄHG*, no. 58, 18–20.

93. *Sonnenhymnen*, text 114, 11(c).

94. Papyrus Strasbourg 7, col. 5, l. 2. On the self-creation of the primeval god see Zandee, *Hymnen*, 38–39.

95. This does not exclude the possibility that the temporal relationship between unity and multiplicity is simply a metaphorical expression of the ontological one, in the sense of "temporizing of essence" (K. Burke); see my article "Die 'Häresie' des Echnaton," *Saeculum* 23 (1972): 115ff., esp. nn. 28 and 31. But I believe I can now see the historical development more clearly than I did then. The term "hidden

unity" *in* (as distinct from *before*) the multiplicity belongs specifically to Ramesside Amun-Re theology.

96. Zandee, *Hymnen*, 75–86; *ÄHG*, no. 138.

97. The Epigraphic Survey, *The Temple of Ramses III in Karnak*, Oriental Institute Publications, vol. 24 (Chicago: U of Chicago P), pl. 23 = *ÄHG*, no. 196, 12–15.

98. E. Hornung, *Der ägyptische Mythos von der Himmelskuh*, Orbis Biblicus et Orientalis 46 (Fribourg: Editions Universitaires, 1982) 26f., 47.

99. Papyrus Boulaq 4, 7.15; Volten, *Studien*, 111–112, 115; see *Saeculum*, 23, 125, n. 63.

100. Sandman, *Texts*, 95, 12–13. On this passage see G. Fecht, *Zeitschrift Für Ägyptische Sprache* 94 (1967): 33; *Sonnenhymnen*, text 54 (x).

101. Sandman, *Texts*, 15, 1–9; see *Sonnenhymnen*, text 253(s).

102. J. C. Goyon, in R. A. Parker, J. Leclant, and J. C. Goyon, *The Edifice of Taharqa* (Hanover and London: UP of New England, 1979), 69–79, 40–41, pl. 27. Cf. *ÄHG*, no. 128. A parallel demotic text has been published by M. Smith, *Enchoria* 7 (1977): 115–149.

103. An illustration of the otherwise largely unpublished representation of the ten *ba*s of Amun in the crypt of the Ptolemaic Opet Temple at Karnak may be found in Claude Traunecker, *Les dieux de l'Egypte*, Que Sais-Je? vol. 1191 (Paris: Seuil, 1992), 97, fig. 8.

104. A similar concept of kingship as an intramundane manifestation of god's creative and preserving power is expounded in Papyrus Leiden 1, 344, vso. 9.9, and Zandee, *Amunshymnus*, 873–876; 11.1–2, and Zandee, ibid., 995f., where the king is called the *ka* of God.

105. Mentioned by Goyon, *Edifice*, 69ff.

106. Norman de Garis Davies, *The Temple of Hibis in El-Khargeh Oasis*, vol. 3, *The Decoration*, The Metropolitan Museum of Art, Egyptian Expedition, vol. 17 (New York, 1953), pl. 31 (the trans. in *ÄHG*, no. 128, 1–2, must be corrected accordingly).

107. See esp. R. Merkelbach and M. Totti, *Abrasax: Ausgewählte Papyri religiösen und magischen Inhalts*, Abhandlungen der Rheinisch-Westfälischen Akademie der Wissenschaften, Sonderreihe Papyrologia Coloniensia, 17, 3 vols. (Opladen: Westdeutscher Verlag, 1990–1992), s.v. "Gebete."

108. Sauneron, *Papyrus magique*, 18, pl. 2, fig. 2 (facing p. 12).

109. Merkelbach and Totti, *Abrasax*, vol. 1, 78; vol. 2, 10–11; vol. 3, 59–65.

110. Preisendanz, *Papyri Graecae Magicae*, no. 12, 238–245 = Hans Dieter Betz, ed., *The Greek Magical Papyri in Translation*, 162. See Preisendanz, no. 13, 762–794 = Betz, *Translation*, 190f.:

> Come to me, you from the four winds,
> Ruler of all, who breathed spirit into men for life,
> Whose is the hidden and unspeakable name
> —it cannot be uttered by a human mouth—
> At whose name even the daemons, when hearing are terrified,
> Whose is the sun, NNN, and the moon, NNN,
> They are the unwearied eyes, shining in the pupils of men's eyes,
> Of whom heaven is head,
> Ether body,

Earth feet,
And the environment water,
The Agathos Daimon,
you are the ocean, begetter of good things and feeder of the civilized
world.
Yours is the eternal processional way in which your seven-lettered
name is established for the harmony of the seven sounds [of the
planets which] utter their voices according too the twenty-eight
forms of the moon, NNN.
Yours are the beneficient effluxes of the stars,
Daemones, and Fortunes, and Fates,
By whom is given wealth, good old age, good children, good luck, a
good burial.
And you, lord of life, king of the heavens and the earth and all things
living in them,
You whose justice is not turned aside,
You whose glorious name the Muses sing,
You whom the eight guards attend,
NNN, you who have truth that never lies.
Your name and your spirit rest upon the good.
Come into my mind and my understanding for all the time of my life
And accomplish for me all the desires of my soul.

111. On the concept of the "limitlessness" of god, cf. "who concealed himself, whose limits cannot be attained," Papyrus Leiden I, 344, vso. 2, 8–9; Zandee, *Amunshymnus*, 120–126. Cf. Papyrus Berlin 3049, 16, 6, and Urk 8, 116: "whose circuit has no limits."

112. This is one of the very few instances where in texts other than those from Amarna the sun is called *ḫprw* of the god. This doubtless refers to the concept of the divine "transformations" in which the sun forms the last stage of the cosmogonic and transformational process of the primeval god.

113. Here *ḥḥw* clearly means "millions" and not, as Sethe suggested, the "all pervasive air" personifed in the god Hah (sect. 201). The god Hah does not occur in this connection until the Ptolemaic period (see E. Drioton, *Annales du Service des Antiquitées Egyptiennes* 44 [1944]: 127[c]).

114. *Conceptions*, 170: "'Millions,' enormous and unfathomable, but not infinite multiplicity are the reality of the world of creation, of all that exists." Is it really legitimate to speak of *ḥḥw* as if it were something finite? It obviously does not mean a finite number (such as a million as distinct from a million and one); rather, it refers to incalculable abundance. It should also be borne in mind that the idea of infinity, expressed in *ḥḥw*, is a category of chaos, just like the concept of "undifferentiated unity." When the cosmogonic concept of differentiation is meant, the phrase "one who becomes three" is used, not "one who becomes millions" (de Buck, *Coffin Texts*, 2, 39; cf. E. Otto, "Altägyptischer Polytheismus. Eine Beschreibung," *Saeculum* 14 [1963]: 267 and 274). See also the text on the coffin Cairo *Catalogue Général* 6234: "I am the one, who became two / I am the two who became four / I am the four who became eight"; see Maspero, in *Receuil de Travaux* 23 (1901) 196–197.

115. See Leiden stela V, 70 = *ÄHG*, no. 90, where the sun god is addressed as

"that ḥḥw whose limits are not known, scarab whose body is not known." The text derives from a time close to the Amarna period and thus belongs to the "New Solar Theology." It probably means the "boundless" omnipresence of the light.

116. Papyrus Leiden I, 344, vso. 3, 2–3 = Zandee, *Amunshymnus*, 168–176.

117. Emile Chassinat, *Le temple d' Edfou*, vol. 3 (Cairo: Imprimerie de l'Institut Français d'Archéologie Orientale, 1928), 34.9–10.

118. *ḥprw.f m ḥḥw:* stela of Ramesses III = Kenneth A. Kitchen, *Ramesside Inscriptions*, vol. 6 (Oxford: Blackwell, 1969), 452.8.

119. Urk, 8, sect. 138b = Kurt Sethe, *Thebanische Tempelinschriften aus griechisch-römischerer Zeit*, ed. Otto Firchow (Berlin: Akademie Verlag, 1957), 110. Of Yahweh, on the contrary, it is said: "'One' is his name" (Zekh. 14:9).

120. On this meaning of ḥḥw see *Sonnenhymnen*, text 149(c).

121. Hymn to the primeval god in the "Livre que mon fleurisse" in Papyrus Berlin 3030, 8–9; Papyrus Louvre 3336, 1, 1–16; Papyrus Brussels published by Louis Speelers in *Recueil des Travaux* 39 (1917): 28ff.

122. *Ex voto* inscription from Capua, first or second century C.E. = *Corpus Inscriptionum Latinarum*, 10, 3800: "Te tibi una quae es omnia dea Isis." See Dunand, "Le syncretisme isiaque," 82, n. 1. L. Vidman, *Sylloge inscriptionum religionis Isiacae et Sarapidae* (Berlin: Akademie Verlag, 1969), no. 502; V. Tran Tam Tinh, *Le culte des divinités orientaux en Campanie* (Leiden: Brill, 1972), 41ff., 77, 199–234.

123. Hymn of Isidorus from Medinet Madi; see above, Chapter 2, n. 66.

124. *Corpus Hermeticum*, 4.10 = Arthur D. Nock and Jean-André Festugière, *Corpus Hermeticum*, 4 vols. (Paris: Collection Budé, Les Belles Lettres, 1973–1980), vol. 1, 64; *Asclepius*, sect. 20 = vol. 2, 321.

125. *The Expulsion of the Triumphant Beast*, 240.

7. Abolishing the Mosaic Distinction

1. Yehoshua Amir, "Die Begegnung des biblischen und des philosophischen Monotheismus als Grundthema des jüdischen Hellenismus," *Evangelische Theologie* 38 (1978): 2–19.

2. See Lactantius, *De Ira Dei*, and my "Politische Theologie."

3. See Walzer, *Exodus and Revolution*.

4. See Jacob, *The Radical Enlightenment*.

5. See Warburton, *Divine Legation*, vol. 2, 149ff.

6. See Manuel, *The Eighteenth Century Confronts the Gods*, 47–53.

7. See Rüdiger Schott, "Das Geschichtsbewusstsein schriftloser Völker," *Archiv für Begriffsgeschichte* 12 (1968): 166–205. Aleida Assmann, in A. and J. Assmann, "Schrift, Tradition und Kultur," *Zwischen Festtag und Alltag*, ed. Wolfgang Raible (Tübingen: Narr, 1988), 25–50, esp. 35f.

8. See Luckmann, "Kanon und Konversion."

9. Odo Marquard, "Lob des Polytheismus: Über Monomythie und Polymythie," in *Philosophie und Mythos. Ein Kolloquium*, ed. Hans Poser (Berlin: W. de Gruyter, 1979), 40–58; cf. Jacob Taubes, "Zur Konjunktur des Polytheismus," *Mythos und Moderne: Begriff und Bild einer Rekonstruktion*, ed. Karl Heinz Bohrer (Frankfurt: Suhrkamp, 1983), 457–470.

Index